Foundations of Joomla

Bintu Harwani

Apress®

Foundations of Joomla

ISBN-13 (pbk): 978-1-4842-0750-5

ISBN-13 (electronic): 978-1-4842-0749-9

Managing Director: Welmoed Spahr
Lead Editor: Ben Renow-Clarke
Technical Reviewer: Massimo Nardone
Editorial Board: Steve Anglin, Mark Beckner, Gary Cornell, Louise Corrigan, Jim DeWolf,
    Jonathan Gennick, Robert Hutchinson, Michelle Lowman, James Markham, Susan McDermott,
    Matthew Moodie, Jeffrey Pepper, Douglas Pundick, Ben Renow-Clarke, Gwenan Spearing,
    Matt Wade, Steve Weiss
Coordinating Editor: Kevin Walter
Copy Editor: Nancy Sixsmith
Compositor: SPi Global
Indexer: SPi Global
Artist: SPi Global

Distributed to the book trade worldwide by Springer Science+Business Media New York, 233 Spring Street, 6th Floor, New York, NY 10013. Phone 1-800-SPRINGER, fax (201) 348-4505, e-mail orders-ny@springer-sbm.com, or visit www.springeronline.com. Apress Media, LLC is a California LLC and the sole member (owner) is Springer Science + Business Media Finance Inc (SSBM Finance Inc). SSBM Finance Inc is a Delaware corporation.

For information on translations, please e-mail rights@apress.com, or visit www.apress.com.

Apress and friends of ED books may be purchased in bulk for academic, corporate, or promotional use. eBook versions and licenses are also available for most titles. For more information, reference our Special Bulk Sales–eBook Licensing web page at www.apress.com/bulk-sales.

Any source code or other supplementary material referenced by the author in this text is available to readers at www.apress.com. For detailed information about how to locate your book's source code, go to www.apress.com/source-code/.

This book is dedicated to:

My mother, Mrs. Nita Harwani. My mother is next to God for me. Whatever I am today is just because of the moral values taught by her

And

Brian Acton and Jan Koum, the founders of WhatsApp, am amazing instant messaging app for smartphones. I am a big fan of the WhatsApp app because it keeps me connected with my respected teachers, lovely friends, students, and relatives. It's a great energy booster for me. WhatsApp is so successful that it inspires millions of programmers around the world.

Contents at a Glance

Contents

About the Author

Bintu Harwani is the founder and owner of Microchip Computer Education (MCE), which is based in Ajmer, India. MCE provides computer education in all programming, web developing and smartphone platforms. Harwani is also a well-known speaker and author of several books. His latest books include *Foundation Joomla*, published by Apress; *jQuery Recipes*, published by Apress; *Core Data iOS Essentials*, published by Packt; *Introduction to Python Programming and Developing GUI Applications with PyQT*, published by Cengage Learning; *Android Programming Unleashed*, published by Sams Publishing; *The Android Tablet Developer's Cookbook* (Developer's Library), published by Addison-Wesley Professional; *UNIX & Shell Programming*, published by Oxford University Press; *PhoneGap Build: Developing Cross Platform Mobile Applications in the Cloud*, published by Auerbach Publications; and *Learning Object-Oriented Programming in C# 5.0*, published by Cengage Learning PTR.

To know more, visit Harwani's blog at `http://bmharwani.com/blog`.

About the Technical Reviewer

 **Massimo Nardone** is an experienced Android, Java, PHP, Python, and C++ programmer; technical reviewer; and expert. He holds a Master of Science degree in computing science from the University of Salerno, Italy. He worked as a PCI QSA and Senior Lead IT Security/Cloud/SCADA Architect for many years and currently works as Security, Cloud, and SCADA Lead IT Architect for Hewlett Packard Finland. Nardone has more than 20 years of work experience in IT, including security, SCADA, cloud computing, IT infrastructure, mobile, security, and WWW technology areas for both national and international projects. He has worked as a Project Manager, Cloud/SCADA Lead IT Architect, Software Engineer, Research Engineer, Chief Security Architect, and Software Specialist. Nardone worked as visiting lecturer and supervisor for exercises at the Networking Laboratory of the Helsinki University of Technology (Aalto University). He has been programming and teaching how to program with Perl, PHP, Java, VB, Python, and C/C++ for almost 20 years. He holds four international patents (in the PKI, SIP, SAML, and Proxy areas).

Acknowledgments

I owe a debt of gratitude to Ben Renow-Clarke, Senior Editor, Web Development for his initial acceptance and giving me an opportunity to create this work. I am highly grateful to the whole team at Apress for their constant cooperation and contribution to create this book.

My gratitude to James Markham, who as a development editor offered a significant amount of feedback that helped to improve the chapters. He played a vital role in improving the structure and quality of information.

I must thank technical reviewer Massimo Nardone for his excellent and detailed reviewing of the work and the many helpful comments and suggestions he made.

Special thanks to copy editor Nancy Sixsmith for first-class structural and language editing. I appreciate her efforts to enhance the contents of the book and give it a polished look.

I also thank the formatter for doing excellent formatting and making the book dramatically better.

Big and ongoing thanks to Coordinating Editor Kevin Walter for his great job and sincere efforts with the whole team to get the book published on time.

A great big thank you to the editorial and production staff and the entire team at Apress, who worked tirelessly to produce this book. I really enjoyed working with each of you.

I am also thankful to my family—my small world: Anu (my wife) and my two little darlings Chirag and Naman—for allowing me to work on the book, even during the time when I was supposed to spend with them.

I should not forget to thank my dear students who have been good teachers for me because they make me understand basic problems they face in a subject and enable me to directly emphasize those topics. The endless interesting queries of my students help me write books with a practical approach.

Introduction

Joomla is a content management system (CMS) that helps you build dynamic and functional websites with a minimum of effort. Not only can you make personal web sites to blogs and discussion forums but also to fully functional professional web sites such as e-commerce stores. Joomla provides a very simple-to-use interface that you can use to do the following:

- Post content on your web site, add videos, pictures, and so on

- Moderate comments, if any, and respond to them if required

- Allow users to register at your site and enable them to access your content and even post their content

- Easily create and maintain a web site because all the content that you define for the web site is stored in a database

---

■ **Note**   You don't need any programming skills to create and handle web sites through Joomla because all you have to do is to operate an easy-to-use interface; the rest of the job is handled by Joomla.

Here is a brief description of the content in different chapters of the book:

- *Chapter 1, "Introduction to Joomla"*: This chapter provides an introduction to Joomla.

- *Chapter 2, "Installing XAMPP and Joomla"*: You learn how to install XAMPP, a complete web development environment, and how to install Joomla on a local and remote server. You see how Joomla creates a fully-fledged web site that already contains menus, links, search boxes, articles, newsfeeds, and so on; and that all these features are functional.

- *Chapter 3, "Your First Steps in Joomla!"*: This chapter provides a brief introduction to the Administrator interface and also introduces the home page and the impact of templates on a Joomla web site. You learn to create sections, categories, and real content in the form of articles. You also see how to make articles appear on the front page of the web site and how to link them to menu items.

- *Chapter 4, "Managing Images and Banners"*: You learn how to use Media Manager to manage images in the articles, banners, and other contents of your web site. You also see how to make categories for your banners, create banner clients, create banners for your clients, and use the Banners module for displaying banners on the web site.

- *Chapter 5, "Creating Users and Contacts"*: You learn how to create different types of users for your web site. You also learn how to create contact forms that allow visitors to your web site to contact the authorized person of your site. The focus of the chapter is to define the interaction of visitors with the organization's administration.

- *Chapter 6, "Creating Interaction"*: In this chapter, you learn to create interaction with users and other data providers. You learn how to use newsfeeds to get updated information from other data providers and how to provide related topics from other web sites in the form of web links to enable data sharing.

- *Chapter 7, "Dealing with Menus"*: You learn how to create menus and menu items of different types so that they can be set to display articles, categories, contacts, web links, news feeds, login forms, and more.

- *Chapter 8, "Module"*: You learn about different types of modules and their uses, and see the different front-end and back-end modules provided by Joomla. Using modules, you can configure the site for the site visitors and customize the site's admin interface for the administrator.

- *Chapter 9, "Adding Extensions"*: You learn how to add more features to your Joomla web site by installing the respective extensions in your site. You see how to download and install templates to make your web site appear more dynamic, e-commerce extensions to maintain an online store and sell products via your web site, RSS feed readers to receive RSS feeds periodically from the selected web sites, and chatting components to allow visitors to your web site to converse with each another.

- *Chapter 10, "Making It Global"*: You learn how to configure global settings for Joomla. You also see how to install an editor, make search engine–friendly (SEF) URLs, change the language of the front end of the web site, and provide a multilingual facility to your visitors (the ability to translate the contents of the web site into multiple languages).

CHAPTER 1

■ ■ ■

Introduction to Joomla

Joomla is a content management system (CMS) that helps you build dynamic and functional websites with a minimum of effort. It is possible to make all kinds of web sites with Joomla, from personal web sites to blogs and discussion forums, and even fully functional professional web sites such as e-commerce stores. All this is possible because Joomla is supported with hundreds of freely available plug-ins and extensions that can be easily applied to a web site to increase its capabilities. By default, Joomla provides all the standard web site content such as menus, articles, and modules, all of which can be customized via the Administrator interface. So the overhead of making a web site from scratch is highly reduced because of this system.

In a CMS, the content of the web site (articles, pictures, and so on) is stored in a database, which makes creating and maintaining a web site very simple. Traditional web sites are often bulky and unwieldy because they consist of a large amount of content (several web pages) that displays information to the visitor. The greater the number of web pages, the more difficult it is to maintain that web site. It is for this reason that a group of people usually maintain traditional web site.

In Joomla, however, because all the web content is maintained in a database, its maintenance cost is highly reduced (as you'll see throughout this book, maintaining a database requires less effort than manually changing web content). Moreover, Joomla provides a user-friendly Administrator interface that guides the administrator through maintaining the web site content stored in the database. Even just one person can easily maintain a web site with the help of Joomla's easy-to-use, menu-driven administrative interface. With a little training, a web developer or administrator can easily administer a web site and change its content, navigation features, and structure with just a few clicks of the mouse. Let's dig a bit deeper into what a CMS is and what makes Joomla so special.

What Is a CMS?

As mentioned previously, a content management system (CMS) is a software system that enables you to create, edit, and different types of documents. These documents can include data files, audio/video files, image files, and most other forms of web content. A CMS not only helps manage all this content (without requiring any technical knowledge of HTML) but it also defines different groups of users, each with different roles and responsibilities. The idea is that more than one person in an organization can contribute to creating, editing, and managing content, whereas normal visitors are given limited access privileges— usually just permission to view the content. In short, you can make an easily maintainable web site with the help of a CMS in which creating, editing, and managing content are simple tasks.

In a CMS, the whole of the web site is contained within a database. All links, articles, user information, images, and other parts of the web site are maintained by the administrator using that database. This talk of databases may sound a bit scary, but all the web site maintenance is carried out using the Administrator interface—a user-friendly, menu-driven system that makes the task of updating or managing the content of the web site very easy. The Administrator interface is accessed through the web browser and is simple to operate. All the changes that you make in the Administrator interface are reflected in the database in which the content of the web site is kept.

1

Making a web site from scratch is usually a time-consuming task that requires expertise to develop all the individual site parts. The processes of coding and integrating these different parts are highly error-prone, and thorough testing procedures are needed before new parts can be added to a web site. In a traditional web application, you might have several different criteria for modules that you want to add to your site, such as the following:

- Login system: Provides a means of authenticating a user

- Account Creation module: Provides users with a form to enter information, which is then stored in a database for future use

- Forgotten Password module: Helps users who have forgotten their password or user ID

- Popular module: Displays popular web site content or services

- Banner module: Displays client's banner for advertisement purpose.

- RSS Feed module: Syndicates the web site for others to read

- Feed Reader module: Enables reading of RSS feeds from different web sites

- Search box: Enables users to search web site content

- Multilingual module: Makes it possible to implement multilingual facilities in a web site

- Granting-and-Revoking-Permission module: Facilitates assigning permissions to users to allow them to view (or block them from viewing) certain information

In a CMS system, all these modules are already built for you and are easy to add to an existing site. You just need to configure them and decide on their position and appearance in your web site. Creating a web site is thus very easy—you can have it ready in a couple of hours. Also, maintaining the content of the web site doesn't take much effort; the configuration of the modules provided by a CMS and maintenance of the web content is all done with the easy-to-use Administrator interface.

Why Are CMSs So Popular?

There are many reasons why people choose to use a CMS rather than creating a site from scratch in code, but I'll run through a couple of the big ones. You will always need to update your website to keep viewers returning to it, and a CMS makes this very easy. For example, you may need to do the following:

- Deliver new articles or information about your organization to visitors

- Inform readers about any forthcoming events

- Introduce new services or products

Besides this easy and quick updating, you might also need to add some extra features that do the following:

- Allow users to sign up on your web site with different privileges

- Add a shopping cart module

- Add multilingual support to your web site

- Apply different dynamic styles to your web site

- Add a third-party module to provide extra features such as Google Maps or a search box

To deal with natural demands of webmasters, CMSs appear as helping hands because they store all the contents of the web site in a database and enable the webmaster to manipulate the database contents with an easy-to-operate, browser–driven Administrator interface. So, in simple terms, using a CMS is a way to manage the content of a web site with the click of a mouse button instead of hours spent typing in code.

CMSs are popular because they separate the web content from the presentation. As a consequence, the content developer can concentrate on creating that content, and web designers can focus on giving that content a dynamic appearance by applying different templates (or developing their own custom templates) without interfering with each other. Hence, the content development and presentation process can proceed simultaneously in a CMS.

▧ **Note**   To compare the available CMSs and to determine which is best for your situation, see www.cmsmatrix.org/.

What Is Joomla?

Joomla is one of the most powerful and popular open source CMSs available today. It is a free, open source framework and content publishing system designed for quickly creating highly interactive multilingual web sites, online communities, blogs, and e-commerce applications. It is a server-based application that maintains all the contents of the web site in a database. A web site built with Joomla can be easily administered via a web browser using Joomla's browser–driven Administrator interface.

Joomla provides several built-in modules and components for adding features to your web sites, such as main menus, polls, popular items, search, RSS feeds, and so on. In addition, there are hundreds of third-party modules and components available on the Internet, such as shopping carts, news readers, and language translators that can be freely downloaded and added to a Joomla web site.

One of the best features of Joomla is that it separates the content from the presentation—the raw content stored in the database is given dynamic styling with the help of templates (collections of styles) before it is viewed by the visitor.

Joomla is very successful and is a winner of the Open Source Content Management System Award. It has many more great features (some of which are explained in more detail in the following sections).

Structure of a Joomla Web Site

Figure 1-1 shows that the raw contents of the web site (i.e., the articles, pictures, user information, etc.) are stored in a database. When a visitor selects any link or menu item on a web site, the desired data is retrieved from the database and is displayed. But before the information is displayed to the user, there are several modules and components that are applied to it to filter the required information. For example, there may be several news feeds stored in the database, but only the news feed specified in the News Feed module will be passed. There may be polls on several subjects, but only the subject specified in the Polls module will be passed on to the visitor.

After it is decided what information is to be displayed, the selected template is applied to it. The template consists of styles that give an attractive look to the content. It also defines the design and structure of the web site because it contains the screen position of several modules, such as where the Polls, Search box, and Popular links modules are supposed to appear on the web site. Joomla provides three built-in templates to give a dynamic appearance to your web site, but you can always download more templates from the Internet and install them to be used in your web site.

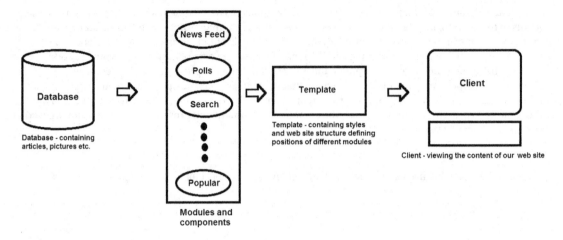

Figure 1-1. *Structure of a Joomla web site*

It is also possible to make your own custom templates, but that is a more complex process and is beyond the scope of this book.

Joomla Characteristics

Joomla is heavily used in developing highly interactive multi-language web sites, blogs, discussion forums, online communities, e-commerce applications, and much more. Joomla has several characteristics that make it an in-demand CMS, including the following:

- Joomla offers a huge number of extensions. You can easily enhance features of your web site by installing more extensions, some of which follow:

  - Dynamic form builders: These components help you take feedback from visitors and accordingly display a form back to them. For example, visitors paying for a product in cash will see a form that prompts them to fill in bank name and account details, and visitors paying via credit card will see a form that has a list of credit cards to choose from and a field to enter the credit card number information.

  - Image and multimedia galleries: These components help you add images to your web site, view image thumbnails, customize image size, apply special effects on images when the mouse is moved over them, and so on. These components also allow you to add music and animations to your web site.

  - E-commerce and shopping cart engines: These components help you create and manage shopping carts, complete with PayPal support, in minutes. Examples of these components are MijoShop, VirtueMart, and HikaShop.

  - Forums and chat software: Forums are used for discussing subjects, getting the views of visitors, replying to queries, and so on. Kunena is a Joomla component that can add a forums facility to your web site. Similarly, several chat components are available, including ActiveHelper and BlastChat.

- Calendars: Calendar extensions can display monthly calendar information. You can switch to the calendar of any month and year, and the date on which you click will be retrieved for processing.

- E-mail newsletters: To contact visitors of your web site and get their feedback, e-mail is the best communication medium. Joomla provides many e-mail marketing newsletter components for doing this job, including jNews, Newsletter Subscriber, Phoca Mail, and others.

- Data collection and reporting tools: These components search through data to collect the requested information and display reports — such as sales reports, market survey reports, and sales forecasting reports — in tabular or chart formats.

- Banner advertising systems: These components are used for managing and displaying advertising banners on your site. You can also specify the period for which the banner will be published on your web site (e.g., for a specified number of hits or for an unlimited period).

- You can easily install any of these hundreds of extensions to increase the functionality of your web site.

- Joomla has an active community of more than 200,000 users and developers.

- Working with Joomla is very simple. Its user-friendly, menu-driven system and tools allow even nontechnical users to add or edit web site content.

- Joomla is very easy to install and setup when compared with other CMSs such as Workdpress and Drupal.

- Joomla runs on Windows, Linux, FreeBSD, Mac OS X, Solaris, and AIX.

- With Joomla, you can build completely database-driven sites.

- With Joomla, you can upload images to be used anywhere in the site. Joomla has a Media Manager component that allows you to upload images. These uploaded images can then be used on any number of web pages (also called articles).

- Joomla contains image libraries that can store all type of picture formats (including PNG, GIF, and JPEG) along with other document types, such as PDF, DOC, and XLS.

- Joomla contains an Automatic Path-Finder tool, which allows you to place an image from the image library (Media Manager) and have Joomla set its path automatically.

- With Joomla's Remote author contribution tool, authors can add articles, news, and links to your web site remotely. Joomla supports different groups of users, each having different rights and permissions (e.g., authors, editors, publishers, and managers), which enables authorized users to contribute to the web site from anywhere.

- For every article, Joomla provides two options, "E-mail a friend" and "Print," so you don't have to write code to provide these facilities.

- Joomla provides two inline text editors for adding or editing articles and information: TinyMCE and XStandard Lite. These WYSIWYG editors help you apply different fonts, styles, and sizes to your text.

- Joomla supplies several ready-to-use modules that can be used directly in your web site, including Polls, Popular, RSS Feed, and Banner.

- With Joomla, you can change the sequence of appearance of modules on your web site.

- Administrators can administer the web site remotely with the help of a browser.

- You can apply different templates to give a dynamic look to your web site. (A template contains styles and screen positions for placing modules and components.) Joomla provides several templates by default that you can immediately apply, and you can also download many more.

Advantages of Joomla

There are several advantages of using Joomla to build your web site:

- Joomla is absolutely free and easy to install.

  - Joomla offers many extensions to enhance the features of your web site. For example, in just a few minutes you can add extensions that provide discussion forums, chat features, and shopping carts to your site.

  - Many free plug-ins are available at the Joomla site home page.

  - Joomla's home page provides great support to beginners and developers by supplying links for tutorials, tools, and discussion forums.

  - Joomla supports multiple languages.

  - Joomla can be controlled remotely using a web browser. Its web site can be easily maintained from anywhere by using its browser-based Administrator interface.

  - Joomla supports XAMP technology. The X in XAMP designates the three operating systems that it supports (Windows, Linux, and Mac OS X); and *AMP* refers to the three pieces of server software that it is built upon: Apache, MySQL, and PHP.

  - Joomla can manage web site content using any of the popular web browsers. It is fully tested on Firefox 13 and Internet Explorer 8; and newer Safari 5.1+, Opera 11.6+, Chrome XY+, and Yandex 14.10+.

Disadvantages of Joomla

Joomla has a couple of disadvantages, too. Let's have a quick look at them:

- Even though Joomla has many modules and templates, there are not many options for more advanced users, and some plug-ins and modules are not free.

- Joomla offers more than 3,000 extensions, which can be hard to keep track of.

- Some of the Joomla plug-ins have compatibility issues, so you might need to write PHP code to resolve them.

- The learning curve of Joomla is longer when compared with other open source platforms.

Summary

In this chapter, you saw how Joomla has influenced the web development industry and why it is such a powerful tool. Here are some important points to remember:

- Joomla is a CMS that enables you to create a fully featured web site in a few hours. It is supported with hundreds of extensions and plug-ins, and can easily make any kind of web site.

- Joomla provides a GUI–based Administrator interface that makes the process of web site maintenance easy.

- A CMS reduces the cost of web site maintenance because all the web content is organized in a database, making it easier to maintain than it would be in individual web pages.

- With Joomla, you don't have to make a web site from scratch because it provides a default web site with menus, articles, and modules that can be easily customized to suit your needs.

- Joomla supports most operating systems, including Windows, Linux, and MAC OS X.

- Joomla is free, supports multiple languages, stores all types of picture formats, and is compatible with most web browsers.

In Chapter 2, you will learn the Joomla installation process, both on local and remote servers. For local installation, you will be installing and using the XAMPP software. The characteristics of XAMPP and how it is installed and configured will be covered in detail.

■ ■ ■

Installing XAMPP and Joomla

You now know that Joomla is a CMS that stores all the information of a web site in a database and provides a bundle of built-in modules that can be readily added to make a rich web application in a couple of hours. To work with Joomla, you need three applications, a web server, the PHP scripting language, and a database server. Instead of downloading and installing these three applications individually (which is a difficult task), you can download and install just one application: XAMPP. XAMPP is a project that provides a complete web development environment in one easy package—perfect for your needs.

In this chapter, you will learn how to install XAMPP, a complete web development environment in one easy package, and install Joomla on a local server and a remote server. A *remote server* is a machine containing special software that is used for hosting a web site. These servers are called remote servers because they are found in another location (often a long way away) from where you are, and you usually access them using FTP client software. While the web site is under construction, there is no need to run everything on a remote server, and it is much quicker and easier to run the site from your everyday (local) machine. You can do so by installing some software on your machine that will make it into a local server on which you can test your web site.

Web Request Life Cycle

Before diving into the Joomla installation prerequisites, it's important to have some background on the web request life cycle. Web applications normally work in a request-response mode. The user (usually called a *client*) sends a request for some information to the web server via a web browser. The web server processes the request by executing certain scripts/programs that may involve fetching desired information or updating the RDBMS. The web server then sends the response in the form of an HTML document back to the client, as shown in Figure 2-1.

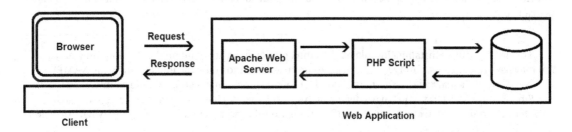

Figure 2-1. *Web request life cycle*

In terms of Apache PHP (a popular web-scripting language) and MySQL, the following list describes the steps in the web request life cycle:

1. The client sends the request to the Apache web server in terms of HTTP GET or POST messages.

2. The Apache web server parses the request, locates the desired PHP script, and executes it.

3. Depending on the user's request, the PHP script either fetches the desired information from the MySQL database or updates its contents.

4. The MySQL database returns the desired information and the status of the database to the PHP script.

5. The PHP script combines the database information with an HTML template and sends it to the Apache web server program.

6. Apache sends an HTTP response in the form of the HTML document to the user's browser.

Prerequisites to Installing Joomla on the Local Server

As discussed earlier, Joomla is a server-based application made in PHP that has to be installed on a web server. It also requires a database server, another piece of software running remotely or locally to help maintain the database, to store the contents of the web site. So before you install Joomla, the following applications must be installed on your local PC:

- Web server: Apache web server (version 2.x or higher)

- PHP scripting language: PHP (version 5.4 or higher)

- Database server: MySQL (version 5.1 or higher)

You are free to choose any other web server that is compatible with PHP if you'd rather not use Apache. For example, you can use the Nginx server or Microsoft IIS instead of Apache.

Joomla is platform-independent and can run on several OSs, including Linux, Mac OS X, and Windows. I use Windows 8 for Joomla in this book because it is very convenient, and it is easy to use Joomla on Microsoft Windows.

■ **Note**   Microsoft is teaming up with the Joomla community to make it easy and convenient to host Joomla on Windows.

The prerequisite of installing Joomla on the Linux platform may depend on the distribution you use. You may have Apache, PHP, and MySQL packages preinstalled; and you may not need to install XAMPP at all. Even if any of the packages are not installed, the process of their installation is quite simple.

Similarly, on Mac OS X, you have a default web server (Apache) in your system that just needs to be activated. You only need to download the PHP Apache module and executable versions of MySQL for Mac OS X, and then install them.

XAMPP

As discussed, to develop any web sites with Joomla, you need a web server, a database, and the PHP language installed on your computer. XAMPP, which is an Apache distribution developed by Kai "Oswald" Seidler and Kay Vogelgesang, contains Apache, MySQL, and PHP. In fact, that's what the *AMP* in XAMPP stands for: Apache, MySQL, and PHP. The final *P* is for Perl, another scripting language. The first letter in the acronym, *X*, means cross-platform; it implies that XAMPP is available for the Windows, Mac, and Linux operating systems. XAMPP is very easy to install and automatically configures the Apache web server along with MySQL, PHP, and Perl.

Installing XAMPP doesn't make any changes to the Windows registry, which makes removing it from the system an easy task: you can just delete its folder from the disk drive (although removing it using Control Panel is considered a better option). XAMPP is a compilation of free software and is free to copy under the terms of the GNU General Public License (GPL). To make XAMPP convenient for developers, it is configured with all features turned on.

Installing XAMPP

XAMPP is very easy to install. Just navigate to `www.apachefriends.org`, click the XAMPP link on the web site, and then click the correct version for your operating system. Scroll down to the Download section and click the Installer file download under the Basic Package heading. I downloaded the Windows version, XAMPP 5.6.3; at the time of this writing, it is the latest available Windows version. The downloaded file is named `xampp-win32-5.6.3-0-VC11-installer.exe`. Just double-click this EXE file to install it. It is a better option to install it at the root of the local disk drive (I used disk drive C:).

The first screen you'll see is a welcome screen, as shown in Figure 2-2.

Figure 2-2. *Welcome screen of XAMPP setup wizard*

Click Next and you'll see a dialog box allowing you to specify which components you want to install. A *component* is an executable file that performs specific functions without the need of any user intervention. The components are usually auto-starts, meaning that they automatically start when the operating system is booted and run in the background as long as the system is running. Some components don't start automatically; they require manual startup.

Apache and MySQL are essential requirements for Joomla, so you must select the check boxes Apache and MySQL. You can also select the FileZilla FTP Server, as shown in Figure 2-3, but it is optional.

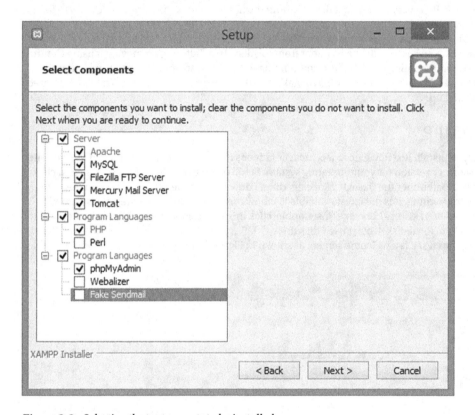

Figure 2-3. *Selecting the components to be installed*

■ **Note** FileZilla is an FTP server used for remote administration. It is used if you need to transfer files to your web server from a remote computer. If you already have an FTP server installed on your machine, you can skip it. You just have to carefully handle the server address and FTP username and password to avoid any unauthorized access.

Click the Next button. You will be prompted to specify the location to install XAMPP. Specify the C:\xampp folder, as shown in Figure 2-4 (note that you can install it in any folder you choose).

Figure 2-4. *Specifying the folder to install XAMPP*

Click Next to continue in the Setup Wizard. The following dialog box introduces Bitnami for XAMPP and provides a link to know more about Bitnami. Click Next to continue. The next dialog box informs you that XAMPP is ready to be installed. Click Next; XAMPP will start extracting the files, as shown in Figure 2-5.

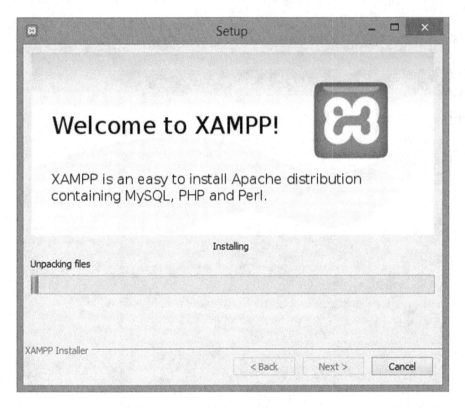

Figure 2-5. *XAMPP files being copied to the specified folder*

XAMPP requires port 80 to work. If you already have a server occupying port 80 (e.g., ColdFusion Server, IIS Server, Skype, etc.), you can't launch XAMPP after installing it due to a port-binding conflict. For example, if you have Skype installed on your machine, you may get an error saying that port 80 is already in use. To avoid a port-binding conflict with any server running on the machine, it is a better option to stop the services of other servers (if any) from the Control Panel.

■ **Note** To understand how port-binding conflicts can be avoided, visit the following web sites: http://complete-concrete-concise.com/web-tools/how-to-change-the-apache-port-in-xampp and https://community.apachefriends.org/f/viewtopic.php?p=206035&sid=9e3fc2dc9f59d8293a5dba3ff5 ab982b.

Finally, you'll see a dialog box showing the completion of the XAMPP Setup Wizard. The dialog box shows a checkbox that determines whether you want to start the XAMPP Control Panel, as shown in Figure 2-6. The checkbox is checked by default.

Figure 2-6. *Dialog box showing successful completion of the XAMPP Setup Wizard*

Using XAMPP Control Panel

The XAMPP Control Panel is the main steering panel from which you can control the workings of Apache as well as MySQL. You can also work with phpMyAdmin through this panel (phpMyAdmin is software for creating and maintaining MySQL databases). You can access your MySQL account using phpMyAdmin.

XAMPP comes packed with phpMyAdmin and an FTP server. Click Finish to complete the installation.

The installation of XAMPP is simple if there are no port conflicts — just double-click its installer file. You may see a number of informational messages and dialog boxes during the installation. Just accept the default options. After a successful installation, the XAMPP Control Panel will be displayed, as shown in Figure 2-7.

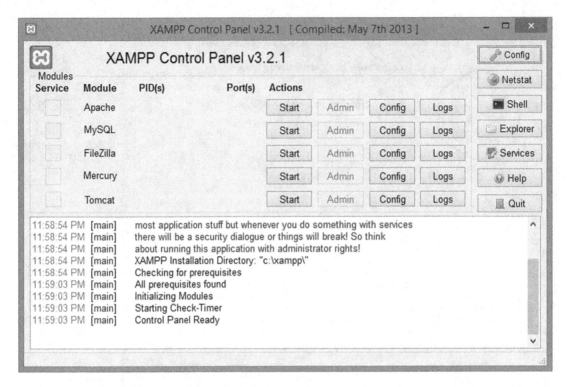

Figure 2-7. XAMPP Control Panel showing the status of services

On the XAMPP Control Panel, you should see that Apache, MySQL, and FileZilla are running (assuming that this is what you selected while installing XAMPP). With the successful installation of XAMPP, you are assured that your PC now contains Apache, PHP, and MySQL, which are necessary for Joomla installation.

Mercury bundled with XAMPP is a mail transport mechanism that provides your web site users with message boxes so that they can communicate with each other and/or receive auto generated messages. It is very straightforward to use. To get started, just click the Start button in the Mercury section of the Control Panel and then click the Admin button to add users. After managing user accounts, a couple of steps configure this package and make it ready for use. Your web site visitors can send/receive e-mail, but because you will be using the PHP mailer function for managing e-mail on your web site, you need not worry about this package at this stage.

From the XAMPP Control Panel, if you click Explorer, you'll get a list of all the subfolders under the xampp installation folder, as well as the files required to start and stop XAMPP (see Figure 2-8).

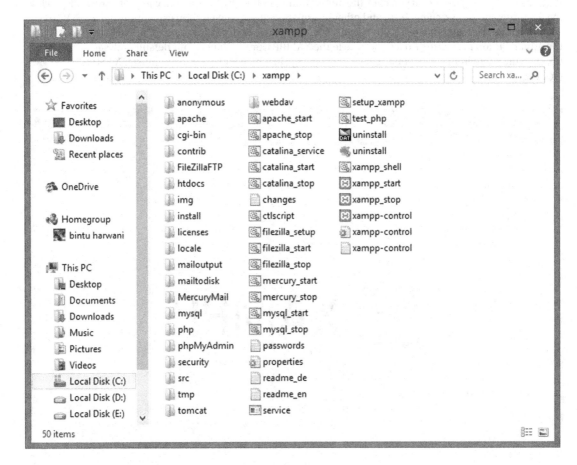

Figure 2-8. *List of files and folders in the xampp directory*

Administering XAMPP

In the XAMPP Control Panel, if you click the Admin button in the MySQL section, you get a screen displaying the environment, server, client, host, and other information about MySQL. You can administer MySQL and set its environment from that page, but because you don't have to do any administration in MySQL, just click the Admin button next to the Apache service in the XAMPP Control Panel. Your default browser will open up, showing a screen that asks you to select the language in which you want to administer XAMPP (see Figure 2-9).

Figure 2-9. *Selecting the language to administer XAMPP*

■ **Note**   Visit `https://docs.joomla.org/XAMPP` to see the XAMPP documentation.

Click the appropriate link to display the administration options in the language of your choice. The first page that opens up is a welcome page. On the left side is a navigation bar, as shown in Figure 2-10.

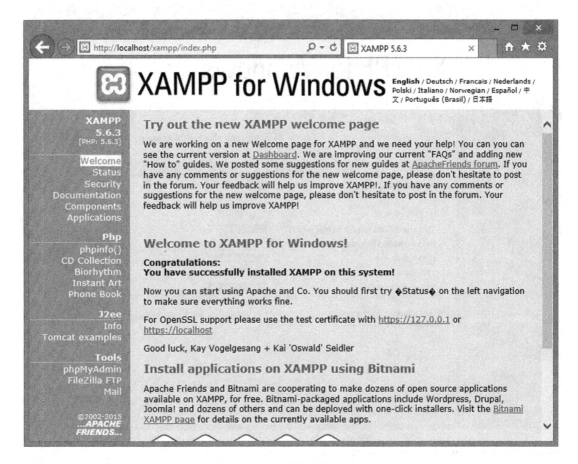

Figure 2-10. Welcome screen displayed upon opening XAMPP

Click the Status link on the navigation bar to display the status of the service(s) running on your computer, as shown in Figure 2-11.

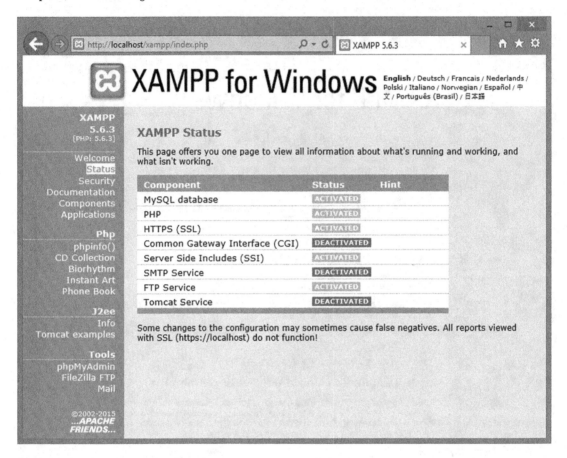

Figure 2-11. *Displaying the status of all the services*

You can see that MySQL, PHP, HTTPS, Common Gateway Interface (CGI), Server Side Includes (SSI), and FTP Service are all activated. Only SMTP Service (required for sending/receiving e-mail) is not working. Currently, you shouldn't be worried about any other services except PHP and MySQL (required for installing Joomla), so your job is done. If you click the phpMyAdmin button from the navigation bar on the left side, it will open phpMyAdmin, a software package used for creating and maintaining MySQL databases. Let's take a look at it now.

Using phpMyAdmin

As previously stated, phpMyAdmin is used to create and maintain MySQL databases. The initial database management interface screen (shown in Figure 2-12) can look a little bewildering, but you don't need to worry about a lot of that information for now.

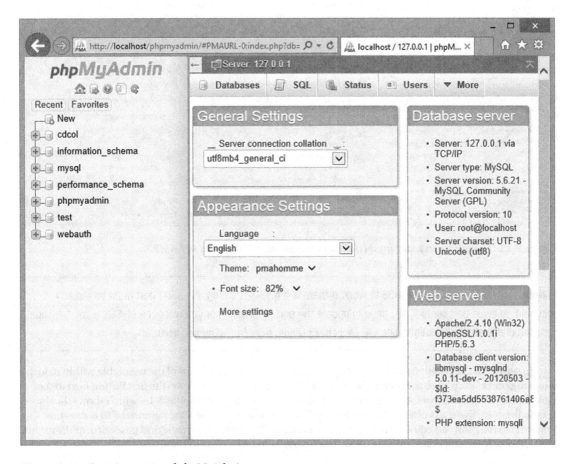

Figure 2-12. *Opening screen of phpMyAdmin*

The left frame in phpMyAdmin is used for navigation. The databases that you create are displayed in this area, along with the tables (if any) under their respective database names. You can click any database or table to work with it. By default, seven databases are provided: cdcol, information_schema, mysql, performance:schema, phpmyadmin, test, and webauth. When selecting any database, you see the list of tables in it. For example, if you select the mysql database from the navigation bar, you see the list of tables in it (see Figure 2-13).

Figure 2-13. *Default tables in the mysql database automatically provided in XAMPP*

■ **Note**   MySQL requires port 3306 to work. If there is a MySQL running, the 3306 port must be already occupied; to avoid port conflict, you have to update the port information or you will get a MySQL error message. For solutions to similar questions, see `www.apachefriends.org/faq_windows.html`.

To see the list of default users of the `mysql` database, browse the contents of the user table within it. Just select the check box next to the user table and click the Browse icon in that row (the first button next to the table name). You'll find that there are five rows in the user table shown in Figure 2-14, which shows that by default there are five users of the `mysql` database. (Users are the people who are authorized to access the `mysql` database.) You can edit the contents of these rows to change the username and password, and you can also add new users and delete existing users. The five default users are as follows:

- `root` (Host: `localhost`): This user can access the `mysql` database only locally.

- `root` (Host: `127.0.0.1`): This user can access the `mysql` database locally and from the Internet. That is, a person can log in remotely and access the `mysql` database. In that case, the host column in the user table of the `mysql` database should be set to the IP address of the remote MySQL server.

- `pma` (Host: `localhost`): This user is used by the phpMyAdmin application.

- " " (Host: `localhost`): No username is provided, and you can assign it any name. It will have the same privileges as `pma` and can be used to perform necessary database functions via phpMyAdmin.

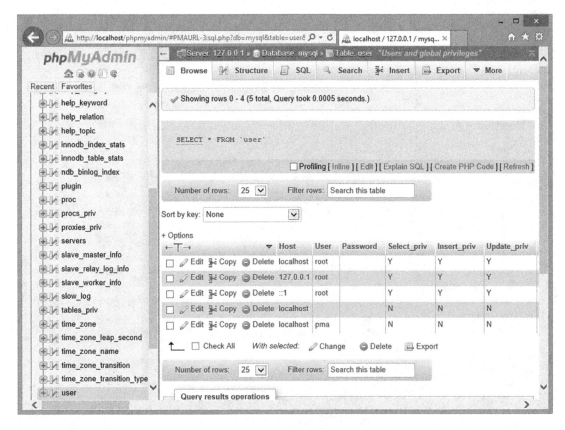

Figure 2-14. Displaying rows of the user table in the MySQL database

For security reasons, you should change the password of root (keeping default passwords is too risky). Because you will be accessing the mysql database locally, you will edit the root user that has the value localhost in its Host column.

Select the first row (which has the value root in its User column and localhost in its Host column) by checking the box for this row and then select the Edit tool in that row (the Edit tool looks like a pen). The table will open in edit mode, and you can alter its contents, as shown in Figure 2-15.

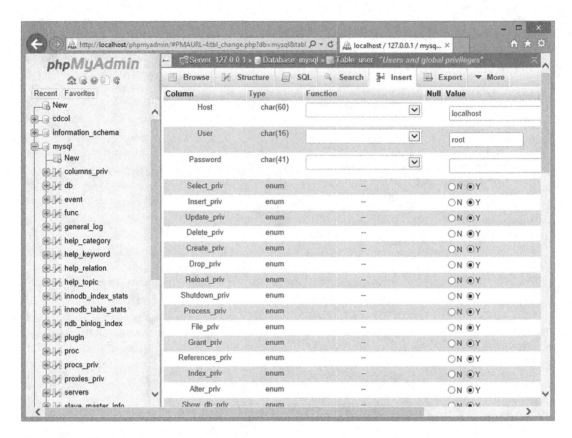

Figure 2-15. *Changing the root user's password*

Enter a password for the root user. I used mce here, but you can use whatever you want. Click the Go button at the bottom to save the password. You can skip this step if you are using an already existing (installed on the machine) version of MySQL.

If you don't want the password to be stored in the user table as plain text, you can use the PASSWORD function from the Function drop-down box to encrypt the password.

You need to change default password of the mysql database for security reasons. After saving the password, you'll see a screen like the one shown in Figure 2-16.

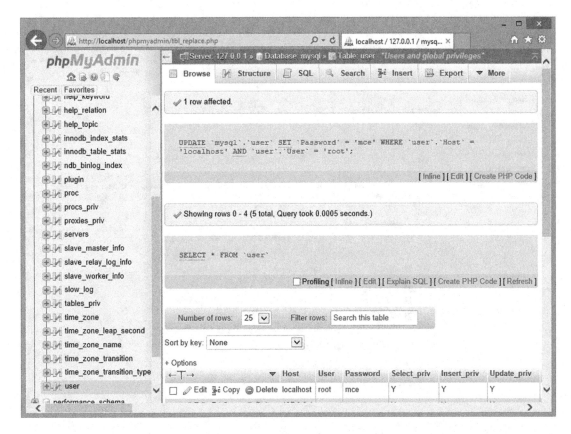

Figure 2-16. *Screen displaying the message that the contents of the user table have been successfully modified*

You get a message that one row has been updated, and the SQL command that carried it out is displayed below. The message confirms that the password of the root user has been changed.

Creating a Database

Because Joomla will store all the raw contents of your web site (articles, images, user information, etc.) in a database, you should now create a database. I'll show you how to create a database in MySQL. I call mine joomladb, but you can use any name you like. Open the initial screen of phpMyAdmin by clicking the Home button at the top left, underneath the phpMyAdmin banner. Type the name of the database to be created in the Create New Database text box and click the Create button, as shown in Figure 2-17. Don't worry about the rest of the settings; leave everything else as-is for now.

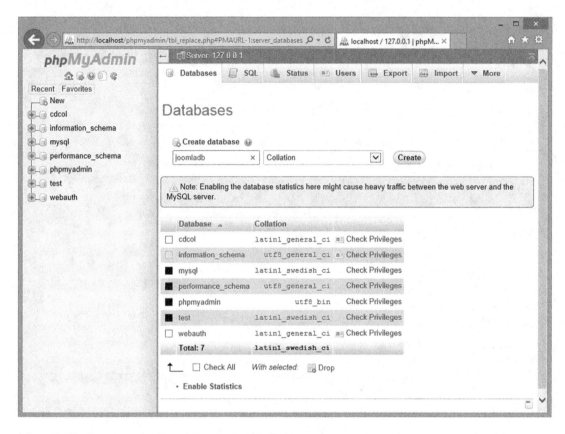

Figure 2-17. *Creating a database by name: joomladb*

■ **Note**   If you don't create a database, the Joomla 3.0 installer will automatically create a database for you during the installation process. The only condition is that the specified user account must exist and should have sufficient privileges to create a new database.

You'll get a message informing you that the database has been successfully created, and a message that the database created (which I'll refer to as joomladb from here on) has no tables in it (see Figure 2-18). However, you don't need to create any tables manually because it will all be done automatically by Joomla when you start adding features to your web site.

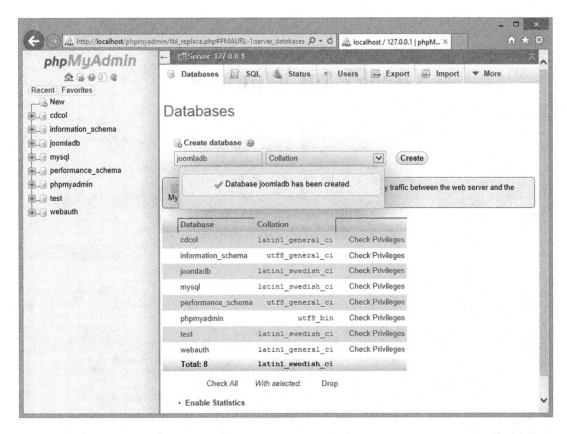

Figure 2-18. *Window displaying message of successful database creation*

Requiring User Authentication

This step is required only if MySQL is not already installed on your machine; skip it if it already exists. The final thing that you'll do before installing Joomla is make phpMyAdmin a little more secure by requiring users to authenticate themselves before opening phpMyAdmin (it isn't essential for installing Joomla, but it is good practice). You will do this by assigning a password to phpMyAdmin. To do so, return to the XAMPP admin screen and select the Security tab in the navigation bar. You will see the screen shown in Figure 2-19.

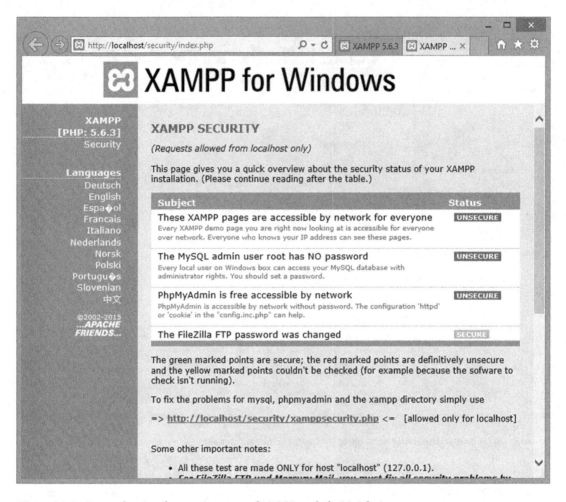

Figure 2-19. *Screen showing the security status of MySQL and phpMyAdmin*

Click the http://localhost/security/xamppsecurity.php link to open the security console, as shown in Figure 2-20. Specify the password for MySQL SuperUser: root in both the New Password and Repeat The New Password text boxes.

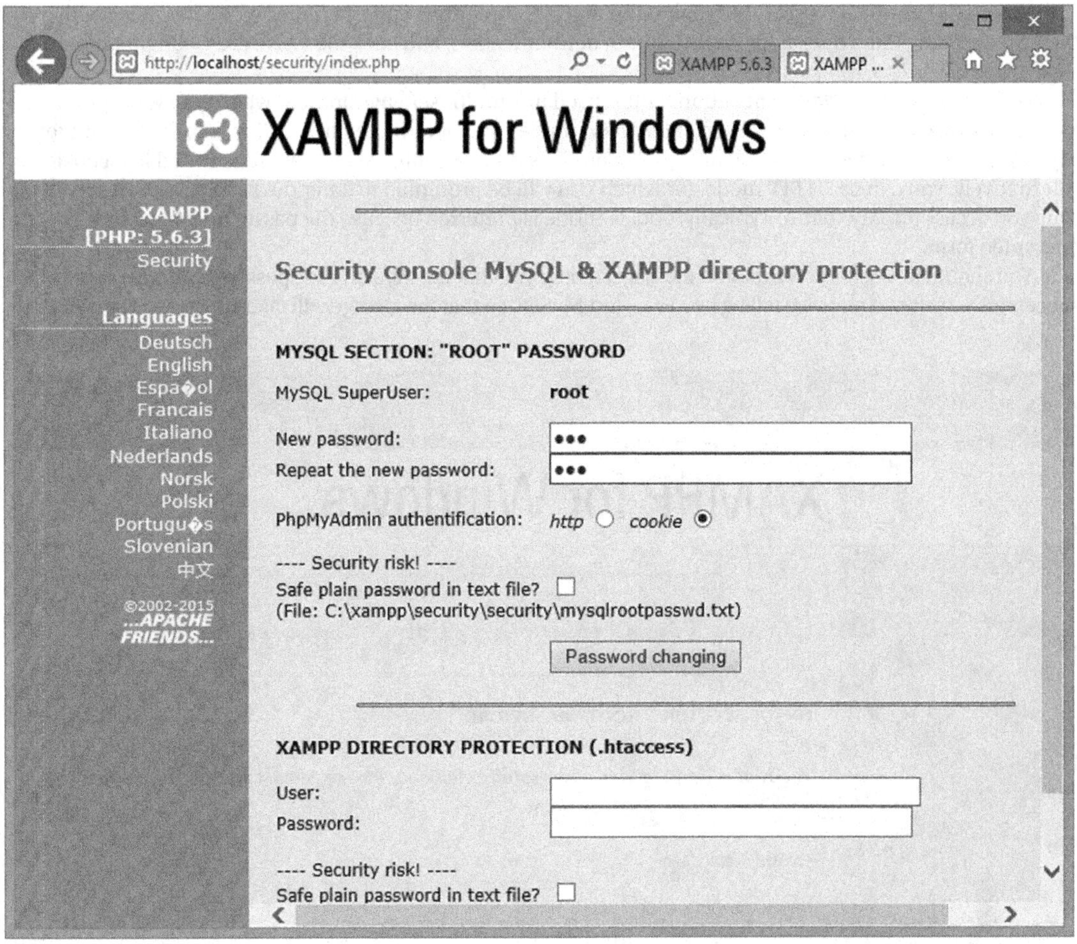

Figure 2-20. *Specifying the option for phpMyAdmin authentication and root password*

■ **Note** The superuser has all the privileges for maintaining the databases. The superuser can create more users, delete existing users, assign and revoke permissions to other users, create backups, and even restore databases in case of system crashes.

You can also assign superuser rights to any user by performing the following steps:

1. Open the cmd window.

2. Login as root on MySQL.

3. Execute the following SQL command:

   ```
   GRANT ALL PRIVILEGES ON *.* TO 'any_user'@'%';
   ```

Enter any password you like, but make sure that it is something you can remember. Then select either the http or cookie radio button for PhpMyAdmin authentication, and click the Password Changing button to save the password.

HTTP and cookie are authentication modes used in a multiuser environment where you want users to be able to access their own database only. These modes also determine how phpMyAdmin connects to MySQL as the root superuser. By default, cookie mode is used, in which the password is stored in a cookie. Alternatively, you can use HTTP mode, for which you will be prompted to enter the root password every time you access phpMyAdmin. Typically, cookie mode is preferred because the password is stored in encrypted form.

You should now get a confirmation message, telling you that the MySQL root password change was successful as well as a message telling you to restart MySQL so that the change will take effect (see Figure 2-21).

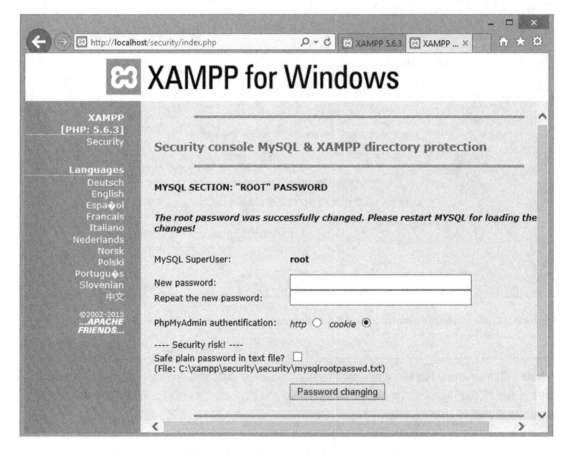

Figure 2-21. *Message displaying the successful change of the MySQL root password*

Restart MySQL by clicking the Stop button in the MySQL section of the XAMPP Control Panel (refer to Figure 2-7). The MySQL server is stopped, and the button will change to Start. Click it to restart MySQL. To invoke the XAMPP project, click the Admin button in the Apache section of the XAMPP Control Panel. The XAMPP project will be invoked and its welcome screen will be displayed, as shown in Figure 2-22.

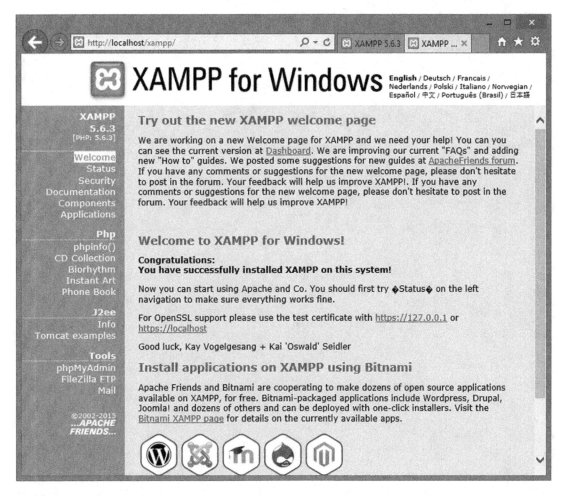

Figure 2-22. *Welcome screen of the XAMPP project*

If you find an error here, something is wrong with the password you entered. To fix that error, go to the phpmyadmin directory of the xampp directory and open the config.inc.php file. In it, search for the following line:

```
find $cfg['Servers'][$i]['password'] = '';
```

Add your password in the single quotes after the = (equals) sign. For example, if you want to set the password to world2009, the line will be changed to the following:

```
$cfg['Servers'][$i]['password'] = 'world2009';
```

Save the file; and you will be able to invoke the XAMPP project. The welcome screen that may appear is shown in Figure 2-22.

If you now invoke phpMyAdmin by clicking the phpMyAdmin button from the navigation bar, it will not open directly as before; it will prompt the user to enter the password for the root user (see Figure 2-23).

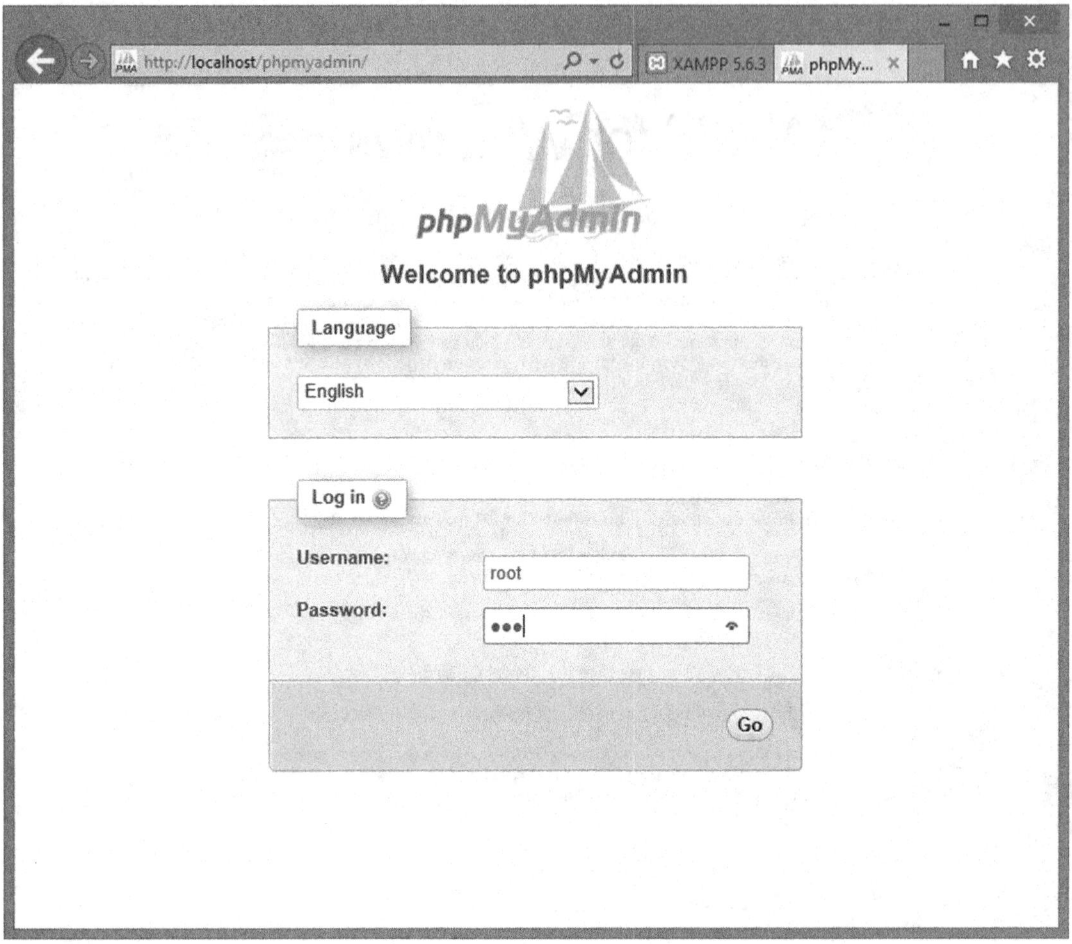

Figure 2-23. *Login screen for opening phpMyAdmin*

Until you enter the correct password in the preceding page (you have to enter the same password that you specified in the security console — refer to Figure 2-20), phpMyAdmin will not open, and you cannot maintain the MySQL database.

Now that the prerequisite conditions of Joomla installation have been successfully met (i.e., you've installed XAMPP, which has automatically installed PHP, MySQL, and Apache), you can install Joomla on the local server (Apache) installed on your PC.

Installing Joomla Locally

To install Joomla on a local server, you have to first download it from www.joomla.org/download.html. The latest Joomla version available for download at the time of this writing is Joomla3.4.1. The archive file that is downloaded is namedJoomla_3.4.1-Stable-Full_Package.zip. You have to unzip the Joomla ZIP file into a subfolder of the htdocs directory of XAMPP. That is, you have to first make a subfolder inside the htdocs directory of your XAMPP project, in which you will store all the Joomla files and folders. Recall that you installed the XAMPP project in the default c:\xampp folder, so open this folder and go to its htdocs directory. Now make a subfolder in the c:\xampp\htdocs directory. I called mine joomlasite, but the name doesn't matter. The only thing left to do now is to copy the Joomla files and folder into this joomlasite subfolder.

Download the latest Joomla package from the Internet by going to www.joomla.org and clicking the Download Joomla button. It is packaged in a ZIP file, so you need the appropriate software, such as WinZip, to unpack it. I downloaded the Joomla package, which is in the form of a Joomla_3.3.6-Stable-Full_Package.zip file, but this may vary depending on the latest release available on the Internet. Unzip the file to any folder and copy all the unzipped files and folders of the Joomla package into the joomlasite subfolder (created in the c:\xampp\htdocs directory).

Joomla version 3.3.6, the latest version of Joomla, includes the following added features:

- It allows you to preview your web site after making changes.

- It has an improved user interface that allows you to easily manage media files (images, songs, videos, etc.).

- It includes a new plug-in manager.

- It allows multi-CSS file editing.

- It has full support for Atom 1.0 and RSS 2.0 feeds.

- It has better internationalization support, including full UTF-8 support, RTL support, and translation using INI files.

- It contains several components that help develop Ajax applications easily.

Joomla is installed using a browser. So open your browser and point it to the following address: http://localhost/joomlasite/ (assuming you have copied the Joomla files and folder into the joomlasite subfolder of the htdocs folder). A Joomla installer will be invoked that installs Joomla through a step-by-step approach. Each step prompts you to enter required certain information. Step 1 of the installer, the Main Configuration screen, will display (see Figure 2-24).

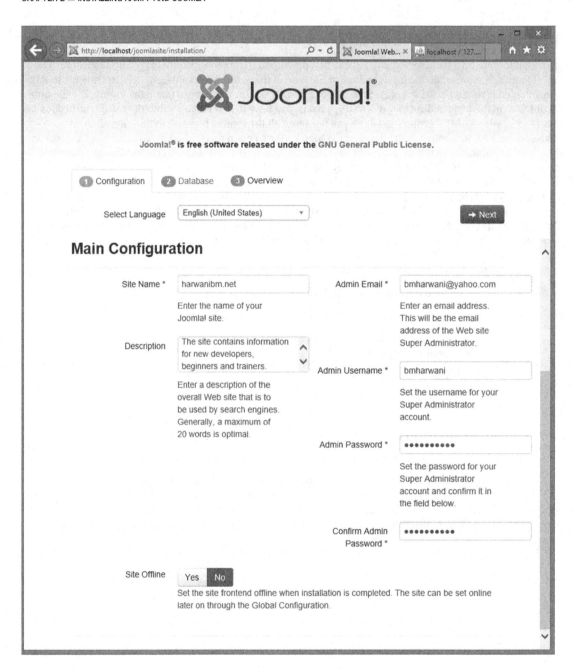

Figure 2-24. *Step 1 of Joomla installation*

■ **Note**   If your server is not properly configured to run Joomla, you get a system status page instead of installation steps that inform the pending requirements for installing Joomla. After installing the required components, reload the page to begin the Joomla installation.

Step 1

Step1 of the installation wizard is the Main Configuration screen shown in Figure 2-24.
The Main Configuration screen prompts for the following information:

1. The Select Language box prompts you for the language to be used for the installation steps. Choose your preferred language from the drop down list or don't make any changes to select the default language: English (United States).

2. In the Site Name box, enter the name for your Joomla site. I'm using the name harwanibm.net, but you can use whatever name you want for your site.

3. In the Description box, enter a brief description for your Joomla site. This description will become your site's default metadata.

4. In the Admin Email box, enter the valid e-mail address of the site's administrator.

5. In the Admin username box, enter the admin's username.

6. In the Admin Password box, enter the admin's password.

7. In the Confirm Admin Password box, re-enter the admin's password to confirm it.

8. The Site Offline button determines whether to make the site online (visible to visitors) or offline (invisible to visitors). Clicking the Yes button will make the site offline, but it can be made online later through Global Configuration.

9. Click the Next button in the upper-right corner of the page to move on to the next step.

The information entered here can be changed after installation via the Joomla Global Configuration Manager.

Step 2

Step 2 of the installation wizard is the Database Configuration screen shown in Figure 2-25.

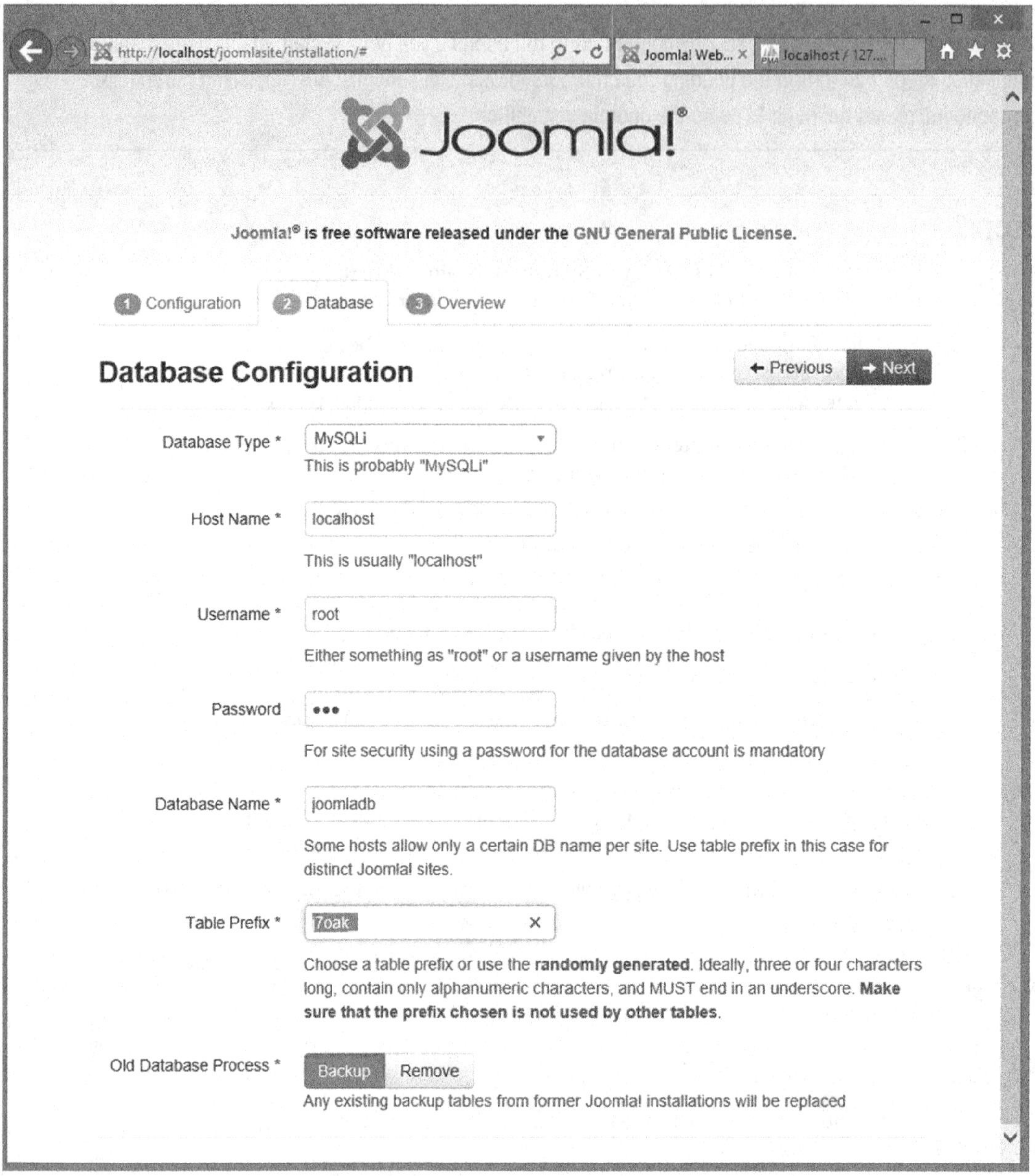

Figure 2-25. *Screen for specifying database configuration settings*

The Database Configuration screen prompts you to enter the following information:

1. From the Database Type combo box, select the type of database that your server is using. To install Joomla on Microsoft SQL Server, you need to install drivers for PHP for SQL Server and enable Microsoft SQL support in your PHP installation.

2. In the Host Name box, enter the hostname for your database. Because Joomla is being installed on the local server, simply enter **localhost** in this box.

3. In the Username box, enter the username for the database. Enter **root** as the username in this box.

4. In the Password box, enter the password associated with the username. Recall that via phpMyAdmin you set the root user's password to mce (or whatever password you chose) by altering the contents of the user table of the mysql database.

5. In the Database Name box, specify the name of the database that you earlier created via phpMyAdmin in MySQL. Recall that the MySQL database that you created through phpMyAdmin was named joomladb. This database will now be used for storing the content of the Joomla web site.

6. In the Table Prefix box, you can enter a set of characters that end with an underscore or you can leave it unchanged to its default value.

7. The Old Database Process, which is used when replacing an existing Joomla, determines whether you want to backup or delete the tables of the former Joomla installation. Because you are installing Joomla for the first time, whether you choose the Backup or Remove button, there will be no effect.

■ **Note** Even if a database is not already created, the Joomla 3.0 installer can create the database for you during the installation process. Make sure that the specified user account exists and has sufficient privileges to create a new database.

After entering the preceding information, click the Next button in the upper-right corner to move on to the next step.

Step 3

Step 3 is the "Finalisation" screen that helps you determine whether you want to install Joomla with or without sample data (see Figure 2-26).

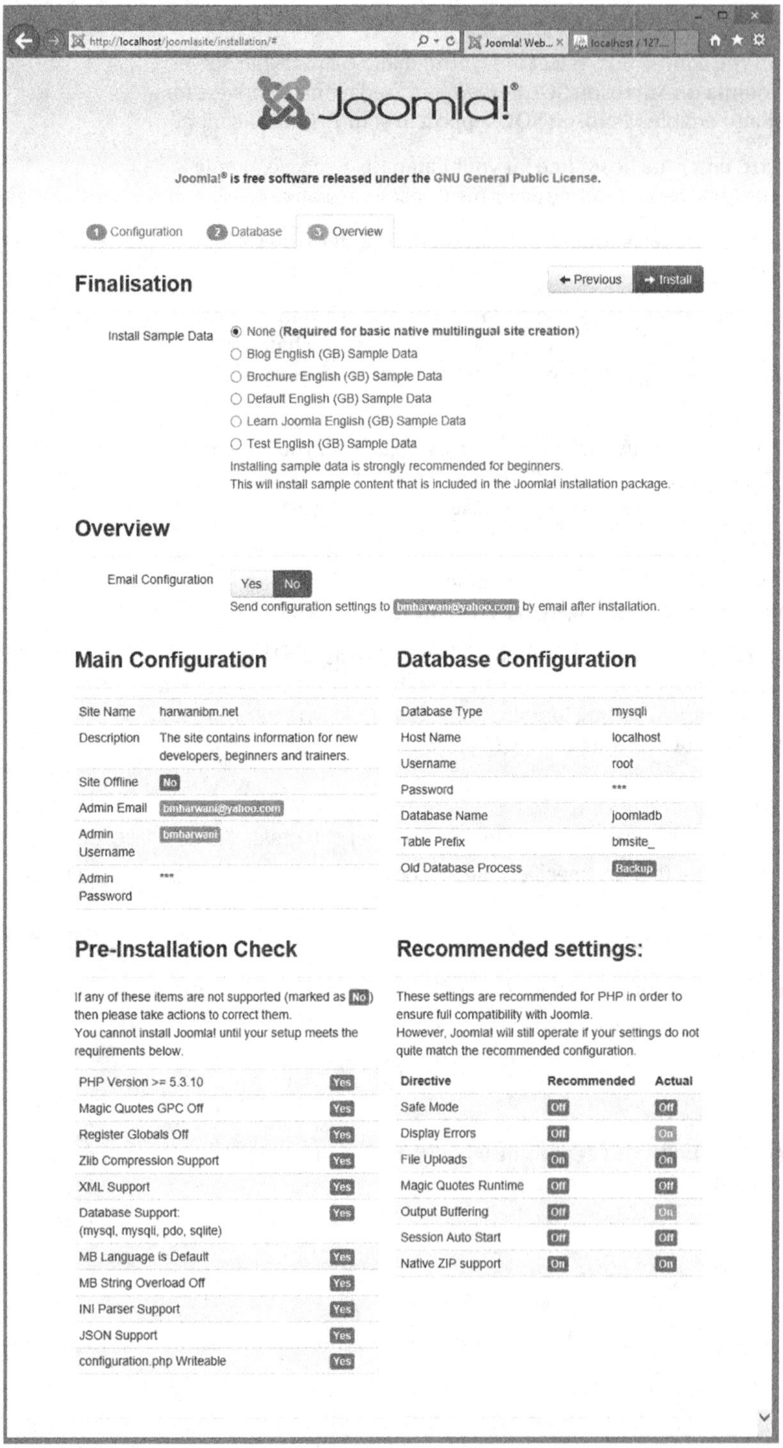

Figure 2-26. Finalization step of installing Joomla

The step also allows you to review and check whether the information entered in the earlier steps is correct. After revising the information and finding it correct, choose the desired type of sample data to be installed along with Joomla and click the Install button to initiate the Joomla installation. If this is your first time working with Joomla, I highly recommend that you install the sample data, which will help you understand the structure of a web site and the role of different menus and modules. Obviously, using sample data saves a lot of time when compared with creating a site from scratch.

The sample data, which includes a set of menus, navigation links, sections, and categories, is extremely useful for beginners learning the workings of Joomla and its different modules.

A brief description of different sample data options is as follows:

- *None*: A very basic web site will be created that will contain nothing but a menu and a login form. No content or modules will be created for you. This option is not recommended for a beginner.

- *Blog English (GB) Sample Data*: The site that appears like a blog will be created. Few articles will be published on the home page. The right sidebar will display blog features such as a list of recent posts, a blog roll, and a list of most popular posts.

- *Brochure English (GB) Sample Data*: The site in a brochure format will be created. Meant for small business, the home page will be set as a static page that shows only one article. The sidebar will show additional informational about the site through links such as About Us, News, Contact Us, Login Form, and so on.

- *Default English (GB) Sample Data*: The site similar to the brochure format will be created, but the sidebar will contain a Latest Articles module instead of a simple text module.

- *Learn Joomla English (GB) Sample Data*: A site will be created that contains information on how Joomla 3.0 works. The home page includes articles and examples for beginners, upgraders, and professional Joomla users. The sidebar includes links that will point at the Joomla community.

- *Test English (GB) Sample Data*: A site will be created that helps test Joomla 3.0. It is designed for users who want to contribute to Joomla 3.0. The home page article features information on how to run tests and report bugs to Joomla; the sidebar provides links for simple testing.

Choose the Blog English (GB) Sample Data option from the list of available options because it will create a very simple blog site for you. After selecting this option and clicking the Install button, Joomla files will be immediately installed, along with the sample data on your local server.

Finally, you'll get a Finish screen displaying the message Congratulations! Joomla Is Now Installed. You'll also get a message telling you to remove the installation directory from the `joomlasite` subfolder (in the `c:\xampp\htdocs` directory), as shown in Figure 2-27. This is a compulsory condition for successful installation of Joomla because of security reasons.

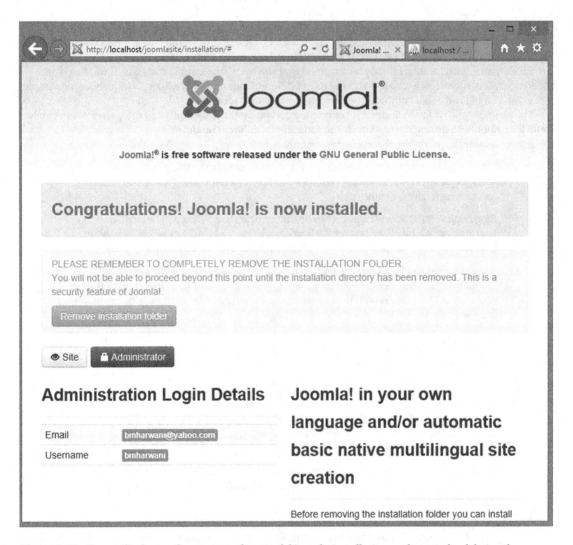

Figure 2-27. *Screen displaying the message of successful Joomla installation and a note for deleting the installation directory*

Deleting the Installation Folder

To delete the installation folder, click the Remove Installation Folder button. You can also delete the installation folder manually by using Windows Explorer or with the command line. After removing the installation folder, you get the confirmation that it was successfully deleted. The figure shows two buttons, Site and Administrator, which can be used to open the Joomla site and Joomla administration interface to manage its content.

By clicking the Site button, the Joomla web site will be displayed, as shown in Figure 2-28.

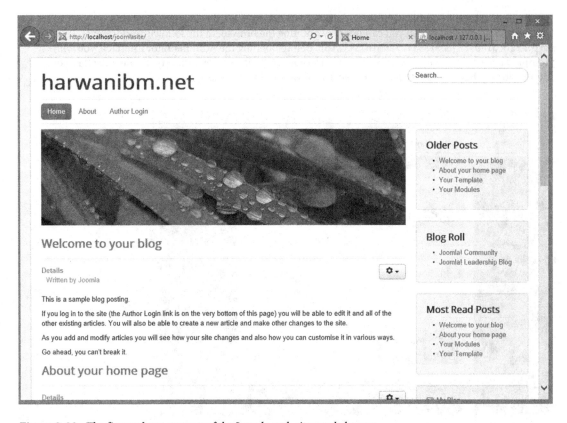

Figure 2-28. *The first welcome screen of the Joomla web site made by you*

The page that appears is actually your new web site. The reason why all that content is already there is because you clicked the Install Sample Data button earlier. You will be changing this web site throughout the rest of the book to make it your own. This web site can now be accessed anytime by pointing the browser at `http://localhost/joomlasite` (replace `joomlasite` with whatever you called your web site earlier).

■ **Note**   I'll be using `joomlasite` throughout the book, so remember to change the name to whatever you called your own web site whenever you see it appear.

To administer this Joomla web site and manage its content, you have to use the Administrator interface, which you can open by pointing the browser at the following address: `http://localhost/joomlasite/administrator`. Before opening the Administrator interface, you will prompted to specify the super-administrator's username (`bmharwani`) and password (the password you entered during the Joomla installation earlier), as shown in Figure 2-29.

Figure 2-29. *Opening the Joomla Administrator interface by entering the username and password*

In the Administrator interface, you find a Control Panel and menus to manage the web site contents, as shown in Figure 2-30.

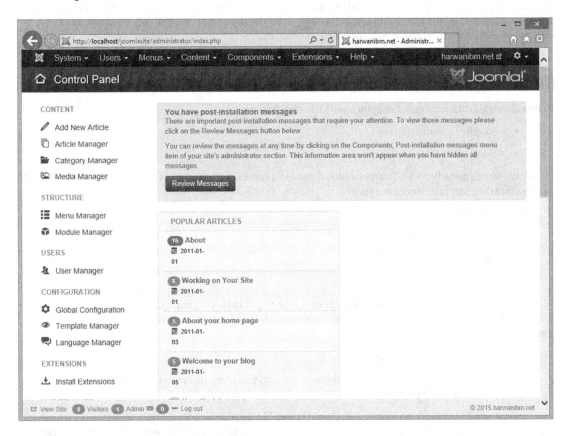

Figure 2-30. *Screen showing different managers and menus of the Joomla Administrator interface*

■ **Note**   From Chapter 3 onward, you will learn how to use these managers and menus to maintain your Joomla web site.

That's it for installing Joomla on your local machine. The next thing you need to do if you want the rest of the world to be able to see your Joomla site is to install Joomla on a remote server. When you do so, the hostname, username, and password are provided by the hosting company.

Having your web site hosted involves the procedure of uploading your web site to a public server to be viewed and accessed by the rest of world. It gives you the ability to show your presence on the Internet. Web-site hosting has become the most common medium to advertise services, facilities, and products provided by an organization. It has also become a great medium to get feedback from customers around the globe. The server space for hosting web sites is provided by various web-hosting companies.

Web-hosting companies offer an environment in which people can have their piece of cyberspace on the Internet 24/7 without great cost. These companies provide the space in which you can keep your web site, news, bulletins, documents, data, and post office (mail server) to accept mail. You just need to pay for the disk space used on the server and any extra charges for database support. The core components in a web-hosting environment are the web server, FTP server, mail server, and database server.

Installing Joomla on a Remote Server

To install Joomla on a remote server, you have to do two things:

- Register a domain name
- Book a web space on a server

If you do not already own a domain name, there are a great many services available on the Web that will enable you to register one. Here are a few:

- www.dreamhost.com/
- www.hostgator.com/
- in.godaddy.com
- www.hostpapa.in

I have registered a domain by name (bmharwani.net at godaddy.com) and booked approximately 100GB of space on a server via a web-hosting provider company. Before you proceed, ensure the following about your hosted account:

- PHP is installed and enabled.
- You have a MySQL database for the web site and you know its database name, username, and password.

You just need to upload the Joomla ZIP file to the public_html folder on the remote server (or whatever folder is provided by your hosting company) and then unpack it. You can even use File Manager to extract the files. Open the browser and type in your domain name (in my case, www.bmharwani.net), after which you will see the first Joomla installation screen. The rest of the procedure should then be exactly same as local installation.

Using One Click Installers

Another way to install Joomla is to use the one-click installers (also called auto installers) provided by the web-hosting service provider, available in the Control Panel. Fantastico is one of the most commonly used auto installers provided by most hosting companies. The Control Panel, also called cPanel, is a premier software package that makes life easier for web hosts and web site owners. It offers easy-to-use, powerful tools that perform essential tasks easily. It provides a GUI interface to help web site owners manage their sites, and includes video tutorials and onscreen help that enable hosting customers to manage their own accounts without requiring any help from support staff. It also includes virus protection, root kit detection, and a host of other tools to keep servers secure. To access cPanel, open the browser and point it at the following address: www.bmharwani.net/cpanel.

You will be asked to specify the username and password. Enter the username and password supplied to you by the web-hosting service provider while booking the web space. After the correct username and password are entered, cPanel will open (see Figure 2-31).

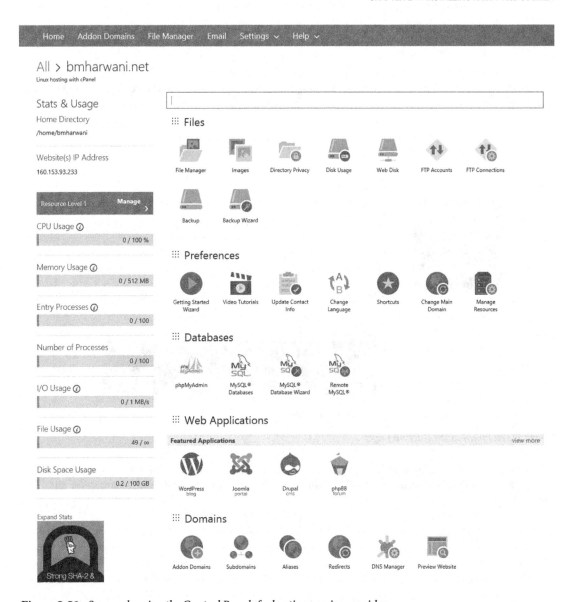

Figure 2-31. *Screen showing the Control Panel of a hosting service provider*

Figure 2-31 shows the Control Panel of a hosting service provider that provides executables for various CMSs. These executables are easy-to-use files that facilitate the installation of many open source applications on web-hosting accounts. These executables are in fact the wizards that upload files and configure databases with just a few mouse clicks. The figure shows the executables for WordPress, Joomla, Drupal, and other CMSs that are automatically provided by a hosting service provider.

To execute the Joomla wizard, click the Joomla icon under the Web Applications category; you should see a screen displaying a small introduction to Joomla along with its home page link (see Figure 2-32).

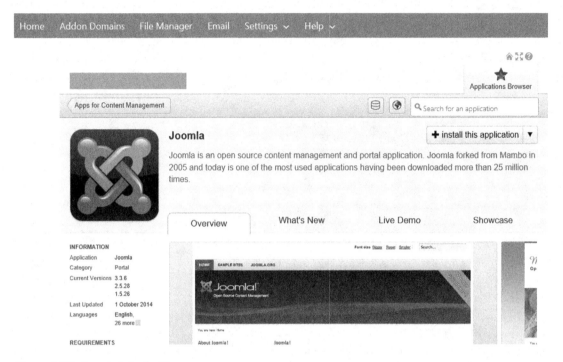

Figure 2-32. *Joomla introduction page*

Select the Install This Application link because you are installing Joomla for the first time in your web space. The screen shown in Figure 2-33 will pop up for you to enter admin and database settings for the Joomla site.

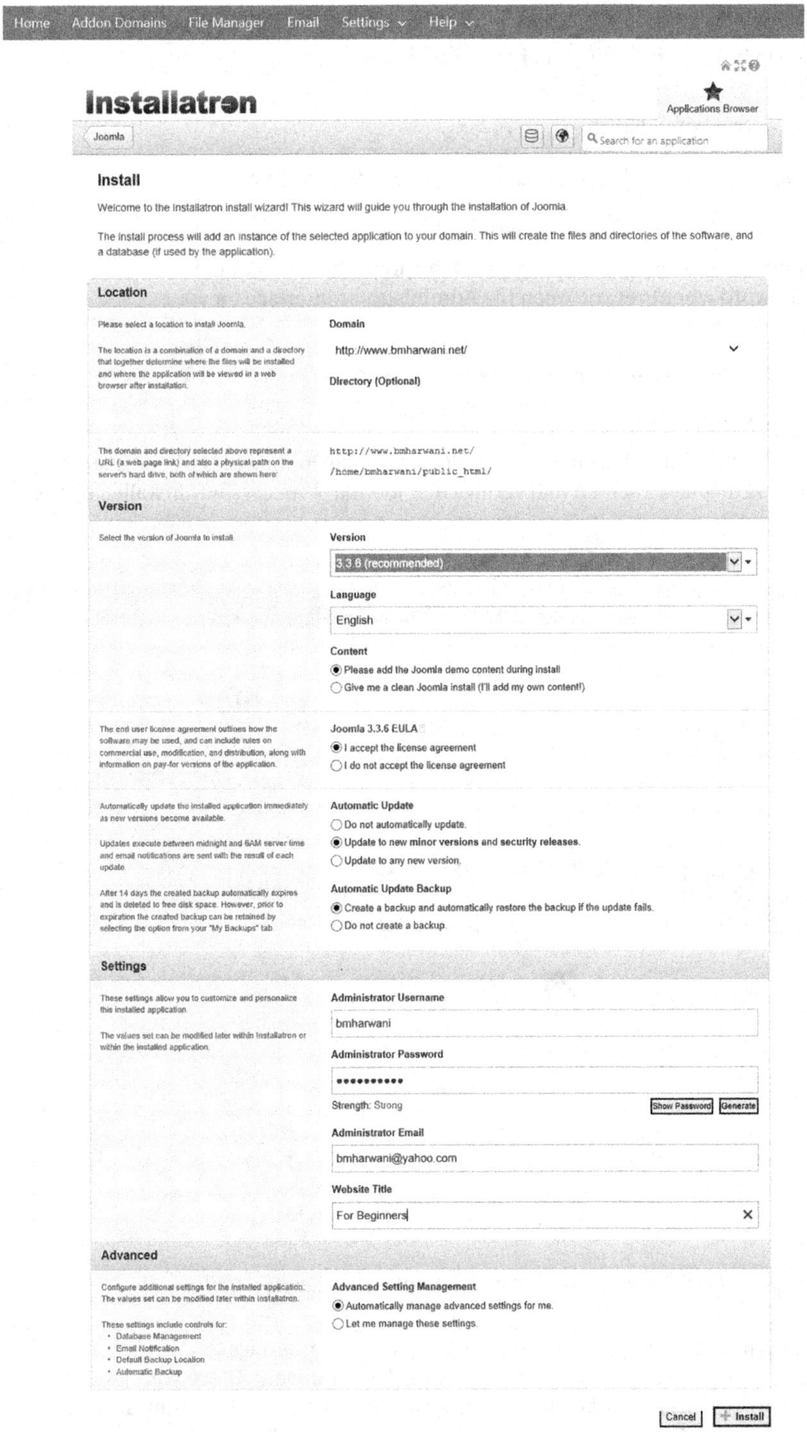

Figure 2-33. Screen for specifying Joomla web site information and administrator details

You will be asked to specify certain information, including the following (refer to Figure 2-33):

- The domain name to install Joomla on: enter the name of your web domain here (mine is bmharwani.net).

- The Joomla version to install: select the latest (3.3.6).

- The language to be used for installing Joomla: leave it at the default (English).

- The end user license agreement: accept the agreement.

- The administrator username and password: you will be prompted to enter the username and password whenever you open the Administrator interface for your Joomla web site.

- The e-mail ID of the administrator: enter your e-mail address.

- The web site title: enter the web site title here (mine is For Beginners).

After entering all the preceding information, click the Install button. The Joomla files will be installed on your remote server. Figure 2-34 displays a screen that verifies that Joomla is successfully installed on the remote server.

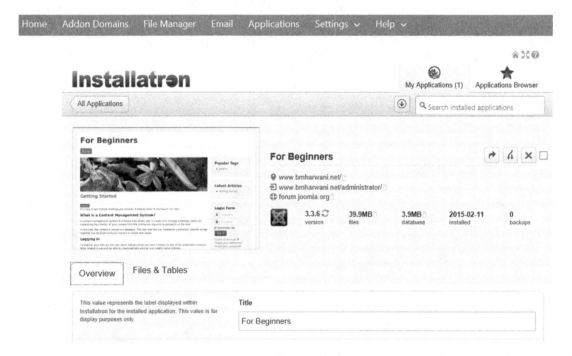

Figure 2-34. *Screen displaying joomla site preview and information aboutits files and tables*

Also, you are given the URLs to access the web site and the Administrator interface: http://bmharwani.net/ and http://bmharwani.net/administrator/, respectively. To see your Joomla web site, you point the browser at http://bmharwani.net/; and to manage its content, you open its Administrator interface by pointing the browser at http://bmharwani.net/administrator/. If you click the Files & Tables button, you'll get complete information about the MySQL tables automatically created for you (see Figure 2-35).

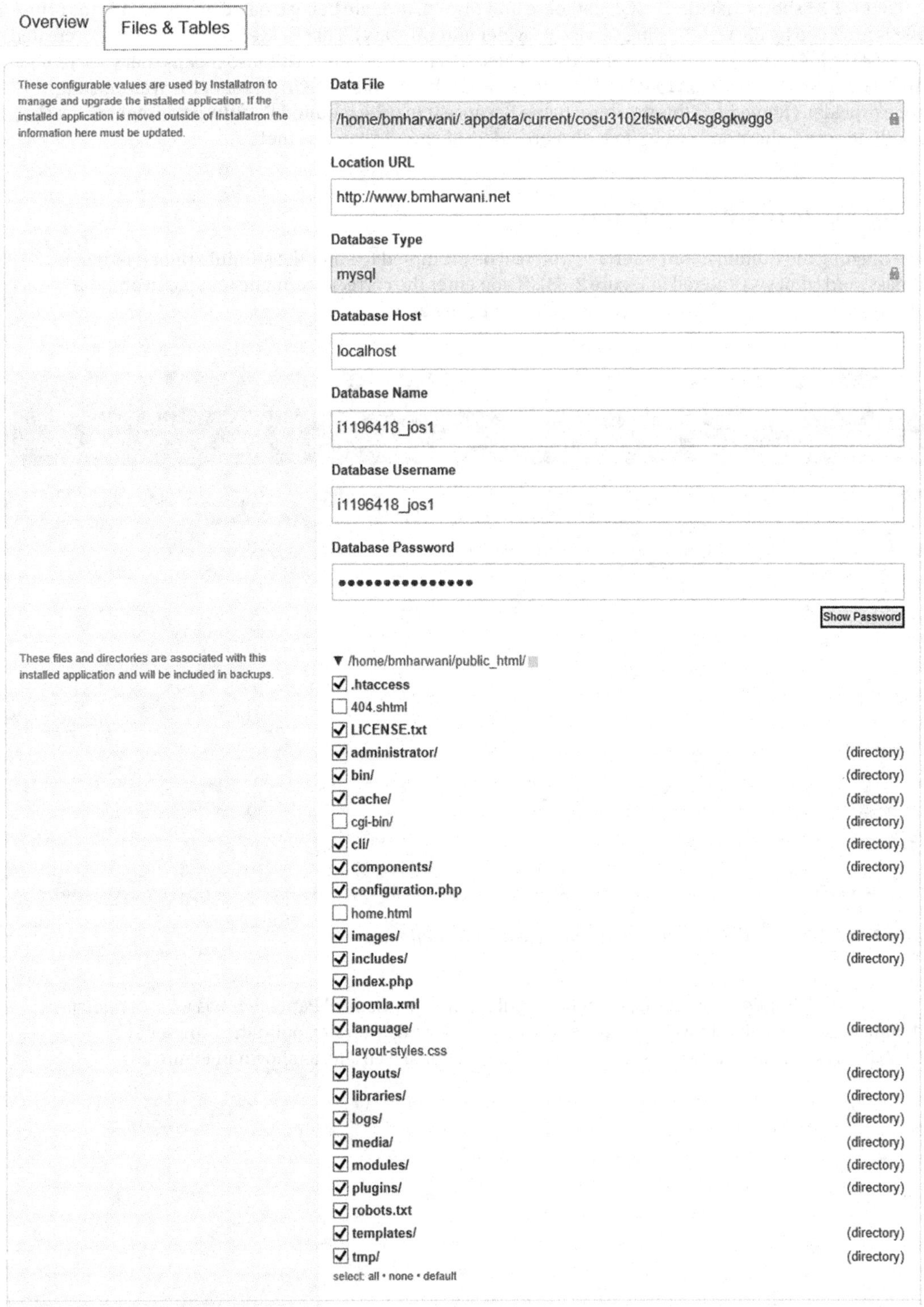

Overview   Files & Tables

These configurable values are used by Installatron to manage and upgrade the installed application. If the installed application is moved outside of Installatron the information here must be updated.

Data File

/home/bmharwani/.appdata/current/cosu3102tlskwc04sg8gkwgg8   🔒

Location URL

http://www.bmharwani.net

Database Type

mysql   🔒

Database Host

localhost

Database Name

i1196418_jos1

Database Username

i1196418_jos1

Database Password

•••••••••••••••

Show Password

These files and directories are associated with this installed application and will be included in backups.

▼ /home/bmharwani/public_html/ ▨
- ☑ .htaccess
- ☐ 404.shtml
- ☑ LICENSE.txt
- ☑ administrator/   (directory)
- ☑ bin/   (directory)
- ☑ cache/   (directory)
- ☐ cgi-bin/   (directory)
- ☑ cli/   (directory)
- ☑ components/   (directory)
- ☑ configuration.php
- ☐ home.html
- ☑ images/   (directory)
- ☑ includes/   (directory)
- ☑ index.php
- ☑ joomla.xml
- ☑ language/   (directory)
- ☐ layout-styles.css
- ☑ layouts/   (directory)
- ☑ libraries/   (directory)
- ☑ logs/   (directory)
- ☑ media/   (directory)
- ☑ modules/   (directory)
- ☑ plugins/   (directory)
- ☑ robots.txt
- ☑ templates/   (directory)
- ☑ tmp/   (directory)

select: all • none • default

Figure 2-35. *Screen displaying the MySQL database name, username, and URL to access the Joomla web site*

49

Figure 2-35 shows that the MySQL database and MySQL user are being created as i1196418_jos1 (this name is provided by the web-hosting service provider and can vary). That is, the MySQL database is created as i1196418_jos1, and the MySQL user is also created as i1196418_jos1. This also means that your Joomla web site will be stored in the i1196418_jos1 database on the remote MySQL server of the web-hosting service provider. (Remember this database name because it may be required for future maintenance tasks.) The URL to access the Joomla web site is also provided: http://bmharwani.net.

Using Administer Interface

While opening the Administrator interface, you will be prompted to enter the administrator username and password (that you entered in Figure 2-33). If you enter the correct username and password, the Administrator interface will be invoked, as shown in Figure 2-36.

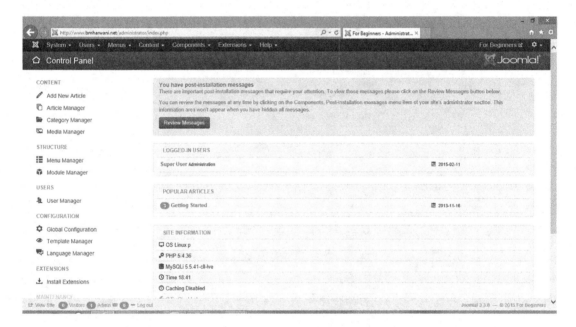

Figure 2-36. *Opening the Administrator interface of the Joomla web site*

When the Administrator interface opens, you'll be shown a Control Panel that has a list of managers and menus used to maintain web site content. To see the Joomla web site, point the browser at http://bmharwani.net/; and you should see a fully functional web site, as shown in Figure 2-37.

Figure 2-37. *Fully functional Joomla web site with default content*

The content and modules that you see are provided as sample data, which you can remove at any time through the Administrator interface. If the Joomla site doesn't open, and you get some "Hello" message instead, it means that there is a file named index.html in your home directory that is preventing your index.php file (the home page of your Joomla web site) to execute. Web-hosting companies usually provide a default opening file (index.html) when creating a web space account. This index.html file just displays a "Hello" or "Welcome" message. It has to be deleted to invoke the opening web page (index.php) of your Joomla site. The location of the home directory is specified by the web-hosting service provider, and it is usually public_html.

Connect to your domain with some FTP client software, go to the public_html folder, and delete any file with the primary name index. After you take care of this, your job should be done! Just refresh the browser, and a fully functional Joomla web site will be displayed on the screen.

Summary

In this chapter, you learned how to install an XAMPP project (a prerequisite for installing Joomla) and took a step-by-step walkthrough of installing Joomla on a local and a remote server. The next step is learning how to maintain Joomla web site content using the managers provided in the Control Panel of the Administrator interface; you will learn how to do that in Chapter 3.

■ ■ ■

CHAPTER 3

Your First Steps in Joomla

Chapter 2 looked in detail at the installation of the XAMPP framework and the Joomla package. While installing Joomla, you were prompted to specify the name of the Joomla web site you wanted to create (in this case, harwanibm.net). As a result, Joomla created a full-fledged web site that already contained menus, links, search boxes, articles, polls, news feeds, and so on; and all these features were functional. This automatically generated content can be updated, deleted, and added to at any time.

This chapter will cover the following:

- A brief introduction to the Administrator interface

- The home page: what it is and why it is important

- The impact of templates on a Joomla web site

■ **Note**   As mentioned in Chapter 2, the entire content of the web site so far is stored in the MySQL database named joomladb (although you could have called it anything), which you created when you installed Joomla. This is what is meant by a CMS: the whole web site is managed in one place, and what is a better place than a database?

Key Terms

Before you get started, there are two important terms that will crop up repeatedly throughout this book, so it will be useful to define them now: front end and back end (see Figure 3-1).

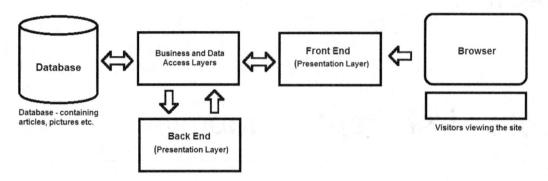

Figure 3-1. Block diagram demonstrating the relation between front and back end

Front end refers to the web site; the part that's accessed by users or visitors and that displays the content of the web site. The front end is called up by opening a browser window and pointing at the address. In this case, the address is `http://localhost/joomlasite` (remember that `joomlasite` was the folder in which you unpackaged Joomla, and at this stage you are dealing with the local server). The Business layer includes the business rules on the basis of which database is updated using the Data Access layer via executing SQL statements. The Back End represents the interface through which the Business and Data Access layers are managed, and hence the database. The front end of your Joomla web site will appear as shown in Figure 3-2.

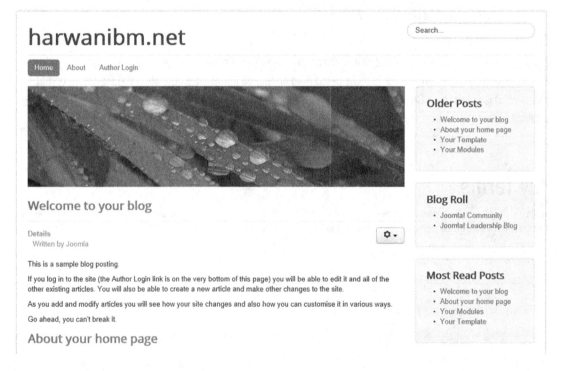

Figure 3-2. Default Joomla web site

The *back end* is the Administrator interface, which you use to manipulate the contents of your web site. It provides a Control Panel and other tools essential for maintaining the web site. To reach the Administrator interface, open a browser window and point it at the address `http://localhost/joomlasite/ administrator`.

Elements of the Administrator Interface

As discussed in Chapter 1, a CMS is a computer software system for organizing and managing documents, including web content. Because Joomla is a CMS, it provides a Control Panel and tools for you to manage your web site and its contents, and this Control Panel can be accessed by using the Joomla Administrator interface. To manage web site content, open your browser and point it at `http://localhost/joomlasite/ administrator` to open the Joomla Administrator interface.

From now on, you will have two windows open on your computer system: one with the browser pointing at `http://localhost/joomlasite` (showing your Joomla web site), and the other pointing at `http://localhost/joomlsite/administrator` (displaying the administrator tools and managers). You will manage the web contents through the Administrator interface and then switch to the Joomla web site browser window and refresh it to see the effect of the changes made to the Joomla web site. You can also view your updated Joomla web site directly from the Administrator interface. The Preview link at the top right quickly opens up the home page of the Joomla web site in a new window (in Internet Explorer) or a new tab (in Firefox).

Before the Administrator interface opens, you will be prompted to log in, as shown in Figure 3-3. Enter the administrator name and password that you specified while installing Joomla.

Figure 3-3. *Login screen of the Administrator interface*

The first screen contains a set of buttons for the various Joomla managers, which are collectively called the Control Panel, and menus to manage your web site contents (see Figure 3-4).

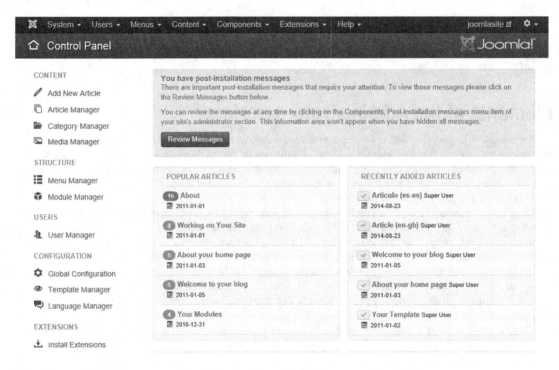

Figure 3-4. *Administrator screen displaying the Control Panel (managers) and menus*

Some of the most important features of Joomla can be found in this panel, and you'll spend a lot of time here. It is a sort of control tower for your web site, in which you can maintain its content and appearance. Each of the managers in the interface has a specific function, so let's take a look at them and see what they can do.

Control Panel

In the Control Panel, you'll find a menu bar that contains drop-down menu items allowing access to all the main Joomla functions. It also has a set of buttons that represent the most common actions, providing shortcuts to some of the menu items. Finally, it provides a utility toolbar at the top right that, among other things, allows you to view of the front end of your Joomla web site (the way it will appear to the user).

The Control Panel contains the following managers:

- Add New Article

- Article Manager

- Category Manager

- Media Manager

- Menu Manager

- Module Manager

- User Manager

- Global Configuration

- Template Manager

- Language Manager

Instead of running through all these managers sequentially, you'll focus on those managers that will enable you to quickly get up and running and develop some content for your Joomla web site. Before creating the content, let's take a look at the relationship between four key parts of Joomla that you'll need to understand to get the most out of the Administrator interface: menu items, menus, categories, and articles.

A *menu item* appears as a link on a web site that, when selected, displays some kind of information. Several menu items are collectively placed under one menu heading. In other words, a *menu* is a collection of several menu items.

Information in a web site can be divided among *categories* and any level of *subcategories*. Suppose that you want to display information about electronic and clothing products on your web site, where electronic products consist of subcategories such as Camera and Cell Phone; and clothing products consist of subcategories such as Men and Women. In that case, you need to create two categories for your web site: Electronics and Clothing. The Electronics category will have two subcategories to start with (Camera and Cell Phone), and the Clothing category will have two subcategories (Men and Women), as shown in Figure 3-5.

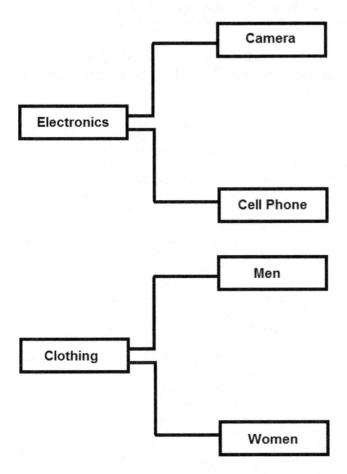

Figure 3-5. *Electronics and Clothingcategorieswith two subcategories each*

To display information for different types of clothing (for the Men category), you can create one or more articles and link them with the Men category of the Clothing category. An *article* is a web page that can contain text, images, and animations to provide information about a product or service. You can create several articles for a category. A category can have any number or level of subcategories (also known as child categories), and each category and subcategory can store one or more articles.

Using the Category, Article, and Menu Managers

Before you begin creating a web site, here is a quick introduction to the Article, Category, and Menu Item Managers:

- **Article Manager:** Articles contain the actual information or content that you want your web site visitors to see. An article comprises text and may also include images and other multimedia content.

- **Category Manager:** To manage articles and to handle them with ease, they are categorized into categories. A category is a title that groups related articles. By accessing a category, you access all the articles within it.

- **Menu Manager:** This manager enables you to create and manage menus and menu items. By selecting the respective menu item, the web site visitor can access the desired content in your site.

Let's make a web site that looks something like the one shown in Figure 3-6. As shown in the figure, you'll add a new menu item, New Electronics Products arrival. When selected, this menu item will display the Camera subcategory of the Electronics category.

Figure 3-6. *Menu item displaying the Camera subcategory of the Electronics category*

■ **Note**   Joomla provides several default categories and articles in your web site to give you an idea of how they are related. You can unpublish any of them to remove them from the web site and create your own contents instead.

Let's Make This

Before you get started, here is a brief overview of what your example web site will look like and how it will function. Though you can create several categories in your web site, for this exercise you'll keep it simple and just create one of each: a Camera subcategory inside an Electronics category. When your visitors select the Camera category, they will see the list of articles in that category, as shown in Figure 3-7.

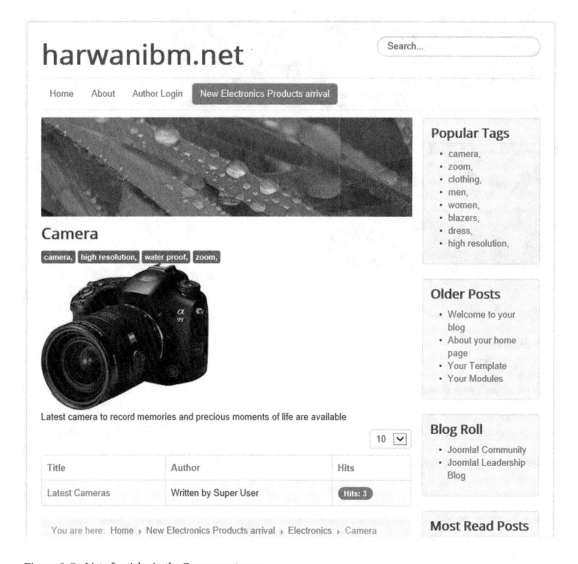

Figure 3-7. List of articles in the Camera category

Again, to keep the example simple, you'll also just display a single article when the Camera category is selected: "Latest Cameras." When the article title is selected, it will display the content of that article, as shown in Figure 3-8.

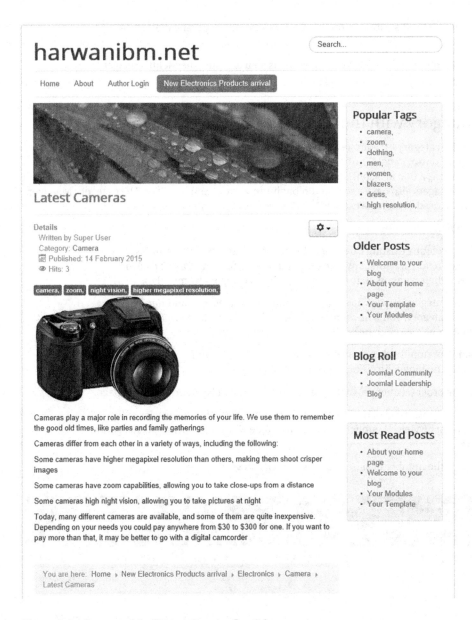

Figure 3-8. *Content of the "Latest Cameras" article*

To create some simple content for your example web site, you can use two managers found in the Control Panel: the Category Manager and the Article Manager. To create this simple content, follow these steps:

1. Create the Electronics category using the Category Manager.

2. Create the Camera subcategory in the Electronics category using the Category Manager. The Electronics category will be the parent category of the Camera category.

3. Create an article ("Latest Cameras") in the Camera category using the Article Manager.

4. Create a menu item (New Electronics Products arrival) using the Menu Manager and linking it to the Electronics category.

Creating a Category with the Category Manager

To build the Electronics category for your web site using the Category Manager, click the Category Manager button in the Control Panel. The Category Manager will open, as shown in Figure 3-9. Notice that each manager window has a title in a consistent location to help you locate your position in the Joomla environment. Most managers also have a similar toolbar button layout and behavior. The Category Manager, as the name suggests, is used to manage categories, which entails the following:

- Creating new categories.

- Editing or deleting existing categories. A category cannot be deleted unless it is empty (i.e., before deleting any category, you have to first erase all its categories along with their contents so that you don't delete a category by mistake).

- Copying a category, along with its articles from one category to another. When copying a category, you'll be prompted to specify the category to which the selected category's contents are to be copied.

- Publishing or unpublishing a selected category. If you unpublish a category, its articles will no longer be visible on your web site.

- Setting the order (sequence) that the category will be displayed on the home page.

- Setting the Access level of the category (i.e., deciding whether the articles of the category can be viewed publicly or are meant to be viewed by only a specific group of users).

- Displaying the number of subcategories in each category.

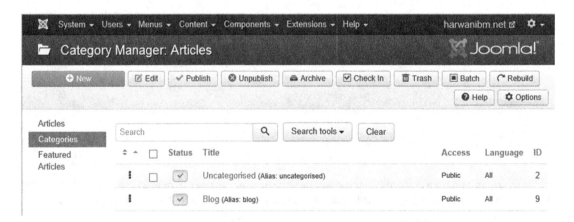

Figure 3-9. *Category Manager*

The Category Manager toolbar contains several buttons that provide quick access to several functions. Table 3-1 gives a brief description of Category Manager toolbox tools.

Table 3-1. *Brief Explanation of the Category Manager Toolbar*

Tool	Description
New	Used to add a new category.
Edit	Edits the selected category. Used to modify the category's information.
Published	Shows whether the category is currently in the published or unpublished state. A check mark indicates that the category is published (i.e., its subcategories and their corresponding articles will be visible on the web site), and a red X indicates that the category is unpublished. To publish any category(ies), select from the list and click this button.
Unpublish	Select the required number of categories from the list and click this button to unpublish them.
Archive	Select the required number of categories from the list and click this button to move them to the archive.
Check In	Select the required number of categories from the list and click this button to close them and mark them as Check In. No editing can be performed on the opened category. In an opened state, a category is blocked from use by other administrators. To make it editable, a category needs to be closed and marked as Check In.
Trash	Moves the selected category(ies) to the trash.
Batch	Used to apply batch processing on a set of selected categories. To copy or move certain selected categories or to apply actions such as assigning tags, setting the language, setting the Access level, and so on for a set of categories, select them from the list and click the Batch button. A pop-up dialog box will open, as shown in Figure 3-10. The action selected from the combo box(es) will be applied on the selected categories as a batch.

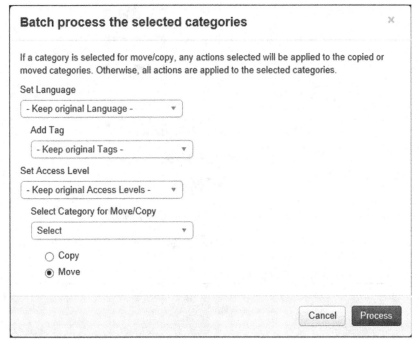

Figure 3-10. *Dialog box for performing batch processes on the selected categories*

(*continued*)

Table 3-1. (*continued*)

Tool	Description
Rebuild	Rebuilds the category table. Usually used when several operations are performed on categories and you want to see the outcome of those operations in the category list.
Help	Clicking this button will open the new browser window and navigate to the online help files related to the active topic.
Options	Opens the Article Manager Options screen. Select the Categories tab in that screen to display options (see Figure 3-11) that can be used to configure Category Manager.

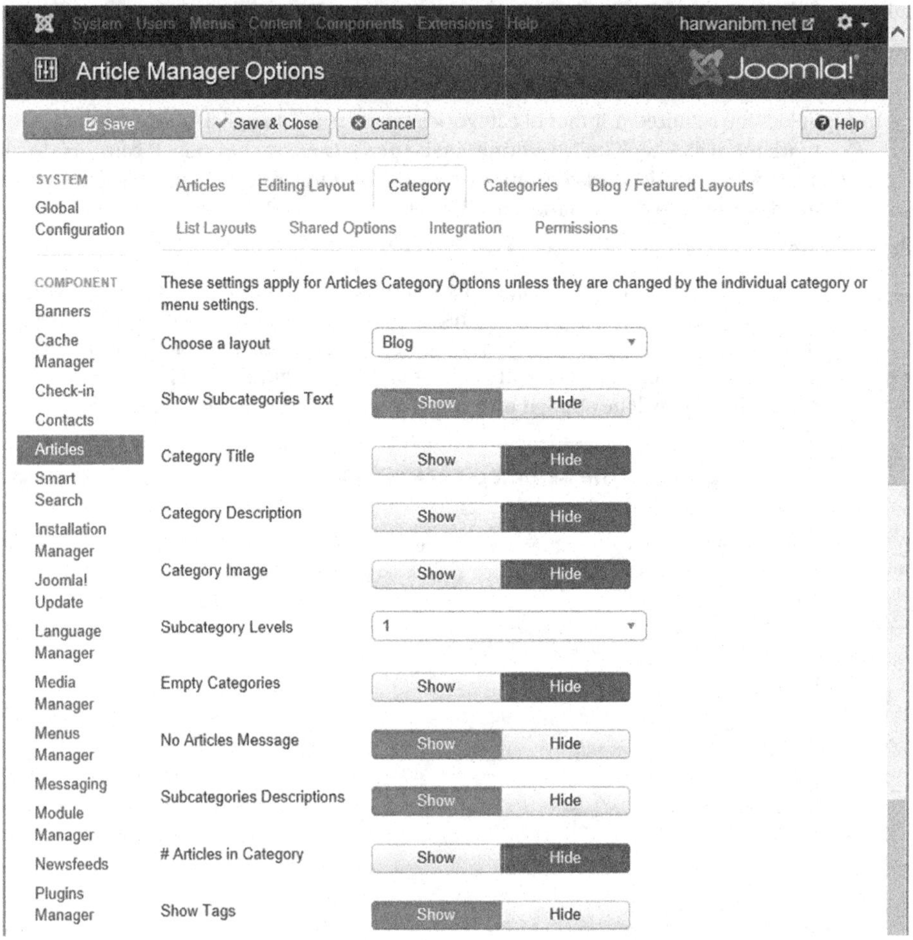

Figure 3-11. *Configuring Categories globally*

(*continued*)

Table 3-1. (*continued*)

Tool	Description
	You can use the parameters to do the following: • Change the layout of the site • Show or hide the category title, description, and image • Determine the number of subcategory levels to be displayed • Show or hide empty categories • Show or hide the subcategories' text and description • Determine the count of the articles in a category • Show or hide category tags

Below the toolbar, the Category Manager shows a Search box that can be used for searching categories. You can type a word or phrase into the Search box and then click the magnifying glass icon to display the list of categories that match the entered phrase. To clear the screen and display the full list of categories, click the Clear button. The Search tools button applies more filters (see Figure 3-12) to display the desired categories precisely. The filters are as follows:

- **Select Max Levels:** Determines the number of levels of categories to display.

- **Select Status:** Displays the categories that match the selected status —whether they are published, unpublished, archived, or trashed. It is also very useful for searching inactive categories.

- **Select Access:** Displays the categories that match the selected Access level. The Access level can be Guest, Public, Super Users, Registered, or Special. The Access level represents a group that is authorized to view and access the given category (you will learn about Access levels later in this chapter).

- **Select Language:** Displays the categories that match the language chosen from this combo box.

- **Select Tag:** Displays the categories that match the selected tag. Tags are the keywords that define and distinguish the categories from the rest.

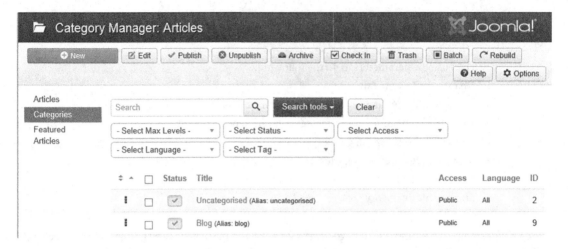

Figure 3-12. Category Manager showing combo boxes for advanced search

The Sort Table By button helps to display the categories sorted in ascending or descending order of the selected column of the category. For example, if you select the Title ascending option from the combo box, the categories will be sorted in the ascending order of the titles. Also, you can sort any column by clicking the column header. The last combo box determines the number of categories to display in the table. The default value displayed in the combo box is 20 and has values in multiples of 5. You can use it to display 5, 10, or 15 categories in the table. You can alter the default value of the categories to be displayed by changing the List Length parameter in the Global Configuration Manager.

■ **Note**   To reset any of the preceding filters, change the combo box back to its default setting.

The main content area of the screen displays a table that shows all the categories in a Joomla site. The usage of each column is the following:

- **Vertical double arrows:** Shows the order in which the category items are displayed on the page of the web site and enables you to change their order. You can click the arrows to change the sort order. You can also click and hold the three squares (to the left of the checkbox column) and drag the category to change its order location in the Category Manager.

- **Check boxes:** Click a check box to select a category. Check boxes are used to apply batch action on several categories collectively. Simply click the check boxes of the desired categories and select the required tool from the toolbar.

- **Status:** A green check mark indicates that a category is published. Click this check box to toggle the state of the category between published and unpublished.

- **Title:** Displays the full name of the category. Click the category title to open it in edit mode.

- **Access:** Displays the Access level set for the category (i.e., which level of users can access the category). The Access levels are as follows:

    - **Guest:** Content with this Access level is for users who are not logged in.

    - **Public:** Content with this Access level can be seen by all people, whether logged in or not. This is the default Access level for all Menu Items, Articles, Categories and Modules.

    - **Registered:** Content with this Access level can be seen by only those users who are logged in.

    - **Special:** Content with this Access level can be seen only by users with author status or higher (you will learn more about Access levels later).

    - **Super User:** Content with this Access level is meant only for super users, who are the only users who can access or edit the content.

- **Language:** Displays the languages in which the category is available.

- **ID:** Displays the system-generated ID number of the category as defined in the database.

To create a new category, click the New button in the toolbar at the top left of the Category Manager to create a new category. A screen displays, in which you specify information for the new category, as shown in Figure 3-13. On this screen, you can specify a variety of information for the category, including the Title, Access level, Image, and Description.

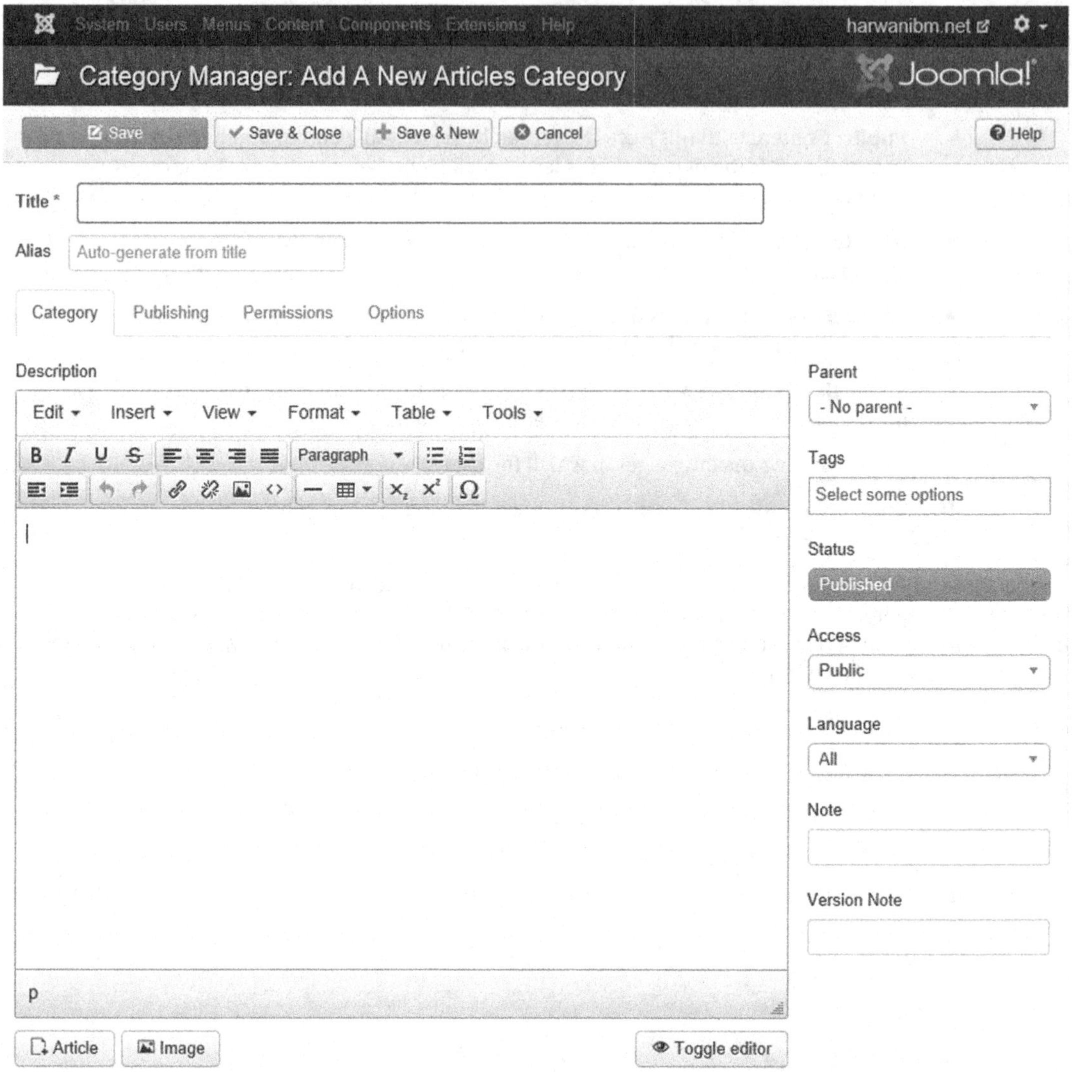

Figure 3-13. *Page for creating a new category*

■ **Note** Categories are generally used to categorize articles into groups so that you can easily search and manage desired articles.

For the Title, enter the name for your new category: **Electronics**. Alias is a sort of secondary name for the category that is used internally by Joomla. You can leave it blank here (and anywhere else); Joomla will fill it in automatically, or you can give it your own meaningful name. If you specify it, it must be lowercase, and it cannot contain any spaces (hyphens are the only allowed symbol and should be substituted for spaces). The alias is used in search engine–friendly (SEF) URLs (which help search engines display your web site content and also help you control the text that you want to appear in the URL). For this exercise, enter **Electronics** for the alias.

In the Description text box, you can enter a few lines to describe the category. You can also insert an image into the description using the Image button at the bottom. Click the Image button, and you'll be presented with the images available in the Media Manager. Joomla provides some images by default, but you can also upload your own images into the Media Manager.

■ **Note** The Media Manager is used to maintain web site images. All the images are stored and maintained in `joomla_root/images` (extensions, plug-ins, and templates keep their images in their own image directories). The Images directory already contains some default subdirectories containing images. Using the Media Manager, you can upload images from other directories into the `joomla_root/images` folder and you can also delete any undesired images.

It is very easy to upload new images into the Media Manager. Just click the Browse button in the Upload area, as shown in Figure 3-14, to locate the folder that contains the image file to upload (preferably in PNG or JPG format). Assuming that you have an `electronics.jpg` file on your local drive, select the image file.

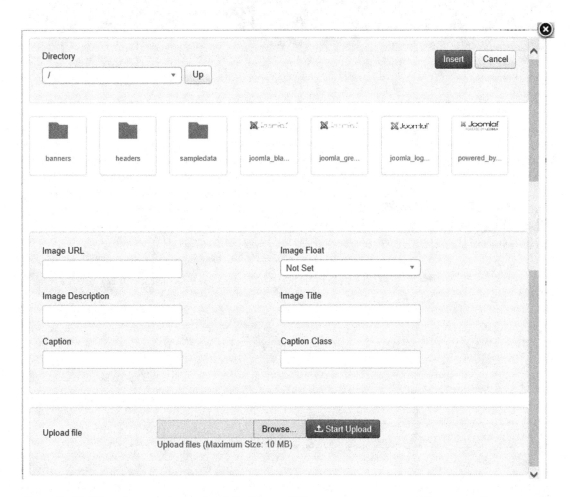

Figure 3-14. *Uploading new images in Media Manager*

■ **Note**   Images can be uploaded and added to the site through FTP. But in case you don't have FTP access to the web server, Media Manager is preferred. It is usually best to upload all the images, videos, documents, and other files that you will use on your web site to the Media Manager before creating the web site contents because all the content can be accessed from the Media Manager while developing the site.

When you select an image thumbnail, the URL of the image will be displayed in the Image URL field. In the Image Description field, you can enter a short description of the image. In the Image Title field, enter the title of the image, which will be displayed when a visitor hovers the mouse over the image. After entering information for the image, when you click the Start Upload button, the image will be uploaded to the Joomla `images/stories` folder, and a Completed message will appear to show that the uploading is done. You want the Electronics category to be represented by an image, so (assuming that you have an image called `electronics1.jpg` in your local drive), upload it into the Media Manager. Also, enter the information of the Electronics category, as shown in Figure 3-15.

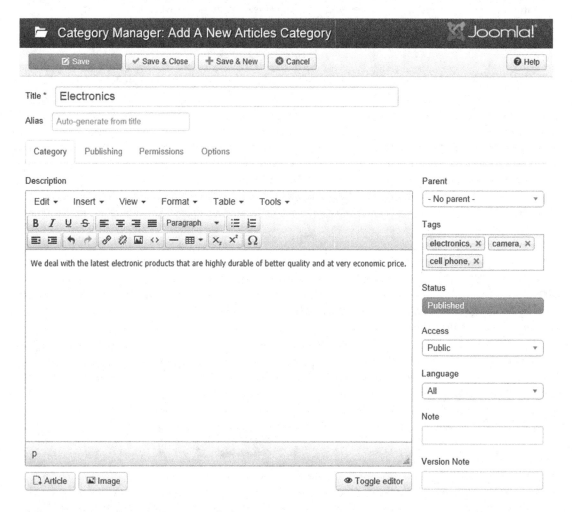

Figure 3-15. Creating a new category called Electronics

From the Parent drop-down list, select the category to which you want the current category (Electronics) to belong. Select the No Parent option because you want the Electronics category to be at the top of the hierarchy. In the Tags box, type in the unique tags to represent the electronics category. Let's assign the tags **electronics**, **camera**, and **cell phone**.

Set the Status to Published to make the category visible on the web site (unpublished categories don't appear), and set the Access level to Public to make the category accessible to anyone. Set Access level to Public to make the category visible to all users of the web site.

In the Language combo box, select the language to be assigned to this category: leave it at the default language (All/English (UK)). In the Note box, you can assign a small text note related to the new category. In the Version Note box, enter an optional note for this version of the category. For example, you can assign the 1.0 version to this category. When modified, assign version 1.1 to this category to show that it is the enhanced version of 1.0.

Below the Title box is the Publishing link. When clicked, it will display the information related to creating and modifying the category. The page (see Figure 3-16) will also prompt for other information as listed here:

- **Created Date:** Displays the date and time the category was first created. The date and time are generated and entered by the system automatically.

- **Created by:** Displays the user who created this category.

- **Modified Date:** Displays the date and time when this category was last modified. Again, they are generated and entered by the system automatically.

- **Modified by:** Displays the user who made the last modification.

- **Hits:** Displays the number of hits for this category.

- **ID:** Displays the unique ID of the category.

- **Meta Description (Optional):** Enter a small description of the category that usually appears in the results of search engines.

- **Meta Keywords (Optional):** Enter a comma-separated list of keywords to describe the category. Previously, search engines used meta keywords while searching content on the web, but now search engines have become more intelligent, so meta keywords are not useful.

- **Author:** Enter the author of this category.

- **Robots:** Choose the option that helps make your site visible to search engines. The available options are Use Global/Index, Follow/No index, Follow/Index, and No follow/No index, No follow. Here are the meanings of Index and Follow:

  - **Index:** Determines whether you want a search engine to index the contents of this page.

  - **Follow:** Determines whether you want a search engine to follow and crawl the links on this page.

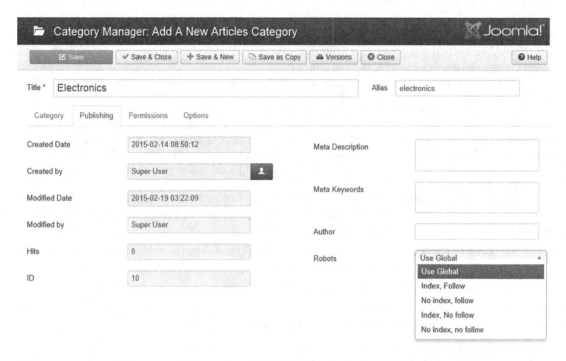

Figure 3-16. *Page displaying Publishing information of the category*

To modify permissions related to the current Electronics category, click the Permissions link. Permissions are usually inherited from the Global Configuration settings, but you can override them through the Permissions link. Short descriptions of the combo boxes shown on the page (see Figure 3-17) follow:

- **Create (Inherited/Allowed/Denied):** Determines whether to allow or deny Create permission for users in the Public group

- **Delete (Inherited/Allowed/Denied):** Determines whether to allow or deny Delete permission for users in the Public group

- **Edit (Inherited/Allowed/Denied):** Determines whether to allow or deny Edit permission for users in the Public group

- **Edit State (Inherited/Allowed/Denied):** Determines whether to allow or deny Edit State permission for users in the Public group

- **Edit Own (Inherited/Allowed/Denied):** Determines whether to allow or deny Edit Own permission for users in the Public group

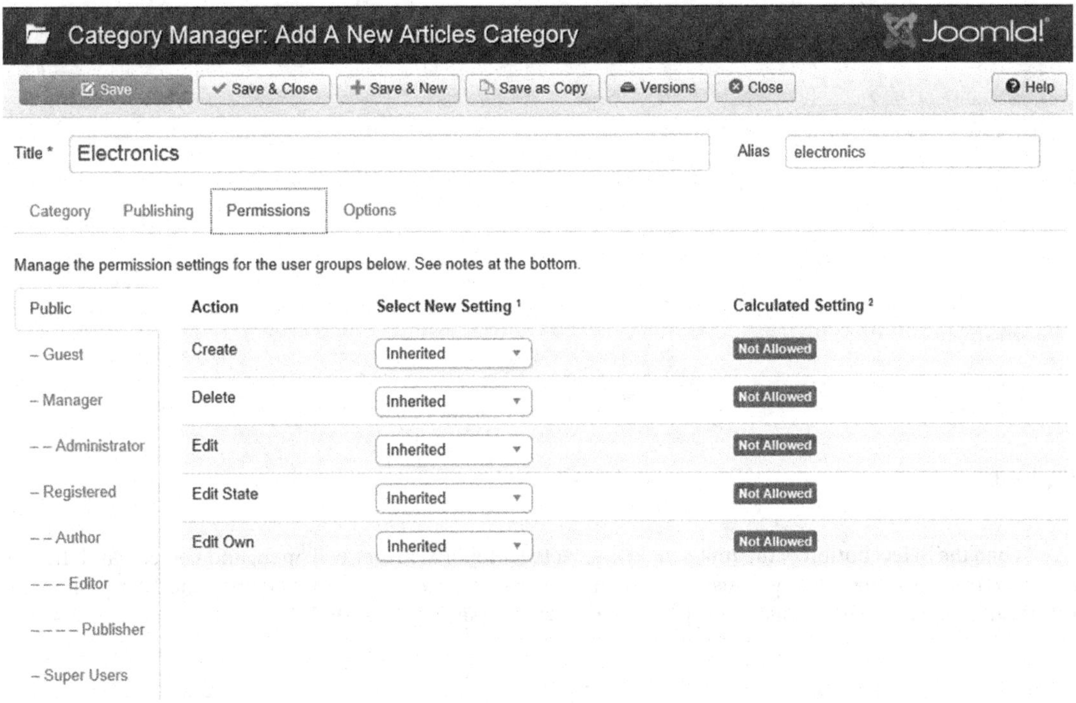

Figure 3-17. *Page for setting permissions related to the current category*

To represent the Electronics category with an image, select the Options link in the Category Manager. A dialog box to select the image displays (see Figure 3-18).

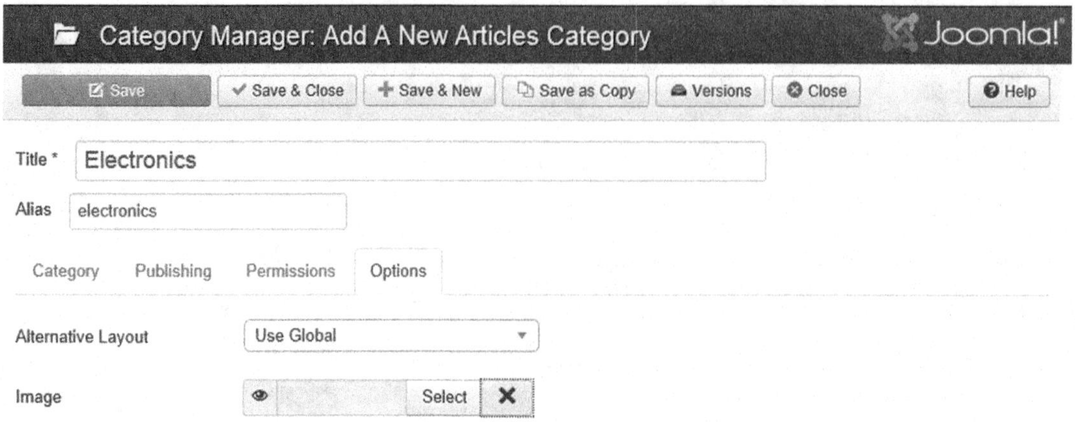

Figure 3-18. *Options tab*

When the Select button of the Image field is selected, Media Manager will open, and you can find the electronics1.jpg image that you just uploaded in it. Select the electronics1.jpg image and click the Insert button to assign the image to the Electronics category (see Figure 3-19).

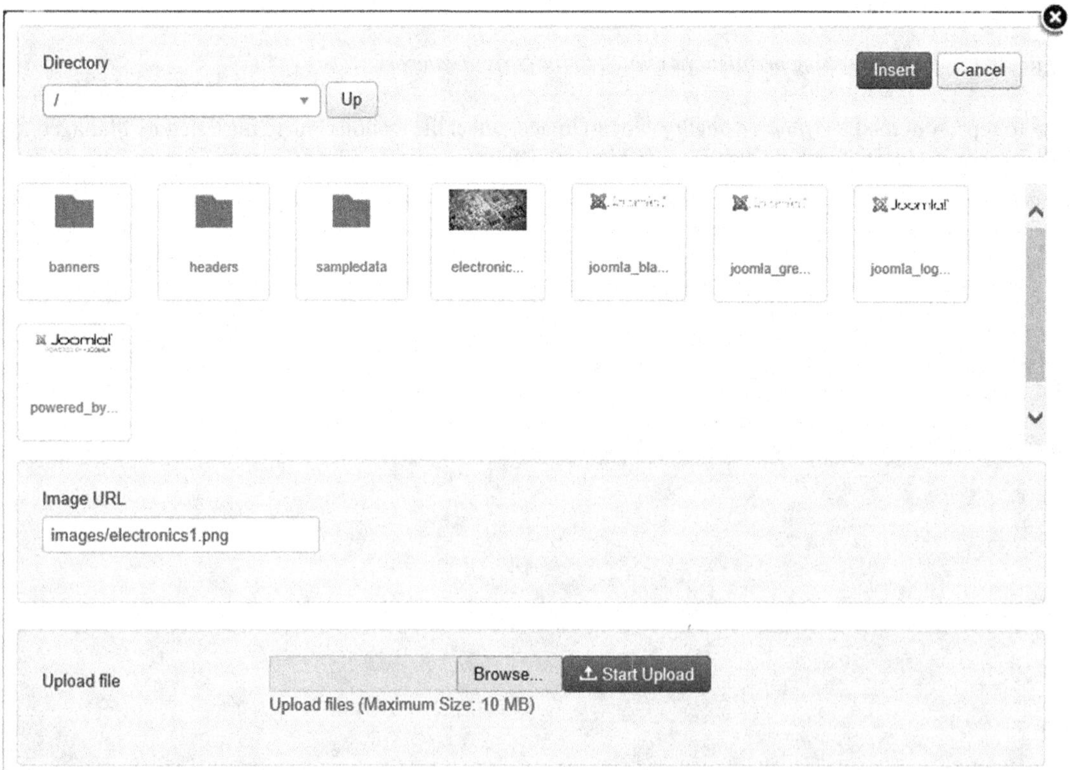

Figure 3-19. *Selecting the electronics1.jpg image file for the Electronics category*

In the Category Manager, the toolbar at the top shows the tool buttons as listed here:

- **Save:** Saves the category without exiting from the workspace. Usually used to save the work.

- **Save & Close:** Saves the new category and exits the workspace.

- **Save & New:** Saves the new category, closes the current workspace, and opens another New Category workspace to add another category.

- **Cancel:** Cancels the current task and exits the workspace.

- **Help:** Opens the browser and displays online help files related to the active screen.

After inserting the necessary information for the new category, click the Save & Close button in the toolbar to save it. The newly created Electronics category will be displayed in the Category Manager, as shown in Figure 3-20.

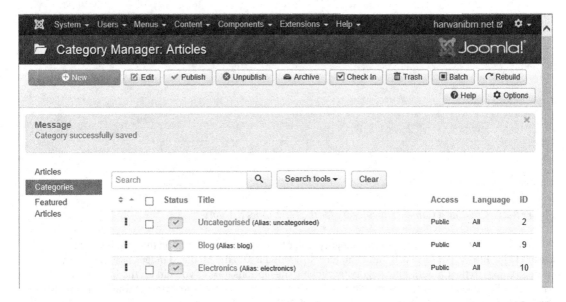

Figure 3-20. *A new Electronics category is added to the Category Manager*

Creating a Camera Subcategory

Now that you've created a category, repeat the procedure to create a subcategory called Camera for the Electronics category. While creating a subcategory of any category, just mention the category name in the Parent combo box. To declare the Camera category as a subcategory of the Electronics category, its Parent combo box should be set to point at the Electronics category, as shown in Figure 3-21.

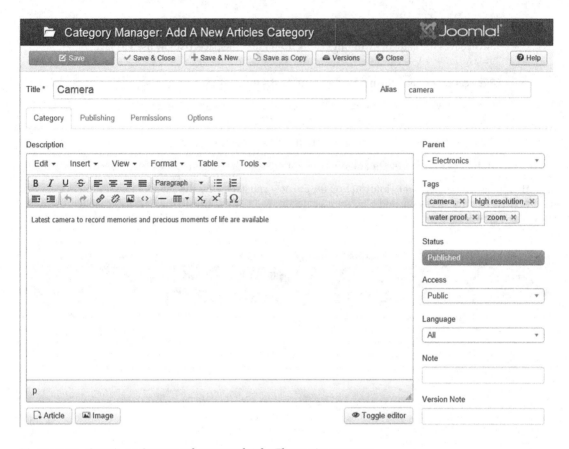

Figure 3-21. *Creating a Camera subcategory for the Electronics category*

Enter the details of the Camera subcategory (refer to Figure 3-18). Assuming that you have the camera1.jpg file in your local drive and you have uploaded it into the Media Manager, assign that image (camera1.jpg) to the Camera subcategory by clicking the Options link, as you did for the Electronics category. Click the Save & Close button to save the Camera subcategory. The Category Manager will display the newly created Camera subcategory (see Figure 3-22).

		Status	Title	Access	Language	ID
		✓	Uncategorised (Alias: uncategorised)	Public	All	2
		✓	Blog (Alias: blog)	Public	All	9
		✓	Electronics (Alias: electronics)	Public	All	10
		✓	— Camera (Alias: camera)	Public	All	12

Figure 3-22. *Category Manager showing the Electronics and Camera categories*

Now that you have created a category and a subcategory, it is time to create an article.

Creating an Article with Article Manager and Publishing It in a Category

Articles contain the actual information or content that you want your web site visitors to see. Besides text, articles can contain images and other multimedia content. The information in your articles may appear on the home page of the web site so that visitors can view the article directly on opening the web site or it may appear when a visitor selects a particular menu item or link on the web site.

■ **Note** Joomla extensions extend the functionality of Joomla web sites. There are five types of extensions: Components, Modules, Plugins, Templates, and Languages. Each of these extensions handles a specific function. A plug-in is used to add small functions to an existing component or module. For example, a search plug-in can be used to search a desired product from a shopping cart component, and a bookmark plug-in can be used to place bookmarks on the desired content. A component is an independent application (having its own functionality, database, and presentation). Adding a component to your web site is like adding an application. Examples of components are shopping carts and guest books. Modules are meant for adding new features to an existing component (application) of your web site (e.g., you might add a login module or a digital counter module to your shopping cart component).

Because you'll be displaying some content that provides information about new cameras, you'll write an article and attach it to the Camera category. To do so, you need to open the Article Manager, so either select the Content ➤ Article Manager menu option or click the Article Manager button in the Control Panel. The Article Manager will open and display a list of articles under different categories (provided by Joomla in the default web site), as shown in Figure 3-23.

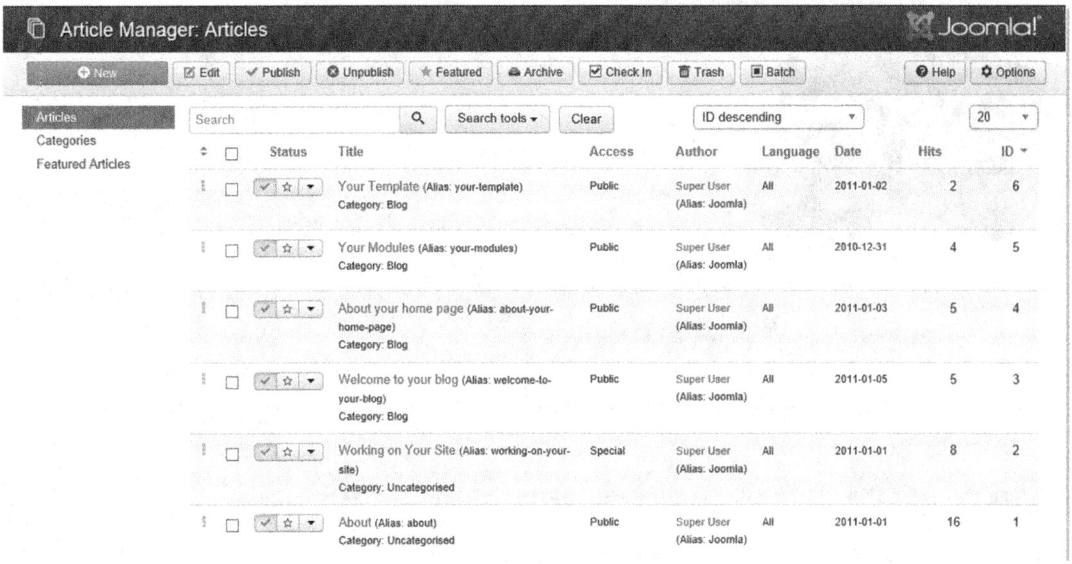

Figure 3-23. *Article Manager*

As its name suggests, the Article Manager is used to manage articles. It contains tools with which users of certain groups (e.g., administrators) can add new articles, edit existing articles, unpublish the article(s) (making them disappear from the web site), move or copy the articles from one category to another, and so on.

The Article Manager table contains some important information about each article, such as the author of the article, the Access level (which sets whether the article is for public view or only for users belonging to certain groups), whether the article should be displayed on the home page (the first page of the web site), the date the article was created, and the number of times it has been accessed by visitors.

To add a new article, you can either click the New button from the toolbar or click the Add New Article button in the Control Panel. An editor box will appear, which allows you to type the content for the article, as shown in Figure 3-24. In the Title box, specify Latest Cameras as the name of the article. For the Alias, specify latest-cameras. Set the Published option to Yes to make the article visible on the web site. Set the Home page option to No because you don't want the article to appear directly on the opening screen of your web site, but only when a menu item is selected on the web site. From the category drop-down list, choose Camera.

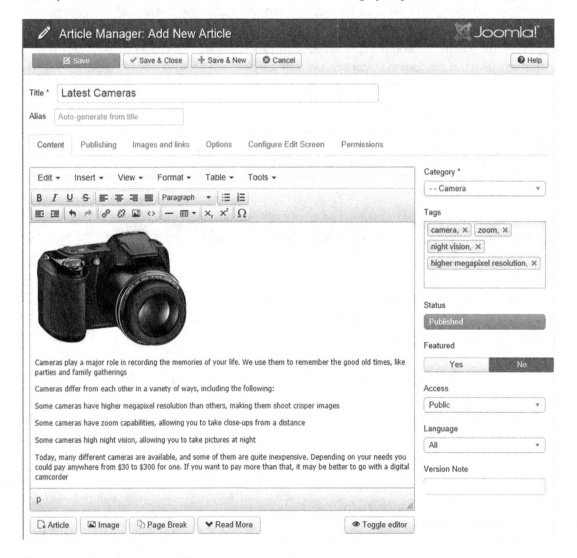

Figure 3-24. *Creating a new article*

■ **Note**   While adding an article, you must specify a category in which the article will be displayed.

The editor provides formatting tools for formatting your text and a variety of buttons that allow you to perform various tasks. If you're used to using a word processing application, you'll find the buttons here fairly straightforward. However, I'll quickly run through a few of the ones that may be unfamiliar to you: the buttons for inserting images, page breaks, and read-more links.

There are two buttons for inserting images into articles: the Image button in the TinyMCE editor toolbar (see Figure 3-25) and the Image button at the bottom left of the editor (refer to Figure 3-24).

Figure 3-25. *Image button in the TinyMCE editor*

The button in the editor toolbar is bit difficult to use because it requires the URL of the image to insert and it doesn't allow you to add new images in the Media Manager. When you click the Image button in the toolbar, the Insert/Edit Image dialog box displays, as shown in Figure 3-26.

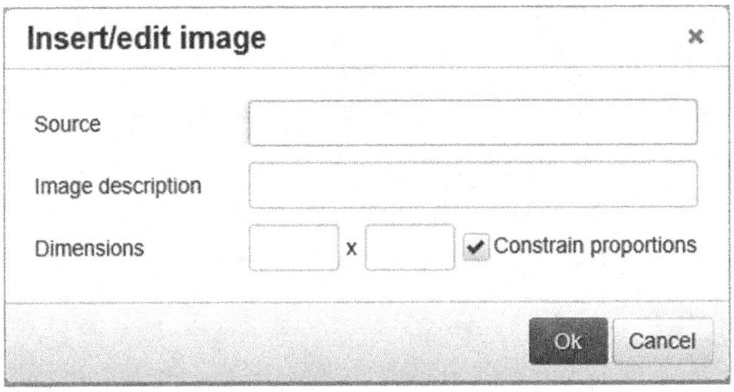

Figure 3-26. *Insert/edit image dialog box*

In the Source field, you can specify the URL of an image available on the Internet, and you can also specify the URL of an image already uploaded to the Media Manager. Assuming that an image called cam1.jpg already exists in the Media Manager, you can insert it by specifying its URL here as c:\xampp\ htdocs\joomlasite\images/stories/cam1.jpg and then clicking OK.

On the other hand, if you select the Image button at the bottom of the editor, you'll see a screen like the one shown in Figure 3-14. This dialog box allows you to upload new images to the Media Manager and insert selected images into the article.

This dialog box provides a list of predefined images (the images that are provided by Joomla as well as those that you have uploaded). It also provides an Upload interface to upload the images from other directories into the Media Manager's Images directory (the directory in which all the images for the web site are kept, except for templates and third-party modules, which will be discussed later). The uploaded images can be inserted into the article.

The Page break button at the bottom left of the editor (refer to Figure 3-24) places a dotted line in the article as you are editing it. When viewing your web site, the visitor is shown only the part of the article up to the page break line, and a Next Page link is shown at the end of the page. The portion of the article after the page break is displayed when the Next Page link is clicked, and it runs until the next page break or the end of the article.

The Read More button is used when you have a large article and you want to display a brief summary or introduction of the article first and then include a link for the reader to read more. If interested, the reader can click the Read More link to see the whole article.

After entering the information for your article, click Save & Close to save it. The message Successfully Saved Article will appear, and the article name will be listed in the Article Manager, as shown in Figure 3-27.

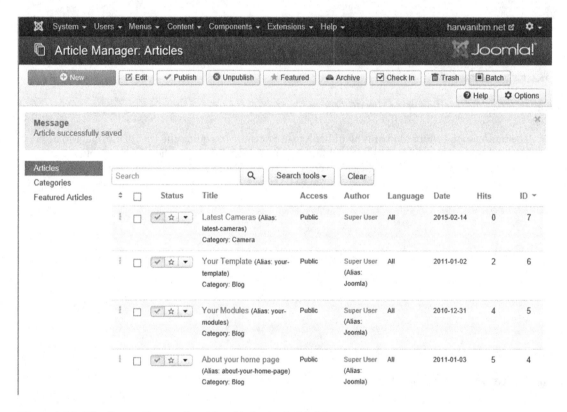

Figure 3-27. *The "Latest Cameras" article added to the Article Manager*

Creating a Menu Item to Access the Category

A menu item is a link that appears on the web site that users can select to see the desired information. There are two steps to create a menu:

1. Create the menu.

2. Create a module for the menu.

To create a menu, open the Menu Manager by clicking its button in the Control Panel. A range of menus is provided by Joomla by default (see Figure 3-28), and each menu is a collection of certain menu items. Every menu item is defined as a specific menu item type, and it is the menu item type that decides what kind of information the menu item is supposed to display (explained in detail in Chapter 7).

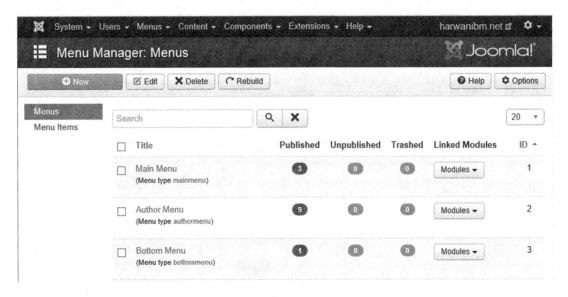

Figure 3-28. Menu Manager

You can create a menu item in any of the menus in the Menu Manager. Let's create a menu item in the Main Menu. Just click the Main Menu title and you'll see all the menu items under the Main Menu that are provided by Joomla (see Figure 3-29).

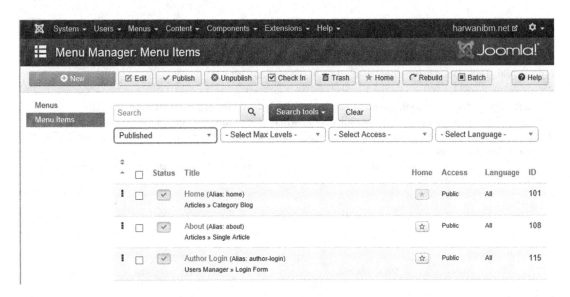

Figure 3-29. Menu items under the Main Menu

To add a new menu item, click the New button. You'll see a screen for specifying the menu type, as shown in Figure 3-30. The menu type plays a major role in deciding how to display the information (i.e., when the menu item is selected, whether to display the article directly, to display all the article titles of a particular category, or to display all the categories of the site or subcategories of a particular category).

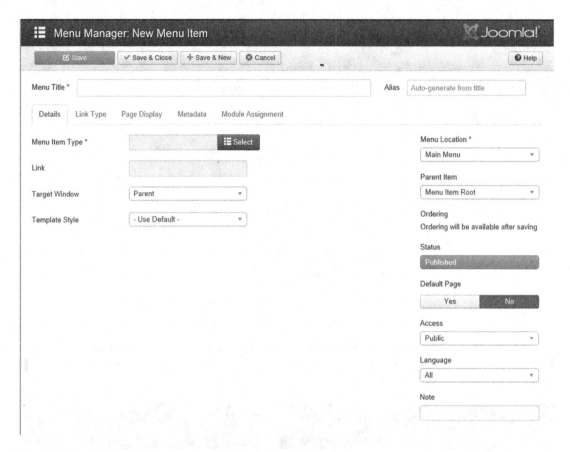

Figure 3-30. *Page for creating a new menu item in the Main Menu*

If the user selects the menu type that displays all the article titles of a particular category, the article contents will be displayed when the user selects the article title. If the user selects the menu type that displays all the subcategories of a particular category, the user must select the category title to see the list of articles under any category.

The list in Figure 3-31 shows that menu items can point to a variety of contents, including articles, contacts, news feeds, and so on.

Figure 3-31. *List of menu types*

Let's see the available options in the Article node. Select the Articles node, and you'll be presented with the options shown in Figure 3-32.

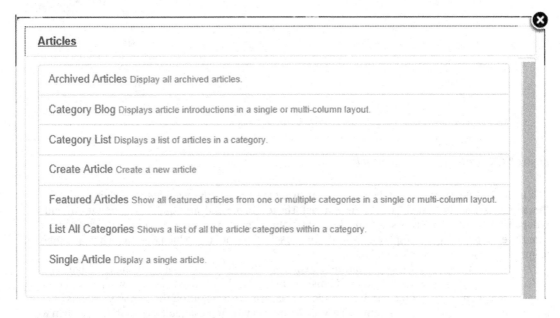

Figure 3-32. *Expanding the Articles node*

Select the Category Blog menu type, which will display all the subcategories of the selected category. When a subcategory is selected, it will display the list of articles in that subcategory; when the title of an article is selected, it will display the information stored in that article. After selecting Category Blog, you'll be presented with a screen for specifying the rest of information of the menu item (see Figure 3-33).

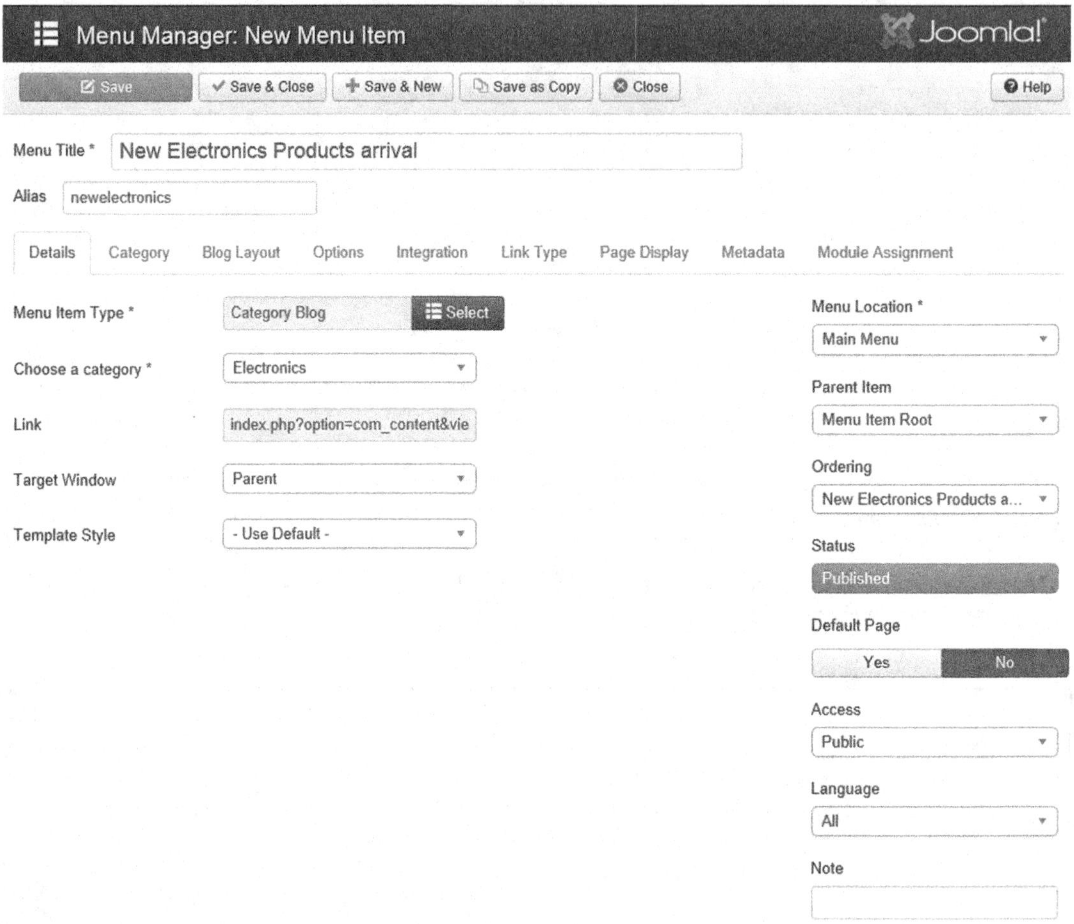

Figure 3-33. Specifying the menu item information

In the Title field, enter the menu item that you want to appear in the Main Menu: in this case, **New Electronics Products arrival**. The alias is optional. The text in the Link field appears automatically and is dependent on the menu type selected. This text lets the menu item know which object it is linked to; it cannot be edited. From the Display In drop-down list, select the menu in which this menu item is supposed to appear. In this case, select Main Menu.

In the Parent Item list box, select the menu item that will act as a parent of the menu item that you are creating (used when creating submenu items). In this case, select Top because you want to create an independent menu item. Set the Published option to Yes to make it visible on the web site. Order is for setting the sequence of the menu item in the Main Menu. Leave it at the default so that the menu item will appear as the last position in the Main Menu. Set the Access level to Public to make the menu item publicly accessible.

After you enter the information as described (refer to Figure 3-33), click Save & Close to save the menu item. The menu item will be saved and added to the menu item list, as shown in Figure 3-34. Notice that it displays Articles ➤ Category Blog below the title, which means that the menu item will display all the subcategories of the specified category.

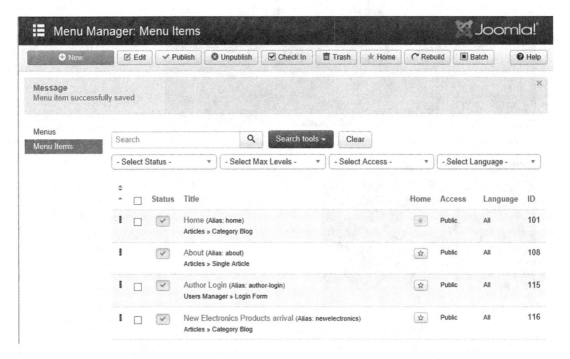

Figure 3-34. *Menu item created*

Viewing the Contents

Now that you've performed all the steps to create the web site contents, it is time to see the result. Open the browser window pointing to your web site and refresh it, or just click the Preview button at the top right of the Menu Item Manager. On the front end, you'll find that the menu item New Electronic Products Arrival appears in the Main Menu. Select this menu item; it will display the subcategories under the Electronics category and the number of articles that these categories have, as shown in Figure 3-35.

Figure 3-35. *Menu item displayingthe Electronics category and its subcategories*

Select the Camera subcategory of the Electronics category; the description titles of all the articles under this category will be displayed, as shown in Figure 3-36.

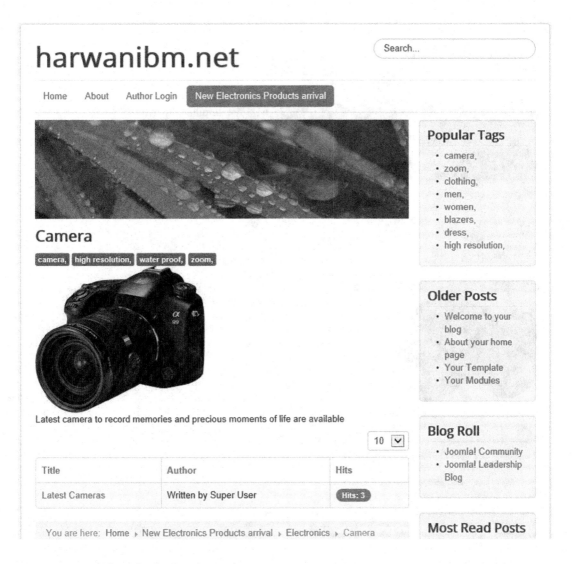

Figure 3-36. *Article under the Camera category*

Select the link for the "Latest Cameras" article; its content will be displayed on the screen, as shown in Figure 3-37.

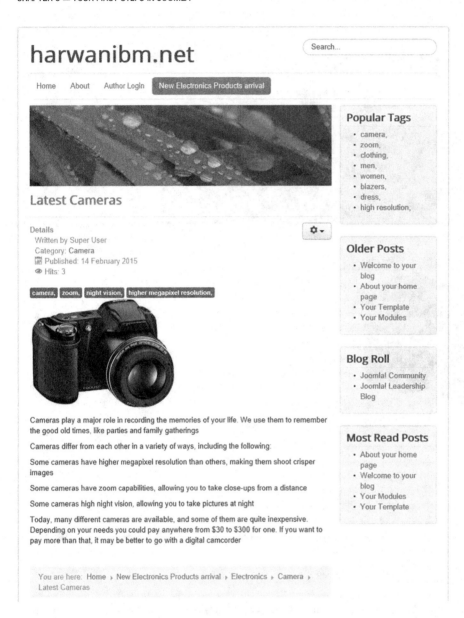

Figure 3-37. *Displaying the article content*

Because you selected Category Blog for the menu item type (refer to Figure 3-33), you first got the subcategory (Camera) of the selected category (Electronics) on selecting the New Electronic Products Arrival menu item from the Main Menu. When you selected the Camera subcategory, the title of the article ("Latest Cameras") in that category was displayed, and when you selected the article title, the information stored in that article was displayed. But you can always change the menu type to display the kind of information that you want to be displayed when clicking the menu item

Working with the Home Page

The home page is the first welcome page when you open any web site. It can be any other page also, but usually it is the first page of the web site (see Figure 3-38).

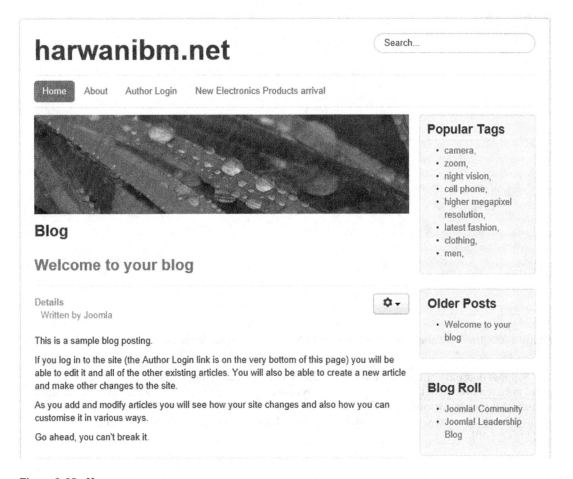

Figure 3-38. *Home page*

The articles that you see in Figure 3-38 are provided by Joomla by default. Open the Article Manager from the Control Panel to see the list of sample articles that are provided by default (see Figure 3-39).

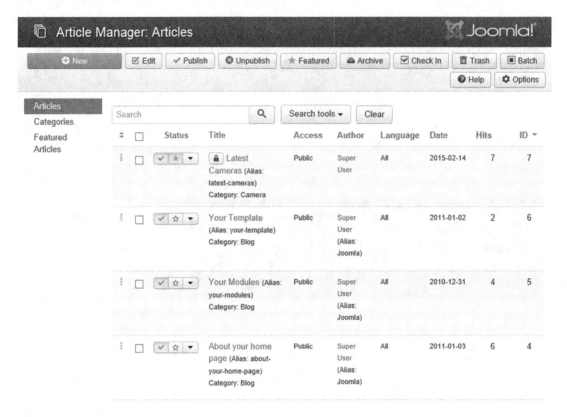

Figure 3-39. *Article Manager showing default articles displayed on the home page*

Suppose that you want the three articles "Your Template," "Your Modules," and "About your home page" to be removed from the home page. Just select the check boxes of these three articles and click the Unpublish button in the toolbar. You'll find that the check mark in the Published column of the selected articles changes to a red X, which means that these articles will no longer be shown on the home page (see Figure 3-40).

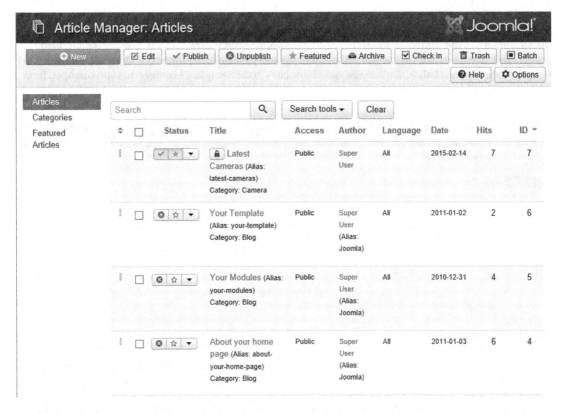

Figure 3-40. *Unpublishing unwantedcontents*

To see the effect in your web site, open the web site browser window and click the Refresh button. You'll see the result in which all the articles except those that you set to Unpublish are visible.

Okay, you now have a basic web site, but it doesn't look very exciting yet. The easiest way to change the appearance of a Joomla site is by applying a template. There are hundreds of templates available that cover every kind of design, so I'm sure you'll find something that suits you. For now, though, you'll start by looking at the templates that came preinstalled with Joomla.

Applying a Different Template

A template is the predefined structure that gives a dynamic look to a web site. A template consists of cascading style sheets (CSS) and a layout that defines the positions of components and modules in it. When a template is applied to a web site, the location of the modules and components are relocated according to the layout in it, and the styles are applied to the content of the web site.

By default, Joomla provides two front-end templates and two administrative templates. The front-end templates determine the appearance of the web content; and the administrative templates determine the appearance of the administrative interface that the administrator uses to create web content, upload images, and install extensions. The two front-end templates provided are protostar and Beez3; the back-end templates are isis and Hathor. You can see these templates in the Template Manager that you can open from the Control Panel (see Figure 3-41).

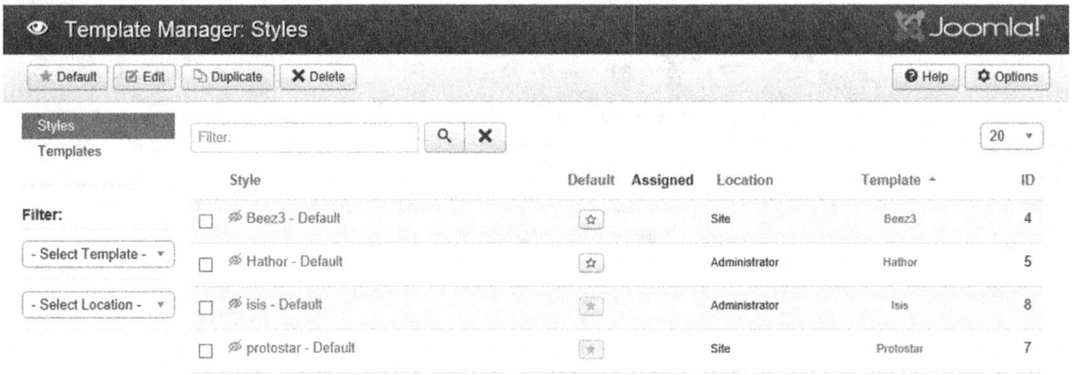

Figure 3-41. *Template Manager showing different built-in styles*

Besides using these templates, you can also add templates to the system through the Extension Manager. Some templates are available for free and some require a payment. You can even create your own custom templates if you have knowledge of PHP programming.

Click the Templates tab in the Template Manager to have a detailed look and feel of installed templates, as shown in Figure 3-42.

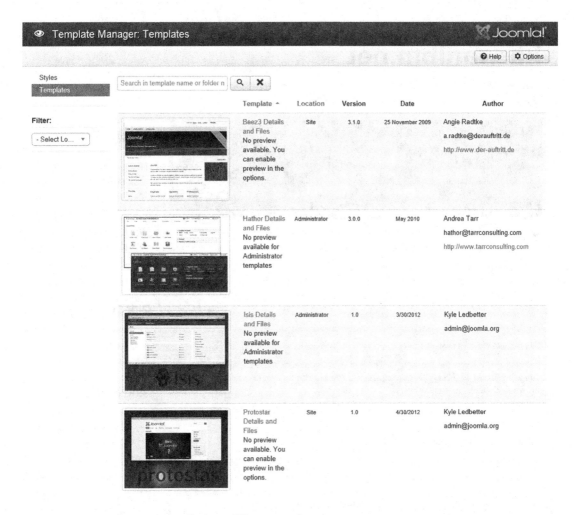

Template Manager: Templates

Template ▲	Location	Version	Date	Author
Beez3 Details and Files No preview available. You can enable preview in the options.	Site	3.1.0	25 November 2009	Angie Radtke a.radtke@derauftritt.de http://www.der-auftritt.de
Hathor Details and Files No preview available for Administrator templates	Administrator	3.0.0	May 2010	Andrea Tarr hathor@tarrconsulting.com http://www.tarrconsulting.com
Isis Details and Files No preview available for Administrator templates	Administrator	1.0	3/30/2012	Kyle Ledbetter admin@joomla.org
Protostar Details and Files No preview available. You can enable preview in the options.	Site	1.0	4/30/2012	Kyle Ledbetter admin@joomla.org

Figure 3-42. *Template Manager showing different templates*

The default home page appears in the applied front-end templates styles. The default applied template for the frontend is marked with a star. You can see in the figure that protostar–Default is applied to the home page by default. The protostar template is very simple and uses Bootstrap to make it easily adjust to various screens of mobile devices without applying major style sheet modifications. The home page in protostar–Default appears in Figure 3-43.

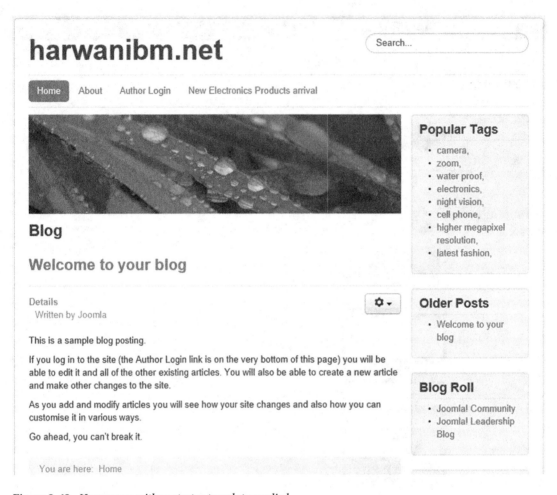

Figure 3-43. *Home page with protostar template applied*

Let's change the default template for the home page to Beez3. To do so, click the check box to the left of the style (Beez3–Default) and click the Default tool button in the toolbox at the top. The star changes from protostar to Beez3.

Switch to the browser window that is displaying your web site (the one pointing at http://localhost/joomlasite) and click Refresh. The effect of the template on the Joomla web site will appear, as shown in Figure 3-44. Notice that the location of the modules and contents has changed, and the CSS present in the current template have changed the appearance of the web site altogether.

Font size Bigger Reset Smaller   Search...

HOME   ABOUT   AUTHOR LOGIN   NEW ELECTRONICS PRODUCTS ARRIVAL

Joomla!®
Open Source Content
Management

We are volunteers!

You are here: Home

CLOSE INFO

Popular Tags

Home Blog

- camera,
- zoom,
- water proof,
- electronics,
- night vision,
- cell phone,
- higher megapixel resolution,
- latest fashion,

Welcome to your blog

Written by Joomla

Older Posts

This is a sample blog posting.

Welcome to your blog

If you log in to the site (the Author Login link is on the very bottom of this page) you will be able to edit it and all of the other existing articles. You will also be able to create a new article and make other changes to the site.

Blog Roll

- Joomla! Community
- Joomla! Leadership Blog

As you add and modify articles you will see how your site changes and also how you can customise it in various ways.

Most Read Posts

Go ahead, you can't break it.

- Welcome to your blog

My Blog

Figure 3-44. *Home page with Beez3 template applied*

You can also download third-party templates and create your own templates (these will be covered in later chapters). As an introduction, this is enough for you to know about templates.

After this quick start on how to create content in your Joomla web site, let's take a look at the rest of the buttons available in the Control Panel. You can use this chapter for reference if you ever need a reminder of what the various managers do.

Other Control Panel Managers

There are a number of other managers in the Control Panel that haven't been covered yet, including the Module Manager, the User Manager, Global Configuration, the Template Manager, and the Language Manager. They are described in the following sections.

Module Manager

The Module Manager is a collection of several independent executable units in which each executable unit can be a collection of any of the following:

- Menus
- Popular articles or related articles
- Advertisements, banners, or random images

The main benefit of collecting several related items in a module is to gain better control. For example, you could make a module become invisible on the web site (which would be easier than unpublishing the individual items), apply a CSS style uniformly to all items in a module, change its Access level or position, and so on. By default, Joomla provides several built-in modules, and you can add more using the Module Manager. When you open the Module Manager, the list of modules present in it is displayed, as shown in Figure 3-45.

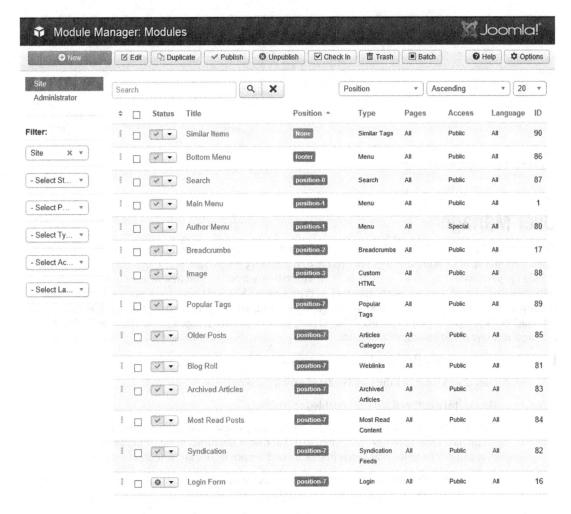

Figure 3-45. *Module Manager showing built-in modules*

Language Manager

The Language Manager is used to manage the installed languages. You can define the default language for your web site with this manager. This is the language used in the Administrator interface. The example Language Manager in Figure 3-46 shows that only one language is currently displayed (English), but you can always install more languages by using the Extensions Install/Uninstall option.

Figure 3-46. *Language Manager*

User Manager

The User Manager is used to manage users. A user might be a simple visitor who is registered at your web site, an employee of your organization, or even you. When you create users, you assign them to groups that decide the permissions assigned to them (e.g., whether they can edit or add new articles to the web site, or only view them). With the User Manager, you can create users, delete existing users, edit user information (password, e-mail ID, group membership, etc.), block existing users from accessing the web site, and so on. The User Manager displays a list of all the current users, as shown in Figure 3-47. The table in the User Manager displays the following information:

- Username (the ID with which the user logs in).

- User status (whether the user is logged in or logged out).

- User state (whether the user is enabled or blocked).

- User group: A user can be assigned any of the groups described following. Each group has certain privileges assigned to it that define the limits or rights of the user in that group. The groups, in ascending order of their privileges, are as follows:

  - Registered: Users of this group cannot edit or submit articles, and can access only the contents that are assigned the Registered Access level.

  - Author: Users of this group can submit new articles, but these articles must be approved by a member of the Publisher group or higher. Users of this group cannot edit existing articles.

  - Editor: Users of this group can submit new articles or edit existing articles. The articles must be approved by a member of the Publisher group or higher.

  - Publisher: Users of this group can submit, edit, and publish articles.

  - Manager, Administrator, and Super Administrator: Users of this group can do all the previous actions, and they can also log into the back end for better control over the web site.

- User ID.

- Date when the user last visited the site.

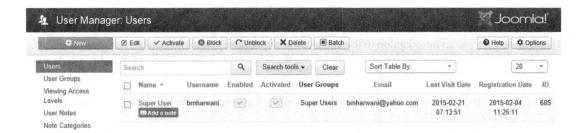

Figure 3-47. *User Manager*

Global Configuration

Global Configuration is used for specifying certain configuration settings that can have a deep impact on the overall appearance and operation of your web site. Most of the settings listed in Global Configuration are automatically configured during the installation and that you can modify per your requirements. For example, you can change the Location Settings if you are in a different time zone. You can perform a variety of functions for your web site with this tool, such as these:

- Specify the web site metadata that is used by search engines to locate your web site. Metadata contain keywords that describe your web site.

- Specify the lifetime of the session. The session is created when a user logs into your site and is deleted when that user logs out. When you specify the lifetime of the session, the session is deleted automatically after the specified time. The lifetime is important for visitors who forget to log out of the web site. By default, the value of the Session Lifetime field is 15 minutes, and the user is automatically logged out if there is no activity during this time period. (While working on the exercises in this book, I suggest increasing this time limit to avoid having to log in repeatedly.)

- Specify the mail settings to indicate the mailer to use for e-mailing (e.g., PHP, Sendmail, SMTP, etc.). If you use SMTP as a mail server, you can also specify the SMTP username and password. Specifying the mail settings is required if you want to send and receive e-mail from your web site.

- Allow or disallow new user registration on your web site.

- Enable or disable web services (e.g., Google Search, Google Maps, etc.). Web services are facilities provided in the form of web methods that can be invoked by your application to add more functionality to your web site. For example, invoking Google Search will allow your visitors to search the Net from your site, and they will get exactly the same output that they would get while searching from Google.

- Allow or disallow the FTP facility. If FTP is allowed, you can specify the FTP username and password here.

- Specify the location of media files and temporary files.

- Specify the database name (to store the contents of your web site), its type, and its hostname.

Summary

This chapter gave you an introduction to the managers of the Control Panel found in the Administrator interface. You learned how to publish and unpublish articles from the home page of the web site, and how to change the default template used by your web site.

In the next chapter, you will learn about the Media Manager. You will also learn how to create banner categories, enter information for banner clients, and create a banner for a client. Finally, you will learn to use the Banner module to display a banner on your web site

CHAPTER 4

■ ■ ■

Managing Images and Banners

In the previous chapter, you saw how to create sections, categories, and (above all) real content in the form of articles. You also learned how to make articles appear on the front page of the web site and how to link them to menu items.

In this chapter, you'll learn how to add colors to your web site and make it a source of income for you. The chapter includes the following topics:

- What the Media Manager is

- How to make categories for your banners

- How to enter information for your banner clients

- How to create a banner for your client

- How to use the Banners module to make a banner appear on the web site

Working with Media Manager

The Media Manager is a component that enables you to manage all the images used in your web site in articles, menus, categories, sections, and so on. Using this manager, new images can be uploaded, existing images can be edited, and new directories can be created.

All the images in your web site are stored in the `joomla_root/images` folder, except for the images for any extensions, which are stored in their respective image directories. The term *extensions* refers collectively to the components, modules, plug-ins, and templates that are installed in a Joomla web site to enhance its features. A template is a collection of styles for giving a dynamic appearance to your web site. The remaining types of extensions—components, modules, and plug-ins—are closely related:

- A *component* is an independent application with its own functionality, database, and presentation. Installing a component in a web site is like adding an application to the site. A forum, shopping cart, newsletter, and guest book are all examples of components, which may consist of one or more modules.

- A *module* is used to add new functions (features) to a component (application) of a web site—for example, a login module, a sign-in module of a guest book component, or a subscription module of a newsletter component. A module isn't a stand-alone application; it is an application's running unit.

- A *plug-in* is a function that can be applied to a particular component or complete web site—for example, a search plug-in that visitors can use to search a forum or a bookmark plug-in to place bookmarks on the desired contents of a Joomla web site.

■ **Note** Plug-ins were called *mambots* in Joomla 1.0, but have been called *plug-ins* since Joomla 1.5.

Making a Client Banner, Step by Step

Let's look at an example that combines all three extensions. A shopping cart is a component that has several modules, including those for maintaining inventory, storing payment information, and printing bills. Plug-ins can be added to this component, such as a plug-in to change the price of a particular product or a search plug-in to search for a desired product from the shopping cart.

To open the Media Manager, point the browser to the Administrator interface: the address http://localhost/joomlasite/administrator. In the Administrator interface, select Content ➤ Media Manager from the menu bar or Media Manager from the Quick Icons on the Dashboard; the Media Manager will open (see Figure 4-1). It already contains images in the banners, headers, and sampledata folders. Joomla provides these images in the default web site, and you can use them directly in your web site.

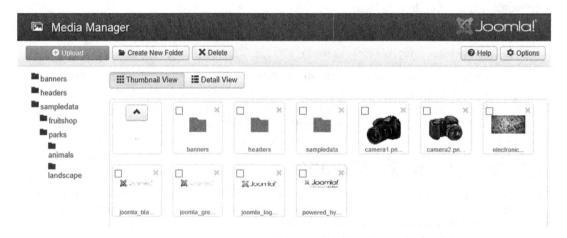

Figure 4-1. *Media Manager*

■ **Note** The camera1.png, camera2.png, and electronics1.png images that you see in Figure 4-1 are not the default images; you uploaded them in Chapter 3.

You can also upload new images. To do that, the first step is to create a folder in the Media Manager, which is discussed next. Remember that moving or copying images between folders is not possible in the Media Manager, however. In the next sections, you will learn to create a folder, copy image(s) in it, and display a banner ad using them.

Creating a Folder

It is best to create a separate folder for any new images uploaded in the Media Manager. To create a folder within the joomla_root/images folder, do the following:

1. Click the Create New Folder button from the toolbar. Type the name of the new folder in the text box to the right. Call your folder trialimg.

2. Click the Create Folder button, as shown in Figure 4-2.

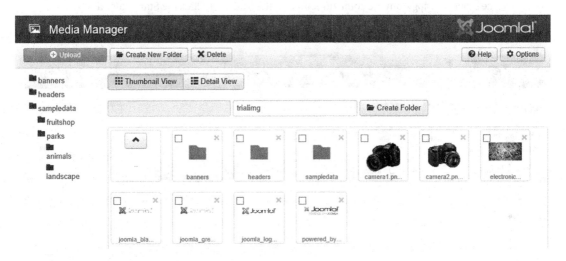

Figure 4-2. *Creating the trialimg folder*

A new folder named trialimg will be created and will appear in the Folders list of the Media Manager. To upload images to the trialimg folder, make it the active folder by clicking it in the Folder list. Because it currently contains no images, it will appear blank, as shown in Figure 4-3.

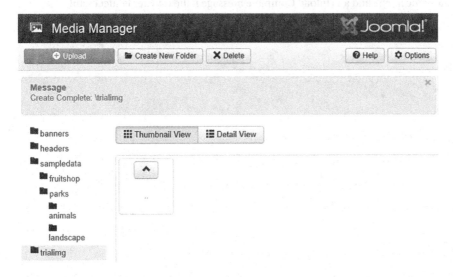

Figure 4-3. *The trialimg folder contains no images*

Uploading a File

To upload an image from your computer to the Media Manager's active folder (in this case, trialimg, which is a subdirectory of the joomla_root/images directory), use the Upload button shown at the top in the toolbar. Besides using the Upload button, you can also use an FTP program to upload media to the desired folder.

1. Click the Browse button to locate an image (in JPG, GIF, BMP, or PNG format) on your computer and then click the Start Upload button to transfer a copy of the file from your computer to the active trialimg directory (I'm using an image named cellphone1.jpg from the some directory on the D: drive). Click the Start Upload button (see Figure 4-4).

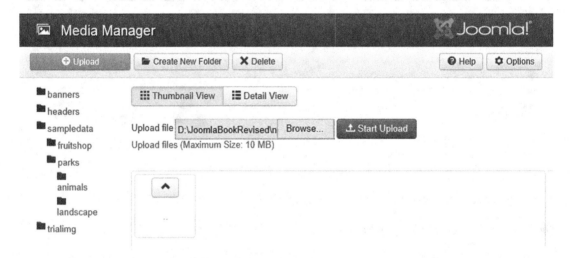

Figure 4-4. *Image loaded into the trialimg folder*

You'll see a preview of the image and an Upload Complete message if the transfer is successful (see Figure 4-5).

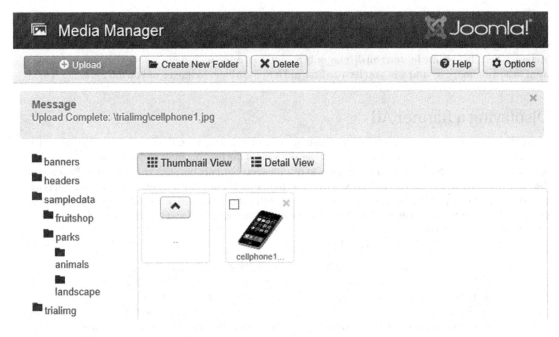

Figure 4-5. Uploading an image file

Upload one more image file (in this example, I'm using an image named cellphone2.jpg from a directory on the D: drive) and click the Start Upload button. You now have two images, cellphone1.jpg and cellphone2.jpg, uploaded in the trialimg subdirectory of the joomla_root/images folder, as shown in Figure 4-6.

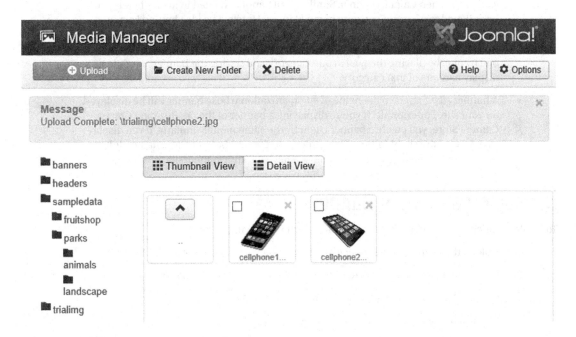

Figure 4-6. Two images loaded in the trialimg folder

These images can now be easily inserted into any article, menu, or category. If you did not upload the file to the proper directory, you can always delete it, navigate to the correct directory, and reload it. When you create the contents of your web site via the Administrator interface, you'll see a button for inserting images. When clicked, the button will display only the images found within the Media Manager, so if you want to add an image to your site, you have to first add it to the Media Manager, as you did here.

Displaying a Banner Ad

Web sites have become a good source of advertisements, and many organizations look for high-traffic sites that can display their banner (an image that carries the logo of the organization and advertises its products or services). Organizations pay web site owners to display their banners because visitors to the site who click the banner will be sent to that organization's web site, hence increasing the awareness of their products or services and eventually increasing their business. The organizations whose banners you will display on your site are called clients. There can be more than one banner for a client, and you can choose to display the banners of several clients.

Before you proceed with displaying banners on your web site, you need to understand the following terms:

- A *banner* is an image file (with a hyperlink pointing to the client's URL) that is displayed on a web site. If, for example, an organization named Chirag that deals with cameras and camcorders wanted you to display the banners of both these products randomly, you would make two banners named, for example, Chirag Camera banner and Chirag Camcorder banner. Similarly, if an organization named Johnny Electronics also wanted you to display the banner for its product, Camera, you could name that banner Johnny Camera banner. (You can assign any name to a banner.)

- A banner *category* is used to categorize similar banners. For example, all banners related to the Camera product (of any organization) can be assigned to a banner category named Camera Banner. Similarly, all banners related to luxury hotels can be assigned to a banner category named Luxury Hotels. The idea behind keeping the banners categorized is to make it easy for you to find specific banners while assigning them to different clients. Also, you can display several banners randomly, one by one, by placing them all in one category and setting the Banners module to display banners of that category.

- A banner *client* refers to the name of an organization whose banner will be displayed on your site. For example, if you're displaying a banner of the organization Chirag Camera Store, you create a banner client by the same name. Similarly, if you display a banner for the client Johnny Electronics, you create a banner client named Johnny Electronics. (Note that a banner client can have multiple banners.)

Displaying a Client's Banners

To display your client's banners on your web site, take the following steps:

1. Upload the client's banner image file to the banners folder of the Media Manager.

2. Create a category for the banner using the Banner Category Manager.

3. Create a banner client using the Banner Client Manager.

4. Create a banner using the Banner Manager.

5. Use the Banners module to display the banner on the web site.

Uploading the Client's Banner Image File

To display the client's banner on your web site, you must upload its banner image to the banners folder of the Media Manager. To do so, click the banners folder in the Folders list in the Media Manager to make it the active folder. You'll see all the banner images it already contains (provided as sample data by Joomla), as shown in Figure 4-7.

Figure 4-7. *Banners in the joomla_root/images/banners folder*

Let's assume that you want to display the banner for the Chirag Camera Store client, and that its banner image file is on your local computer and is named ChiragCamera.png. You'll upload it into the banners folder of your joomla_root/images directory using the Upload File section.

The default banner size is 468 pixels wide and 60 pixels high. So to maintain compatibility, it is best to make the banner using the same dimensions for your clients, too.

You can upload the banner image file just as you uploaded the camera image earlier. Once you upload it, you can see it in the banners folder of the Media Manager, as shown in Figure 4-8.

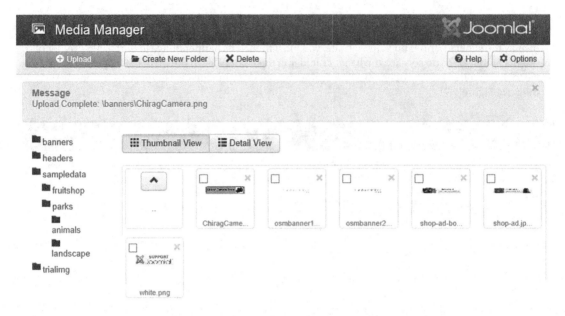

Figure 4-8. *A new banner added to the joomla_root/images/banners folder*

The full-size banner image is shown in Figure 4-9.

Figure 4-9. *Actual view of the new banner added*

After uploading the banner image, your next step is to define a category for it. You can categorize banners so that similar banners can be found in one place.

Creating a Category for the Banner Using the Banner Category Manager

The idea behind creating a banner category is to categorize similar banners. For example, you can keep all banners advertising the latest cellular phones in a category named Cellular Banner and all banners advertising the latest cameras in a category named Camera Banner. You can also create banner categories with names that describe their sizes, such as Standard Banner, Half Banner, Narrow/Wide Skyscraper, Box, Rectangle, and so on.

To create categories for banners, open the Banner Category Manager using either of two methods. The first method is to open the Banner Manager (by selecting Components ➤ Banners ➤ Banners from the menu bar); then from the Banner Manager, click the Categories link. The second method is to open the Banner Category Manager directly by selecting Components ➤ Banners ➤ Categories from the menu bar.

Let's open the Banner Category Manager via the Banner Manager. From the menu bar, select Components ➤ Banners ➤ Banners. But before you go further, let's take a quick look at the Components menu and its options.

The Components menu helps you invoke different components in your web site. Components are the content elements that help add various features to your web site; they include banners, contacts, news feeds, polls, and web links. These components increase the functionality of Joomla and their main purposes are the following:

- Advertise for the clients

- Get feedback from visitors

- Develop interaction with visitors

- Share data from other providers in the form of RSS feeds

- Provide links to other similar web content

Now return to the banner category–creation process. When you select Components ➤ Banners ➤ Banners, the Banner Manager opens, as shown in Figure 4-10. You can see that the Banner Manager lists no banners.

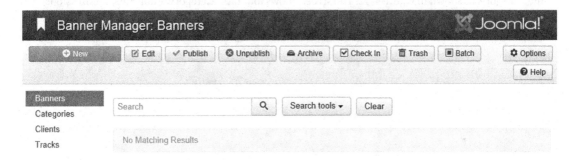

Figure 4-10. *Banner Manager*

The Banner Manager deals with banners that are used for displaying content provided by clients or sponsors for the purpose of advertisement. In Joomla, you can easily configure banners. You can set the banner placement, set it to display for either an unlimited or a defined number of user clicks, and define the categories in which banners of similar types can be stored.

If you click the Categories link, you'll see Category Manager: Banners, also called the Banner Category Manager (see Figure 4-11). It displays a list of banner categories. By default, Joomla provides the banners of the Uncategorized category, but you can unpublish it if you don't want it to appear.

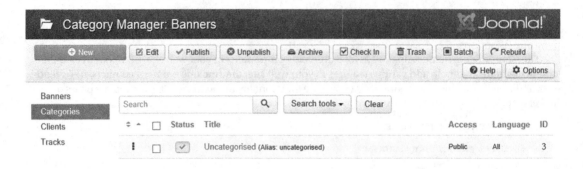

Figure 4-11. *Banner Category Manager*

Creating a Banner Category

Let's create a category named Camera Banner for storing banners that advertise the latest cameras of different clients. Click the New icon in the toolbar. You'll see a screen for entering information about the new banner category, as shown in Figure 4-12. The screen shows four tabs: Category, Publishing, Permissions, and Options. You will first learn how to use the Category tab.

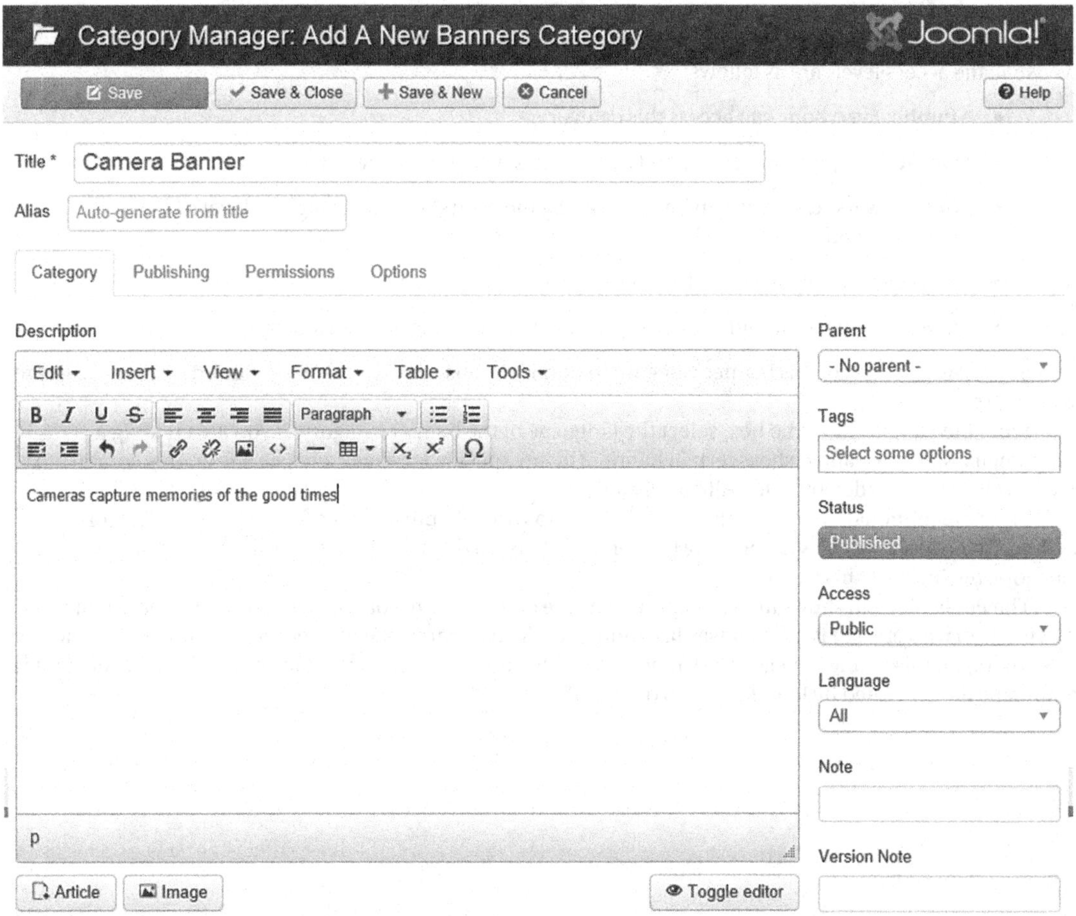

Figure 4-12. *Adding a new banner category*

Enter **Camera Banner** as the title for this banner category. The Alias field is for a sort of secondary name or internal name of the item. Usually it is left blank, but if specified, it has to be lowercase and cannot include spaces. If you leave it blank, Joomla creates an alias for you out of the title by lowercasing it and replacing the spaces with hyphens. That is, if you leave this field blank, Joomla will create the alias camera-banner for you. The alias is used in the URL when the SEF concept is activated. It is the concept by which your web site links are presented and optimized so that search engines can access more of your site. It is enabled from the SEO tab in the Global Configuration section (discussed in Chapter 10). Aliases are used when SEF is activated, which makes Joomla produce friendly URLs rather than normal database-generated URLs.

In the Description box, you can write an introductory description of the category. Several tools are provided for formatting the description.

Because it is a new independent banner category and not a subcategory of any existing category, leave the Parent combo box to its default value: No parent.

In the Tags box, enter one or more optional tags or keywords to distinguish this banner category from others. Tags are also used to relate a banner category with other content, such as articles, contacts, and so on.

Set the Status combo box to the Published option to make the banners of this category visible on your web site. The Access Level field is used to specify which level of users can access this banner category. As usual, the access levels are as follows:

- **Public**: Everybody can access this category.

- **Guest**: Category can be accessed by the users who are not logged in.

- **Super Users:** Category can be accessed by the user(s) who have highest level of authorization.

- **Registered:** Only registered users can access this category.

- **Special**: Only users with author or higher status can access this category.

Set the Access level of this banner category to Public because you want it to be viewed by every visitor to your web site.

From the Language combo box, select the language of the banner category. If you are creating a multilingual site and want to show certain banners in any specific language, choose it from this combo box. Meanwhile, leave the default value All for this field.

The Note (optional) field is for the administrator to write a reminder note for this banner category. Leave it blank for now. The Version Note (optional) field is used to identify the version of this banner category. Again, leave this field blank.

The Publishing tab shows information such as the date when this banner category was created, the username of who created it, when it was last modified, the username of who modified it, the count of the hits (views) on this banner category, the unique identification number, the ID for this banner category that is automatically generated by Joomla, and so on (see Figure 4-13).

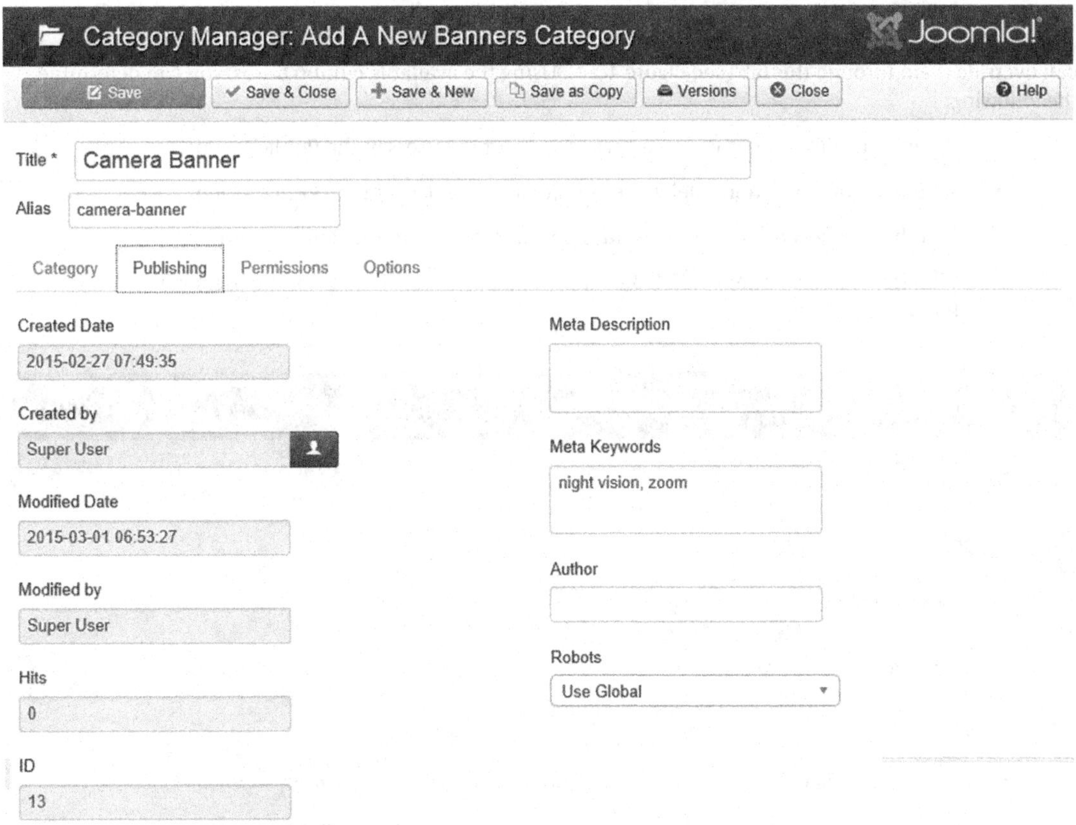

Figure 4-13. *Viewing Publishing information of a banner category*

The screen also allows you to enter some meta information related to the banner category. In the Meta Description (optional) field, enter a short description of this banner category to appear in the search engine results. In the Meta Keywords (optional) box, enter some keywords, separated by commas, that will help display this banner category when related content article, contacts, and so on have been viewed by the user. For example, enter **night vision** and **zoom** as meta keywords in this box. Now whenever any article (or other content) being viewed has either of these keywords, this banner category will show up. You can enter the name of the author for this banner category in the Author field.

As you did in Chapter 3 when creating the article category, choose the desired Robots from the combo box. Recall that robots help you make your site visible to search engines. The available options are Use Global/Index, Follow/No Index, Follow/Index, No Follow/No Index, No Follow. The meanings of Index and Follow are repeated here for your reference:

- **Index**: Determines whether you want a search engine to index the contents of this page

- **Follow**: Determines whether you want a search engine to follow and crawl the links on this page

The Permissions tab shows the combo boxes that enable you to modify permissions related to the current Banner category. Permissions are usually inherited from the Global Configuration settings, but you can override them through this tab (see Figure 4-14). Using the available combo boxes, you can determine the following:

- Whether to allow or deny Create permissions for the users in the Public group

- Whether to allow or deny Delete permissions for the users in the Public group

- Whether to allow or deny Edit permissions for the users in the Public group

- Whether to allow or deny Edit State–Published State permissions for the users in the Public group

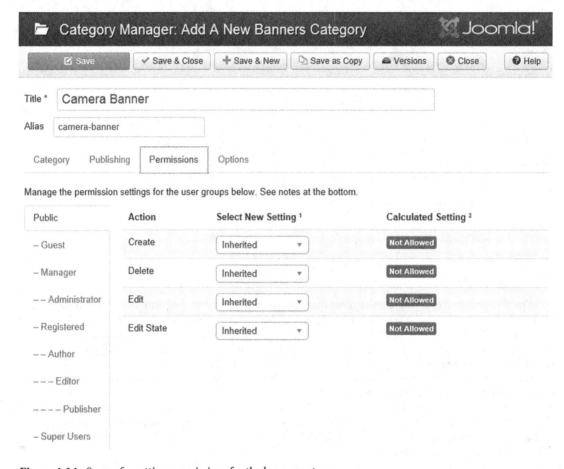

Figure 4-14. *Screen for setting permissions for the banner category*

The Options tab helps assign an image to the banner category. After clicking this tab, you see the screen shown in Figure 4-15. The Alternative Layout combo box can be used for overriding the current layout. When the Select button is clicked, the Media Manager will open and show the images that are already uploaded in it. You can upload new images if required. Select any of the images by clicking the Insert button to represent the current banner category.

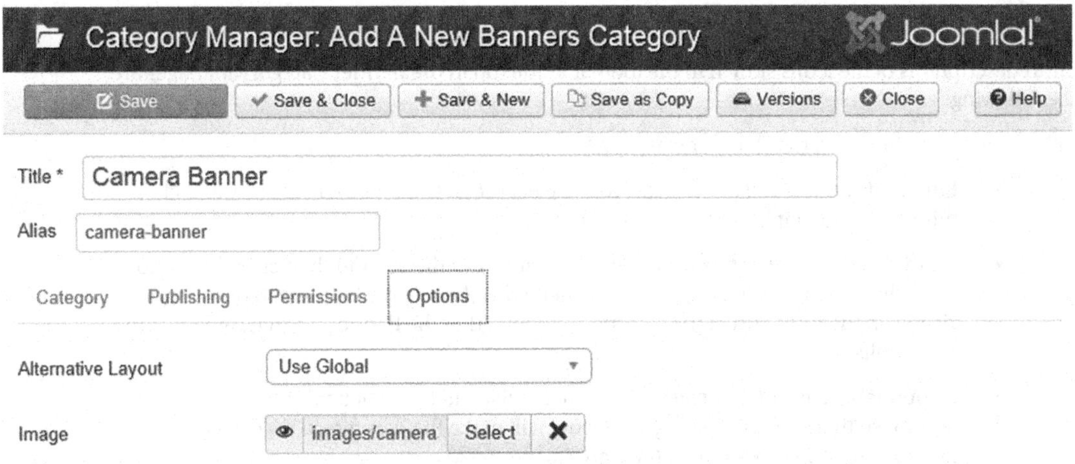

Figure 4-15. *Screen for assigning an image to the banner category*

After entering the information for the new category, as discussed previously, click the Save & Close icon to save it. You'll see the message Category Successfully Saved; and the new category, Camera Banner, will appear in the Banner Category Manager list, as shown in Figure 4-16.

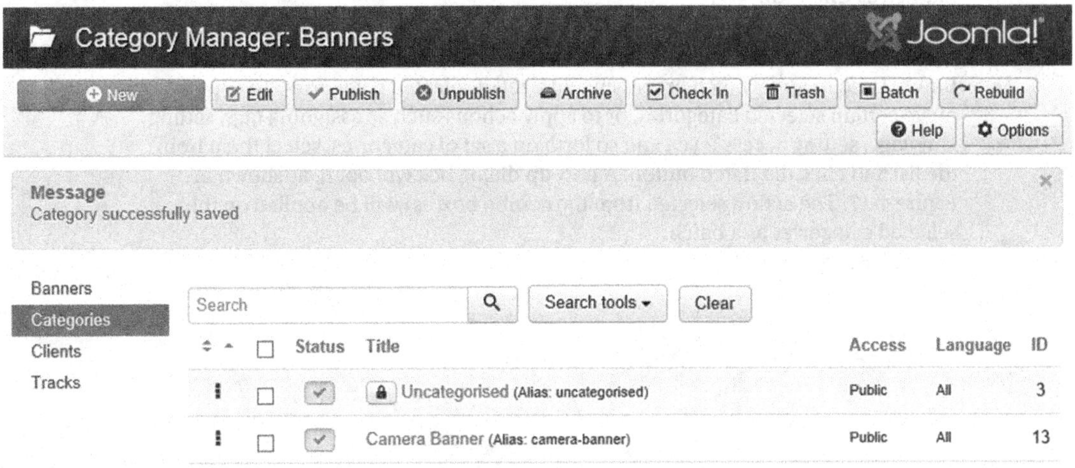

Figure 4-16. *Creating the new banner category, Camera Banner*

Category Manager Toolbar

Short descriptions of the icons shown in the toolbar at the top in the Banner Category Manager are the following:

- **New**: Creates a new banner category.

- **Edit**: Edits an existing banner category. Select the desired banner category and click this icon to open it in edit mode.

- **Publish**: Select one or more banner categories from the list and then click this button to publish them. Publishing a banner category will make the banners in that category visible on the front end of the web site, provided that the banners in that category are also published.

- **Unpublish**: Select one or categories from the list and then click this button to unpublish them. Unpublishing a category will make the banners in that category invisible from the front end of the web site.

- **Archive**: Select one or more categories from the list and then click this button to move them to the archive.

- **Check In**: Select the required number of categories from the list and click this button to close them and mark them as Check In. No editing can be performed on the opened banner category. In an opened state, a banner category is blocked from use by other administrators. To make it editable, a banner category has to be closed and marked as Check In.

- **Trash**: Moves the selected banner category(ies) to the trash.

- **Batch**: Used to apply batch processing on a set of selected categories. To copy or move certain selected categories, or to apply actions such as assigning tags, setting language, setting access level, and so forth on a set of categories, select them from the list and click the Batch button. A pop-up dialog box will open, as shown in Figure 4-17. The action selected from the combo box(es) will be applied on the selected categories as a batch.

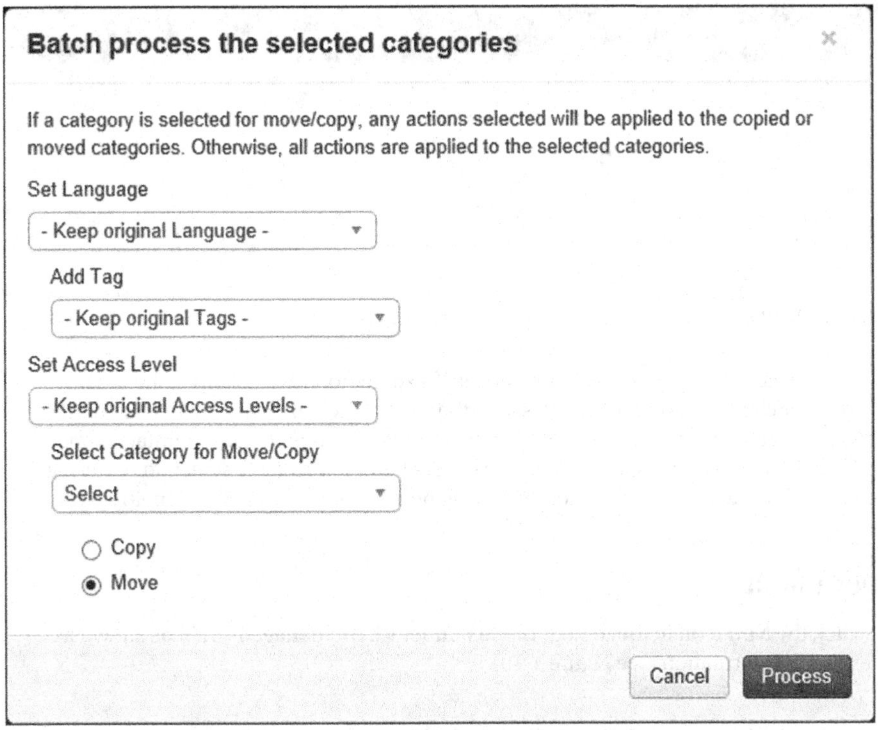

Batch process the selected categories   ✕

If a category is selected for move/copy, any actions selected will be applied to the copied or moved categories. Otherwise, all actions are applied to the selected categories.

Set Language

[- Keep original Language -   ▼]

Add Tag

[- Keep original Tags -   ▼]

Set Access Level

[- Keep original Access Levels -   ▼]

Select Category for Move/Copy

[Select   ▼]

○ Copy
◉ Move

[Cancel]   [Process]

Figure 4-17. *Screen for applying batch operations on banner categories*

- **Rebuild**: Rebuilds the category table. Usually used when several operations are performed on categories, and you want to see the outcome of those operations in the category list.

- **Help**: Opens the new browser window and navigates to the online help files related to the active topic.

- **Options**: Opens the Banner Manager Options that can be used to configure the banners. For example, you can use it to track impressions and number of clicks on the banner, determine the purchase type of the banner, and so on.

Now you need to define the client for whom you'll be displaying the banner on your web site.

Creating a Banner Client Using the Banner Client Manager

The banner client stores the information for the organization whose banner you're going to display on your web site. To create clients for your banners, use the Banner Client Manager. To open the Banner Client Manager, either click the Clients link in the Banner Category Manager or select Components ➤ Banners ➤ Clients from the menu bar. You'll see the Banner Client Manager, as shown in Figure 4-18. It displays a list of all the banner clients and their information, if any, and lets you add new clients, or edit or delete existing clients. Currently, the list is empty because there are no banner clients provided by default. Remember that you have to define at least one Banner Client and one Banner Category prior to starting to add the first new Banner.

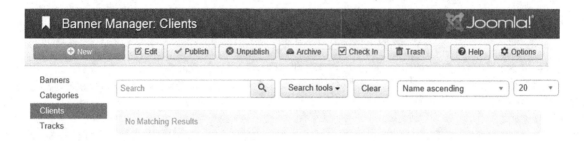

Figure 4-18. *Banner Client Manager*

The icons in the Banner Client Manager toolbar are fairly self-explanatory. For example, the Trash icon is used to delete a banner client. Users just need to select the check box of the client to delete and then click this icon. Similarly, the Edit icon is meant for editing client information (client name, contact name, e-mail ID, and so on). The New icon is used to create a new banner client: it displays a screen for entering information about the client. The Help icon is used for displaying help screens from Joomla's help server.

Creating a Banner Client

To create a new client, click the New icon in the toolbar of the Banner Client Manager. You'll be shown a screen for entering the client's information (see Figure 4-19).

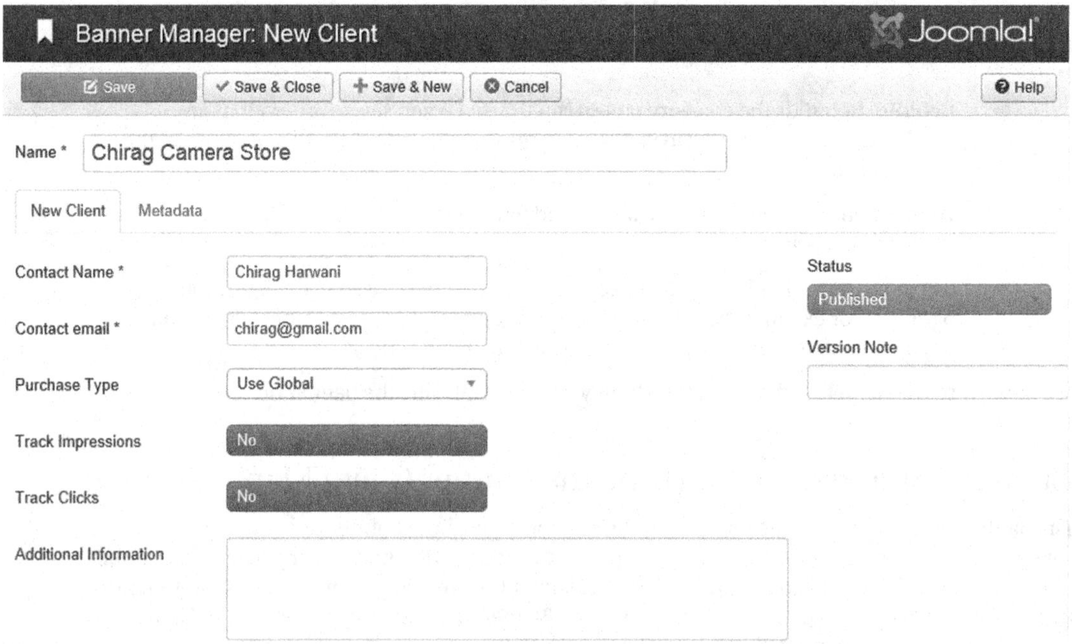

Figure 4-19. *Creating a new banner client*

The screen shows two tabs: New Client and Metadata. First, focus on the New Client tab. In the Name field, enter the company or organization name whose banner you will publish. Enter a dummy banner client name: **Chirag Camera Store**. In the Contact Name field, specify the name of the authorized contact person in the organization. Enter the name of the person who will be contacted for payments and other purposes in this field (I entered Chirag Harwani). In the Contact email field, enter the e-mail address of the contact person. Assuming that the e-mail address of Chirag Harwani is chirag@gmail.com, enter the same in this field. This e-mail ID can be used to tell clients about contract expiration, remind them about contract renewal, and so on.

From the Purchase Type combo box, select the period to display the client's banner. The available options are Daily, Weekly, Monthly, Yearly, and Unlimited. Select Yes from the Track Impressions field to count the impressions and display the number in the Banner Tracks. Or leave it to its default value of No if you don't want impressions to be tracked. Similarly, select Yes from the Track Clicks field to count the clicks on the banner and display it in the Banner Tracks. In the Additional Information (optional) field, enter additional information related to the client. Set the Status to Published to display the client's banner on the site.

Version Note (optional) is for entering the version number of the banner client.

The Metadata tab displays the fields that help make the client's banner visible on the basis of the content being viewed by the user. The screen that appears after clicking the Metadata tab is shown in Figure 4-20. In the Meta Keywords field, enter the keywords that relate to the client's banner(s). For example, **night vision, zoom** is entered in this field. Now whenever users view the content that contains either of these keywords, the client's banner will appear on the web site. Select Yes from the Use Own Prefix field if you want to apply a prefix to the meta keywords. In that case, you also need to enter the required prefix in the Meta Keyword Prefix field. If you enter the prefix advt_ in the Meta Keyword Prefix field, you also need to modify the meta keywords to appear as advt_night vision, advt_zoom. Applying the prefix on meta keywords improves the searching and hence enhances the performance. If you don't want to apply a prefix on the meta keywords, select No in the Use Own Prefix field.

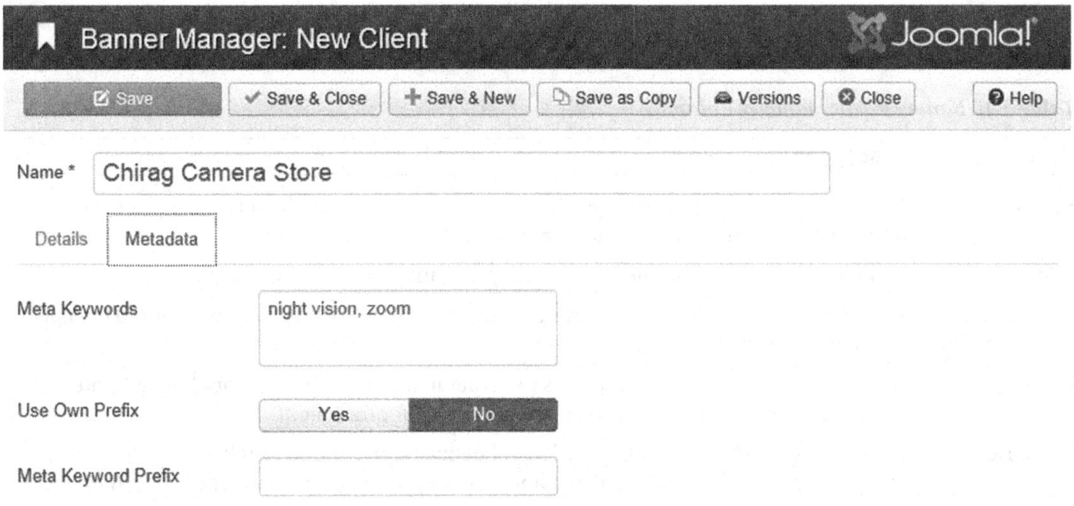

Figure 4-20. *Screen for defining meta keywords for the banner client*

■ **Note**   If you use Meta Keyword Prefix, the Banners module will ignore all the keywords except those that have the prefix `advt_`. Searching for the desired banner will be more efficient and will hence result in better performance.

After entering the information for the client, click the Save & Close button to save it. You'll see the message Client Successfully Saved; and the client organization's name, Chirag Camera Store, will appear in the Banner Client Manager list, as shown in Figure 4-21.

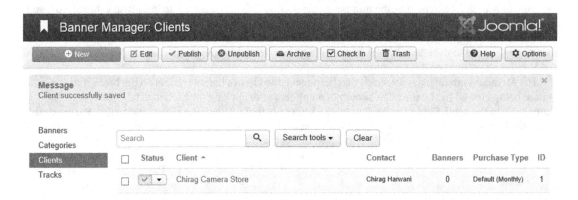

Figure 4-21. *Adding new banner client Chirag Camera Store*

To understand the usage of each column of the Banner Client Manager, see Table 4-1.

Table 4-1. *Banner Client Manager Columns*

Column	Description
Status	Indicates the status of the banner client (whether the banner client is in the published, unpublished, archived, or trashed state).
Client	Displays the name of the client for whom you want to display the banners.
Contact	Displays the name of the person from the client's organization who is authorized to deal with any issues that may arise.
Banners	Displays the total number of banners (whether in the published or unpublished state) that are currently available in the Banner Manager for this client.
Purchase Type	Displays the purchase type (i.e., the kind of banner subscription purchased by the client): whether the period to display client banner is daily, weekly, monthly, yearly, or unlimited.
ID	Displays the unique client identification number that Joomla has assigned to this client. The ID is automatically assigned by Joomla and is not editable.

Now that you've created the client (Chirag Camera Store) and the banner category (Camera Banner), you can open the Banner Manager to actually create a banner for your client.

Creating a Banner Using the Banner Manager

The banner is the actual content that you'll display on your web site and for which the client will pay you. The banner is in the form of an image file (uploaded in the Media Manager) with a hyperlink attached to it that navigates the visitor to the client's home page if the banner is clicked. A banner is associated with a banner category and a banner client, so both must exist before you create a banner. Let's open the Banner Manager to create the client's banner.

From the menu bar, select Components ➤ Banners ➤ Banners to see the Banner Manager, as shown in Figure 4-22. It displays a list of existing banners, if any. Currently, the list is empty because there are no current banners.

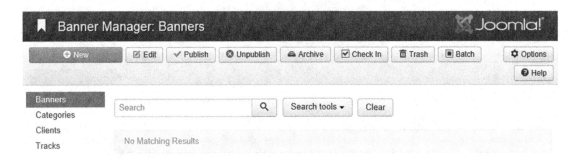

Figure 4-22. *Banner Manager*

Creating a Banner

Let's create a banner. Click the New icon in the toolbar, and you'll see a screen for entering information about the banner you want to create, as shown in Figure 4-23. The screen shows three tabs: Details, Banner Details, and Publishing. Initially, you will focus on the Details tab that opens up by default.

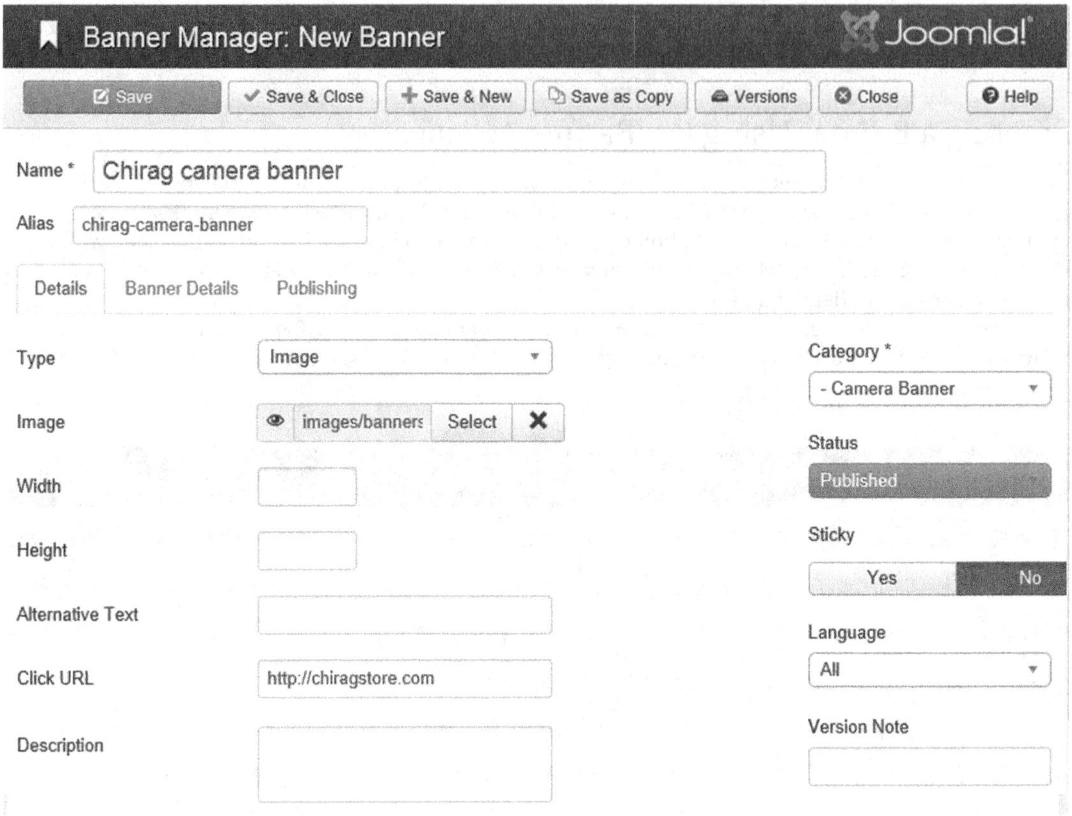

Figure 4-23. *Adding a new banner*

In the Name field, enter the name of the banner. It is better to assign names that resemble their client's name to distinguish them easily. Specify the name as **Chirag camera banner** because you will make this banner for your banner client, Chirag Camera Store.

As mentioned, the Alias field is used in the URL when SEF is activated (again, SEF enables the search engines to access the desired content in an optimized way). Specify the alias as **chirag-camera-banner**.

From the Type combo box, you can select either of the following options:

- **Image**: Used if you want to upload any banner image.

- **Custom**: Used if you want to copy and paste the code provided by your client. If you choose this type, the following Image Selector field will be replaced by the Custom Code field, in which you can paste the supplied banner code.

Using Banners

There are two ways to use banners. One popular and conventional way is to display a banner image that, when clicked by visitors, sends them to the client's URL. For this method, you need to specify the banner client's URL in the Click URL field. This method is preferred when only one banner of a particular client is being displayed. However, you may want to place banners supplied by advertising companies such as Trade Doubler, Commission Junction, or Google's AdSense. If so, you should know that these companies provide the HTML code that contains the banner images and the URLs of the respective clients. You just need to copy and paste the HTML code provided by them into the Customer Code field, and several small banner images will appear on your web site, each pointing to its respective client. In that case, leave the Click URL field blank.

Let's select the Image option from the Type combo box. From the Image Selector field, select the image file to be displayed as the banner. The image is loaded from the `joomla_root/images/banners` folder, so the client's banner image must be preloaded into this folder using the Media Manager (see Figure 4-24). For this example, specify the client banner image file `ChiragCamera.png`, which you uploaded into the Media Manager at the beginning of this chapter. The Banner Image box displays the preview of the selected client's banner image file. Select that image and click Insert button.

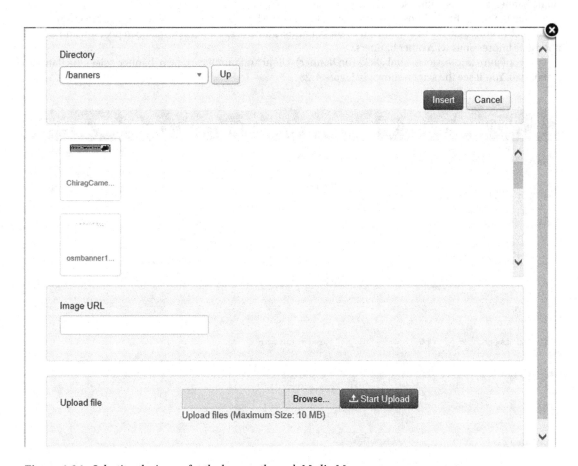

Figure 4-24. *Selecting the image for the banner through Media Manager*

In the Width and Height fields, you can enter the width and height for the banner, or leave these fields blank to make the banner appear in its original size. If you have selected Image from the Type field, you can also enter some text for the image in the Alternative Text field. The text entered in the Alternative Text field appears when the mouse hovers over the banner.

In the Click URL field (refer to Figure 4-23), enter the URL of the client for whom this advertising banner is being made. The visitor will be navigated to this URL if the banner is clicked. Assume that the web site of your client, Chirag Camera Store, is `http://chiragstore.com` and enter the same in this field.

The Description box is used to enter a small description for the banner. This description is not displayed on the web page.

From the Category combo box, select the category to which the banner belongs. Select the banner category you just created: Camera Banner.

Leave the Status combo box value at its default value (Published)to make the banner visible on your web site. You can set the Sticky option to Yes to specify that the banner be sticky. Sticky banners take priority over banners that are not sticky, and their frequency of display is higher. Because you currently have just a single banner, keep this option set to No.

From the Sticky field, choose Yes if you want to mark the banner as sticky. Sticky banners are given preference over non-sticky banners. That is, sticky banners always show in their specified position and do not rotate impressions with other banners.

To configure impressions, total clicks (on banner), client and purchase type of banner, select the Banner Details tab. You'll see the screen shown in Figure 4-25.

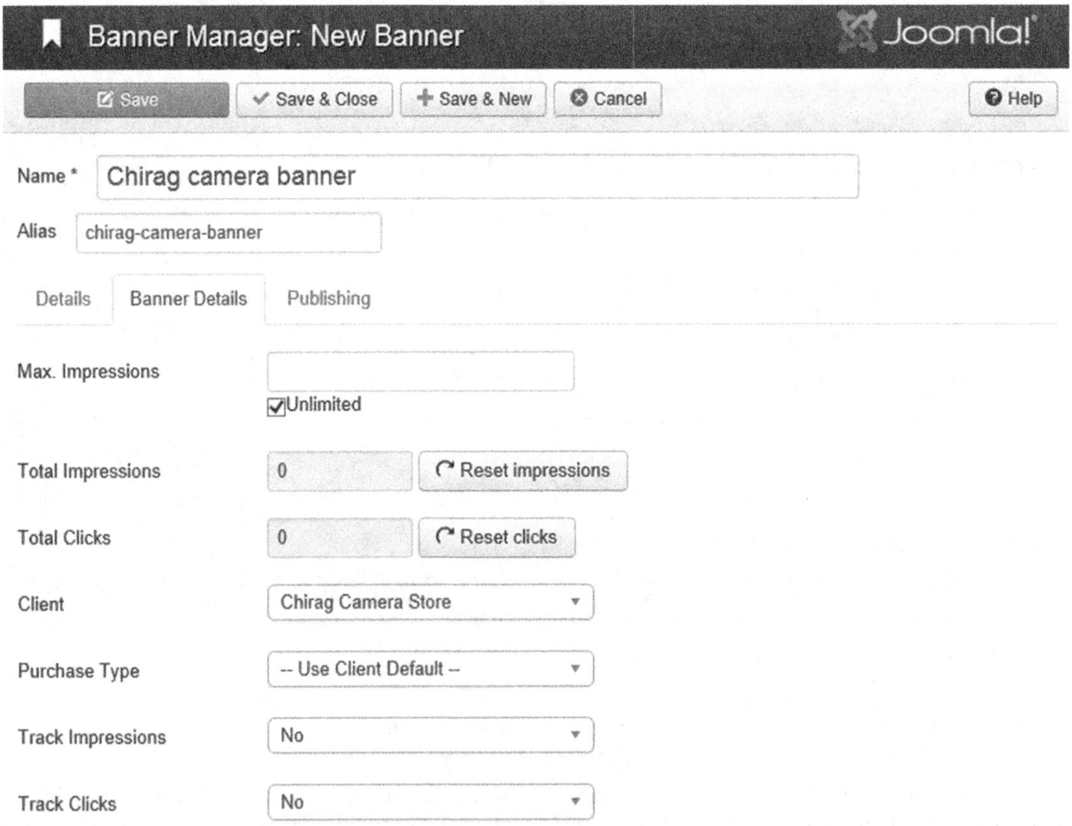

Figure 4-25. *Screen for setting impressions and banner clicks*

In the Max. Impressions box, enter a number that defines how many times this banner will be displayed on your web site. For example, if you enter a value of 1,000 here, it means that this banner will be displayed 1,000 times, after which it will disappear from your web site. Leave this field blank if you will select the Unlimited check box, which allows you to display the client's banner an unlimited number of times.

The Total Impressions field displays the count of the times the banner has appeared on the site. For the new banner, the field displays the value0. Use the Reset Impressions button to reset the value of this field to 0. The Total Clicks field displays the number of times this banner has been clicked by visitors. The Reset clicks button is used to reset the number of clicks to zero.

From the Client combo box, select the client to whom this banner belongs: Chirag Camera Store. From the Purchase Type field, choose the banner subscription selected by the client. The available options are Daily, Weekly, Monthly, Yearly, or Unlimited. The chosen option determines the period for the banner impressions or clicks.

From the Track Impressions field, select Yes to count the banner impressions (i.e., the number of times the banner has appeared on the site) and display that count in the Banner Tracks. From the Track Clicks field, select Yes to count the clicks on the banner and display that count in the Banner Tracks.

Defining Publishing and Meta Info for the Banner

To view publishing information for the new banner and define its meta keywords, select the Publishing tab in the New Banner screen. The publishing information of the new banner will display, as shown in Figure 4-26.

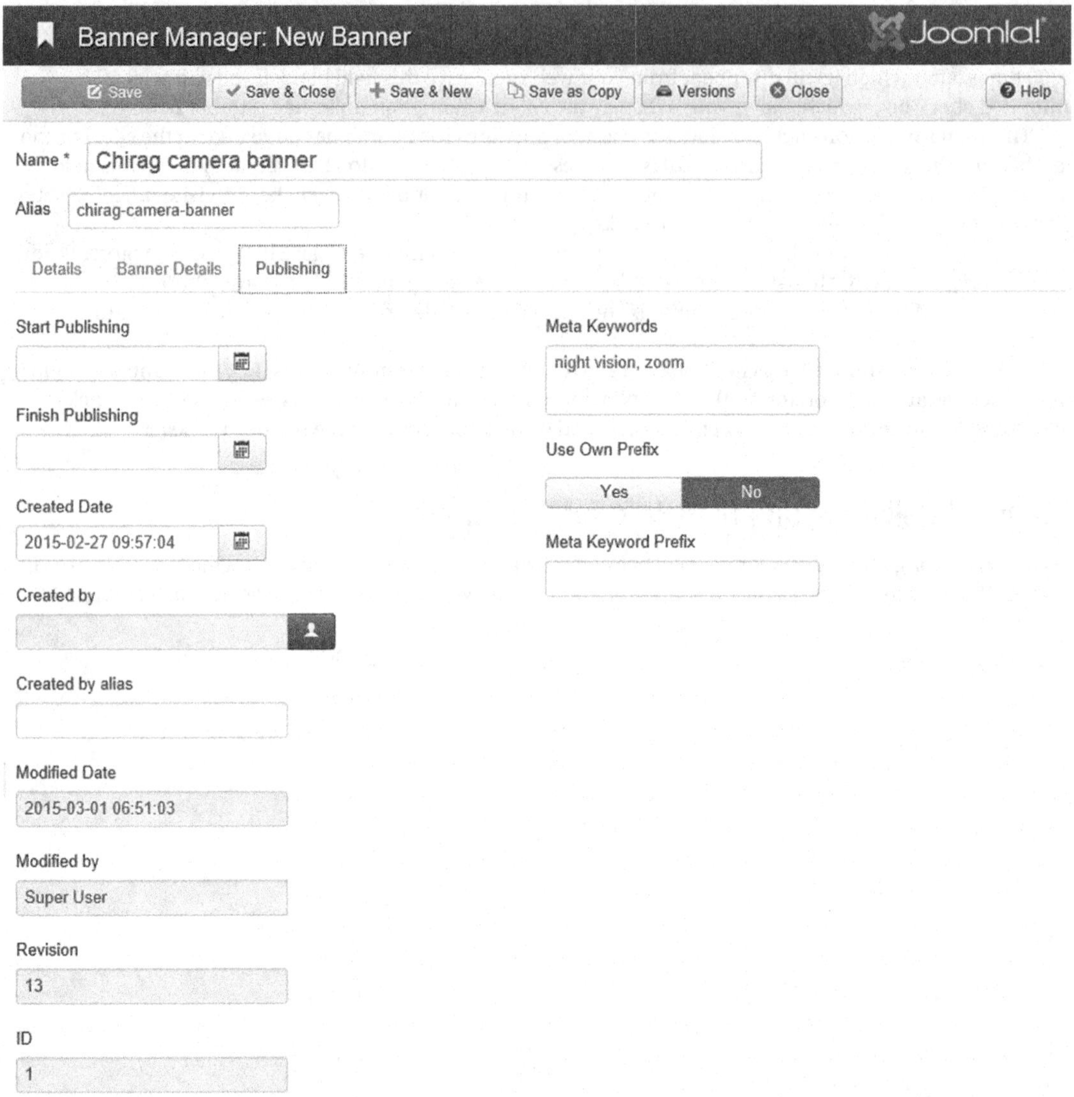

Figure 4-26. *Screen for viewing publishing information of the new banner*

From the Start Publishing field (optional), choose the date from which you want to publish the banner. Leave the field blank to publish the banner immediately. From the Finish Publishing field (optional), choose the date on which you want to unpublish the banner. Leave the field blank to publish the banner indefinitely. The Created Date field is automatically filled with the creation date and time for the banner. In the Created by field, you can specify the user who created the banner. If clicked, the user icon on the right of the field displays the existing users in your Joomla system. In the Created by alias field (optional), you can enter an alias for the user who created the banner. The Modified Date field automatically displays the date when the banner was last modified. The Modified by field automatically displays the username of who modified the banner last. The Revision field automatically displays the count of the number of times the banner has been revised. The ID field displays the auto generated ID for this banner that is used internally by the Joomla system.

The Meta Keywords box is an optional field used for displaying specific banners based on the content of the article being viewed. If you choose Yes to Use Own Prefix, you need to mention the prefix in the Meta Keyword Prefix box. If you enter the prefix as advt_, you have to define the tags in this field with the prefix advt_. These tags will be matched with the keywords of the articles being viewed by the visitor, and the banner whose Tags field matches the keywords of the article will be automatically displayed onscreen. Usually tags refer to important features of the product, and you can have any number of tags, separated by commas.

Applying Meta Tags and Keywords to Banner

Recall the concept of tags from Chapter 3. *Tags* are keywords composed of a few words that briefly highlight important information about an article. When you created the article "Latest Cameras" in Chapter 3, you used the tags camera, zoom, night vision, and higher megapixel resolution (see Figure 4-27). These tags appear in front of your web site under the Popular Tags section. When a visitor clicks any tag, all content that matches the selected tag appears in the front.

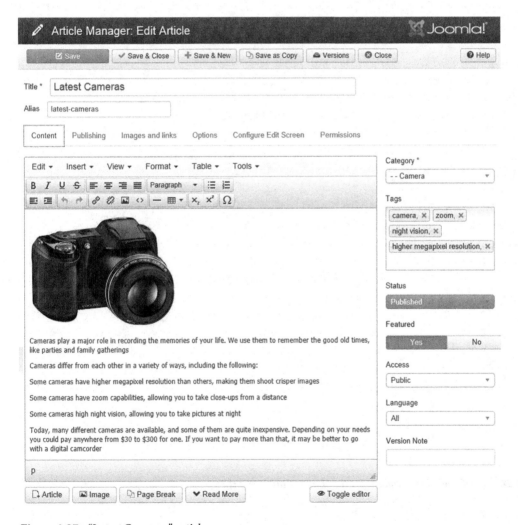

Figure 4-27. "Latest Cameras" article

The meta keywords are meant for search engines. Though most of the search engines have become smarter, meta tags are used by certain search engines to locate web site content. The meta tags are also used to display related banners based on the article being viewed. To relate banners with the "Latest Cameras" article, set its meta keywords as shown in Figure 4-28.

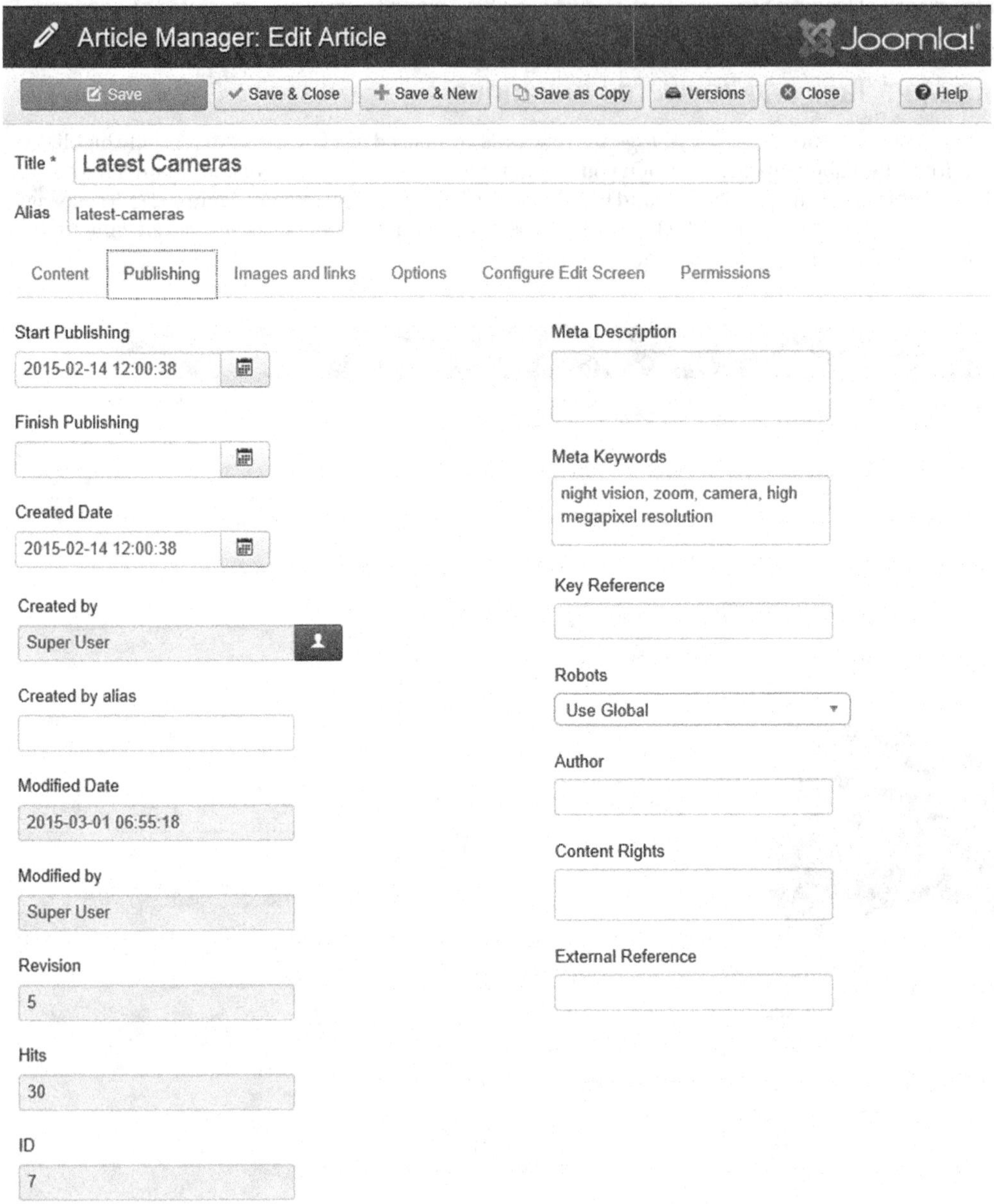

Figure 4-28. *Specifying meta keywords for the "Latest Cameras" article*

Understanding the Banner Manager Toolbar

Back to the Banners module. After entering the information for the banner, as discussed previously, click the Save & Close icon to save it. You'll see a message that reads Item Saved, and a Chirag camera banner entry will appear in the Banner Manager, as shown in Figure 4-29.

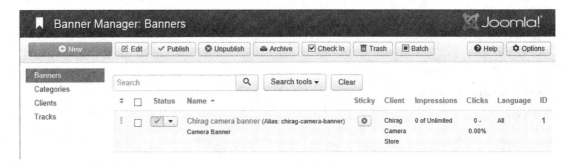

Figure 4-29. *New banner added*

The Chirag camera banner entry in the Banner Manager confirms that your banner has been made.

The toolbar of the Banner Manager has several buttons. Let's have a quick introduction. The Edit button is used to edit the information about the banner that was entered when the banner was created. Information such as the banner name, image, category, and client name can be edited.

The Publish button is used to make banners visible on the web site. To publish a banner, simply select the check box of the banner(s) and click this button. Similarly, the Unpublish button is for making banners invisible on the web site. The Archive button is used to move the selected banners to the archive. The Check In button is used to mark the selected banners as Check In. No editing can be performed on the opened banners; only on the closed banners that are marked as Check In.

The Trash button is used to permanently delete a banner. The Help icon is for opening the Joomla help web site.

The Batch button is for applying batch operations on the selected banners. You can copy, move, and set the client and language for more than one banner through this button. Figure 4-30 shows the combo boxes that open up when Batch is clicked.

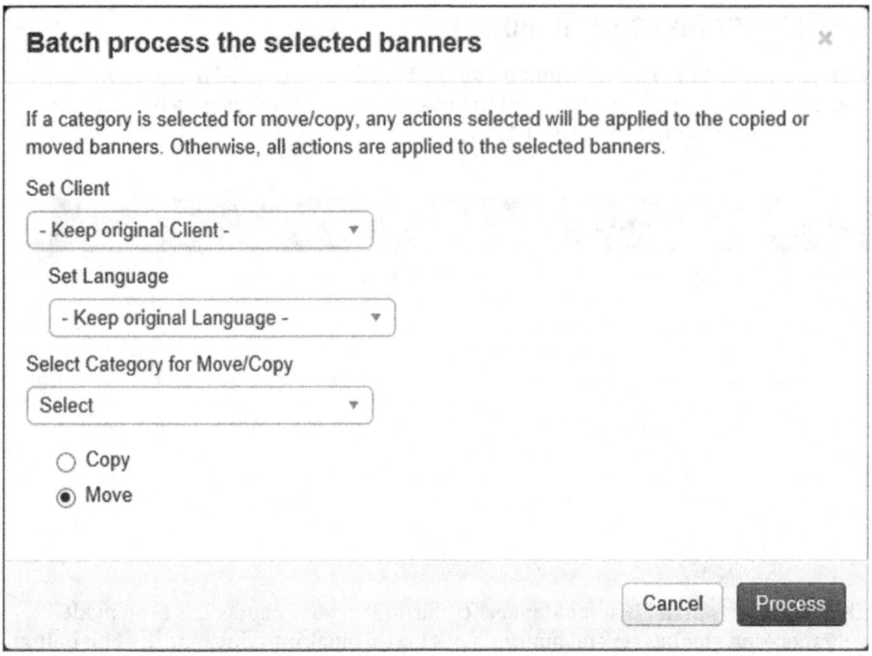

Batch process the selected banners ✕

If a category is selected for move/copy, any actions selected will be applied to the copied or moved banners. Otherwise, all actions are applied to the selected banners.

Set Client

| - Keep original Client - ▼ |

Set Language

| - Keep original Language - ▼ |

Select Category for Move/Copy

| Select ▼ |

○ Copy
◉ Move

Cancel   Process

Figure 4-30. *Dialog box that enables batch processing on selected banners*

Use the Copy radio button to make copies of an existing banner. Select the check box of the banner for which you want to make a copy and choose the Copy radio button from the dialog box. It will make a copy of the banner with the original banner name with a suffix (2) added to its name. For example, if the banner name is Chirag camera banner, its copy will have the name Chirag camera banner (2).

The Options button opens the banner's Global Configuration window, which allows you to set default parameters for banners, as shown in Figure 4-31. The screen shows three tabs: Client Options, History Options and Permissions.

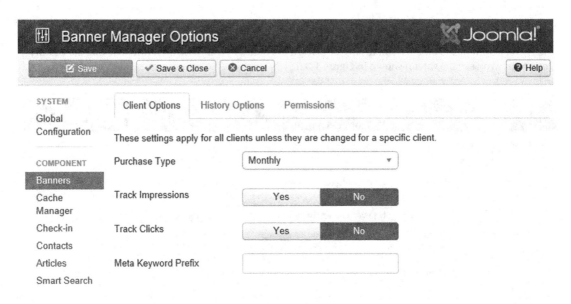

Figure 4-31. Configuring Client Options for the banner

Configuring Client Options for a Banner

First, you will focus on Client Options, which opens by default. The parameters that you set in this dialog box play a major role in deciding when to display a particular banner and how long it will be visible on your web site. The options are as follows:

- **Purchase Type**: Choose the period for banner impressions from this combo box. The available options are Daily, Weekly, Monthly, Yearly, and Unlimited.

- **Track Impressions**: Use this option to decide whether you want to count how many times a banner has been displayed. You should set this option to Yes if the client purchases a fixed number of impressions (wants the banner to be displayed a specific number of times), or set it to No if you want to display the banner an unlimited number of times.

- **Track Clicks:** This option counts how many times a client's banner is clicked. Assuming that the client's banner will be displayed an unlimited number of times, set the values of both Track Impressions and Track Clicks to No.

- **Meta Keyword Prefix**: All the banners of a particular client and category are usually displayed randomly. But sometimes you want to display only the banner that relates to the type of content (article) being viewed by the user. For example, if the visitor is reading an article on cameras, it is wise to display camera-related banners only. In this field, enter the prefix for the tags you will insert in the banner's Tags field. Enter advt_ as the tag prefix to designate it as related to the advertisement. You will soon see how this field will help you choose to display the banner on the basis of the content being viewed on your web site.

Configuring History Options for a Banner

The History Options tab enables you to save or discard the banner version history. After clicking the History Options tab, you see the screen shown in Figure 4-32.

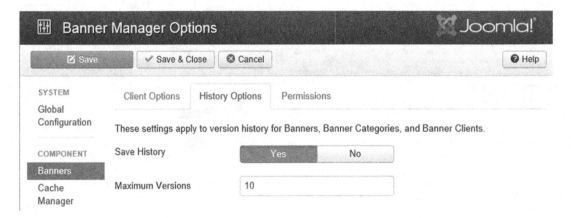

Figure 4-32. *History Options screen*

Set the Save History field to Yes if you want to save the version history for this banner. In the Maximum Versions field, enter the value that defines the maximum number of versions of the banner to store. When the maximum number of versions will be reached, the oldest version will be deleted automatically. If the value for this field is set to 0, versions will not be deleted automatically.

Configuring Permissions Options

The Permissions tab shows the combo boxes that enable you to modify permissions related to the current banner. Permissions are usually inherited from the Global Configuration settings, but you can override them through this tab (see Figure 4-33). Using the available combo boxes, you can determine the following:

- Whether to allow or deny Configure permissions for the users in the Public group. If allowed, users can edit banner options.

- Whether to allow or deny Access Administration Interface permissions for users in the Public group. If allowed, users can access administration interface and apply desired modifications.

- Whether to allow or deny Create permissions for users in the Public group.

- Whether to allow or deny Delete permissions for users in the Public group.

- Whether to allow or deny Edit permissions for users in the Public group.

- Whether to allow or deny Edit State–Published state permissions for users in the Public group.

⊞ Banner Manager Options				🍃 Joomla!®
🖉 Save	✓ Save & Close	⊗ Cancel		❓ Help

SYSTEM
Global
Configuration

COMPONENT
Banners
Cache
Manager
Check-in
Contacts
Articles
Smart Search
Installation
Manager
Joomla!
Update
Language
Manager
Media
Manager

Client Options   History Options   **Permissions**

Default permissions used for all content in this component.

Manage the permission settings for the user groups below. See notes at the bottom.

Public

– Guest

– Manager

– – Administrator

– Registered

– – Author

– – – Editor

– – – – Publisher

– Super Users

Action	Select New Setting ¹	Calculated Setting ²
Configure	Inherited ▾	Not Allowed
Access Administration Interface	Inherited ▾	Not Allowed
Create	Inherited ▾	Not Allowed
Delete	Inherited ▾	Not Allowed
Edit	Inherited ▾	Not Allowed
Edit State	Inherited ▾	Not Allowed

Figure 4-33. *Setting banner permissions*

The columns in the Banner Manager (refer to Figure 4-29) display information about the existing banners of your Joomla web site. The Status column specifies whether the banner is in the published, unpublished, archived, or trashed state. The check mark signifies that the banner is in the published state, and the red X signifies that the banner is in the unpublished state. The Name column displays the name of the banner. Below the banner name is the category in which this banner is placed. The Sticky column specifies whether the banner is set to sticky mode (the frequency of appearance of sticky banners is greater than non-sticky ones). The Client column displays the client name (organization or company name) to whom the banner belongs. The Impressions field displays the number of times the banner has appeared on the web site since it was created. Figure 4-29 shows the impressions of the Chirag camera banner as 0 of Unlimited, which means that the banner has appeared 0 times out of the unlimited number of times assigned to it.

The Clicks column displays the percentage of clicks that were made on a banner in relation to the number of impressions (appearances on the web site) that have taken place. The Language column displays the language assigned to the banner, if any. The ID column displays the unique banner identification number that Joomla has assigned for internal maintenance.

Next, you'll learn about using the Banners module when displaying a banner on your web site.

Using the Banners Module to Display the Banner on the Web Site

Until now, you've been dealing with the Banner component: You made a category for the banner, created clients for the banner, and finally created the banner. Now you need the help of the Banners module to display the banner on the web site.

By using the Banners module, you can configure several settings of the banner—for example, which pages of your web site will display the banner, its position, its access level, and so on. The Banners module is also used for selecting which category of which client's banner will be visible. The Banners module is accessible through the Module Manager.

From the menu bar, select Extensions ➤ Module Manager, and you'll see a list of modules, as shown in Figure 4-34.

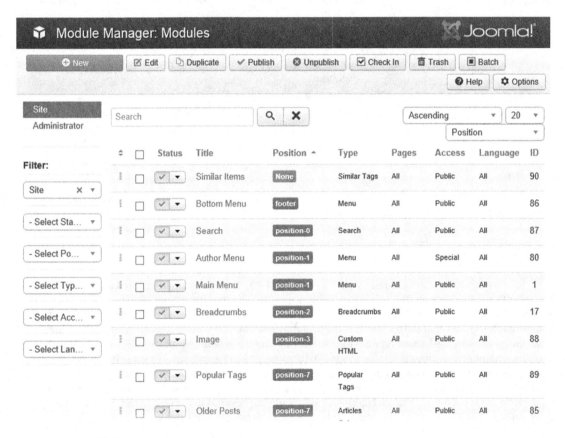

Figure 4-34. *Module Manager*

Understanding Module Manager Columns

Let's see what information the columns of the Module Manager display. The Status column shows whether the module is enabled or disabled. A check mark signifies that the module is enabled and can be used in the web site, and a red X signifies that the module is disabled (temporarily suspended) and won't be visible on the web site.

The Title column displays the name of the module. Joomla provides 20 standard modules and a facility to install more. Selecting a module name opens it in edit mode.

The Position column displays the position on the page where this module will be displayed (left or right). The templates that you use to give a dynamic look to your web site consist of styles and positions. A template internally divides a web page into different positions, including left, right, header, footer, and so on. If the Position column displays the value position-2, the module will appear at the left position on the web page. You can change the display order of modules in a position by selecting the Position drop-down list.

The Type column displays the system name of the module. Recall that Joomla installs 20 standard modules, and each has a unique system name.

The Pages column displays the menu items in which the module will be displayed. The options are All for all menu items, None for no menu items, and Varies for selected menu items.

The Access Level column specifies the category of user that can access the module. The options are Guest, Public, Registered, Special, and Super User.

The ID column displays a unique identification number for the module, assigned automatically by Joomla to identify the module internally.

The toolbar icons in the Module Manager are fairly self-explanatory. For instance, the Publish icon is used to enable a module (if the module was unpublished earlier). Just select a module's check box and click this icon to enable it. Similarly, the Unpublish icon is used to disable a module. Unpublished modules don't appear on the web site. You can also toggle between the published and unpublished state by clicking the icon in the Status column.

Recall that you made a banner named Chirag camera banner and assigned it to the category Camera Banner for the Chirag Camera Store client. To make it appear on the web site, you opened the Module Manager. To activate the banner, you have to create a new module. Click the New icon from the toolbar to create a new module. You will be prompted to select the Module Type. From the list of module types, select the Banners type. A dialog box will open to enter information for the new module, as shown in Figure 4-35.

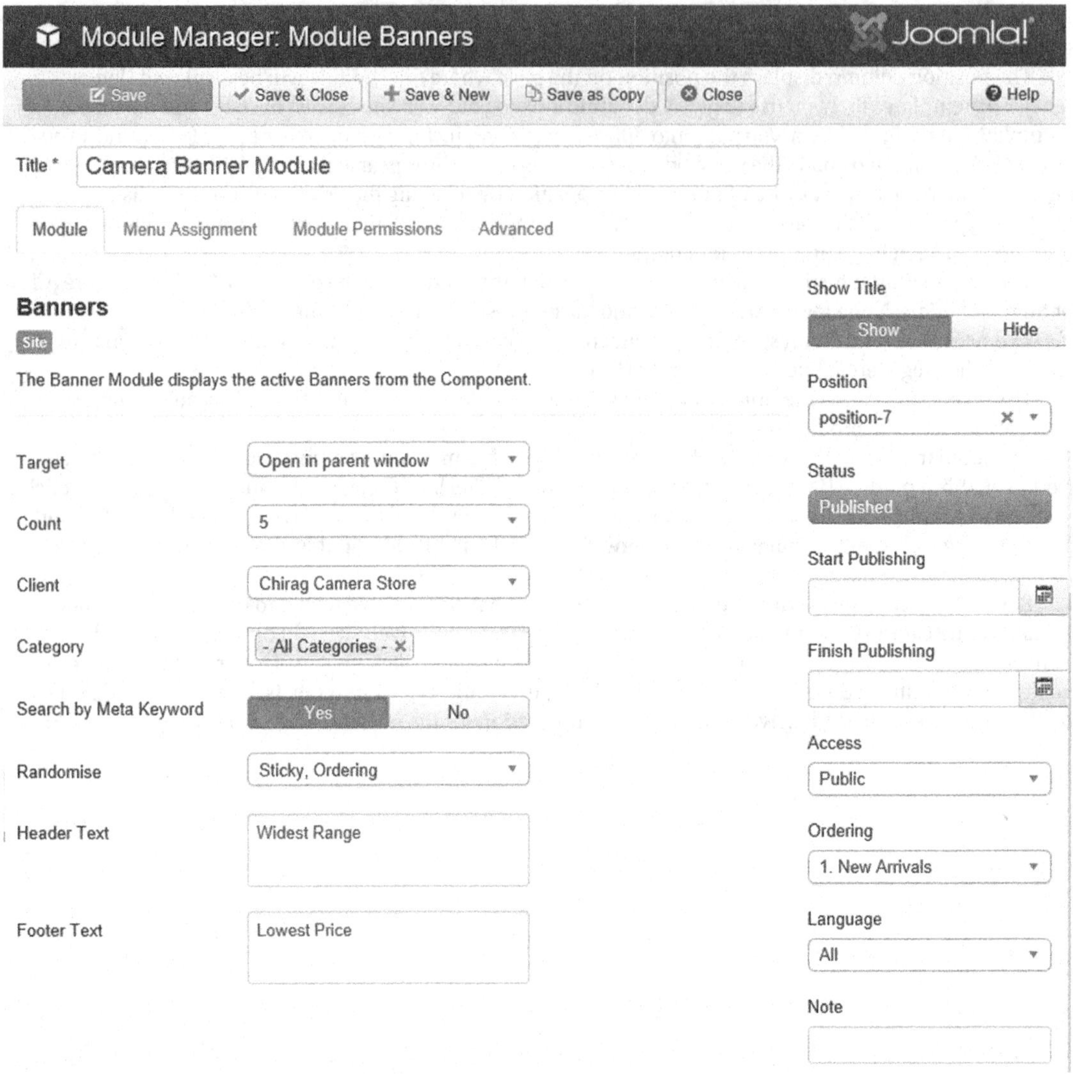

Figure 4-35. *Screen for creating a new module*

This screen contains four sections: Module, Menu Assignment, Module Permissions, and Advanced, which are discussed in the following sections.

Module Section

The Module section shows the fields in which you enter information about the new module. In the Title field, enter the name of the module: **Camera Banner Module**. From the Target combo box, choose where you want to open the link (i.e., when the visitor clicks the banner, the target can open in the same parent window, a new window, or a pop-up window). The available options are Open in Parent Window, Open in New Window, and Open in Pop-Up. In the Count field, enter the number of banners to display simultaneously (the default value is 5). From the Client combo box, select the client whose banners you want to display via this banner module. Select the banner client Chirag Camera Store to display its banner. From the Categories combo box, select the banner category to display: select the Camera Banner category created earlier. The default is All Categories (it will display all banner categories). Select Yes from the Search by Meta Keyword field if you want to display the banner on the basis of the content being viewed. That is, the banner whose meta keywords match with the content being viewed will automatically appear on the site. If this field is set to No, the banner will always display randomly, regardless of the content being viewed.

The Randomise combo box helps to determine the order of banner display. It displays the following two options:

- **Sticky, Ordering**: Sticky banners will display sequentially, followed by a sequential display of non-sticky banners.

- **Sticky, Randomise**: Sticky banners will display in random order.

In the Header Text and Footer Text fields, enter the text that you want to display before and after the banner group, respectively. Enter the text **Widest Range** in the Header Text field and **Lowest Price** in the Footer Text field. Set the Show Title button to Show if you want to display the module title along with the banner on the web site. The Position combo box helps determine the position in which you want the banner to appear on your web site. You can make the banner appear on the left, right, or footer positions (these positions are predefined in the implemented template). Set the Position field to position-7 to display the banner at the right top of the web page.

Set the Status state to Published to make the banner visible on your web site. In the Start Publishing field, enter the date and time from which you want to publish the banner. If left blank, the banner will publish immediately. Similarly, in the Finish Publishing field, enter the date and time on which you want to stop publishing the banner. Again, if left blank, the banner will publish indefinitely. The Access Level field specifies the level of users who can access the module. Select Public to make the banner visible to all visitors to your web site.

The Ordering combo box shows the ordering of all the modules in the chosen position (selected from the Position combo box). From the Language field, choose the language in which you want the banner to appear. Leave the default value: All. Enter a note or description related to the current module in the Note field if desired.

Menu Assignment Section

In the Menu Assignment section (see Figure 4-36), the Menus option allows you select the menus in which you want this banner to appear. The options are the following:

- **On all pages**: Shows the banners in all menus and pages

- **No pages**: Does not show the banner

- **Only on the pages selected**: Shows the banner on the selected pages only

- **On all pages except those selected**: Shows the banner on all pages except the ones that are selected

137

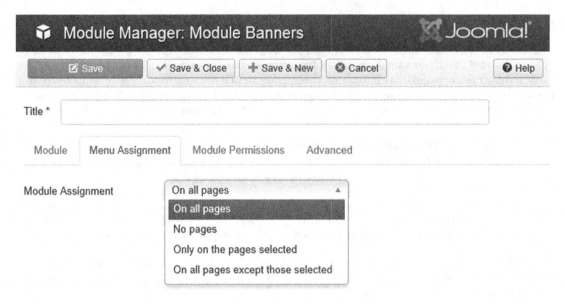

Figure 4-36. *Assigning a module to desired pages of the site*

Because you want the banner to appear on all pages, choose the option On All Pages.

Module Permissions Section

In the previous versions of Joomla, the Module Manager did not include a Module Permissions tab. However, starting with Joomla version 3.2,you can now modify user group permissions for modules. This Module Permissions section shows the combo boxes that enable you to modify permissions related to the current banner module. You can override the Global Configuration settings using this section (see Figure 4-37). Using the available combo boxes, you can determine the following:

- Whether to allow or deny Delete permissions for users in the Public group

- Whether to allow or deny Edit permissions for users in the Public group

- Whether to allow or deny Edit State–Published State permissions for users in the Public group

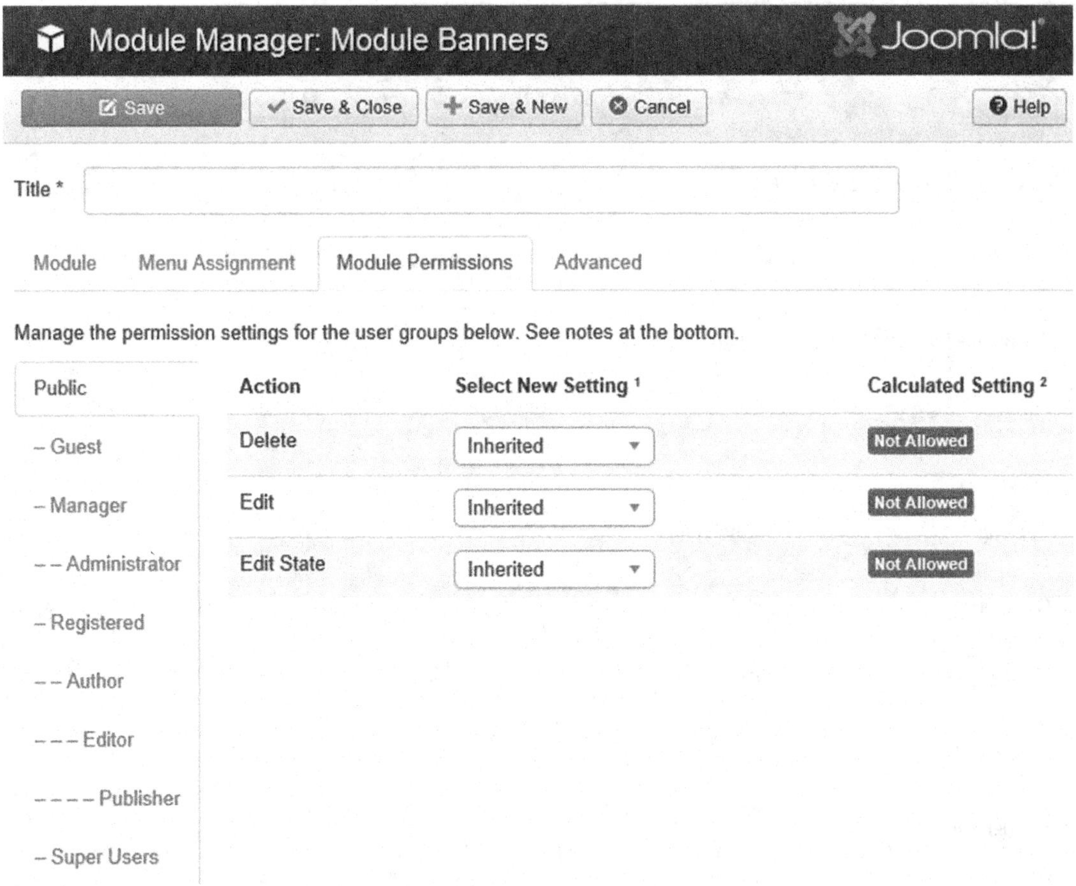

Figure 4-37. *Setting permissions for the new module*

Advanced Section

The Advanced section enables you to apply alternative layouts, styles, and tags to the banner module. The screen shows different combo boxes, as shown in Figure 4-38. From the Alternative Layout combo box, choose the desired alternative layouts for the module (applicable if you have defined alternative layouts in the template. In the Module Class Suffix field, you can define the suffix that you want to apply to the CSS class of the module. It is used to apply different CSS styles to the module. From the Caching combo box, choose the Use Global option to cache the module content. If you don't want caching of this module, select No Caching in this field. In the Cache Time field, enter the time length in minutes before the module is recached. The default value is 900 minutes.

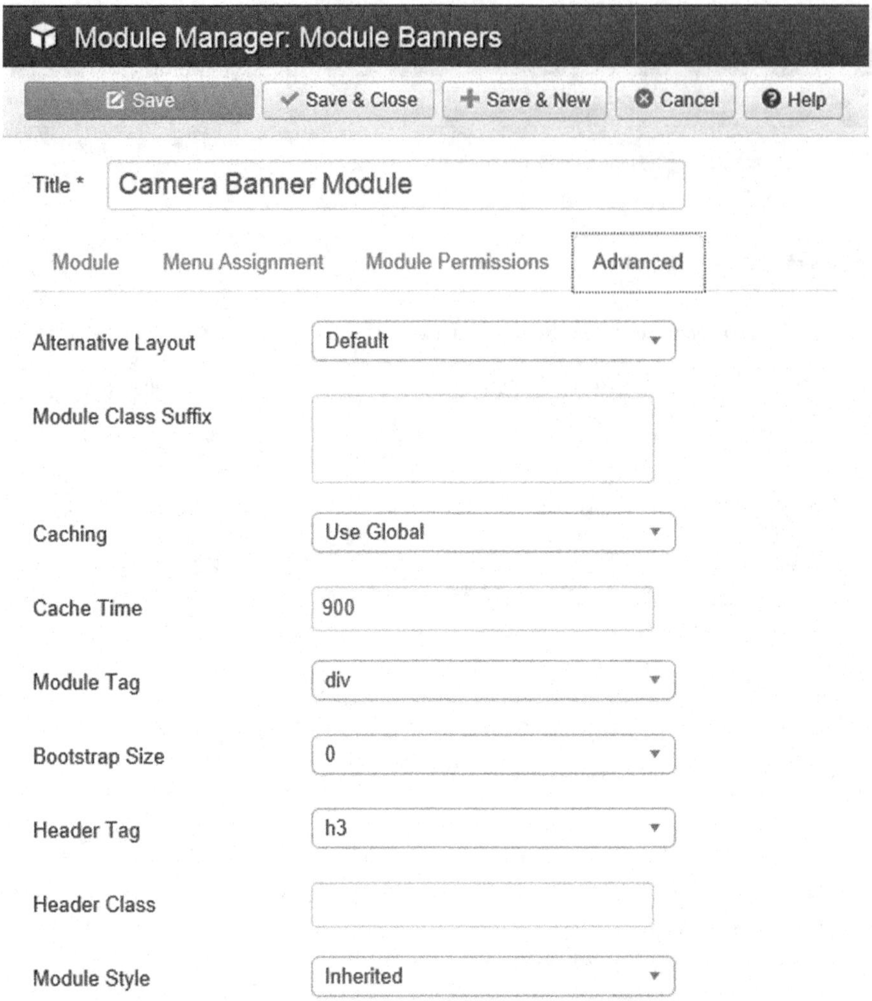

Module Manager: Module Banners

| ☑ Save | ✓ Save & Close | ➕ Save & New | ✖ Cancel | ❓ Help |

Title * | Camera Banner Module

Module   Menu Assignment   Module Permissions   Advanced

Alternative Layout | Default ▼

Module Class Suffix |

Caching | Use Global ▼

Cache Time | 900

Module Tag | div ▼

Bootstrap Size | 0 ▼

Header Tag | h3 ▼

Header Class |

Module Style | Inherited ▼

Figure 4-38. *Page for setting Advanced options for the new module*

In the Module Tag field, you can specify the HTML tag for the module. By default, the div tag is used for the module. From the Bootstrap Size combo box, choose the width of the module that is supplied through the span element. The default value is 0. From the Header Tag combo box, choose the HTML tag to use for the modules header or title. Valid options are theh1, h2, h3, h4, h5, h6, and p tags. In the Header Class field, specify the optional CSS classes to add to the module's header or title element. From the Module Style combo box, choose the style to override the templates style.

Displaying the Finished Product

After entering the module information as discussed previously, save the banner module by clicking the Save & Close icon in the toolbar. You can now see the banner of your client on your Joomla web site. Open the browser window that displays your web site and click the Refresh button. Initially, the banner will not appear because you have set the banner to display when its meta keywords match with the content being viewed.

To display the banner, invoke the "Latest Cameras" article by selecting the menu item New Electronics Products Arrival. You'll find that the Chirag camera banner appears at the right top of the web site (see Figure 4-39).

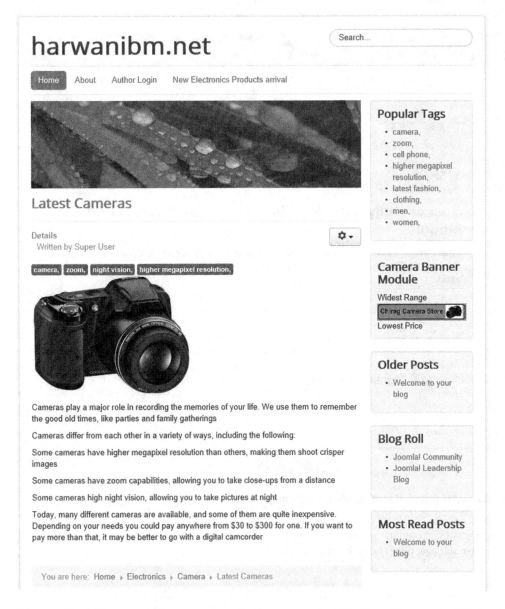

Figure 4-39. *Chirag camera banner automatically appears when the "Latest Cameras" article is selected*

Installing a Banner Component

You can even install freely available banner components from the Internet using the Extension Manager. One such banner component is FlexBanner, which you can download from http://extensions.joomla.org/extensions/extension/ads-a-affiliates/banner-management/flexbanner. The downloaded archive file is com_flexbanners_4.0.21.zip. Open the Extension Manager by selecting Extensions ➤ Extension Manager. In the Install tab of the Extension Manager that opens by default, you will find the Extension package file field. To the right of the Extension package file, click the Browse button to locate the downloaded archive file and click the Upload & Install button to install it. After the successful installation of the banner component, you see this message: Installing Component Was Successful(see Figure 4-40).

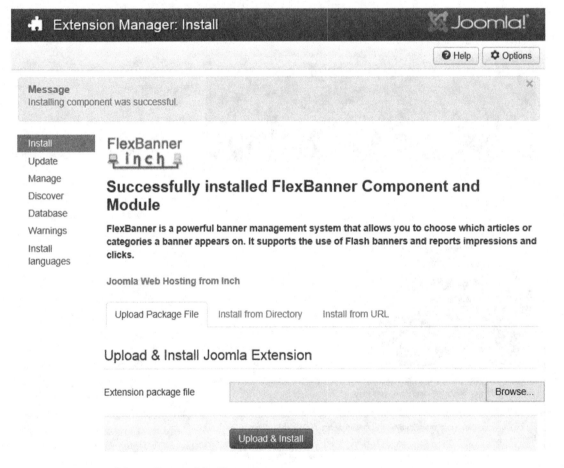

Figure 4-40. *Successful installation of the FlexBanner component*

Open the FlexBanner component by selecting the Components ➤ FlexBanners option. You see the FlexBanner Banner Manager page shown in Figure 4-41.

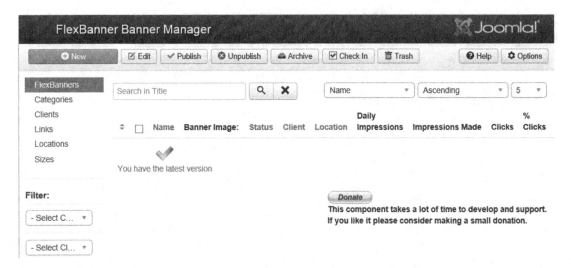

Figure 4-41. *FlexBanner Banner Manager page*

The procedure of creating and displaying banner is the same as discussed previously. The steps are repeated for your reference:

1.   Create a banner category.

2.   Create a client for whom the banner is to be made.

3.   Define the link to which you want the visitor to navigate when the banner is clicked.

4.   Optionally define the location of publishing the banner.

5.   Assuming that you created a banner category called Camera Banner, a banner client called Chirag Camera Store, a location called Right Side (to represent the right side of the site), and a link called bmharwani that points at www.bmharwani.com, you can create the banner for the defined category and client that navigates to the specified link (see Figure 4-42).

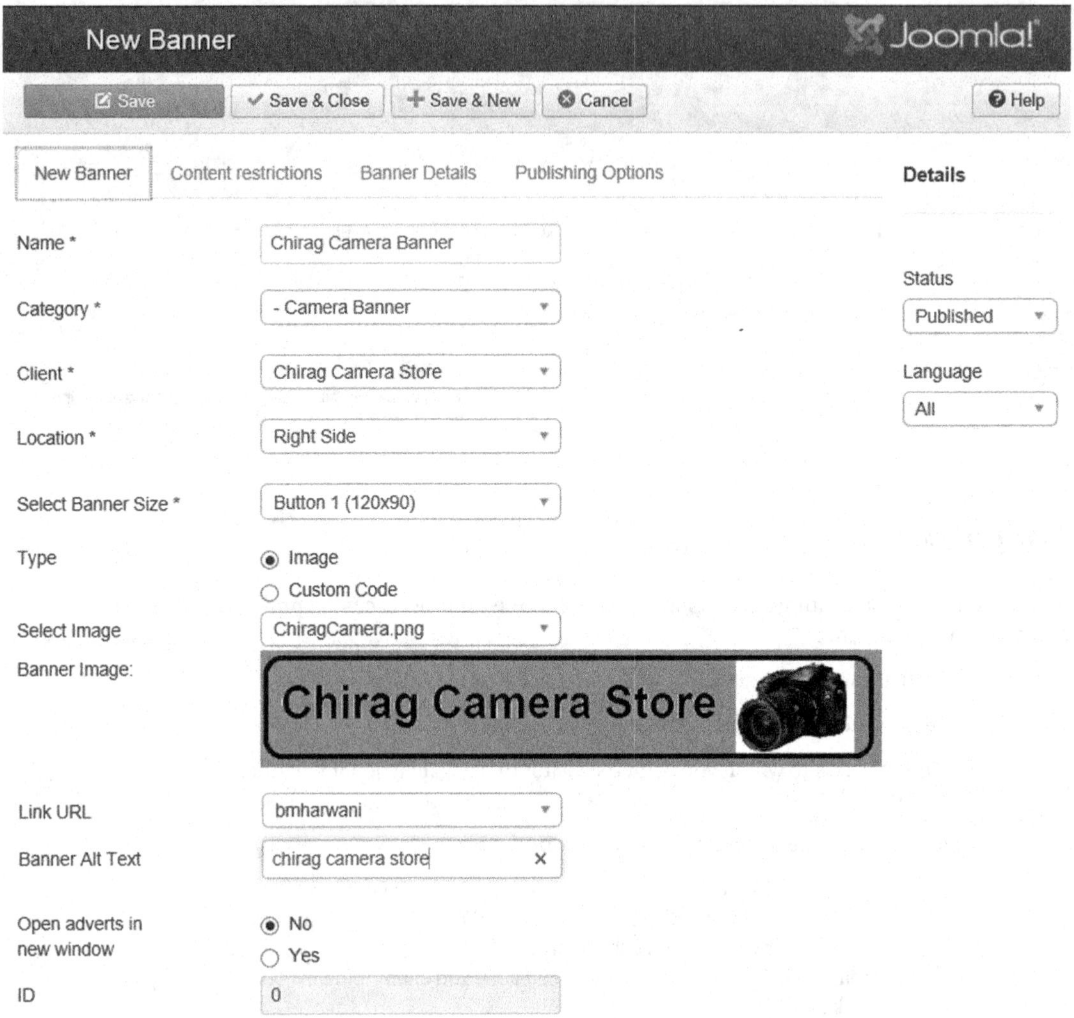

Figure 4-42. *Creating a new banner in FlexBanner Banner*

6. From the Module Manager, enable the FlexBanners module and specify its display position on the web site. You should display the banner at position-7 of the site (i.e., at the right top of the site), as shown in Figure 4-43.

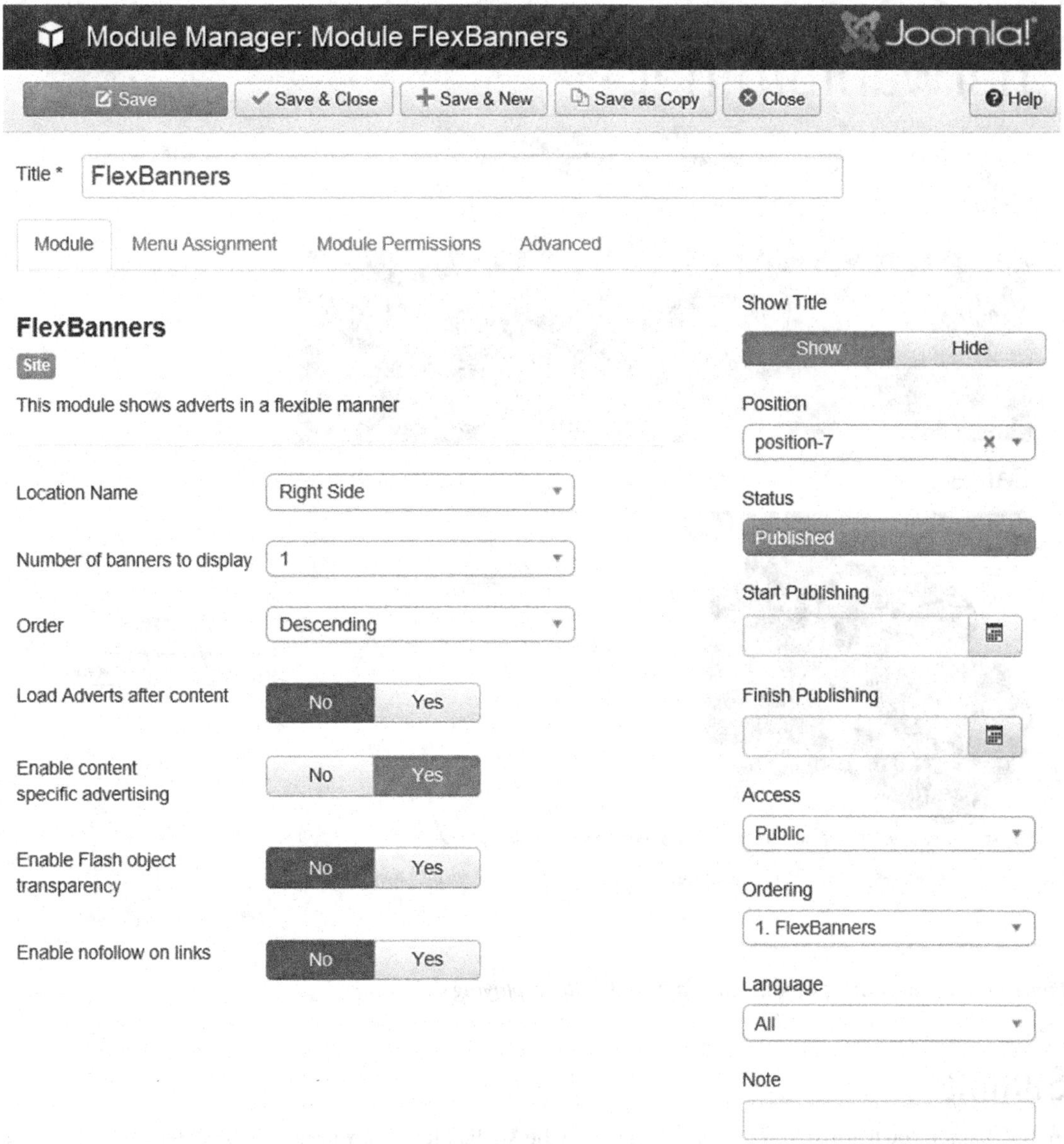

Figure 4-43. *Enabling the FlexBanners module and publishing at required position*

7. View the banner from the front side of the site, as shown in Figure 4-44.

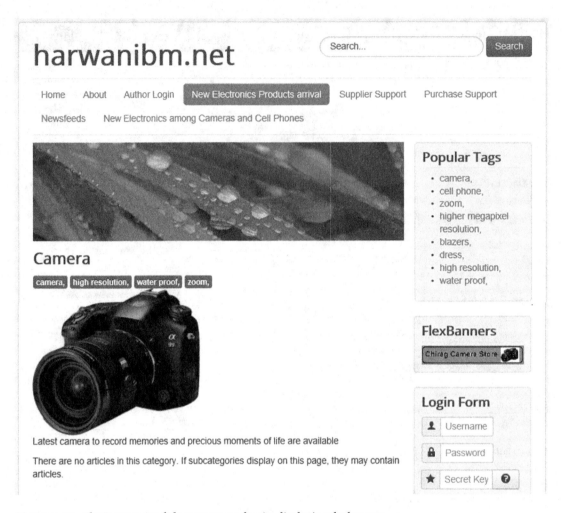

Figure 4-44. *FlexBanners module appears on the site displaying the banner*

Summary

In this chapter, you learned how to upload images to the Media Manager. You saw, step by step, how to create a category and a client for banners, and also how to create banners. Finally, you learned how to edit the Banners module to display the banners of the specific client and category.

In the next chapter, you'll see how users are created for your web site. You'll also explore the different categories of users and their roles in web site maintenance. Additionally, you'll learn to create contact forms to allow the visitors to your web site to contact you (i.e., the web site owner or any authorized person in the respective department of your organization).

■ ■ ■

CHAPTER 5

Creating Users and Contacts

In Chapter 4, you saw the role that the Media Manager plays in managing images in the articles, banners, and other contents of your web site. You also saw how to create a category and clients for the banners. Finally, you created the banner for a specific client and used the Banners module to activate it.

In this chapter, you'll create different types of users for your web site. There are several types of Web site users. One type comprises general visitors to your web site; they can generally only view the content of your site, and don't have permission to edit information or upload their own content. Another type of user can contribute to your web site by writing articles, but cannot edit existing content. There may also be users who cannot only contribute articles but also can edit and even publish them on your web site. So, you will see how these different types of users can be created for your Joomla web site, and what rights each type has.

You'll also create a contact form and allow visitors to your web site to contact the authorized person in a selected department to get desired information. Contact forms are the forms you usually see when you select the Contact Us link on any web site: blank forms with text boxes for you to enter your query and submit it. The information typed by visitors in these contact forms is e-mailed to the concerned person or department (which I will refer to from now on as the *contact*). If the contact is a department, it will be linked to a person who is authorized to receive information on behalf of the department and can take necessary action.

In this chapter, you'll learn about the following:

- User Manager
- Different types of user groups
- Creating users
- Creating a Contacts category
- Creating contacts
- Creating menu items to link to contacts

What Is a Contact?

The main agenda in this chapter is to create a contact form on your web site, which a visitor can fill in and click a button to send to you. On a standard web site, the main contact will be one of the following:

- The concerned person of the organization (in smaller organizations).
- The department of an organization. The department contact is usually linked with an authorized person who is forwarded queries for necessary actions. In large organizations, each department has its own contacts, and each is linked to an authorized person.

Remember that if the contact is a department of an organization, it has to be linked to a user who is responsible for receiving the e-mail sent to it. Consequently, I'll first show you how users are created for a web site.

If you specify a person as a contact, you don't need to link the contact to any user because all the e-mail will be sent to that person directly.

Working with the User Manager

The User Manager provides tools for creating, viewing, editing, and deleting users for your web site. Users play a major role in managing contents of a web site. You can perform several functions with the User Manager, including these:

- Seeing whether a user is logged in or not

- Blocking a user from logging into your site

- Seeing the last time a particular user visited your site

- Changing the state of a user from Logged In to Logged Out

Different Types of User Groups

The users you create can be assigned to a group, depending on what you want them to be able to do on your web site. A newly created user is assigned a group to designate the user's access level. The user groups in Joomla are predefined, and you cannot create your own groups. Table 5-1 describes all the available groups.

Table 5-1. *List of User Groups*

Group	Description
Public	The group that is at the top level in the hierarchy and hence the parent of all other groups. It is a utility group for administrators, and there are no restrictions on this group. Because a Public group is the parent of all other groups, any restrictions placed on a Public group will be inherited by all its child groups.
Guest	A group made for all nonauthenticated users that is used for displaying only specific content to the users who are not logged in. The content that is meant for Guest will not be visible to authenticated users, only to nonauthenticated users.
Manager	A group that manages content. Users assigned to the Manager group can add, delete, and edit content, among other things.
Administrator	A group that administers the site. Users in this group can do all the tasks of a manager group, along with tasks such as adding or removing modules, users, templates, and so on.
Registered	Visitors who have registered on your site are assigned to this group by default. They can view pages and menu items that are assigned the Registered or Public access level, but they cannot submit or edit articles.
Author	Users who can submit articles for approval (from the front end only). These articles must be approved by a member of the Publisher group or higher. Users in the Author group can edit their own content, but not that of other users.

(continued)

Table 5-1. *(continued)*

Group	Description
Editor	Users who can submit articles and edit existing articles of other users, too (from the front end only). These articles must be approved by a member of the Publisher group or higher. That is, the users in this group cannot publish articles.
Publisher	Users who can submit, edit, and publish articles (from the front end only).
Super users	The most powerful user group in the system. The users in this group can do all the back-end tasks to manage a site. They can add and remove content, restrict or allow user(s), configure the site using Global Configuration Manager, and much more.

Creating Users

Now that you know what kinds of groups can be assigned to a user, let's create a user for your web site. To do this, you have to open the User Manager by opening a browser window and entering your Administrator interface address (`http://localhost/joomlasite/administrator`). From the menu bar, select Users ➤ User Manager. You'll see a screen like that shown in Figure 5-1, which displays the list of all registered users of your web site. The user named Super User belongs to the Super Users group and is automatically created by Joomla.

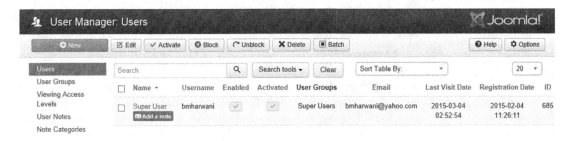

Figure 5-1. *User Manager*

The icons in the toolbar have the usual meanings that you've learned so far.

You don't have to create a user account for everyone who visits your web site, but you do need to create accounts for users who want to maintain your web site. These users need extra privileges to contribute articles, edit existing articles, publish articles, and so on. Each user that the administrator creates for web site maintenance is assigned a group depending on his role in web site administration. Visitors of your web site can also create their own accounts from the front end by selecting the link Create an Account. These self-registered users are assigned the Registered User group by Joomla.

Now let's create a new user. Click the New icon in the toolbar, and you'll see a screen that lets you enter information for the new user. You'll create a user named sanjay. Fill in the information for the new user as shown in Figure 5-2.

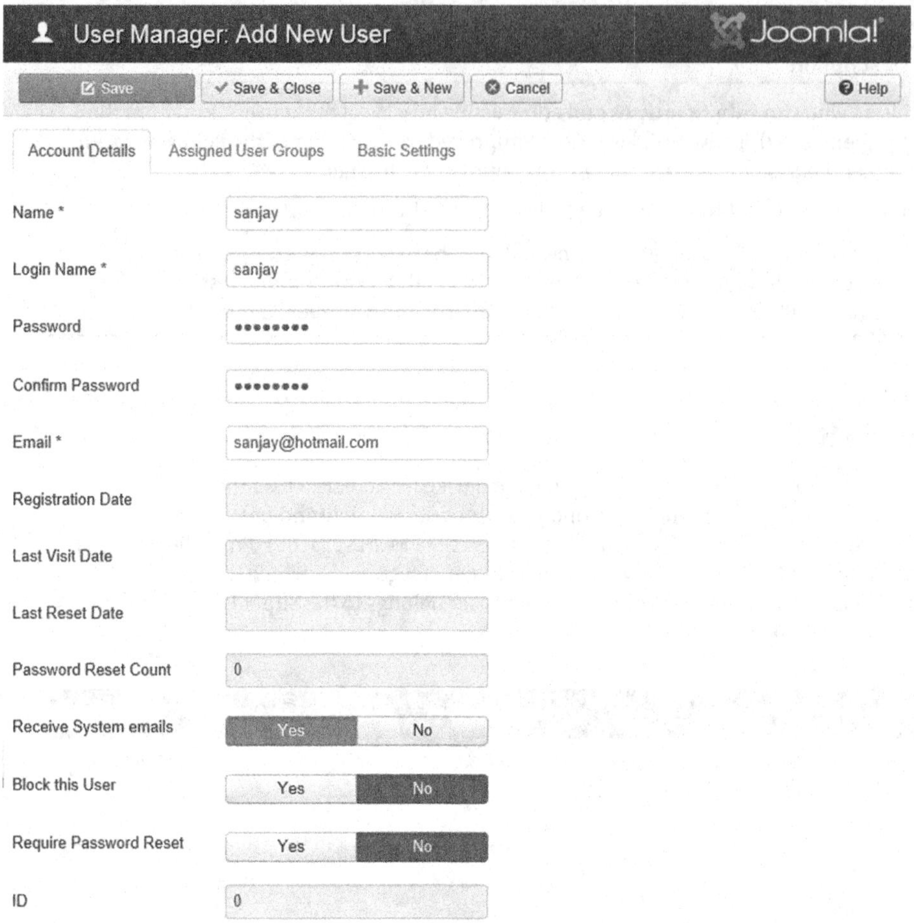

Figure 5-2. *Adding new user sanjay*

The Name field is for specifying the complete name of the user (unlike the Login Name field, it can include spaces). Enter **sanjay** for the name of the user. The Login Name field is for the user ID needed to log in to the web site. As mentioned, it cannot contain spaces and it must be unique for each user. Because you want the new user to log in by entering the name sanjay, type that name here. In the New Password and Confirm Password fields, enter a password for the user (make sure the passwords entered in both boxes are exactly the same).

In the E-mail field, enter the e-mail address of the user: sanjay@hotmail.com. The Registration Date field displays the date on which the user is registered. This date is displayed only when you are editing the information of an existing user. The Last Visit Date field is automatically populated by the date when the user visited the site last time. The date and time when the password was reset last time is automatically populated in the Last Reset Date field. The Password Reset Count field is populated by the count of the times the password has been reset since the last reset date.

Set the Receive System e-mails option to Yes if you want the user to receive system e-mails. This option is visible only to administrators and super administrators. An example of a system e-mail is the e-mail sent by Joomla to new users when they create an account. Set the Block this User option to No when you want the user to be able to log in to your web site. If you want to disable a user from logging in, set this option to Yes. Only members of the Administrator and Super Administrator groups can set this option.

Set the Require Password Reset field to Yes if you want to enable the user to reset the password assigned by the admin. When the user will be logged in for the first time, the Edit Your Profile page will open up with a notice at the top: You Are Required to Reset Your Password Before Proceeding (see Figure 5-3). The user is required to enter the new password and then click the Submit button to assign the new password. The ID field displays the system–generated ID number.

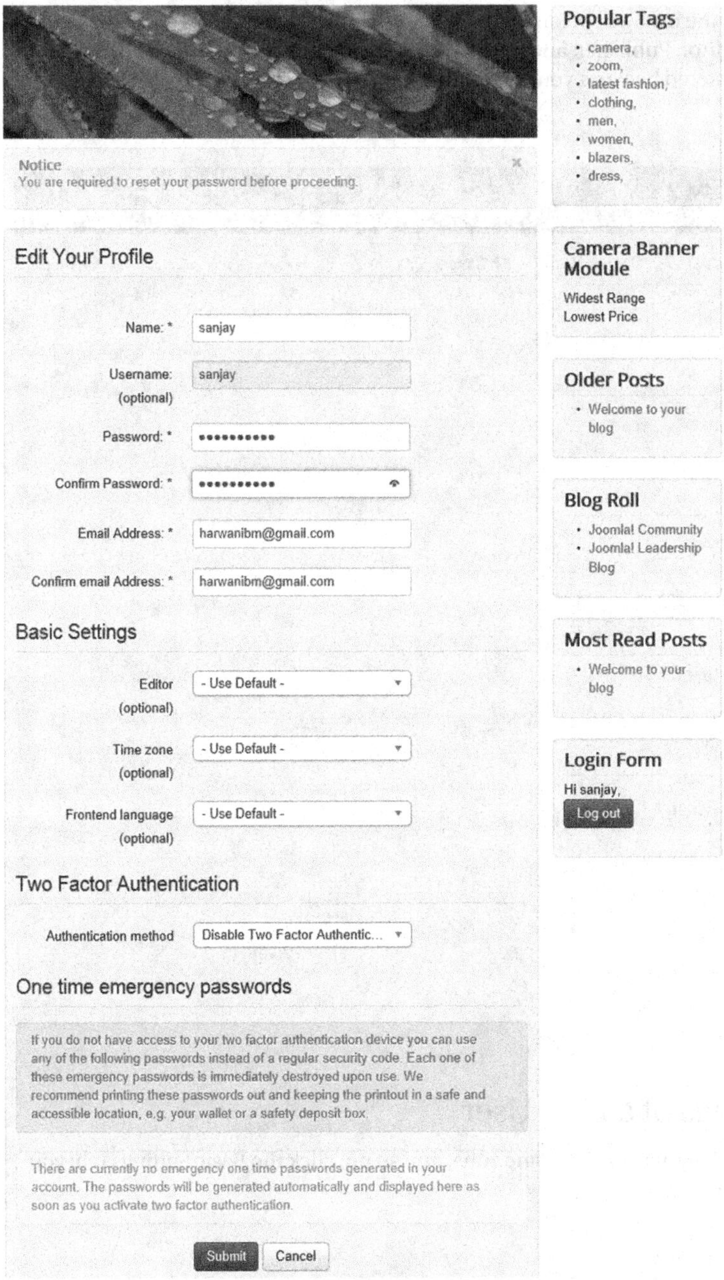

Popular Tags
- camera,
- zoom,
- latest fashion,
- clothing,
- men,
- women,
- blazers,
- dress,

Notice ✕
You are required to reset your password before proceeding.

Edit Your Profile

Camera Banner Module

Widest Range
Lowest Price

Name: *	sanjay
Username: (optional)	sanjay
Password: *	••••••••••
Confirm Password: *	••••••••••
Email Address: *	harwanibm@gmail.com
Confirm email Address: *	harwanibm@gmail.com

Older Posts
- Welcome to your blog

Blog Roll
- Joomla! Community
- Joomla! Leadership Blog

Basic Settings

Most Read Posts
- Welcome to your blog

Editor (optional)	- Use Default -
Time zone (optional)	- Use Default -
Frontend language (optional)	- Use Default -

Login Form

Hi sanjay,
Log out

Two Factor Authentication

Authentication method	Disable Two Factor Authentic...

One time emergency passwords

If you do not have access to your two factor authentication device you can use any of the following passwords instead of a regular security code. Each one of these emergency passwords is immediately destroyed upon use. We recommend printing these passwords out and keeping the printout in a safe and accessible location, e.g. your wallet or a safety deposit box.

There are currently no emergency one time passwords generated in your account. The passwords will be generated automatically and displayed here as soon as you activate two factor authentication.

Submit   Cancel

Figure 5-3. *Profile of user opened in edit mode*

■ **Note** If the Login Module is not visible in the front end of the site, log in to the Administrator backend, open the Module Manager, search for the Login Form module in the list, and enable it.

On clicking the Assigned User Groups tab, you will see the list of available group options, as shown in Figure 5-4. Select the group to which the user will belong. The available choices are Public, Guest, Manager, Administrator, Registered, Author, Editor, Publisher, and Super Users. The default user group is Registered. Let the user group for sanjay be Registered because you want him to be able only to view the web site, not edit it or add anything to it.

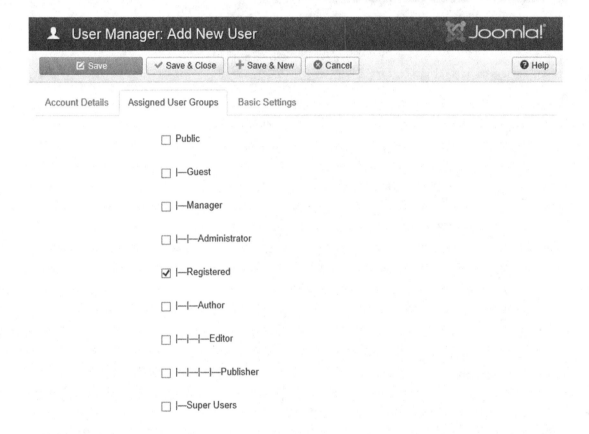

Figure 5-4. *Different user groups*

Configuring Basic Settings of a New User

To implement other settings, such as language, editor, time zone, and so on, click the Basic Settings tab; you will see the fields shown in Figure 5-5.

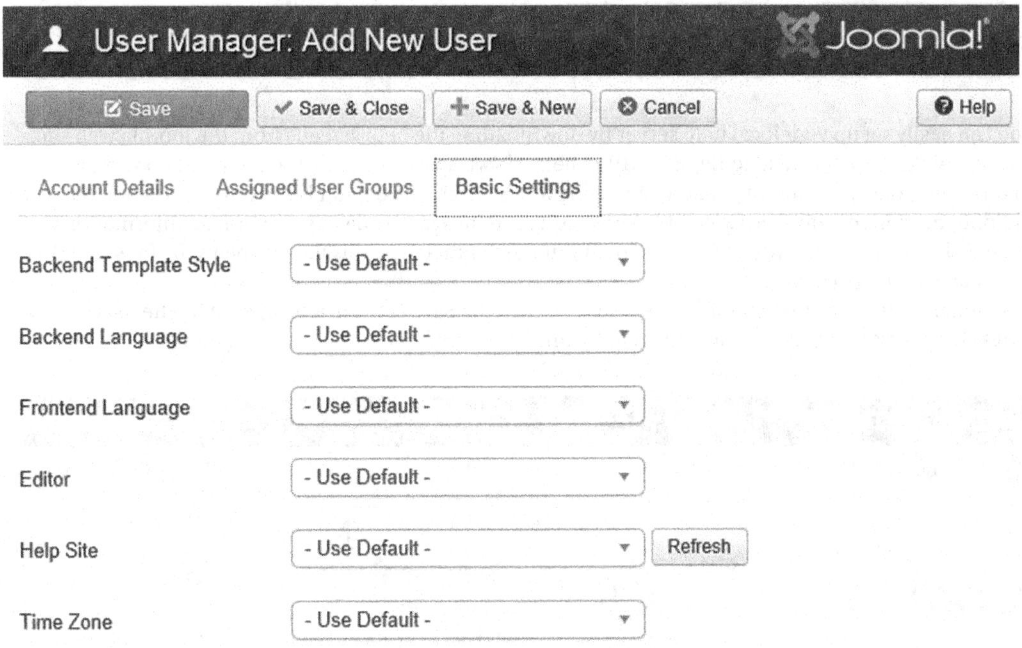

Figure 5-5. *Configuring basic settings of new user sanjay*

From the Backend Template Style combo box, select the desired template. The impact of using the template does not appear on the front side of the site, just on the backend that is used to administer the site. Joomla allows you to administer the web site in one language and access the web site in another language. From the Backend Language field, select the language to be used at the back end (i.e., for administering the web site). For this exercise, let the Backend Language be Use Default (i.e., the language specified in the Global Configuration Manager). Remember that you can see the language options in this combo box only when the Language packs are installed through Language Manager. The Frontend Language field allows you to specify the language to be used while accessing the Joomla web site. Select the same language that you chose for the back end. Again, the default is the language set in the Language Manager. With the new Joomla Language Tool (available since Joomla 3.x), you can install new languages without having to find and manually download them from other sites on the web. In Chapter 10, you will learn how.

■ **Note** If you want to use some other language than the default, you need to install languages of your choice. The procedure to install and use languages of your choice is taught in Chapter 10

In the Editor field, select the front-end and back-end editors for the user. Joomla includes two editors: TinyMCE and CodeMirror. TinyMCE is the default editor; it allows you to edit rich text. It also supports various styles for formatting the text, and enables the content to be displayed on the front end, just as it does in the editor.

The Help Site field is for specifying the location of the help server, which is meant to display the help screens when a user clicks the Help icon on the toolbar. These help screens are displayed by default from a remote server: http:// help.joomla.org. However, you can also set the help server to display help screens from a local server. The local Joomla help server displays help screens that are similar to the remote server, but with the advantage that you can customize them, add extra information to them, and even translate them into the language of your choice.

■ **Note** The local help server must be periodically updated to reflect the latest changes.

You can easily set up your local help server by downloading the help screens from the Joomla web site. Set the value of the Help Site field to English (GB)—`help.joomla.org` to access the remote help server.

In the Time Zone field, you can set the time zone for the user. The default is the time zone set in the Global Configuration section. The Contact Information section is for displaying the contact information if the user is linked to a contact (which you'll learn about next); otherwise, this field displays the message No Contact Details Linked to this User.

After entering the information for the user sanjay, click the Save & Close icon to save it. The user sanjay will appear in the User Manager list, as shown in Figure 5-6.

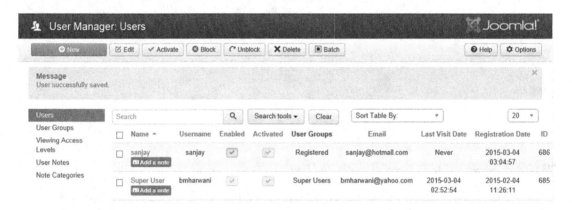

Figure 5-6. *User sanjay created*

Understanding User Manager Columns

The User Manager displays user information, including the complete name and the username used to log in to the web site. The check box in the first column can be used to select user(s) to apply actions using the tools shown in the toolbar above. The Name field shows the full name of the user. On clicking the name, the user's information is displayed in edit mode. As discussed earlier, the Username column displays the name that is used to login to the site. The Enabled column indicates whether the user is enabled or in disabled mode. A green check mark in this column indicates that the user is enabled, whereas a red X indicates that the user is disabled. The Activated column indicates whether the user has activated the account after registration. A green check mark in this column confirms that the user's account is activated.

You can click either of the check boxes to toggle between the two states. When a user registers at your web site, Joomla sends him a system e-mail carrying an activation link that has to be selected by the user in order to activate his account. But a disabled user cannot activate his account even by clicking at the activation link sent to him by e-mail. If the administrator or super administrator blocks a user, that user is disabled. The User Manager also displays the group to which user belongs in the User Groups column. Additionally, the users' e-mail addresses, the date that each was last logged into the web site and the registration dates are also displayed through the Email, Last Visit Date, and Registration Date columns, respectively. The last column of the User Manager table displays the ID number of the user, which is a unique number automatically assigned by Joomla to each user (used for internal maintenance tasks).

Let's Login

To verify that your user sanjay has been created, refresh your Joomla web site. A login form appears on the web site (its location will depend on the template you've chosen). In the login form, enter the username and password for sanjay, as shown in Figure 5-7.

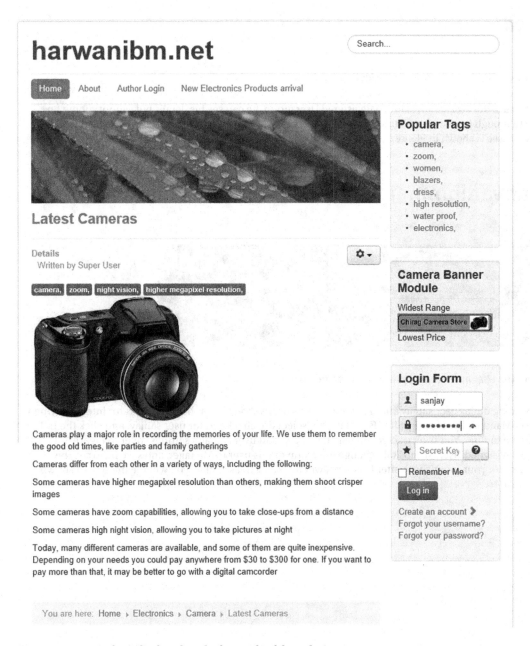

Figure 5-7. *Login form displayed on the front side of the web site*

If the username and password are correct, the login form will change to display a welcome message, as shown in Figure 5-8.

Figure 5-8. *Welcome message on the login form*

Because the user sanjay is in the Registered User group, he can see his details but cannot submit an article (although he can view all the articles that are meant for registered users). The menu that the user sanjay will see is shown in Figure 5-9.

Figure 5-9. *User menu that appears on successful login*

Now log out as user sanjay and try changing this user's group from the Administrator interface. Open the User Manager by selecting Site User Manager, select the check box for user sanjay, and click the Edit icon in the toolbar. You'll get a screen in which you can edit user sanjay's settings (refer to Figure 5-2). Click the Assigned User Groups tab, change the group of this user to Manager, and save it. To see the effect, refresh your Joomla web site. This time, when you log in as sanjay, you will see the screen shown in Figure 5-10.

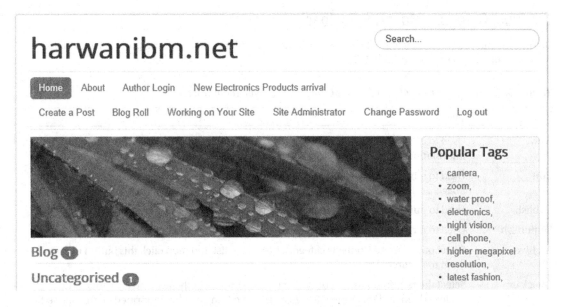

Figure 5-10. Options in the user menu when the user group is changed to Manager

Notice that as a member of the Manager group, sanjay can now submit articles and web links.

Now that you've seen the impact of groups on a user, restore sanjay's user group to Registered because you'll be using it later when dealing with contacts.

Creating a Contacts Category

Next, you need to link your new user, sanjay, to a contact. However, before creating a contact, you need to specify the category (or categories) for the contact. Let's begin by creating a Contacts category, which simply categorizes different contacts. For example, you can create a category by the name of Suppliers so that all the contacts (units within the organization or user) that deal with suppliers are placed in that category. Similarly, a category might be named Technical to group the contacts dealing with technical problems.

First, open the Contacts Category Manager. Open the Administrator interface and select the Components ➤ Contacts ➤ Categories option. You'll see a screen like the one shown in Figure 5-11. Notice that the Contacts Category Manager list already contains a category with the name Uncategorized, which Joomla provides by default.

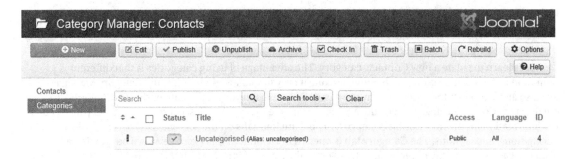

Figure 5-11. Contacts Category Manager

157

Contacts Category Manager Toolbar

Before creating your own Contacts category, you should first understand the purpose of the icons in the toolbar, which are described in Table 5-2.

Table 5-2. *Brief Explanation of the Contacts Category Manager Toolbar Icons*

Icon	Description
New	Used to create a new Contacts category. This icon provides a blank form for entering information about the new Contacts category.
Edit	Used to edit the information for the Contacts category (such as its title, access level, image, and description).
Publish	Used to publish (make visible on the web site) the selected Contacts category.
Unpublish	Used to make the selected Contacts category temporarily invisible from the web site.
Archive	Select one or more Contacts categories from the list and then click this button to move them to the archive.
Check in	Select the required number of Contacts categories from the list, and click this button to close them and mark them as Check In. No editing can be performed on the opened Contacts category. In an opened state, a Contacts category is blocked from use by other administrators. To make it editable, a Contacts category needs to be closed and marked as Check In.
Trash	Used to permanently delete the selected Contacts category. The user is asked for confirmation before it will be deleted.
Batch	Used to apply batch processing on a set of selected Contacts categories. To copy or move certain selected Contacts categories or to apply actions such as assigning tags, setting language, setting access level, and so on for a set of Contacts categories, select them from the list and click the Batch button.
Rebuild	Rebuilds the Contacts category table. Usually used when several operations are performed on Contacts categories, and you want to see the outcome of those operations in the Contacts category list.
Options	Clicking this icon will open the Contact Manager Options that can be used to configure the contacts. You can use it to determine whether you want to hide or show the username, e-mail address, city, state, postal code, and so on; save the contacts history or not; show or hide user articles, profile, links, and so on.(Actually, the Global Configuration window opens up, which is explained in detail in Chapter 10).
Help	Used to open the Joomla help web site. The browser window will navigate to the online help files related to the active topic.

Let's learn to create a new Contacts category. The advantage of using categories is that different items and articles can be grouped together, making it easy to manage them. Also, the Category Manager will also allow you to administer the way the categories are displayed, and create or delete categories. To create a new Contacts category, click the New icon from the toolbar. You'll see a screen that lets you specify the information for the new Contacts category. There are four tabs on the screen: Category, Publishing, Permissions, and Options. The Category tab is opened by default. In this exercise, you'll be creating a Contacts category with the name Suppliers, so enter the information shown in Figure 5-12.

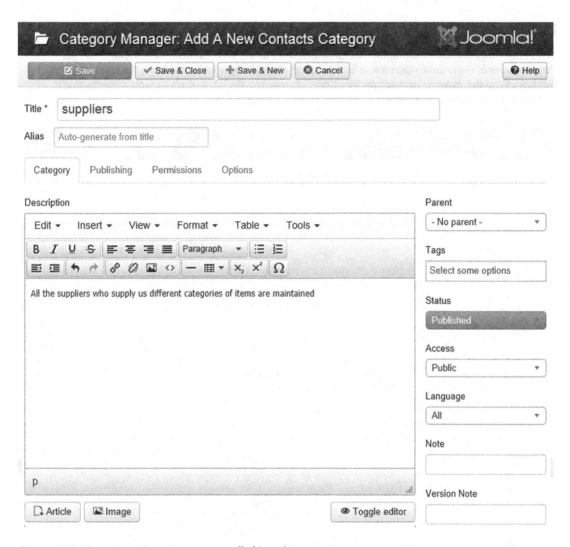

Figure 5-12. *Creating a Contactscategory called Suppliers*

In the Title field, enter the name of the category as it should appear in the database. You're creating a category named Suppliers, so enter the same name here. In the Alias field, you can enter the same text as for the title. In the Description field, you can enter a brief description of the Contacts category in this box.

Because this Contacts category is an independent category, not the child of any existing category, keep the Parent field at its default value: No Parent. You can select some tags to represent this Contacts category. When a user selects any tag that matches any of the Contacts categories, it will show up on the front side of the site.

Leave the Status field to its default value, Published, to publish the Contacts category. Set the value of Access Level to Public because you want every visitor to your web site to be able to access this Contacts category. From the Language combo box, select the language of the Contacts category. If you are creating a multilingual site and want to show certain contacts in any specific language, choose it from this combo box. Meanwhile, leave the default value at All for this field. The Note (optional) field is for the administrator to write a reminder note for this Contacts category. Leave it blank for now. The Version Note (optional) field is used to identify the version of this Contacts category. Again, leave this field blank.

Defining Publishing Info of a Contacts Category

The Publishing tab shows information such as the date on which this Contacts category was created, the username of the creator, when was it last modified, the username of the modifier, the count of the hits (views) on this category, the unique identification number, the ID for this Contacts category that is automatically generated by Joomla, and so on, as shown in Figure 5-13.

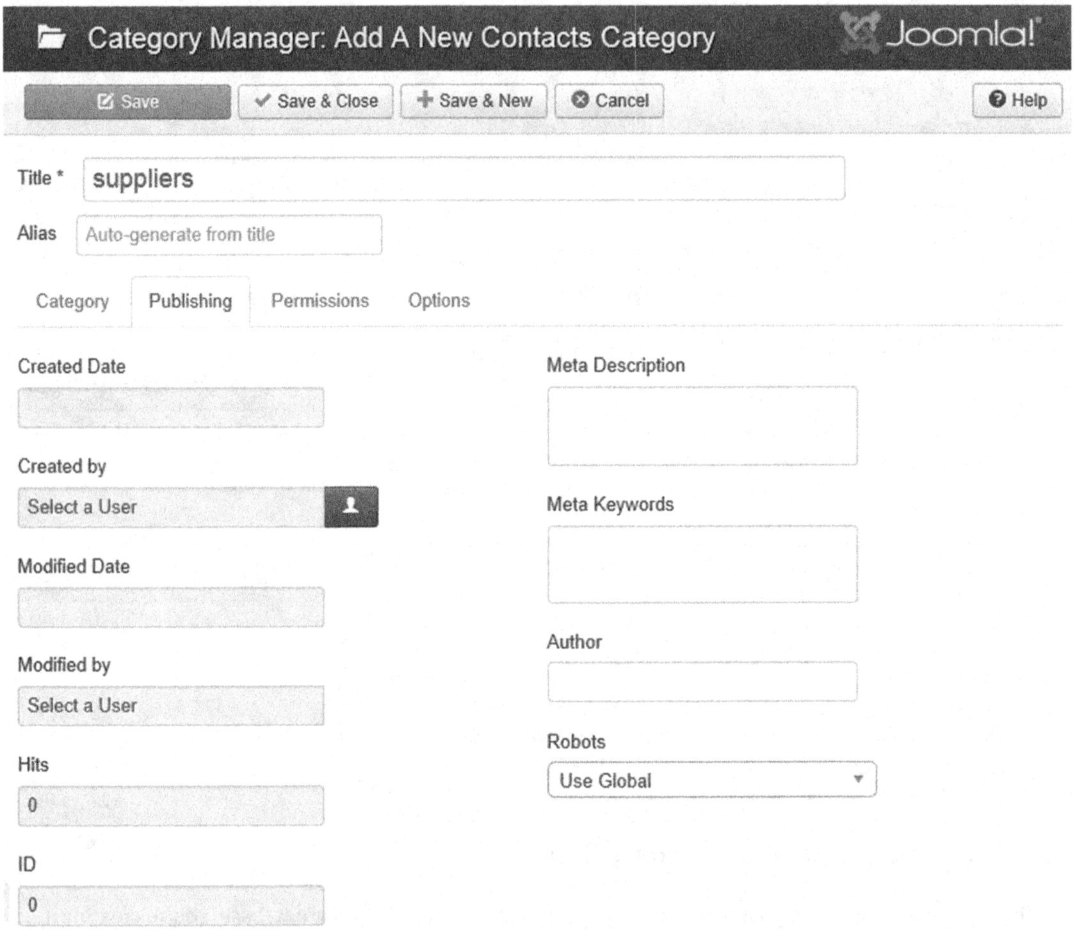

Figure 5-13. *Displaying publishing information of the new Contactscategory:Suppliers*

The screen also allows you to enter some meta information related to the Contacts category. In the Meta Description (optional) field, enter a short description of this Contacts category that usually appears in the results of search engines. In the Meta Keywords (optional) box, enter some keywords separated by commas that will help display this Contacts category when related content article, contacts, and so on are being viewed by the user. You can enter the name of the author for this Contacts category in the Author field. Choose the desired Robots from the combo box. Recall that robots help make your site visible to search engines.

Setting Permissions for a Contacts Category

The Permissions tab shows the combo boxes that enable you to modify permissions related to the current Contacts category. Usually, permissions are inherited from the Global Configuration settings, but you can override them through the Permissions tab (see Figure 5-14). Using the available combo boxes, you can determine the following:

- Whether to allow or deny Create permissions for users in the Public group

- Whether to allow or deny Delete permissions for users in the Public group

- Whether to allow or deny Edit permissions for users in the Public group

- Whether to allow or deny Edit State—Published state permissions for users in the Public group

- Whether to allow or deny Edit Own (the content created by the user) permissions for users in the Public group

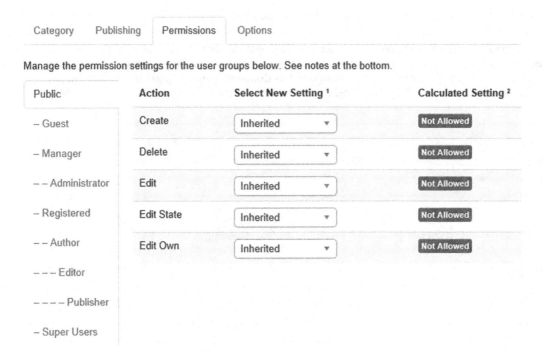

Figure 5-14. Setting permissions for the new Suppliers Contactscategory

Defining an Image for the Contacts Category

The Options tab helps to assign an image to the Contacts category. On clicking this tab, you get the screen shown in Figure 5-15. The Alternative Layout combo box can be used to override the current layout.

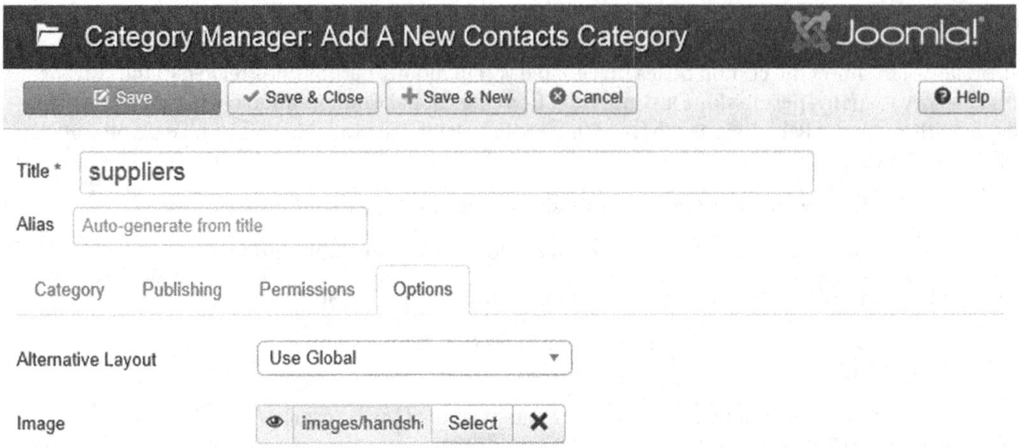

Figure 5-15. *Assigning an image to the Suppliers Contactscategory*

After the Select button is clicked, Media Manager will open, as shown in Figure 5-16. The Media Manager will show the images that are already uploaded in it. You can upload new images if required. I'm usinghandshake.jpg in this example to represent this Contacts category. Select handshake images followed by clicking the Insert button to represent the current Contacts category.

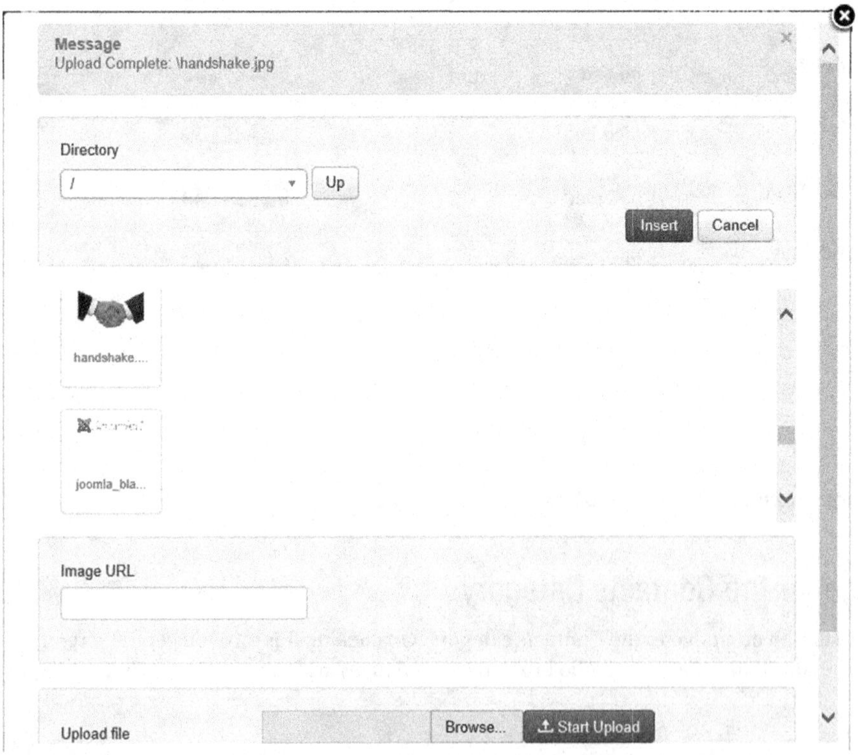

Figure 5-16. *Media Manager showing uploaded images*

After entering the information for the Suppliers Contacts category, click the Save & Close icon from the toolbar to save it. The Suppliers Contacts category will appear in the Contacts Category Manager list, as shown in Figure 5-17.

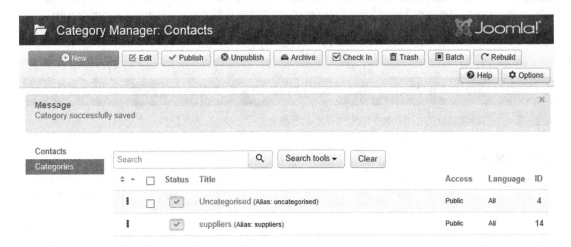

Figure 5-17. *Contacts Category Manager with Suppliers added*

Introduction to Contacts Category Manager Columns

Before proceeding to create contacts, take a look at Table 5-3, which describes the functions of the columns in the Contacts Category Manager.

Table 5-3. *Contacts Category Manager Columns*

Column	Description
Status	Indicates the status of the Contacts category: whether the Contacts category is in a published, unpublished, archived, or trashed state. The check mark means that the Contacts category is in the published state and will be visible on the web site. If you click the check mark, it will toggle the state; that is, the Contacts category will change to the unpublished state. A red X signifies that the Contacts category is in the unpublished state; clicking this sign will again toggle the state.
Title	Displays the name of the Contacts category. Clicking the name will open the Contacts category in edit mode.
Access Level	Displays the level of users who can access this Contacts category. The levels are Public, Registered, and Special. You can click the text link to change the access level. The three levels scroll in a continuous loop when clicked.
Language	Displays the language assigned to the Contacts category, if any.
ID	Displays the category identification number automatically assigned by Joomla when the Contacts category was first created.

Creating Contacts

In general, Joomla's default installation comes with sample contact information to populate the Contact Manager. You will want to create a new contact for your suppliers' Contacts category. To do this, you have to open the Contact Manager. Either select the Contacts link from the Category Manager screen or select Components ➤ Contacts ➤ Contacts from the menu bar. The Contact Manager will open, as shown in Figure 5-18. Initially there is no contact in the list.

Figure 5-18. *Contact Manager*

Introduction to the Contact Manager Toolbar

Let's take a look at Table 5-4, which briefly explains the toolbar icons in the Contact Manager.

You'll be creating two contacts:

- John David: The storekeeper in your organization
- Purchases: The department that you'll link to the sanjay user that you just created

Table 5-4. *Contact ManagerToolbar Icons*

Icon	Description
New	Used to create a new contact. This icon provides a blank form for entering information about the new contact.
Edit	Used to edit the information for the contact, such as the contact's category, linked users, e-mail address, and position.
Publish	Makes the selected contact(s) visible on the web site.
Unpublish	Makes the selected contact(s) not visible on the web site.
Archive	Moves the selected contacts to the archive.
Check in	Closes the selected contacts and marks them as Check In to make them editable by other administrators.
Trash	Used to permanently delete a contact.
Batch	Used to apply batch processing on a set of selected contacts. Batch processing includes tasks such as copying or moving certain selected contacts, assigning tags, setting language, access level, and so on for a set of contacts.
Options	Clicking this icon opens the Contact Manager Options that can be used to configure the contacts. (It opens the Global Configuration settings that are explained in detail in Chapter 10.)
Help	Opens up the Joomla help web site.

The idea behind creating two contacts is that you want the queries made to John David to be e-mailed to him directly, but the queries to Purchases to be e-mailed to the user linked to it—that is, to the e-mail address for sanjay.

Creating the First Contact

Click the New icon to create a new contact with the name John David. You'll be assigning him to the Suppliers category. He isn't linked to any user and he has an e-mail address to which all queries made via the contact form will be sent. The screen that opens up has five tabs: New Contact, Miscellaneous Information, Publishing, Display, and Form. The New Contact tab is opened by default. Enter the information for the contact John David as shown in Figure 5-19.

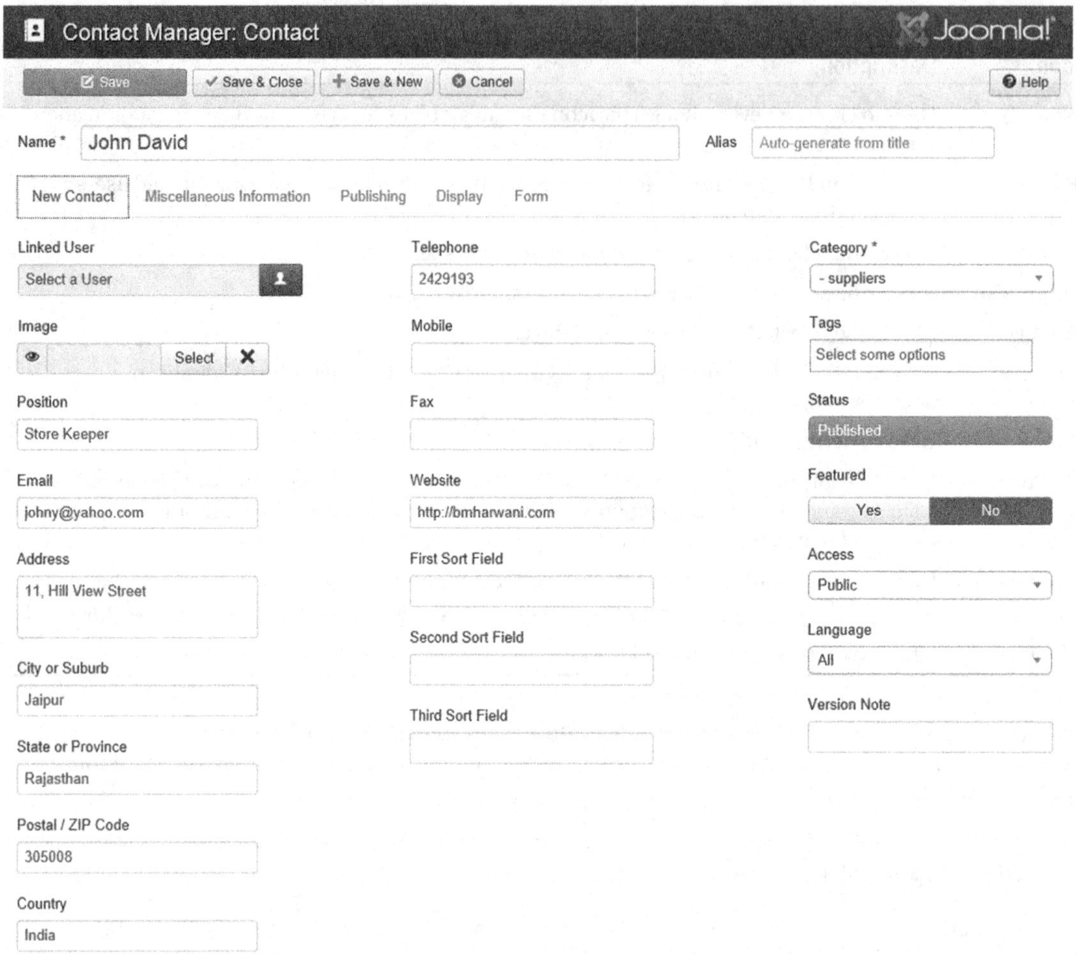

Figure 5-19. *Creating a new contact called John David*

Table 5-5 gives a brief description of each of the fields and the information you need to enter in them.

Table 5-5. *Contact Manager Fields*

Fields	Description
Name	Enter **John David** for the name of the contact.
Alias	This field designates the secondary name for the contact used in the URL when SEF is activated. Although it can be left blank, it must be in lowercase and without spaces (use hyphens instead) if provided.
Linked User	From the drop-down list, select the registered user with whom you want the contact person to be associated. Because John David is the responsible person for his department, leave this field at its default value.
Image	Select an image to represent the contact.
Position	Enter the position that the contact person holds within the web site or organization.
Email	Enter the e-mail address of the contact.
Address	Enter the street address of the contact.
City or Suburb	Enter the name of the town or suburb of the contact.
State or Province	Enter the state or province name of the contact.
Postal/ZIP Code	Enter the postal or ZIP code of the contact.
Country	Enter the country of the contact.
Telephone	Enter the telephone number of the contact.
Mobile	Enter the cell number of the contact
Fax	Enter the fax number of the contact.
Web site	Enter the URL that provides information about the contact. Visitors who click the contact name will be taken to this URL. (You can leave this field blank if you don't know the contact's web site.)
First Sort Field	Used to sort the contacts. Enter the part of the name to be used as the first sort field.
Second Sort Field	Enter the part of the name to be used as the second sort field.
Third Sort Field	Enter the part of the name to be used as the third sort field.
Category	Select the category with which this contact is to be associated. In this case, select the Contacts category that you created: Suppliers.
Tags	Select certain tags if you want the contact to appear when the user selects any of the tags from the front side of the site.
Status	Select the Published status from the combo box to make the contact visible on the web site.
Featured	Select the Yes option if you want this category to be displayed as a featured content.
Access	Select the level of users who can access this contact. The available options are Public, Registered, and Special. In this case, select Public to make the contact publicly accessible.
Language	Select the language of the new contact. If you are creating a multilingual site and want to show certain contacts in any specific language, choose it from this combo box. Meanwhile, leave the default value All for this field.
Version Note	The optional field that can be used to identify the version of this contact. Again, leave this field blank.

Entering Additional Info for the Contact

When you click the Miscellaneous Information tab, you get a screen similar to Figure 5-20. In the provided box, you can enter any miscellaneous or additional information about the new contact.

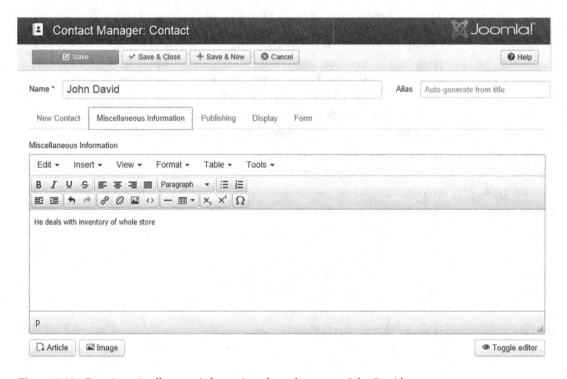

Figure 5-20. *Entering miscellaneous information about the contact John David*

Defining Publishing and Meta Info for the Contact

The Publishing tab shows the publishing details of the new contact (see Figure 5-21). The screen shows information such as the date on which the contact was created, username of the creator, when was it last modified, username of the modifier, number of times the contact has been revised, count of the hits (views) on the contact, unique identification number, contact ID, and so on.

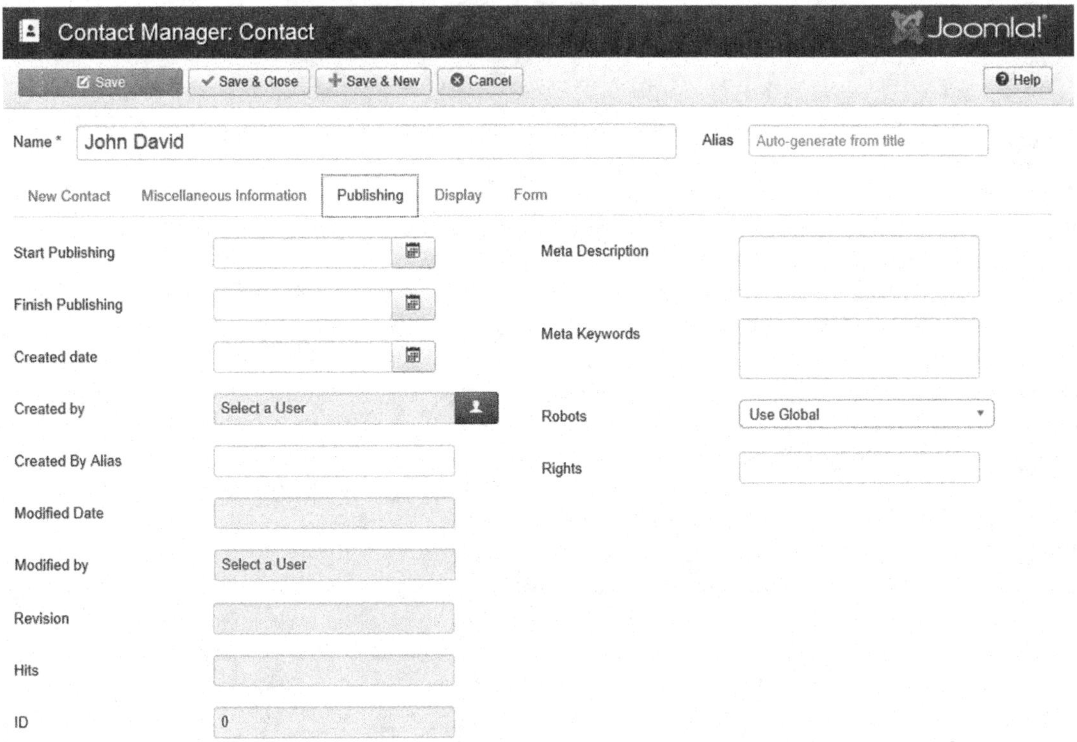

Figure 5-21. *Displaying publishing information of new contact John David*

The screen also allows you to enter some meta information for the contact used by search engines to locate your site. In the Meta Description (optional) field, enter a short description of this contact. In the Meta Keywords (optional) box, enter some keywords (separated by commas) that will help display this contact when related content, articles, and so on are viewed by the user. Choose the desired Robots from the combo box to help make your site visible to the search engines. In the Rights field, you can write the rights that users need to use this contact.

Defining What to Display or Hide

As its name suggests, the Display tab (see Figure 5-22) prompts whether to display or hide certain specific information from the contact's content. Table 5-6 briefly describes the fields shown on the page.

| New Contact | Miscellaneous Information | Publishing | Display | Form |

Show Category	Use Global ▼
Show Contact List	Use Global ▼
Display format	Use Global ▼
Show Tags	Use Global ▼
Name	Use Global ▼
Contact's Position	Use Global ▼
Email	Use Global ▼
Street Address	Use Global ▼
City or Suburb	Use Global ▼
State or County	Use Global ▼
Postal Code	Use Global ▼
Country	Use Global ▼
Telephone	Use Global ▼
Mobile phone	Use Global ▼
Fax	Use Global ▼
Webpage	Use Global ▼
Misc. Information	Use Global ▼
Image	Use Global ▼
vCard	Use Global ▼
Show User Articles	Use Global ▼
Show Profile	Use Global ▼
Show Links	Use Global ▼
Link A Label	
Link A URL	
Link B Label	
Link B URL	
Link C Label	
Link C URL	
Link D Label	
Link D URL	
Link E Label	
Link E URL	
Alternative Layout	Use Global ▼

Figure 5-22. Configuring display settings of new contact John David

Table 5-6. *Contact Manager Display Tab Fields*

Field	Description
Show Category	Determines whether to show or hide the contact's category.
Show Contact List	Determines whether to show or hide the contact list. From the list, users can select the contact whose information is wanted.
Display Format	Used to select the style desired to format the contact form.
Show Tags	Determines whether to show or hide any tags for this contact.
Name	Determines whether to show or hide the contact's name.
Contact's Position	Determines whether to show or hide the contact's position.
E-mail	Determines whether to show or hide the contact's e-mail address.
Street Address	Determines whether to show or hide the contact's street address.
City or Suburb	Determines whether to show or hide the contact's city or suburb.
State or County	Determines whether to show or hide the contact's state or county.
Postal Code	Determines whether to show or hide the contact's postal code.
Country	Determines whether to show or hide the contact's country.
Telephone	Determines whether to show or hide the contact's telephone number.
Mobile phone	Determines whether to show or hide the contact's cell phone number.
Fax	Determines whether to show or hide the contact's fax number.
Webpage	Determines whether to show or hide the contact's web site URL.
Misc. Information	Determines whether to show or hide any miscellaneous information entered for this contact.
Image	Determines whether to show or hide the contact's image.
vCard	Determines whether to show or hide the vCard link for this contact.
Show User Articles	If this field is set to Show, the articles of the user who is linked with this contact will display.
Show Profile	If this field is set to Show, the profile of the user who is linked with this contact will display.
Show Links	Determines whether to show or hide the links.
Link A Label	Enter the text for an additional link for this contact.
Link A URL	Enter the additional URL for this contact.
Link B Label	Enter the text for an additional link for this contact.
Link B URL	Enter the additional URL for this contact.
Link C Label	Enter the text for an additional link for this contact.
Link C URL	Enter the additional URL for this contact.
Link D Label	Enter the text for an additional link for this contact.
Link D URL	Enter the additional URL for this contact.
Link E Label	Enter the text for an additional link for this contact.
Link E URL	Enter the additional URL for this contact.
Alternative Layout	Choose a different layout from the supplied layouts in the implemented template.

Configuring the Contact Form

The Form tab displays options that enable users to submit the contact form (see Figure 5-23). From the Show Contact Form, choose the Show option to display a contact form to the user. Set the Send Copy to Submitter field to Show if you want the submitted contact form to be e-mailed to the contact as well as to the sender. In the Banned Email field, enter the terms (separated by commas) to stop spamming. If an e-mail address includes any of the specified terms, the form will not be submitted. In the Banned Subject field, enter the terms (separated by semicolons) that will stop the form from submitting if found in the e-mail subject line. Similarly, in the Banned Text field, enter the terms (separated by semicolons) that will stop the form from submitting if found in the e-mail form text. Set the Session check to Yes to know whether the cookies are enabled on the user's machine. Cookies are used for session management, and the user cannot submit the form if cookies are not enabled on his/her machine. Set the Custom Reply field to No if you don't want to send the auto reply to the user. Enter the URL in the Contact Redirect field if you want the user to be redirected to a specific URL on submitting the form.

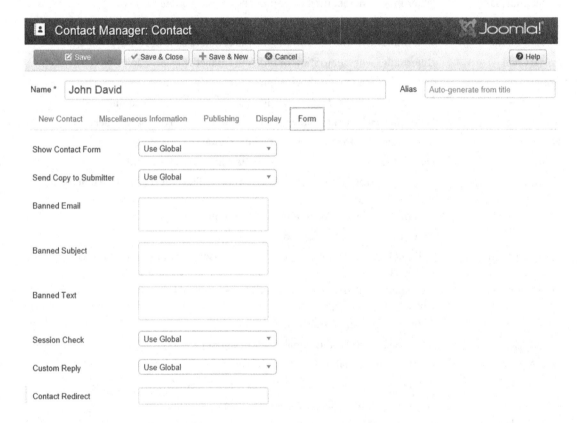

Figure 5-23. *Options displayed in the Form tab*

After entering the information for the contact John David, click the Save & Close icon to save it.

Creating a Second Contact

Now let's create one more contact, Purchases, and link it to the user sanjay. Again, click the New icon on the toolbar of the Contact Manager, and you'll see the form for entering information for a new contact again. Enter the information shown in Figure 5-24.

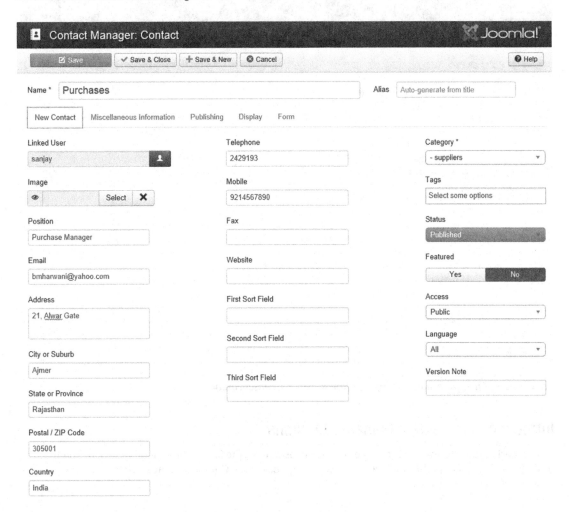

Figure 5-24. *Creating a new contact called Purchases*

Name the new contact **Purchases** and assign it the position Purchase Manager and the category Suppliers. The main things to note regarding this contact are these:

- It is linked to the user sanjay.

- The e-mail address is left blank because it will use the e-mail address of the user sanjay.

Everything else is almost the same as for the contact John David.

Click the Miscellaneous Information tab and enter the additional information of the Purchases contact, as shown in Figure 5-25.

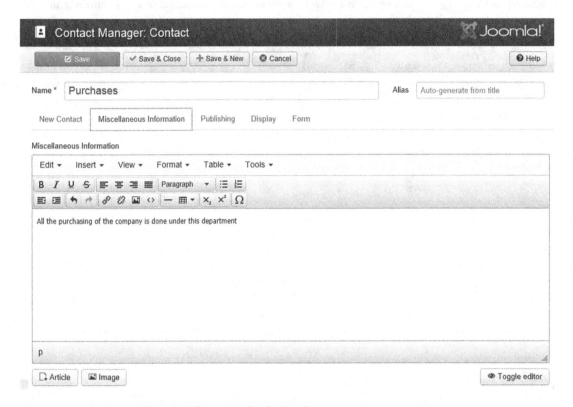

Figure 5-25. *Enter miscellaneous information for the Purchases contact*

Introduction to Contact Manager Columns

After entering the information for the contact Purchases, click the Save & Close icon to save it. You'll find that both contacts, John David and Purchases, appear in the Contact Manager list, as shown in Figure 5-26.

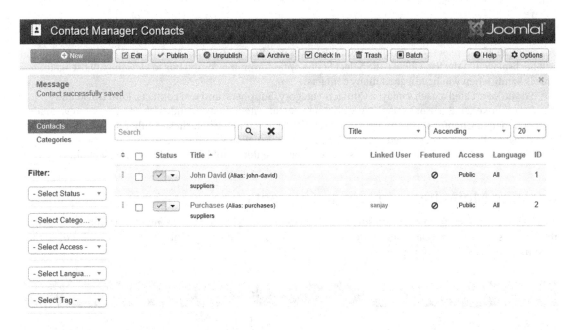

Figure 5-26. *Two contacts added: John David and Purchases*

Table 5-7 will give a brief description of the meaning of the columns in the Contact Manager list.

Table 5-7. *Contact Manager Columns*

Column	Description
Status	Indicates the status of the contact—whether the contact is in a published or unpublished state. The check mark means the contact is in the published state and will be visible on the web site. If you click the check mark, it will toggle the state. A red X signifies that the contact is in the unpublished state.
Title	Shows the name of the new contact. It can be a person, department, or anything else. On clicking a name, the contact will open in edit mode. You can click the Title heading to change the order in which the contacts are displayed.
Linked User	Displays the name of the registered user with whom the contact is linked. A registered user can be linked to more than one contact, but one contact Item cannot be linked directly to more than one registered user.
Featured	Indicates whether the contact is featured. The featured contacts are designated with a black star symbol. You can click the icon in this column to toggle between featured and not featured.
Access	Displays the level of users that can access this contact.
Language	Displays the language assigned to the contact, if any.
ID	Displays the category identification number automatically assigned by Joomla when the contact was first created.

175

The Filter combo boxes are used to display only the desired contacts. You can choose the desired option that is searched for in the contact names, and only the names that match the supplied option are displayed. For example, if you select Unpublished from the Status combo box, only the unpublished contacts (if any) will be displayed in the list. Choose the Select Status option from the combo box to view the full list again. This is handy when you have a great many contacts.

So you've created a user, sanjay; a Contacts category, Suppliers; and two contacts, John David and Purchases (linked to the user sanjay). Now it's time to create menu items to link to the contacts you've made. As mentioned in Chapter 4, a menu item is a text link in a menu that when clicked either invokes the module linked to it or displays the assigned information. The visitor to your web site needs a link to click in order to open the contact forms of the two contacts that you have created. You'll create it in the next section.

Creating Menu Items to Link to Contacts

To access the contacts from your web site, create two menu items in the Main Menu of your web site. Open the Administrator interface and select Menus ➤ Menu Manager from the menu bar. You'll see a list of all the existing menus, as shown in Figure 5-27.

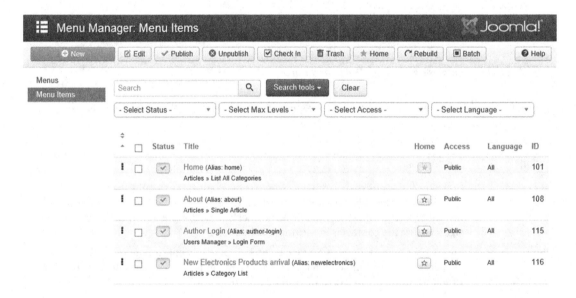

Figure 5-27. *Menu items displayed in the Menu Manager*

Selecting a Menu Item Type

Click the New icon to create a new menu item. You'll see a screen for selecting the menu item type. Recall that you used the Articles node in Chapter 3 for creating menu items to point to the articles. Here, you'll use the Contacts node. The Contacts node will expand (see Figure 5-28) to show you the following menu item types:

- **Featured Contacts**: Displays the featured contacts

- **List All Contact Categories**: Shows a list of contact categories

- **List Contacts in a Category**: Shows the contacts in a specified category

- **Single Contact**: Opens the contact information of the associated contact

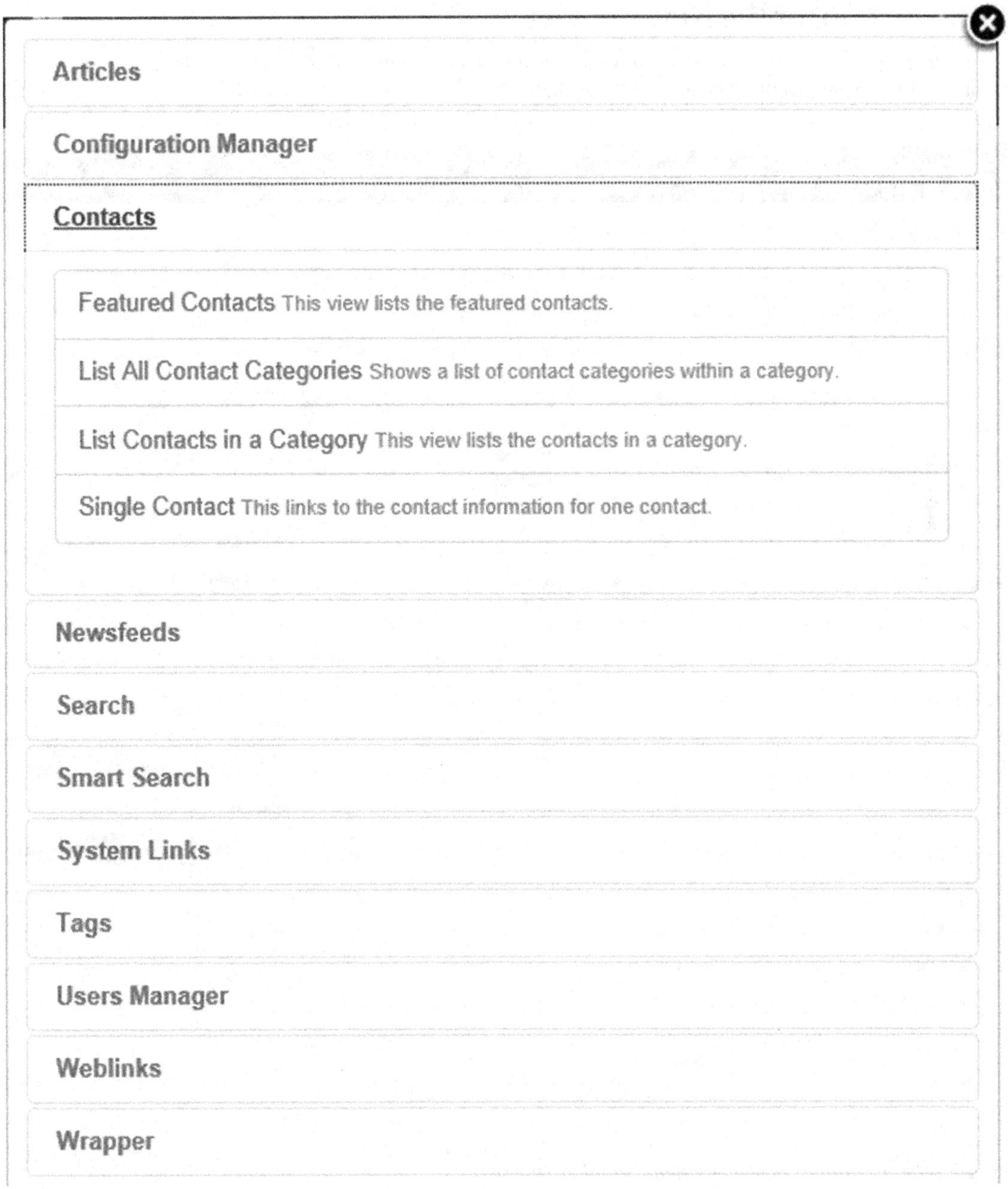

Articles

Configuration Manager

<u>Contacts</u>

Featured Contacts This view lists the featured contacts.

List All Contact Categories Shows a list of contact categories within a category.

List Contacts in a Category This view lists the contacts in a category.

Single Contact This links to the contact information for one contact.

Newsfeeds

Search

Smart Search

System Links

Tags

Users Manager

Weblinks

Wrapper

Figure 5-28. *Different menu item types*

Because you want to open a single contact (when selecting the menu item), select the Single Contact menu item type.

The Single Contact menu item type will activate the contact form directly when the menu item is selected. The List Contacts in a Category menu item type will instead first display the category of the contact; all the contacts in that category will be displayed, and the contact can be selected to send a query.

Entering Info for the New Contact

After selecting the menu item type, you'll see a screen that lets you enter the information for the Single Contact. Enter the information shown in Figure 5-29.

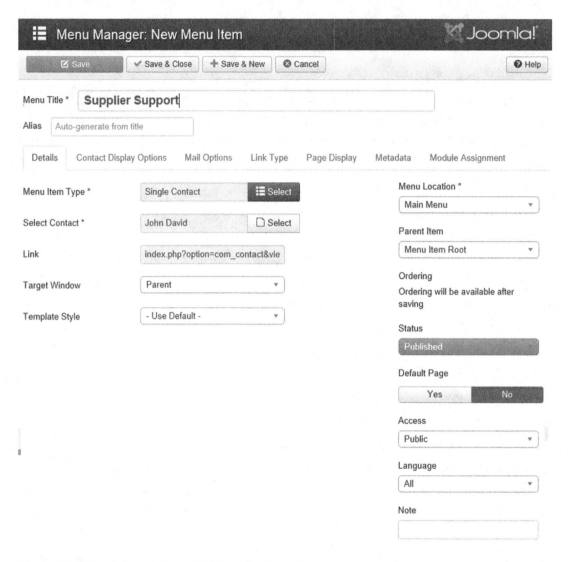

Figure 5-29. *Creating a new menu item: Supplier Support*

The title you want to appear for the menu item is Supplier Support, so enter it in the Menu Title field. The Link field will be automatically filled in, depending on the selected menu item type. The Link field informs Joomla whether to open the contact form directly or display the category of the contact when the menu item is selected. The Menu Location field is used to decide in which menu you want this menu item to appear. Select Main Menu from the drop-down list.

The main thing to note is that the Select Contact field is set to John David—Store Keeper, so that the query sent via the contact form will be e-mailed to this contact.

After entering the information for the menu item Supplier Support, click the Save & Close icon to save it. Similarly, create another menu item with the name Purchase Support, entering the information shown in Figure 5-30. This time, set the Select Contact field to the contact Purchases—Purchase Manager. Because this contact is linked to the user sanjay, a query sent to the contact via the contact form will be sent to the e-mail address of sanjay.

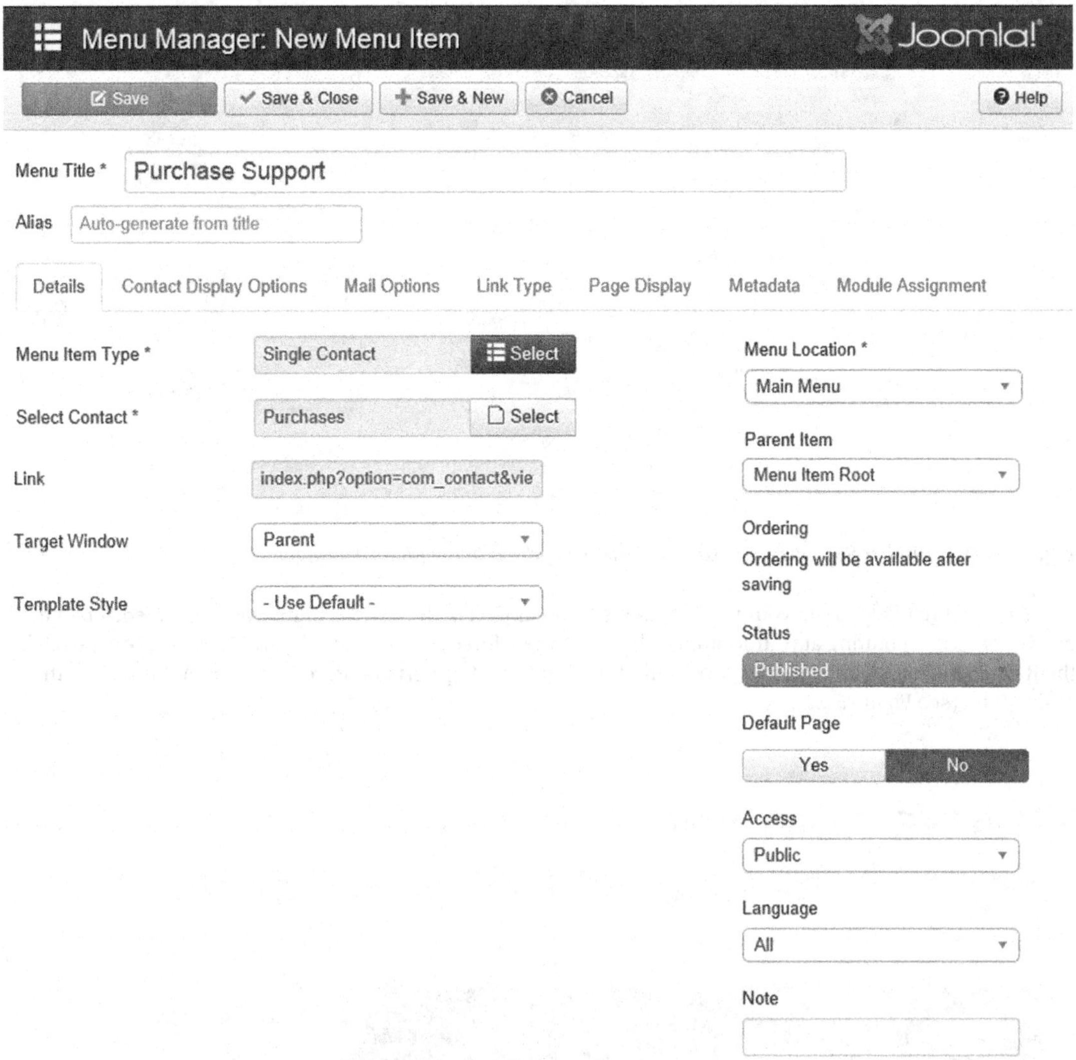

Figure 5-30. *Menu item Purchase Support created*

After entering the information for the menu item Purchase Support, click the Save & Close icon to save it.

You'll find that both Supplier Support and Purchase Support appear in the list of menu items in the Main Menu, as shown in Figure 5-31.

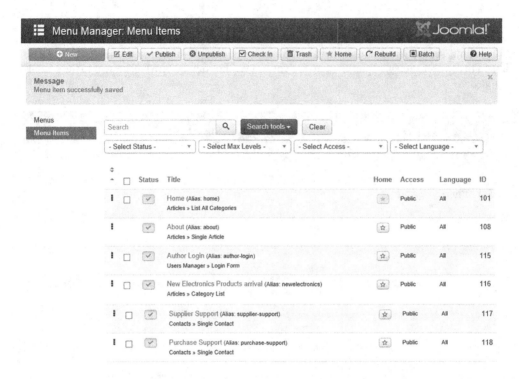

Figure 5-31. *Supplier Support and Purchase Support added to the Menu Manager*

Now you're ready to run your web site and see the impact of the various items you've created. Open the browser window pointing at your Joomla web site (at the address `http://localhost/Joomlasite`) and click the Refresh button. You'll find that two menu items, Supplier Support and Purchase Support, appear in the Main Menu (see Figure 5-32).

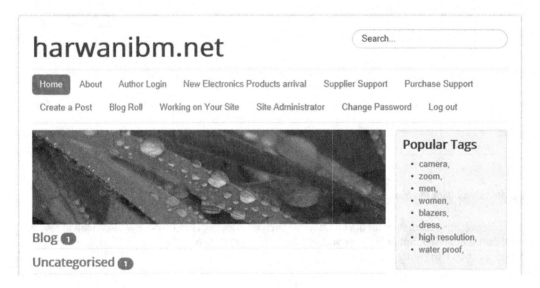

Figure 5-32. *Newly created menu items appear in the main menu*

When you select the Supplier Support menu item, which is connected to the contact John David, his detailed information (address, phone numbers, and so on) will appear at the top of the contact form link, as shown in Figure 5-33.

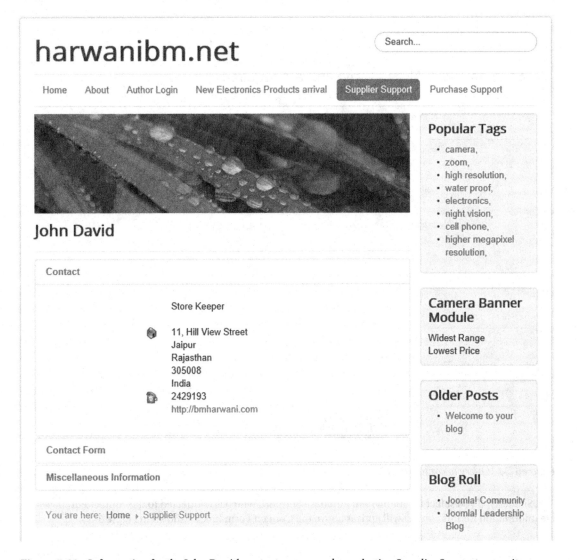

Figure 5-33. Information for the John David contact appears when selecting Supplier Support menu item

On clicking the Contact Form link, the contact form will open, as shown in Figure 5-34, and the query entered in it will be e-mailed to the John David contact. Depending on the installed template, you might get a bit different output. Generally, the output has two parts: information about your site and the form to send an e-mail through the site.

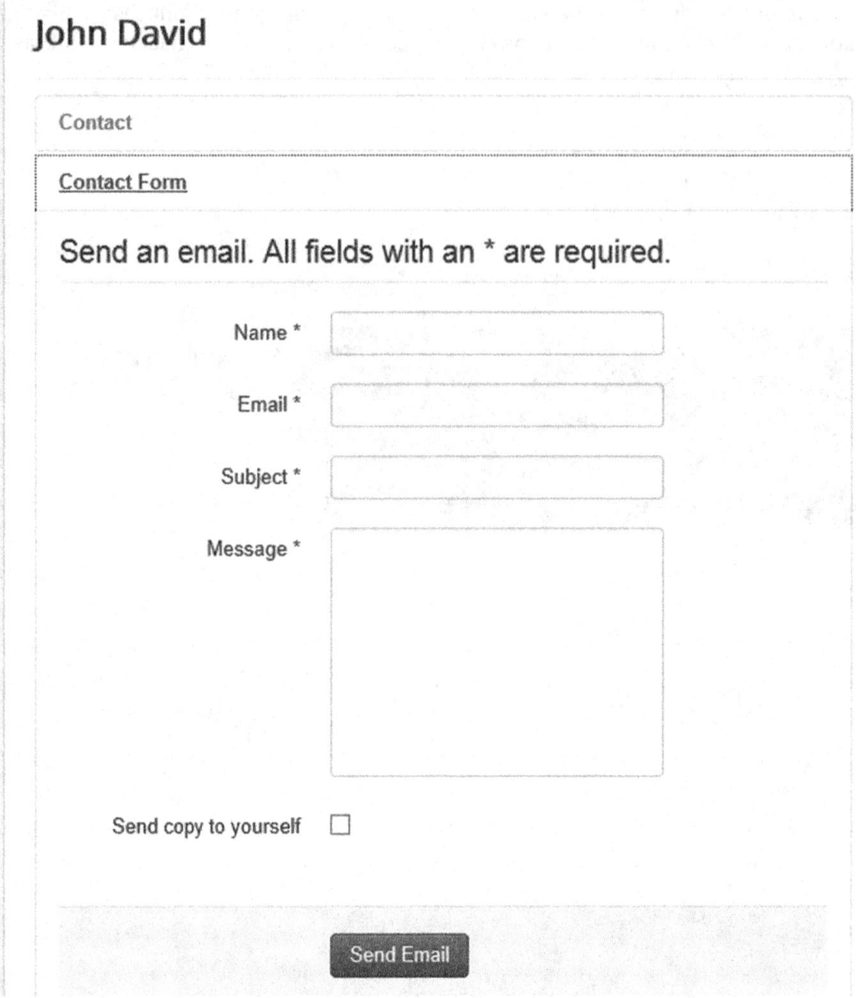

John David

Contact

__Contact Form__

Send an email. All fields with an * are required.

Name * [   ]

Email * [   ]

Subject * [   ]

Message * [   ]

Send copy to yourself ☐

[Send Email]

Figure 5-34. *Query to contact Purchases*

Similarly, if you select the menu item Purchase Support, which is connected to the contact Purchases, the information for this contact will appear above the Contact Form link, as shown in Figure 5-35.

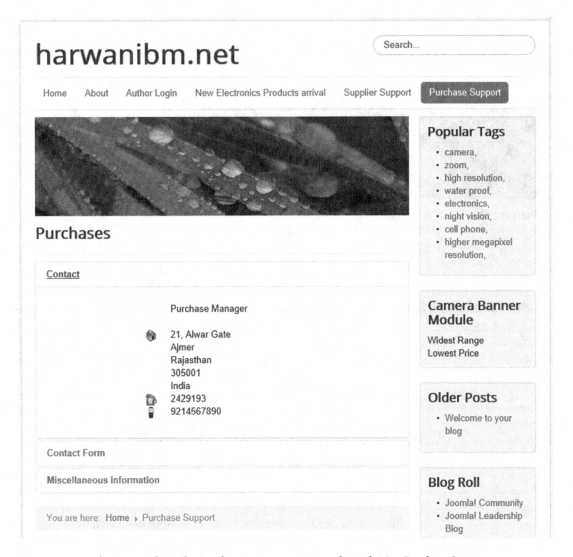

Figure 5-35. *Information about the Purchases contact appears when selecting Purchase Support*

On clicking the Contact Form link, the contact form will open up (see Figure 5-36). In this case, the query entered is sent to the contact Purchases (i.e., the query will be sent to the e-mail address for the user sanjay because the contact Purchases is linked to that user).

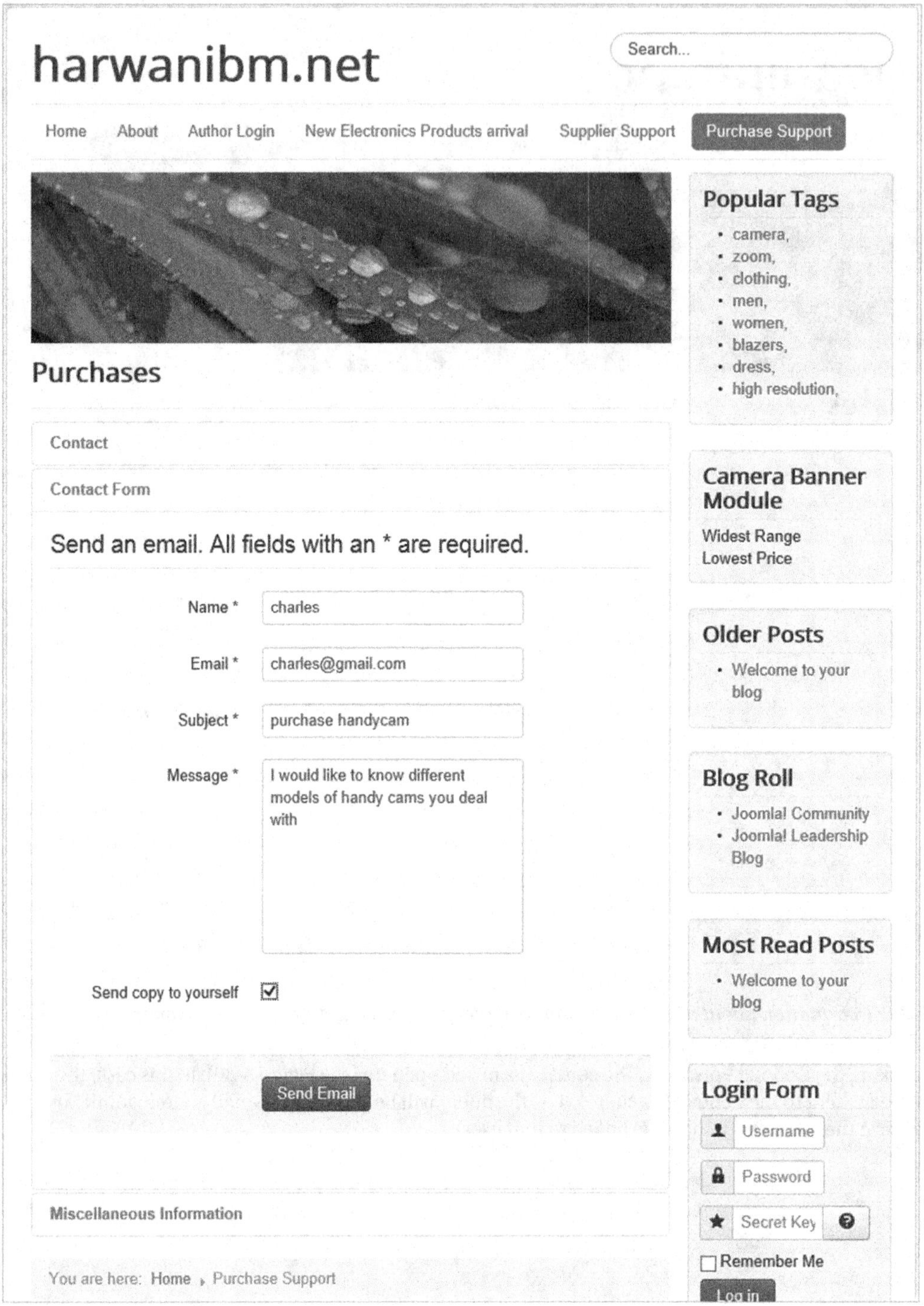

Figure 5-36. *The query being sent to the e-mail address of user sanjay*

The mail function must be configured from the Global Configuration section for e-mail to function properly; this will be explained in Chapter 10.

Summary

In this chapter, you saw a step-by-step method of creating users of different groups. You learned how to create contacts and a Contacts category. Contacts by name and department were both created to help you understand the difference between them when a query is sent via the contact form. Finally, you saw how to create menu items to access the respective contacts.

In the next chapter, you will learn how to develop interactions with the visitors of your web site. Interaction with visitors can be developed by using several methods, including displaying news feeds and prompting them to select desired options from polls.

CHAPTER 6

■ ■ ■

Creating Interaction

In Chapter 5, you saw how to create users, contacts, and categories of contacts so that a visitor to a web site can directly contact the authorized person of the desired department. The purpose of that chapter was to define the interaction of visitors with the authorized person in an organization.

In this chapter, you will increase the interaction with other data providers by using newsfeeds and also enable the visitors to search desired information on your site by using Search and Smart Search components. You'll learn the following:

- How to create categories for newsfeeds
- How to create newsfeeds
- How to use Search and Smart Search components

Newsfeeds

Newsfeeds share data from other providers. There are two ways to display newsfeeds on a web site:

- Use the Joomla Newsfeeds component
- Use the Feed Display module

In this chapter, you will learn to use the Joomla Newsfeeds component. (In Chapter 8, in the discussion on Module Manager, you will learn how to use the Feed Display module to display newsfeeds.)

Before creating a newsfeed, you have to create a category to which the newsfeed will belong. The goal is to categorize similar newsfeeds under the same category.

Creating Categories for Newsfeeds

To create a category for a newsfeed, open the Newsfeeds Category Manager. From the menu bar in the administrator window, select Components ➤ Newsfeeds ➤ Categories; the Newsfeeds Category Manager will open, as shown in Figure 6-1. It displays the newsfeed categories provided by default (which you can unpublish if you don't want them to appear on your web site). You can see that the default newsfeed category provided is the Uncategorized category.

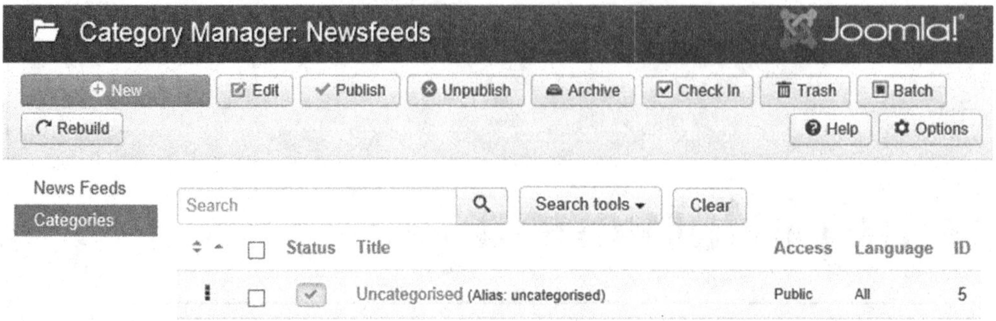

Figure 6-1. Newsfeeds Category Manager

The tools in the Newsfeeds Category Manager toolbar are fairly self-explanatory. As usual, you use Publish to make the selected categories visible on the web site and Unpublish to make the selected categories temporarily invisible (the unpublished categories can be published again any time via the Publish icon). The Trash icon is for permanently deleting a category. The Edit icon is used to edit the information of the category that was entered while creating the category. This information includes the category's title, access level, image, and description. The New icon is for creating a new category of newsfeeds, and the Help icon is for displaying the help screen from the specified help server (in the Global Configuration settings).

The Newsfeeds Category Manager columns display the respective information. For example, the Title column displays the name of the category. Clicking the name opens the category in edit mode. The Status column shows whether the category is visible on the web site. A check mark signifies that the category is visible on the web site; a red X means that the category is invisible. The Access column displays which level of users can access the category. The options are Public, Registered, and Special. The ID column displays the category's unique identification number, which is assigned automatically by Joomla for identifying it internally.

To create a category for your newsfeeds, click the New icon in the toolbar. You'll see a screen that lets you enter information for the new category. The page has four tabs: Category, Publishing, Permissions, and Options (the Category tab is opened by default). The Publishing and Permissions tabs are like the tabs that you have seen earlier: they will display publishing information for the newsfeed category and will help to set permissions for this newsfeed category, respectively.

In the Category tab, enter the information for the new newsfeed category, as shown in Figure 6-2. In the Title field, specify the name for the new category. In this case, enter **Cell Phones**. The Alias field, as mentioned previously, is for SEF purposes, and you can leave it blank (Joomla will generate an alias for you from the title by lowercasing it and using hyphens in place of spaces).

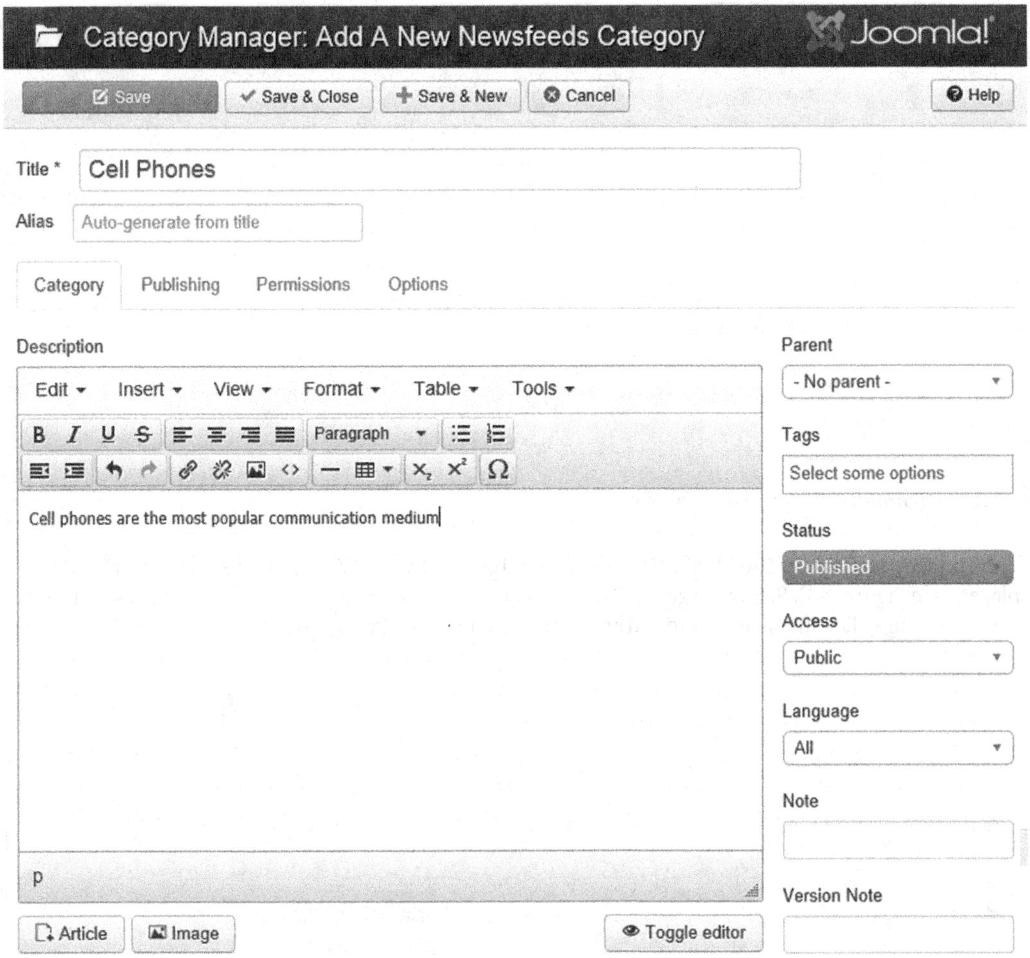

Figure 6-2. *Adding a newsfeed category*

The Options tab displays the fields to assign an image to this newsfeed category. After clicking it, you see the page shown in Figure 6-3. Click the Select button to assign an image to represent this newsfeed category; Media Manager will open up.

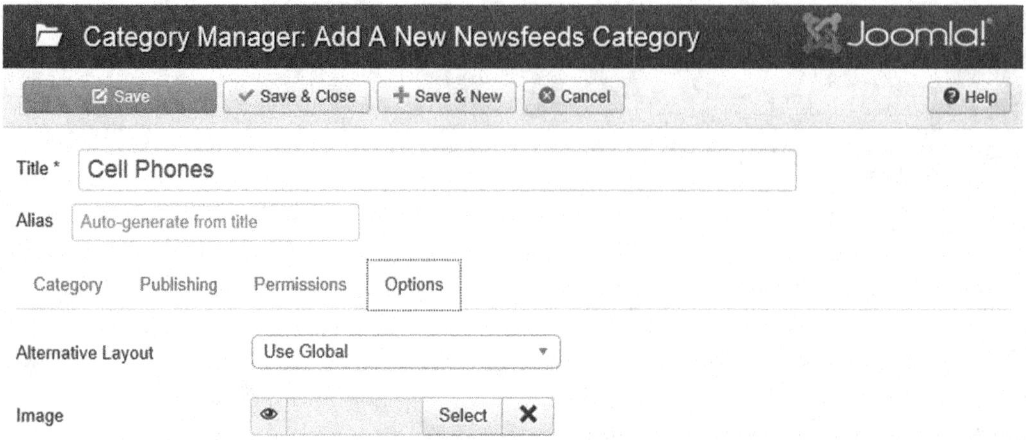

Figure 6-3. *Assigning an image to the newsfeed category*

All the images available in the Media Manager (from the `joomla_root/images/stories` folder) will be displayed (see Figure 6-4). Select image `cellphone1.jpg` (assuming that you already loaded it into the Media Manager) and click the Insert button to assign it to the newsfeed category.

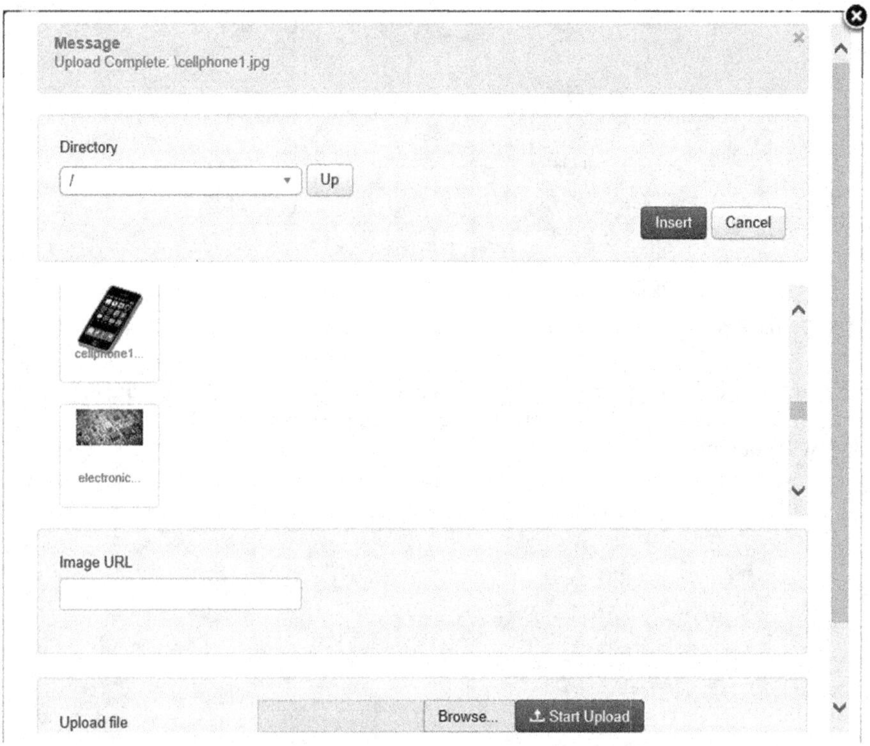

Figure 6-4. *Assigning an image to the newsfeed categoryin the Media Manager*

After entering the information for the newsfeed category, save it by clicking the Save & Close icon. You'll see the message Category Successfully Saved, and your Cell Phones category will appear in the list (see Figure 6-5).

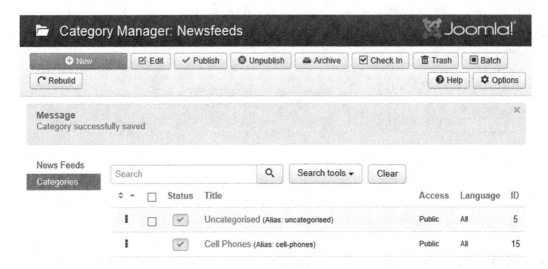

Figure 6-5. *Newsfeeds Category Manager with Cell Phones category added*

Creating Newsfeeds

With the newsfeed category created, you can now create a newsfeed for that category. To create a newsfeed, either click the News Feeds link (above the Categories link) or select Components ➤ Newsfeeds ➤ Feeds from the menu bar. The News Feed Manager: News Feeds page will open and display a list of several news feeds provided by default (if any). Currently, the list is empty because no default newsfeeds are provided (see Figure 6-6).

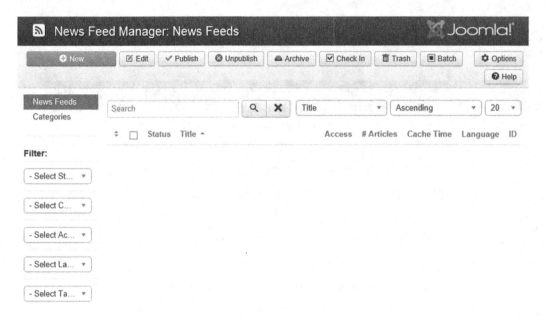

Figure 6-6. *News Feed Manager displaying list of newsfeeds*

Click the New icon in the toolbar, and you'll see a screen that lets you enter information for the new newsfeed. The screen contains the following four tabs:

- **New News Feed:** Enables entering information for the new newsfeed.

- **Images:** Enables assigning image(s) to the newsfeed.

- **Publishing:** Displays newsfeed publishing information. Also enables entering meta keywords and descriptions of the newsfeed.

- **Display:** Shows fields that help configure the newsfeed. For example, you can determine the number of articles to be displayed in the newsfeed, cache time for downloading the newsfeed, direction for displaying the newsfeed, and so on.

The New News Feed tab is opened by default. Enter the information for the new newsfeed as shown in Figure 6-7. In the Title field, enter the name of the newsfeed: **Cell Phones —Fastest Communication**. Although the Alias field can be left blank, enter **cell-phones** in this field. In the Link field, enter the URL of the web site from which you want to get the newsfeeds (in this case, `http://feeds.clickz.com/mobile-all`). From the Category drop-down list, select the category to which this newsfeed should belong: Cell Phones. Set the Status field to Published to make this newsfeed appear on the web site.

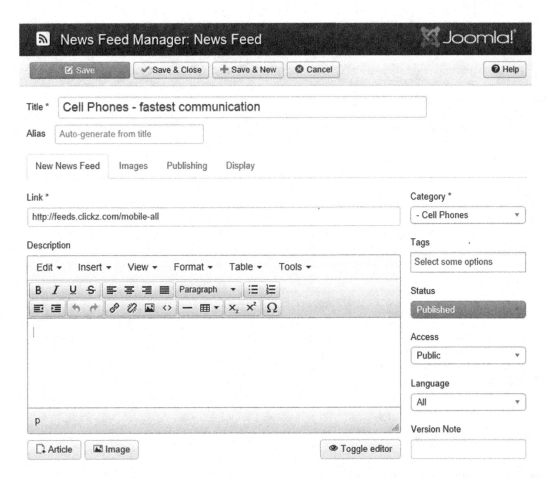

Figure 6-7. *Creating a newsfeed*

Click the Display tab to configure the newsfeed, and you'll see the fields shown in Figure 6-8.

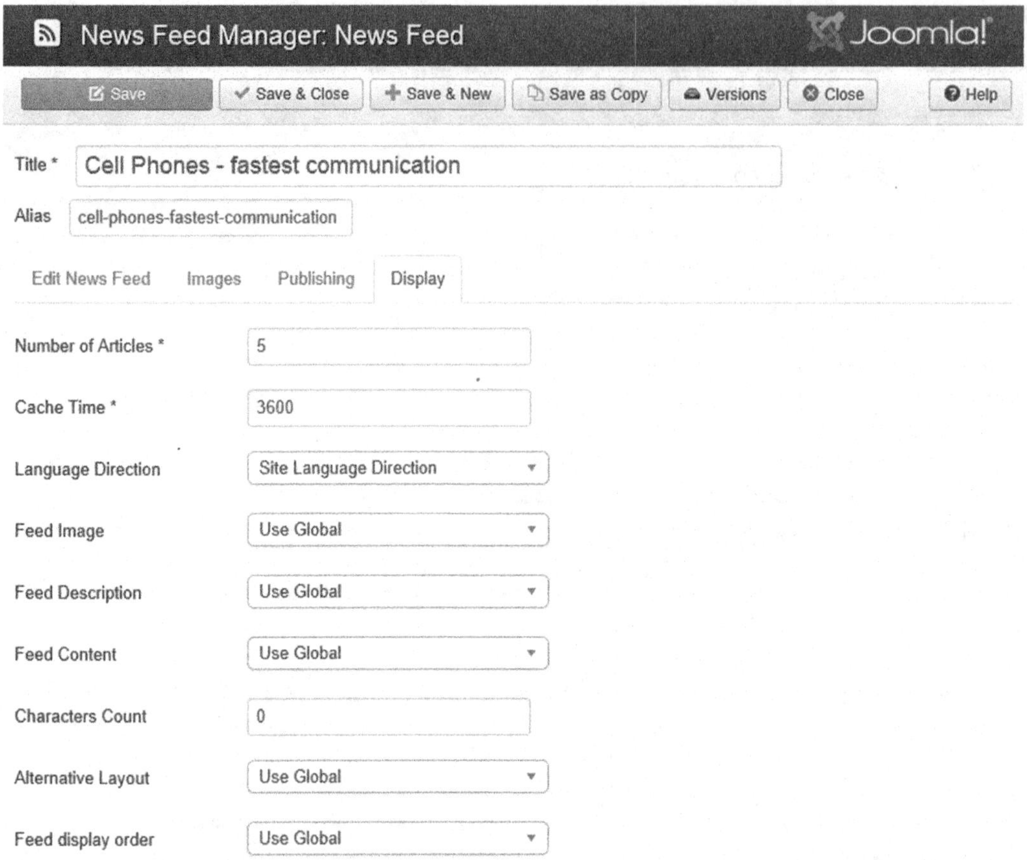

Figure 6-8. *Configuring newsfeed display options*

In the Number of Articles box, specify the number of articles that you want to be accessed from the newsfeed web site and displayed on your web site for your visitors (you can leave it at the default of 5). In the Cache Time field, specify the number of seconds the newsfeed will be saved on your server before being downloaded again from the remote newsfeed web site. The default time is 3600 seconds (1 hour). You can increase this time to reduce the network traffic, but it will make your newsfeeds less up to date.

The Language Direction field is used to specify the direction of the newsfeed content. Its three options are as follows:

- **Site Language Direction:** The direction of newsfeed text will be based on the language in which your web site content is being displayed. For example, if your web site content is being viewed in English, the newsfeed content will move from left to right; if it is being viewed in Hebrew or Arabic, it will move from right to left.

■ **Note** In Chapter 10, you will see how your web site content can be viewed in different languages by using the translation mechanism.

- **Left to Right Direction:** The newsfeed content will flow from left to right, regardless of the language in which your web site is displayed.

- **Right to Left Direction:** The newsfeed content will flow from right to left, regardless of the language in which your web site is displayed.

After entering the information for the newsfeed, click the Save & Close icon to save it. You'll see the message News Feed Successfully Saved, and the newsfeed Cell Phones – Fastest Communication will appear in the News Feed Manager list, as shown in Figure 6-9.

Figure 6-9. *News Feed Manager shows the new newsfeed*

To display a newsfeed, you need to create a menu item and link it to the newsfeed category that you just created. Open the Menu Manager by selecting Menus ➤ Menu Manager. You'll see a list of all the existing menus. Click the New icon to create a new menu item. You'll see a screen that lets you enter the information for the menu item. Enter the information as shown in Figure 6-10.

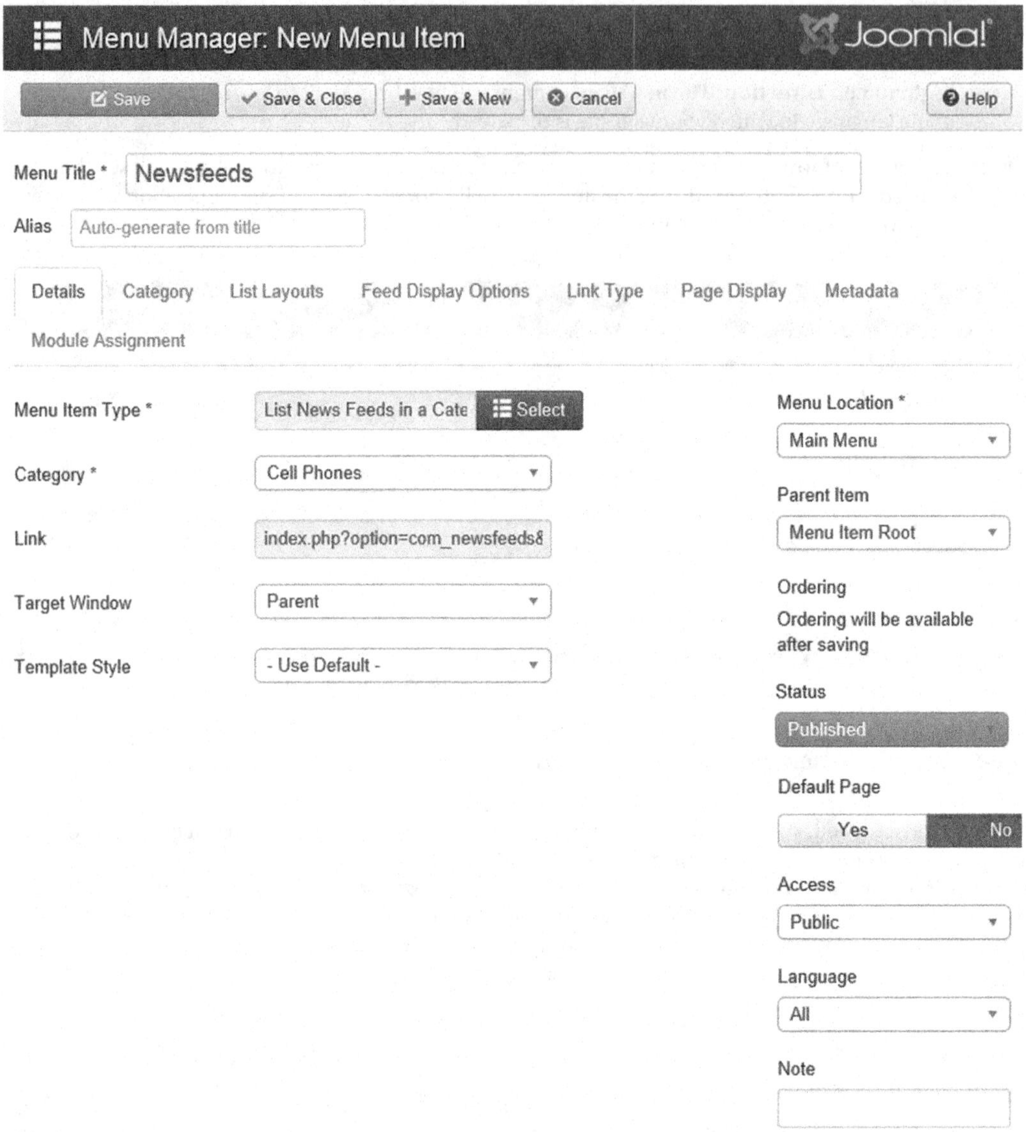

Figure 6-10. *Creating a menu item for the newsfeed*

The title you want to appear for the menu item is Newsfeeds, so enter it in the Menu Title field. The Link field will be automatically filled in, depending on the menu item type selected. The Menu Location field is used to decide which menu you want this menu item to appear in. Select Main Menu from the drop-down list. Because you want to display the newsfeeds from the Cell Phones category that you just created, choose the Cell Phones category from the Category combo box.

When you click the Select button from the Menu Item Type field, you'll see a screen for selecting the menu item type (see Figure 6-11).

Figure 6-11. *Menu item types under the Newsfeeds category*

You will find the following menu item types under Newsfeeds:

- **List All News Feed Categories:** Shows all newsfeed categories within a category.

- **List Feeds in a Category:** Shows all newsfeeds within a category. It shows the links to the newsfeeds in the specified category.

- **Single News Feed:** Shows a single newsfeed.

Select the List Feeds in a Category menu item type.

After entering the information for the menu item Newsfeeds, click the Save & Close icon to save it. You'll see the Newsfeeds title appear in the list of menu items in the Main Menu, as shown in Figure 6-12.

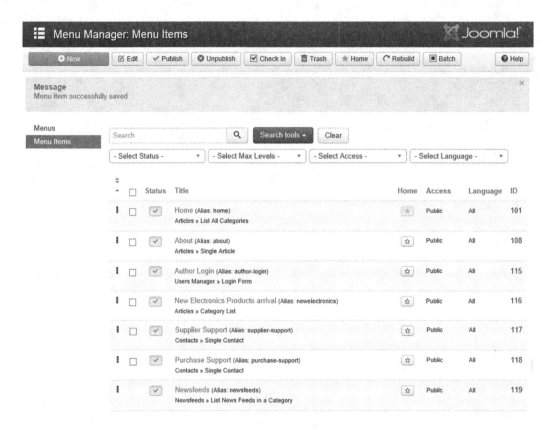

Figure 6-12. *Newsfeeds menu item is added to the Main Menu*

You can now check whether your newsfeed is visible on your web site. Open the browser window, point to the Joomla web site (`http://localhost/joomlasite`), and click the Refresh button. In the Main Menu, select the Newsfeeds menu item and you'll see a screen that displays the newsfeed category Cell Phones that you just created (see Figure 6-13).

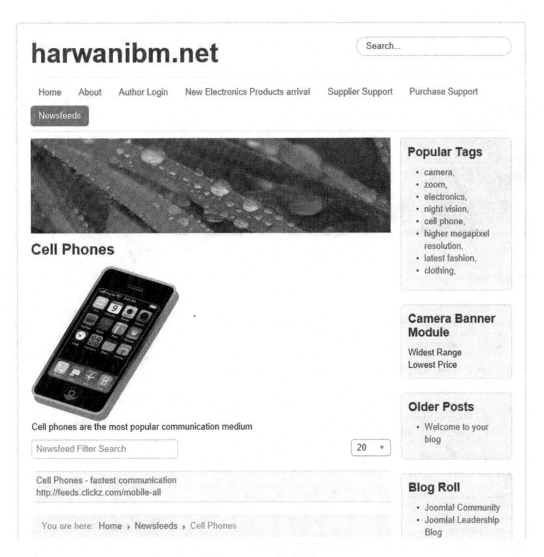

Figure 6-13. *Newsfeed listed under Cell Phones newsfeed category*

The Cell Phones newsfeed category displays the newsfeeds under it; in this case, only the newsfeed Cell Phones - Fastest Communication because it is the only newsfeed you've created in the Cell Phones category. Click the Cell Phones - Fastest Communication link to get the newsfeed from the specified URL: http://feeds.clickz.com/mobile-all. You'll get a list of five articles from the remote newsfeed web site, as shown in Figure 6-14.

harwanibm.net

Home   About   Author Login   New Electronics Products arrival   Supplier Support   Purchase Support

Newsfeeds

Cell Phones - fastest communication

Mobile - Media

1. ### The OS Car Wars

   Cars are fast becoming the next "connected" space, and so the battle for who will gain control over the operating systems is beginning to be waged. Who will win?

   ◈ Email this   ◈ Share on Facebook

2. ### Why Mobile Ad Targeting Can Potentially Be More Accurate Than Desktop

   Marketers are sometimes seeing more accurate data from their mobile video channels than desktop channels. Why is this happening? And how can you capitalize on it?

   ◈ Email this   ◈ Share on Facebook

3. ### Mobile Marketing and the War on Bikes: An Unlikely Comparison

   Does the language marketers use have an effect on how successful our digital campaigns are? If we change the words we use, could we stack the deck in our favor?

   ◈ Email this   ◈ Share on Facebook

4. ### Indonesia Leads Penetration of Global Mobile Facebook Users

   Mobile is a key channel for accessing social media platforms in Indonesia and other emerging Asian markets -- especially for Facebook.

   ◈ Email this   ◈ Share on Facebook

5. ### Is the Apple Watch a Push Notification Killer?

   Apple's CEO Tim Cook unveiled the Apple Watch today, the company's first foray into wearables. But while brands like Uber and W Hotels have already found utility on the watch, others may stumble.

   ◈ Email this   ◈ Share on Facebook

You are here: Home ▸ Newsfeeds ▸ Cell Phones - fastest communication

Popular Tags
- camera,
- zoom,
- women,
- blazers,
- dress,
- high resolution,
- water proof,
- electronics,

Camera Banner Module
Widest Range
Lowest Price

Older Posts
- Welcome to your blog

Blog Roll
- Joomla! Community
- Joomla! Leadership Blog

Most Read Posts
- Welcome to your blog

Login Form
👤 Username

🔒 Password

Figure 6-14. *Five articles related to cell phones display after selecting the newsfeed*

Adding a Search Facility

Joomla provides two search components:

- **Search**: Meant for smaller sites, this type of search is easy to set up.

- **Smart Search**: Meant for larger sites, this type of search provides advanced filters to implement smart searching. Because this search system indexes the entire site and searches from the indexed content, it is faster, too.

■ **Note** Only one of the search components must be active at a time to avoid confusion because both are incompatible.

Using the Basic Keyword Search

The basic keyword search, which is provided by the Joomla Search component, is supported by a variety of plug-ins. The search box that you see on the site provides the basic search facility. This search technique is much slower when compared with indexed search, and it is limited to searching the articles and the selected items that are specified while configuring the plug-ins. As discussed earlier, this type of searching is preferred only for small sites.

Following are two ways to use the Search component:

- Publish the Search module.

- Link to the menu item type named Search Form or Search Results.

Let's begin with publishing the Search module. Joomla includes two search modules, one for each search component:

- Search module for the Search component

- Smart Search module for the Smart Search component

Both modules are the same, except that the Smart Search module also displays an Advanced Search link. Open the Module Manager to list the modules. If you find the Search module in an unpublished state (see Figure 6-15), click the red x status button to publish it.

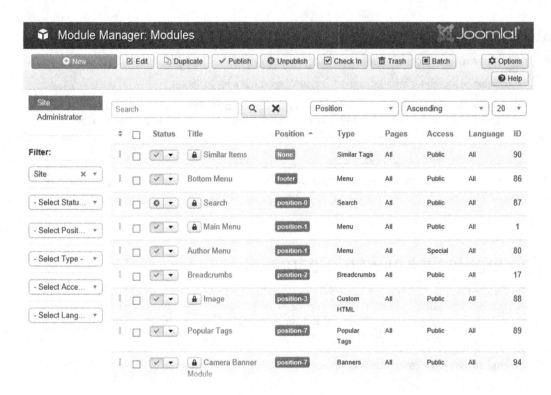

Figure 6-15. *Search module listed in the Module Manager*

Click the Status button; the Search module will open in edit mode, as shown in Figure 6-16. You can use the fields displayed on this page to configure the search module.

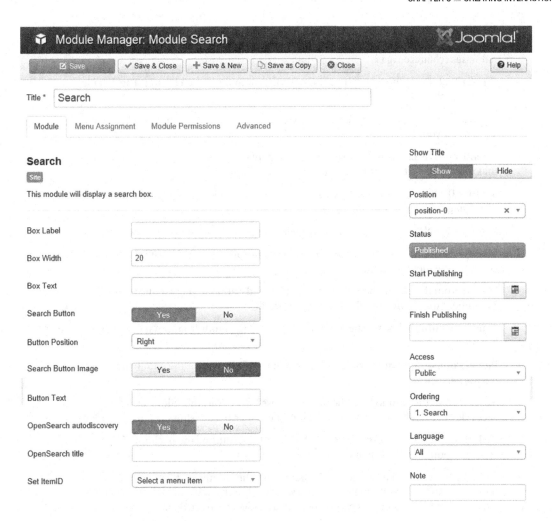

Figure 6-16. *Setting options for the Search module*

The fields are described in the following list:

- **Title:** Displays the module title.

- **Box Label:** Enter the text that you want to appear in the label of the search box.

- **Box Width:** Determines the size of the search text box in characters. Default value is 20.

- **Box Text:** Enter the text that you want to appear in the search text box. The text guides the user and gets overwritten when the user types something in this box.

- **Search Button:** Select Yes to display a Search button.

- **Button Position:** Determines the position of the Search button in relation to the search box. Valid options are Right, Left, Top, and Bottom.

- **Search Button Image:** Select Yes if you want to use an image as a button. The image has to be placed in the `templates/*your template name*/images/` folder with the name `searchButton.gif`.

- **Button Text:** Enter the text that you want to appear in the search button. The default text is Search.

- **OpenSearch autodiscovery:** If your browser supports OpenSearch, select Yes to add support for your site's search.

- **OpenSearch title:** If your browser supports OpenSearch, enter the text in this field that is displayed when your site is added as a search provider.

- **Set ItemID:** From the combo box, assign an ItemID by selecting a menu item for displaying the search results.

- **Show Title:** Select the Show option to display the module's title on the web site.

- **Module Position:** From the combo box, choose the position on the web site where you want the module to appear.

- **Status:** From the combo box, choose the Published option to publish the module. Two other options are Unpublished and Trashed.

- **Start Publishing:** Choose date and time to publish the module automatically in the future.

- **Finish Publishing:** Choose date and time to unpublish the module automatically in the future.

- **Access:** From the combo box, choose the access level of this module. The default access level is Public, which makes the module visible to all visitors.

- **Ordering:** Displays the ordering of all the modules, including the position of the current module in the front end.

- **Language:** From the Language combo box, select the language of the module. If you are creating a multilingual site and want to show search results in any specific language, choose it from this combo box. Meanwhile, leave the default value of All for this field.

- **Note:** In this optional field, you can write a reminder note for this search module. Leave it blank for now.

After configuring the Search module, click the Save & Close button to save the changes and exit. The next step is to enable the search plug-ins by selecting Extensions ➤ Plugin Manager (see the screen shown in Figure 6-17).

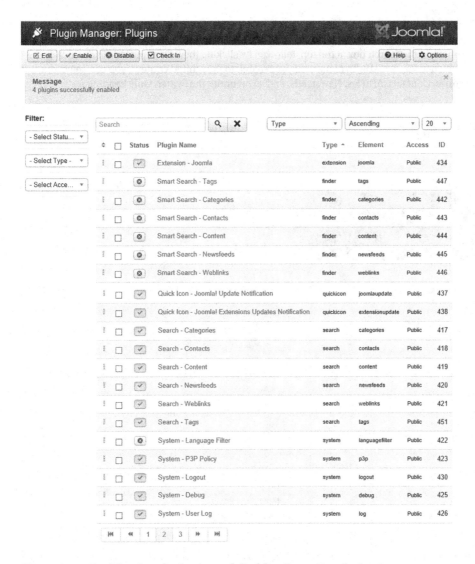

Figure 6-17. *Enabling Search plug-ins and disabling Smart Search plug-ins*

From the list of plug-ins, enable any that are disabled:

- **Search — Categories:** Enables category searching on your site
- **Search — Contacts:** Enables searching of Contacts component content
- **Search — Content:** Enables article searching
- **Search — Newsfeeds:** Enables searching of Newsfeed component content
- **Search — Weblinks:** Enables searching of Weblinks component content
- **Search — Tags:** Enables tag searching

Your Search component is active, and it is time to check it. Open the browser and then open the front end of the site (by pointing the browser at the address `http://localhost/joomlasite`). Let's search for the text *camera* in the site, so write **camera** in the search box at the top, followed by clicking the Search button. The search result will appear as shown in Figure 6-18. To constraint your search to the limited content, you can select the checkboxes for Categories, Contacts, Articles, Newsfeeds, and so on under the Search Only heading.

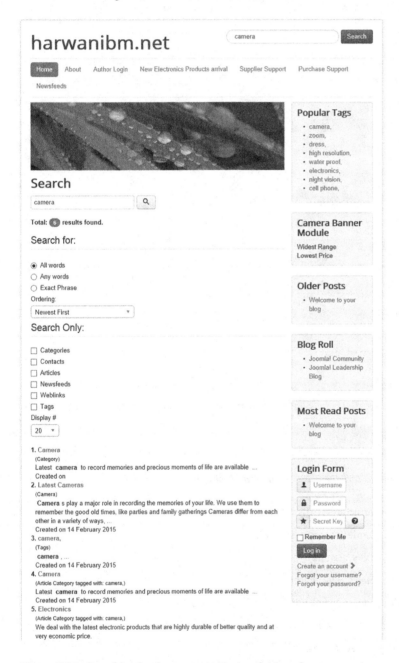

Figure 6-18. *Searching for the cameratext using the Search component*

The second way to use the Search component is to create a menu item and link it to the search page. Open the Administrator interface and select Menus ➤ Menu Manager from the menu bar. You'll see a list of all the existing menus. Click the New icon to create a new menu item. You'll see a screen that lets you enter the information for the menu item. Enter the information shown in Figure 6-19.

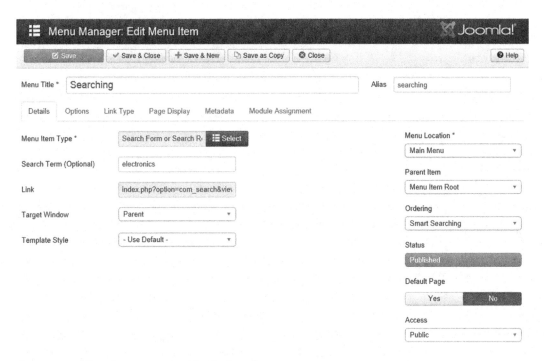

Figure 6-19. *Creating a menu item for the Search component*

The title you want to appear for the menu item is Searching, so enter it in the Menu Title field. The Link field will be automatically filled in, depending on the menu item type selected. The Menu Location field is used to decide which menu you want this menu item to appear in. Select Main Menu from the drop-down list.

After clicking the Select button from the menu Item Type field, you'll see a screen for selecting the menu item type (see Figure 6-20).

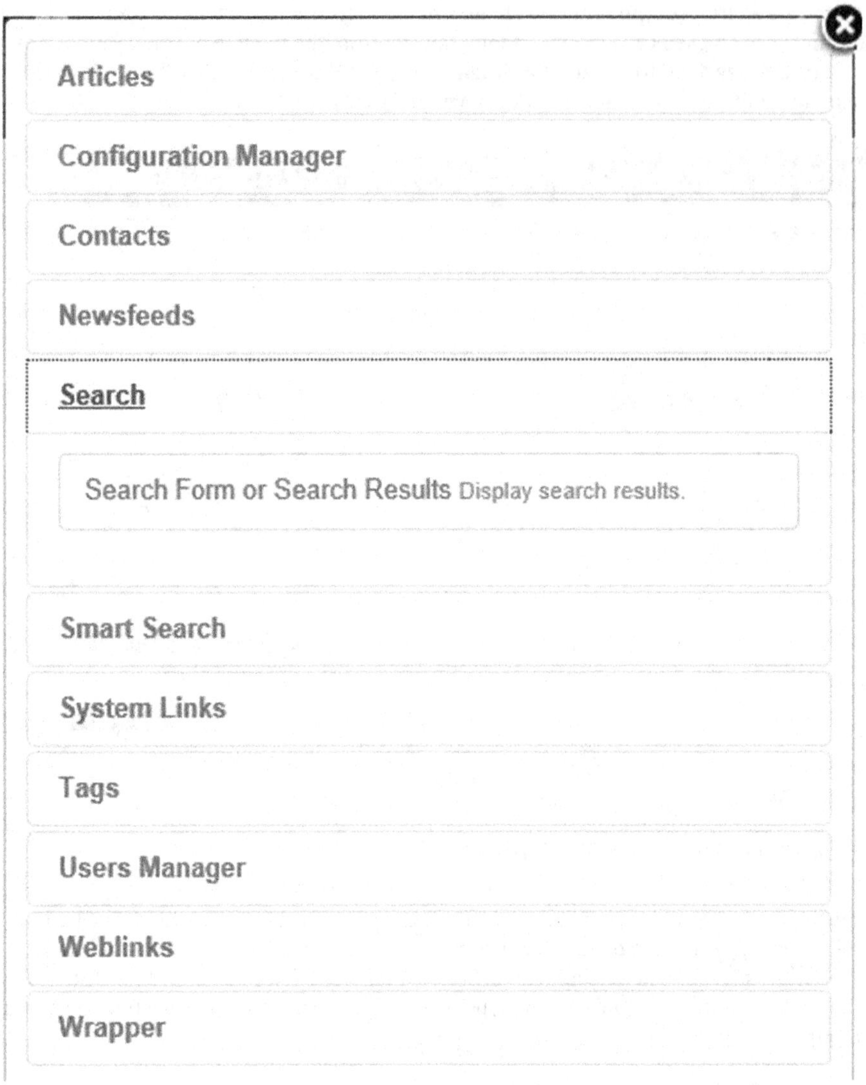

Articles

Configuration Manager

Contacts

Newsfeeds

Search

> Search Form or Search Results Display search results.

Smart Search

System Links

Tags

Users Manager

Weblinks

Wrapper

Figure 6-20. *Menu item types listed under the Search menu category*

The Joomla system includes two menu item types to create menu links to pages that include search forms:

- **Search ➤ Search Form or Search Results:** Used to display a standard search form that asks the user whether to search all words, any words, or an exact phrase that is entered in the search box.

- **Smart Search ➤ Search:** Displays a standard search box and also shows the Advanced Search button that, when clicked, displays the text that helps users get the precise result. It displays the filters that enable users to search in required content type only.

For basic keyword search, select the Search ➤ Search Form or Search Results menu item type.

After entering the information for the menu item Searching, click the Save & Close icon to save it. You'll see the Searching title appear in the list of menu items in the Main Menu, as shown in Figure 6-21.

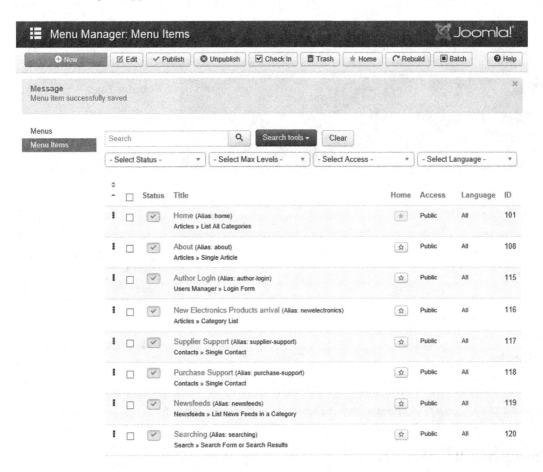

Figure 6-21. *Searching menu item appears in the Menu Manager window*

After refreshing the front end of the web site, you will find the Searching menu item in the main menu of the site, as shown in Figure 6-22. If you click the Searching menu item, the search form appears that can be used for searching the desired content in the site.

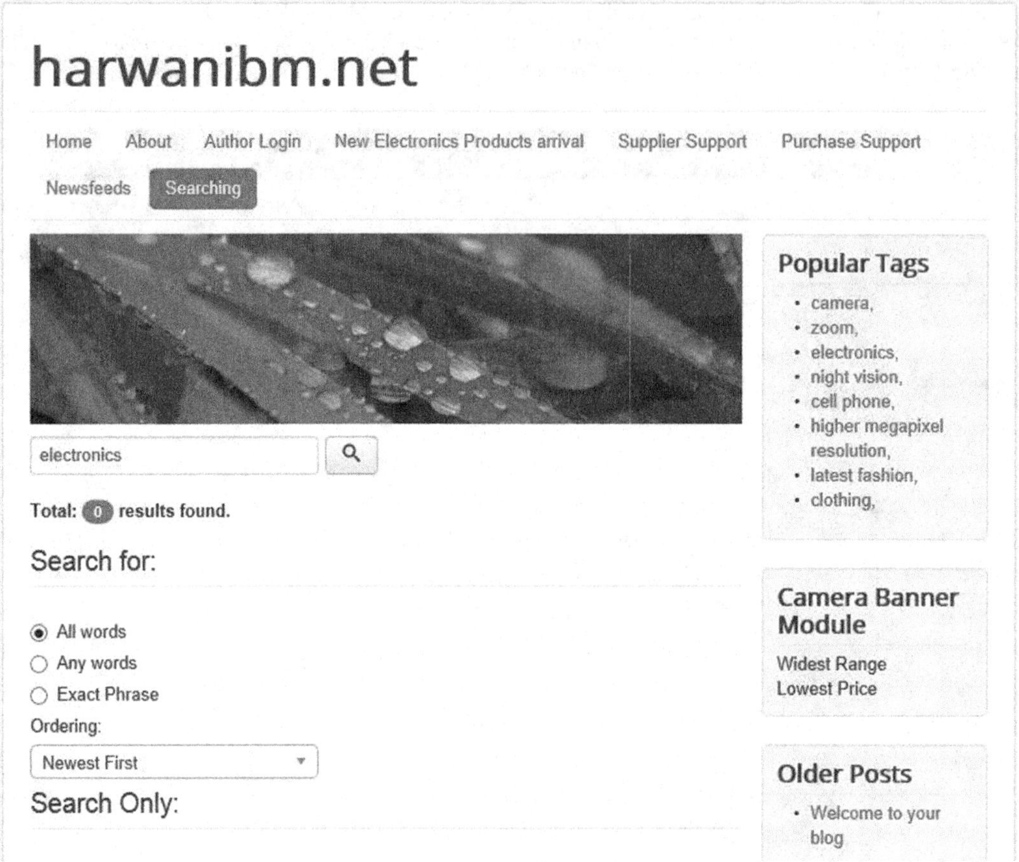

harwanibm.net

Home   About   Author Login   New Electronics Products arrival   Supplier Support   Purchase Support

Newsfeeds   Searching

electronics   🔍

Total: ⬤ 0 results found.

Search for:

◉ All words
○ Any words
○ Exact Phrase

Ordering:

Newest First   ▾

Search Only:

Popular Tags

• camera,
• zoom,
• electronics,
• night vision,
• cell phone,
• higher megapixel resolution,
• latest fashion,
• clothing,

Camera Banner Module

Widest Range
Lowest Price

Older Posts

• Welcome to your blog

Figure 6-22. *The search form appears when the Searching menu item is selected*

Using Smart Search

The Joomla Search component enables administrators to do the following:

• View statistics about what visitors are searching for on a site

• Customize search settings

The Smart Search is mainly used for customizing search settings. As discussed earlier, Smart Search uses indexed content for searching required information. The entire site is indexed whenever searching is done by the user using this technique. Obviously, the search result is delivered very quickly with this search process. Also, special filters can be added to this search technique to display precise results.

To implement Smart Search, follow these steps:

1. Enable the Content - Smart Search plug-in.

2. Index the site.

3. Unpublish the Search module.

4. Enable Smart Search plug-ins.

5. Apply Search Filters (Optional).

6. Configure the Smart Search component.

7. Create a menu item.

Enabling the Content - Smart Search Plug-in

The Content - Smart Search plug-in enables site indexing. You get an error if you try to index the site before enabling this plug-in. To enable it, select the Extensions ➤ Plugin Manager option; you see the screen shown in Figure 6-23. From the list of plug-ins, locate Content - Smart Search, which is disabled by default.

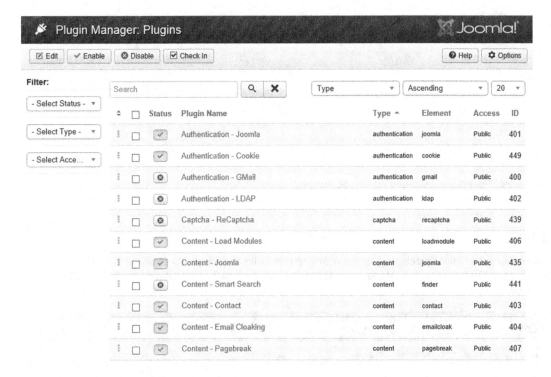

Figure 6-23. *List of plug-ins in the Plugin Manager*

If you have difficulty locating Smart Search plug-ins, you can filter out the rest of the plug-ins temporarily by selecting the Finder option from the Select Type filter drop-down list. The finder filter will display only the Smart Search plug-ins. Initially, all the Smart Search plug-ins are disabled. Click its status (red x) check box to enable it. When enabled, the red x status converts into a green check mark (see Figure 6-24).

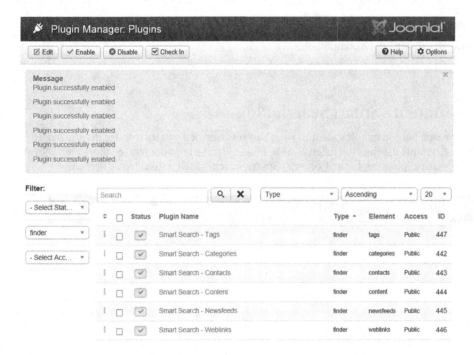

Figure 6-24. *Enabling the Content - Smart Search plug-in*

Indexing the Site

After enabling the Smart Search plug-in, the next step is to index the site. To do so, select Component ➤ Smart Search. The Smart Search: Managed Indexed Content page opens up as shown in Figure 6-25.

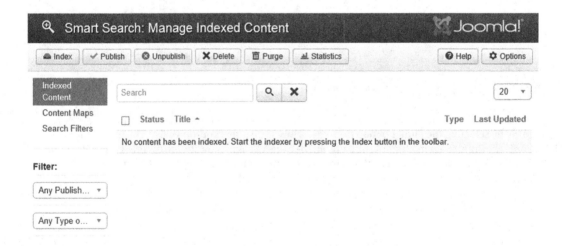

Figure 6-25. *Smart Search: Manage Indexed Content page*

Before you learn how to index the site, Table 6-1 briefly describes the tools shown in the toolbar at the top of Figure 6-25.

Table 6-1. *Smart Search Tools*

Tool	Description
Index	Click it to index the site.
Publish	Publishes the selected items from the list. The published items can be searched.
Unpublish	Unpublishes the selected items from the list. The unpublished items are not included in the search, so they don't appear in the search results.
Delete	Deletes the selected items from the list (i.e., from the index).
Purge	Permanently deletes the present index.
Options	Displays the options to configure the Smart Search component.
Statistics	Displays a brief summary of the indexed content.
Help	Displays online Help of the active screen.

Below the toolbar on the left side are the following three links:

- **Indexed Content:** Displays the Manage Indexed Content workspace

- **Content Maps:** Displays the Content Maps workspace

- **Search Filters:** Displays the Search Filters Manager to apply filters to the search component

By default, the Indexed Content link is selected. Below the three links are two filters that can be applied to the list of indexed items. The first allows you to filter by publication state; the second allows you to filter by type of content.

To index the site, click the Index button on the toolbar. The system begins indexing the site, and you may see the screen shown in Figure 6-26 (top). When indexing is done, you see the window showing the Finish message, as shown in Figure 6-26 (bottom).

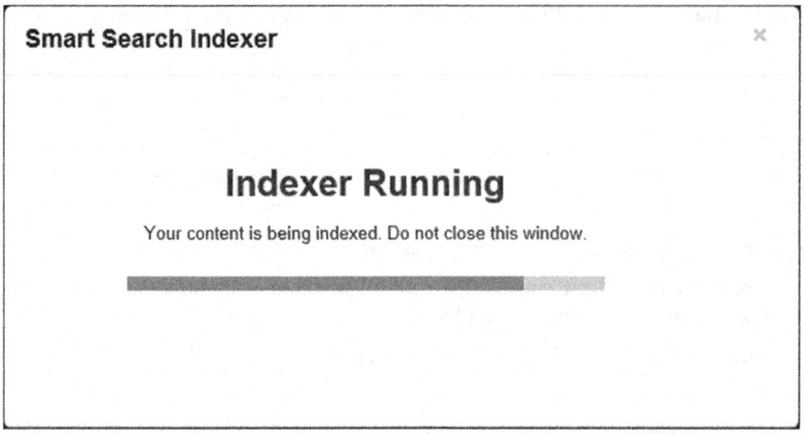

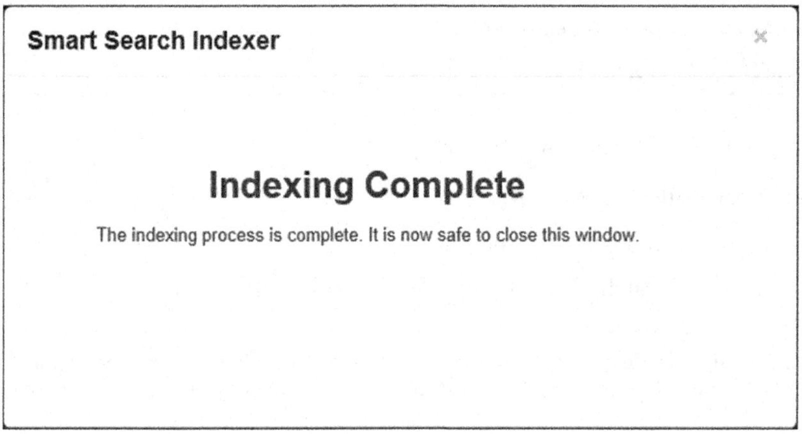

Figure 6-26. *Top:the indexer is indexing site content;bottom: dialog box confirms completion of indexing operation*

Go ahead and close the window; you will see a listing of all the indexed content (see Figure 6-27).

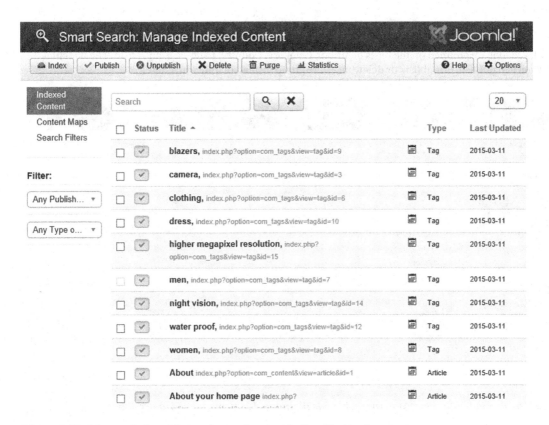

Figure 6-27. *Manage Indexed Content page showing the list of indexed content*

Table 6-2 briefly describes the columns found on the Smart Search: Manage Indexed Content page shown in Figure 6-27.

Table 6-2. *Smart Search: Manage Indexed Content Columns*

Column	Description
Check box	Used to select/unselect indexed item.
Status	Indicates whether the item is in a published or unpublished state. A green check mark means the item is published; a red x means the item is unpublished. Click the check mark to toggle the state.
Title	Displays the full name of the item along with its path. The name and path are separated by a comma.
Calendar icon	Hover the mouse over the icon to view the item's publication information.
Type	Displays the type of the component that is indexed.
Last Updated	Displays when the item was last updated.

The Content Maps link on the left side provides another way to view the indexed content. After its link is clicked, the Content Maps workspace opens up, as shown in Figure 6-28. The items in the index are displayed that are grouped on the basis of Author, Category, Country, Language, and so on. The benefit is that you can publish, unpublish, or delete an entire group instead of individual items.

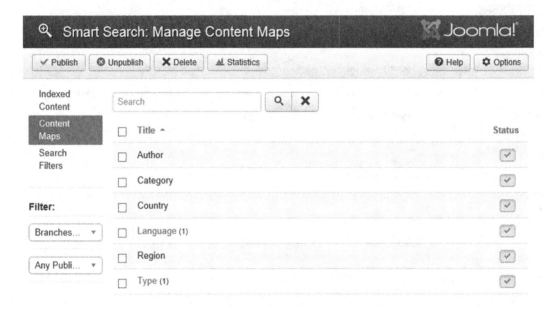

***Figure 6-28.** Manage Content Maps page showing the indexed content grouped under different categories*

Unpublishing the Search Module

Because the Search and Smart Search components are incompatible, only one has to be active at a time to avoid confusion at the front end of the site. So don't forget to disable the basic keyword Search component before enabling the Smart Search component by opening the Module Manager (click Extensions ➤ Module Manager) and unpublishing the Search module, as shown in Figure 6-29.

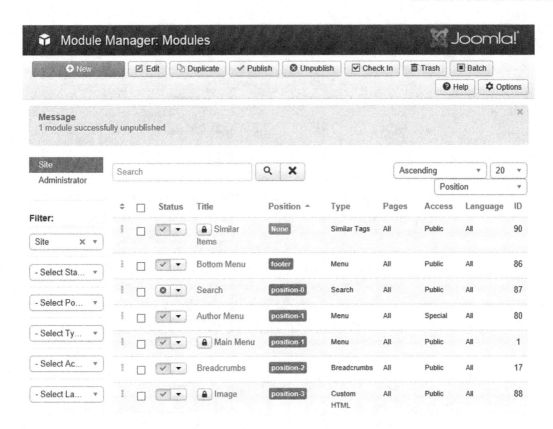

Figure 6-29. *Unpublishing the Search module from the Module Manager*

Enabling Smart Search Plug-ins

Like the basic Search component, Smart Search also includes dedicated plug-ins. Open the Plugin Manager (by clicking Extensions ➤ Plugin Manager) and enable the following listed plug-ins that are associated with Smart Search:

- **Content - Smart Search:** Enables indexing by the Smart Search component. This key plug-in is disabled by default. It must be enabled before you use Smart Search.

- **Smart Search – Categories:** Enables indexing of categories on your site.

- **Smart Search – Contacts:** Enables indexing of Contacts component content.

- **Smart Search – Articles:** Enables article indexing on your site.

- **Smart Search – Newsfeeds:** Enables indexing of the Newsfeed component content.

- **Smart Search – Weblinks:** Enables indexing of the Weblinks component content.

Disable all plug-ins that begin with the word *Search* -, as shown in Figure 6-30.

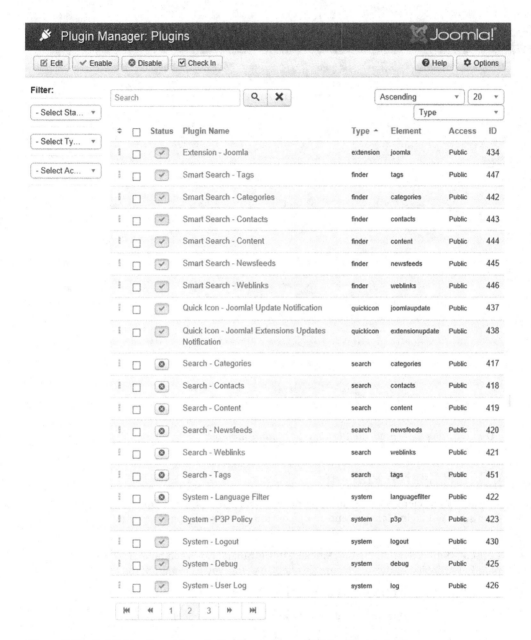

Figure 6-30. *Publishing Smart Search plug-ins and unpublishing Smart plug-ins*

Applying Search Filters (Optional)

Smart Search can be enhanced by implementing custom search filters. To access the Search Filters feature, click Components ➤ Smart Search option. From the page that opens up, click the Search Filters link. You see the screen shown in Figure 6-31.

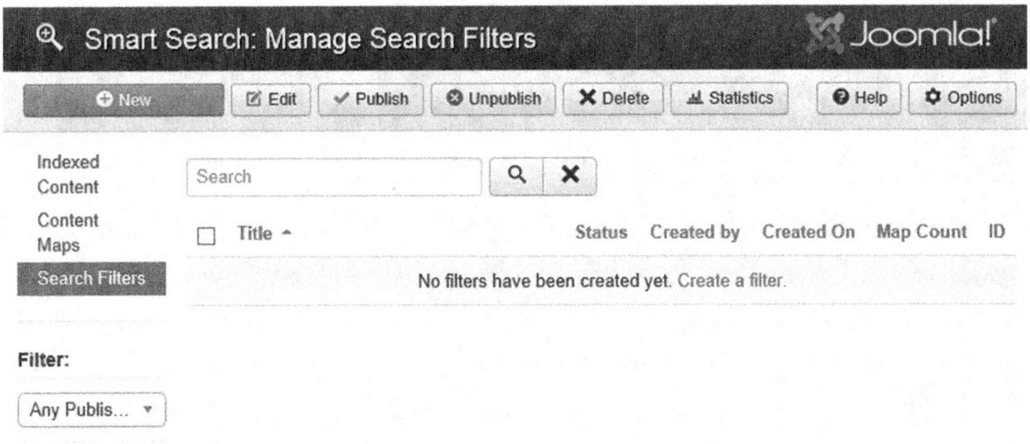

Figure 6-31. *Manage Search Filters page*

To create a new search filter, click the New button on the toolbar. The screen shown in Figure 6-32 will display. Enter a title for your filter in the Title field. Select the options to make the search precise: choosing the required options, search by language, search by type of check boxes, and so on.

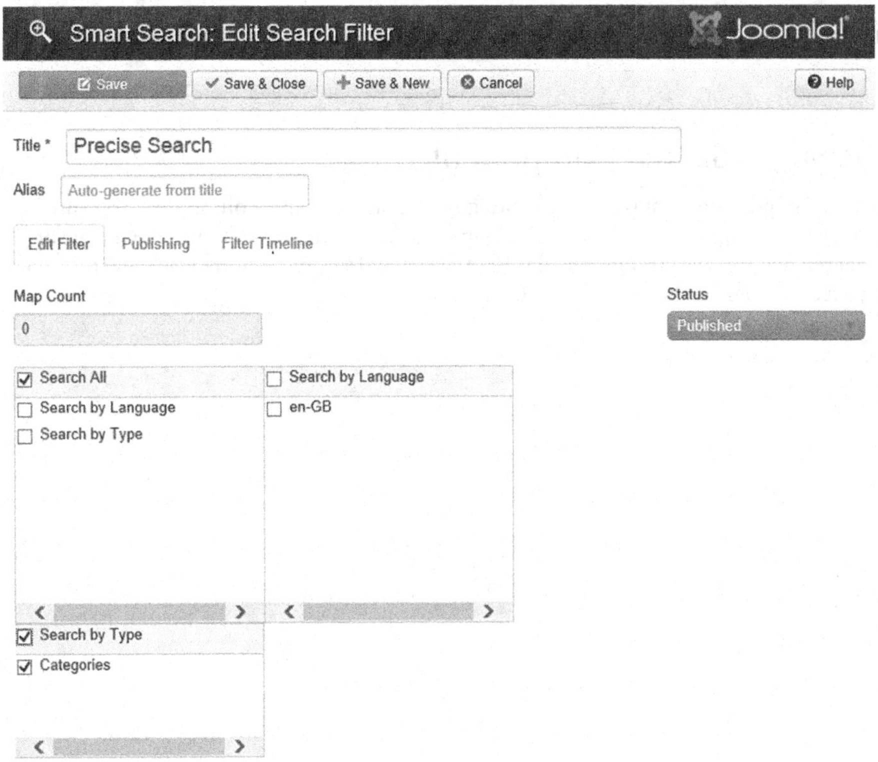

Figure 6-32. *Creating a search filter*

Finally, save the filter by clicking the Save & Close button. Your search filter will be created (see Figure 6-33).

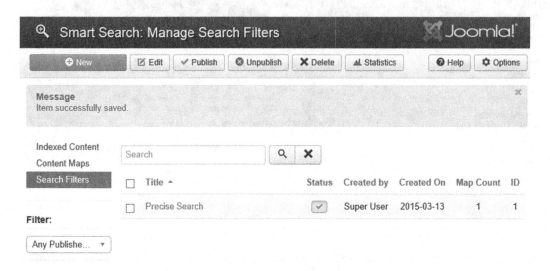

Figure 6-33. *Manage Search Filters page showing the newly created search filter*

■ **Note** The search filter can be used with either the Smart Search module or the Search menu item type.

Configuring the Smart Search Component

To suit your or your visitors' requirements, it is better to configure the Smart Search component. You can access the configuration settings page by either clicking the Options button from the Smart Search page or by clicking the Smart Search link in the Component column of the Global Configuration Manager. The Smart Search: Configuration page appears, as shown in Figure 6-34.

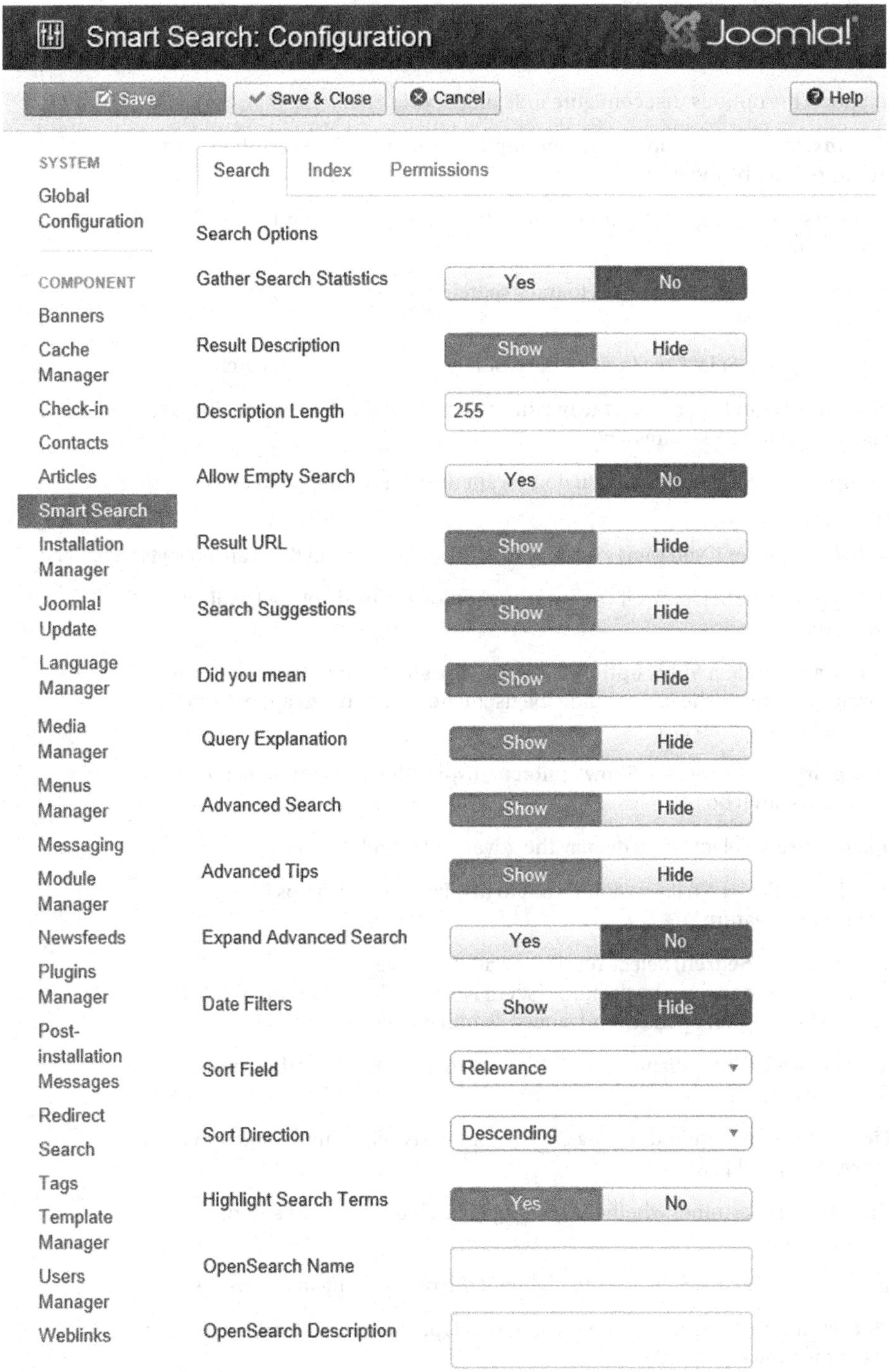

⊞ Smart Search: Configuration		𝕏 Joomla!®

🖺 Save	✔ Save & Close	⊗ Cancel		❓ Help

SYSTEM
Global Configuration

COMPONENT
Banners
Cache Manager
Check-in
Contacts
Articles
Smart Search
Installation Manager
Joomla! Update
Language Manager
Media Manager
Menus Manager
Messaging
Module Manager
Newsfeeds
Plugins Manager
Post-installation Messages
Redirect
Search
Tags
Template Manager
Users Manager
Weblinks

Search   Index   Permissions

Search Options

Gather Search Statistics	Yes	**No**

Result Description	**Show**	Hide

Description Length [255]

Allow Empty Search	Yes	**No**

Result URL	**Show**	Hide

Search Suggestions	**Show**	Hide

Did you mean	**Show**	Hide

Query Explanation	**Show**	Hide

Advanced Search	**Show**	Hide

Advanced Tips	**Show**	Hide

Expand Advanced Search	Yes	**No**

Date Filters	Show	**Hide**

Sort Field [Relevance ▾]

Sort Direction [Descending ▾]

Highlight Search Terms	**Yes**	No

OpenSearch Name [   ]

OpenSearch Description [   ]

Figure 6-34. Search tab of the Smart Search Configuration page

Three tabs are displayed:

- **Search:** Shows the options to configure search and its result.

- **Index:** Shows the options that configure indexing of your site.

- **Permissions:** Shows the options that determine permissions to access the Smart Search component by the users.

The Search tab shows the settings that can be applied to the search form and its results. Following are the options shown by this page:

- **Gather Search Statistics:** Select Yes to track search queries. The tracked statistics data is then displayed.

- **Result Description:** Select Yes to show the result descriptions in the search.

- **Description Length:** Determines the maximum length of the description displayed. The default length is 255 characters.

- **Allow Empty Search:** Select No if you don't want the user to submit an empty search query.

- **Result URL:** Select Yes if you want to display the URL of the items in the search results.

- **Search Suggestions:** Select Yes if you want suggestions to be displayed while the user types in the query.

- **Did You Mean — Select Show option to display the similar text that is entered in the search box:** Shows the text to guide the user if no search result appears on the text entered in the search box.

- **Query Explanation:** Select the Show option to display the explanation of the query entered in the search box.

- **Advanced Search:** Select Yes to display the advanced search option.

- **Advanced Tips:** Select No if you don't want to display the search tips for the advanced search feature.

- **Expand Advanced Search:** Select Yes if you want the advanced search panel to appear in an expanded form by default. If set to No, the advanced search initially appears as a button that opens the advanced search panel when clicked.

- **Date Filters:** Select Yes to display date filters that display the items that match the specified dates.

- **Sort Field:** Select the required sorting criteria for the search results. Valid options are Relevance, Date, and List price.

- **Sort Direction:** Determines whether to arrange search results in ascending or descending order.

- **Highlight Search Terms:** Select Yes to highlight the query string in the results set.

- **OpenSearch Name:** Used if the browser supports OpenSearch. Enter the name that appears in the browser's search box.

- **OpenSearch Description:** Used if the browser supports OpenSearch. Enter the description that appears for the search link when it appears in the browser's search box.

The Index tab shows options for configuring indexing of your site (see Figure 6-35). Indexing consumes system resources, so the options shown on this page enable you to optimize your resources.

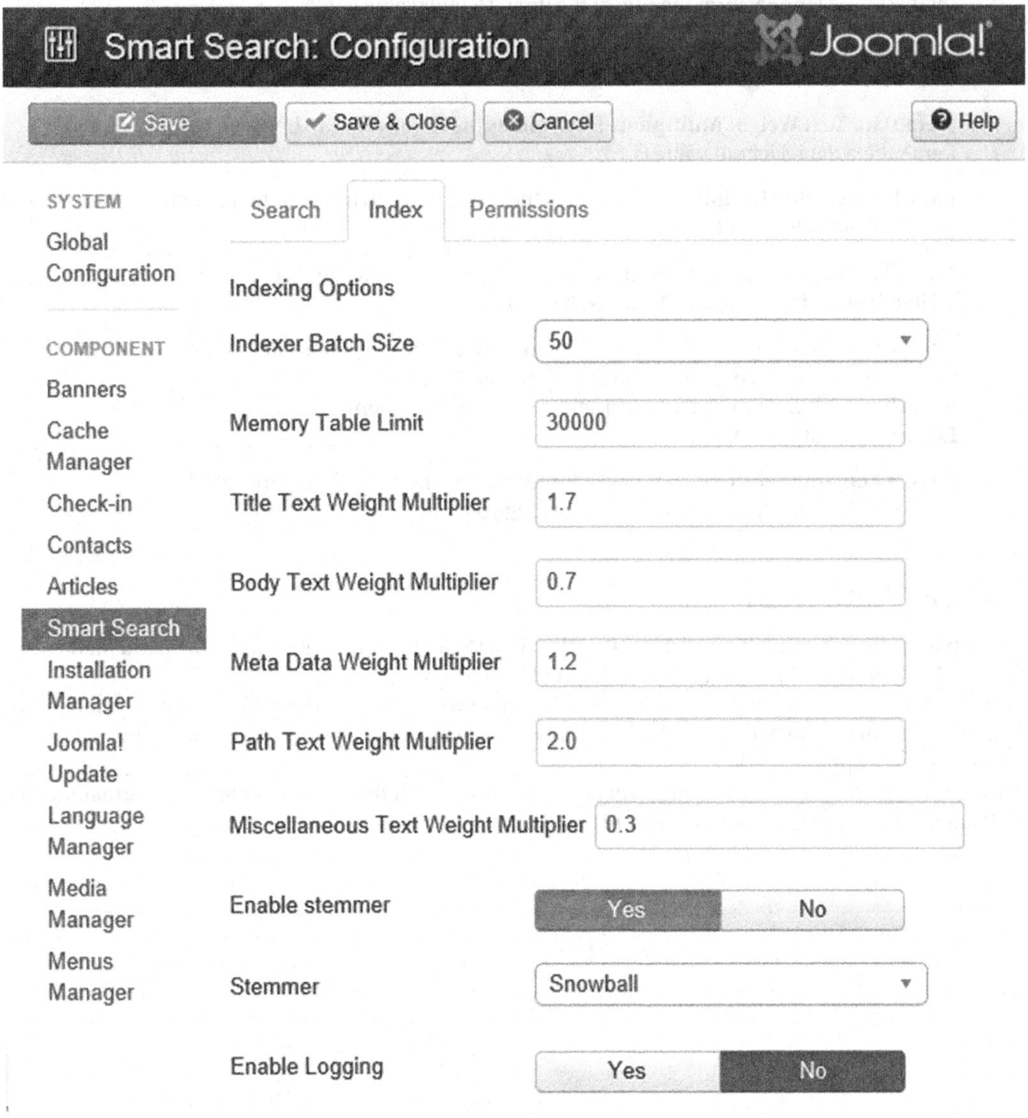

Figure 6-35. *Index tab of Smart Search: Configuration page*

Following are the options shown on this page:

- **Indexer Batch Size:** Select the desired batch size for indexing. Larger batch sizes consume more system resources, but result in faster indexing.

- **Memory Table Limit:** The default value of 30000 is designed to work for most systems.

- **Title Text Weight Multiplier:** Determines the importance to be given to the title field in the search result. Set its value to 1 if you don't want to apply additional emphasis on the title of the item. A value less than 1 reduces the emphasis; more than 1 increases the emphasis on the title of the item. Default value is 1.7.

- **Body Text Weight Multiplier:** Determines the importance to be given to the body text of the item. Default value is 0.7.

- **Meta Data Text Weight Multiplier:** Determines the importance to be given to the item's meta data. Default value is 1.2.

- **Path Text Weight Multiplier:** Determines the importance to be given to the item's path. Default value is 2.0.

- **Miscellaneous Text Weight Multiplier:** Determines the importance to be given to an item's other information. Default value is 0.3.

- **Enable stemmer:** Choose the option from the combo box to enable stemming. If your site is in English only, you can select the English option. If you have a non-English or multilingual site, you can select Snowball. Valid options are Snowball, English Only, and French Only.

- **Enable Logging:** Select Yes to create a log file during indexing that helps to debug any problems that might occur while indexing your site.

Creating a Menu Item

The next step is to create a menu item and link it to the Smart Search component. Open the Menu Manager by selecting Menus ➤ Menu Manager. You'll see a list of all the existing menus.

You can either edit the existing Searching menu item that you created and modify it to be used for Smart Search module, or you can trash the Searching menu item and create a new Smart Searching component. You will use the latter approach.

Click the New icon to create a new menu item. You'll see a screen that lets you enter the information for that item. Enter the information shown in Figure 6-36.

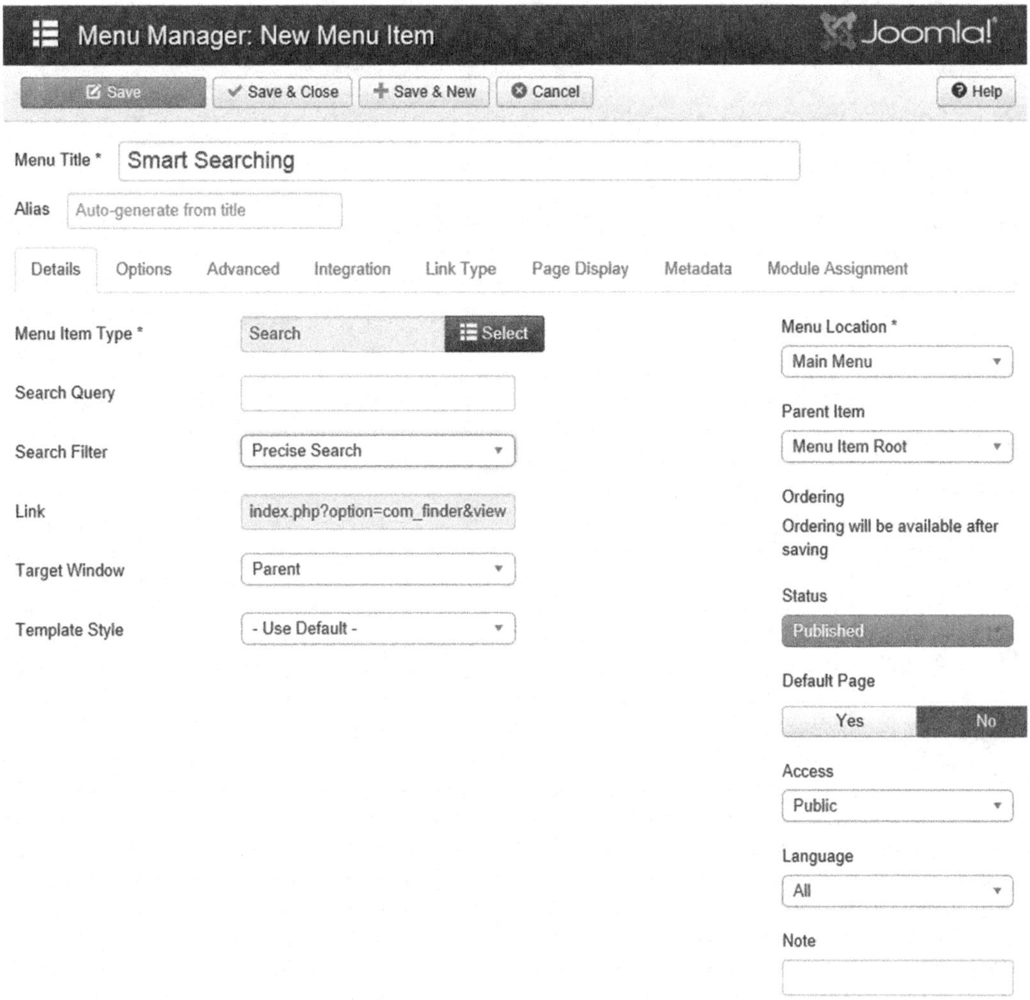

Figure 6-36. *Creating a menu item for the Smart Search component*

The title you want to appear for the menu item is Smart Searching, so enter it in the Menu Title field. In the Search Query field, you can enter the text that you want to be immediately searched when a user selects the menu item. For example, if you enter *electronics* in this field, you will get the search results for the text *electronics* whenever this menu item is selected. From Search Filter, you can apply the search filters, if any. Let's select the Precise Search filter that you already created.

Clicking the Select button from the Menu Item Type field displays a screen for selecting the menu item type (see Figure 6-37). Obviously, you will select the Smart Search ➤ Search menu item type. Recall that this menu item not only displays the search box but also the Advanced Search button that displays the text that guides you get the precise result. Also, it displays the filters that enable users to search in required content type only.

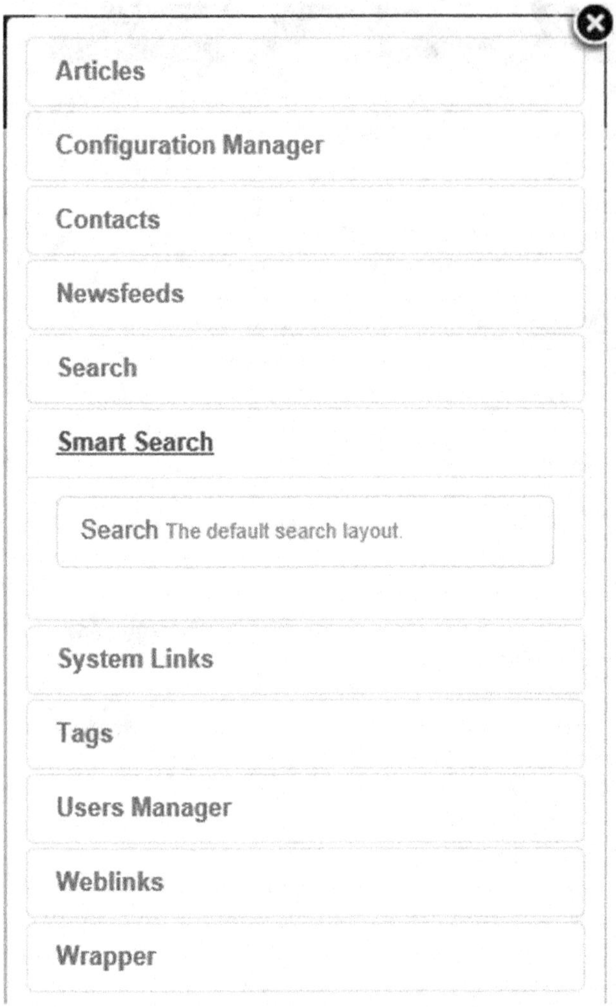

Articles

Configuration Manager

Contacts

Newsfeeds

Search

Smart Search

Search The default search layout.

System Links

Tags

Users Manager

Weblinks

Wrapper

Figure 6-37. *Menu item types listed under the Smart Search menu*

After entering the information for the menu item Smart Searching, click the Save & Close icon to save it. You'll see the Smart Searching title appear in the list of menu items in the Main Menu, as shown in Figure 6-38.

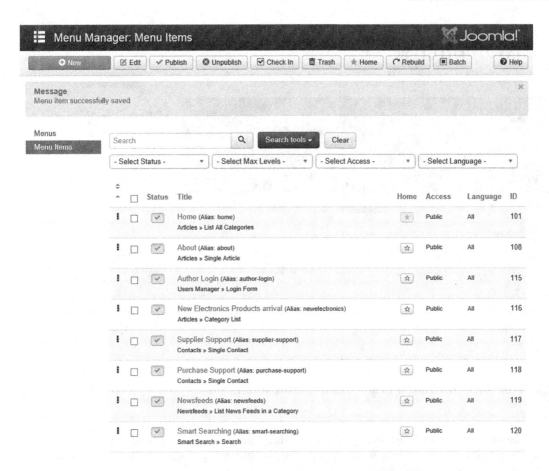

Figure 6-38. *Smart Searching menu item is created and listed in Menu Manager*

When you refresh the front end of the web site, you will find the Smart Searching menu item in the main menu of the site, as shown in Figure 6-39. When the Smart Searching menu item is clicked, the search form appears that can be used for searching desired content in the site. While typing in the search box, suggestions will appear to select from.

Figure 6-39. *Search result displayed of the entered text in the search box*

When you click the Advanced Search button, you will see additional text displayed on the site that guides you to get precise search results. Also, you get filters displayed that you can use to apply the search to limited content of the site (see Figure 6-40).

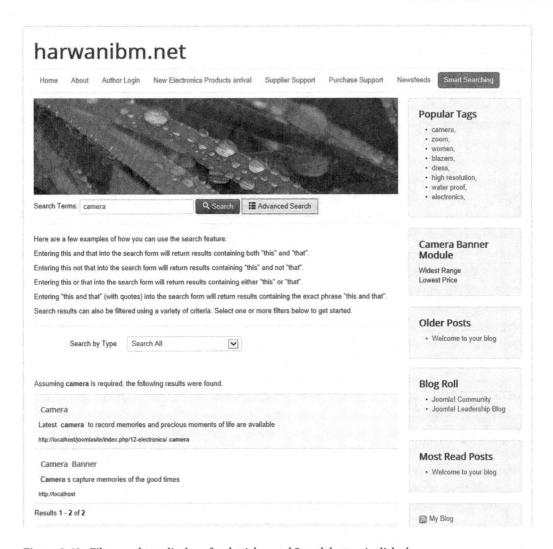

Figure 6-40. *Filters and text display afterthe Advanced Search button is clicked*

Summary

In this chapter, you learned how to create newsfeeds for sharing content from other data providers. You also learned how to use search components when searching desired content in the site.

In Chapter 7, you will learn how to create menus, which are the mode of interface between visitors and the web site. Menus display different options in the form of menu items that a visitor can select to see information.

CHAPTER 7

■ ■ ■

Dealing with Menus

In Chapter 6, you saw how to create interactions with the user and other data providers. You used newsfeeds to get updated information from other data providers and polls to learn visitors' views on a subject. Also, you learned how to provide related topics from other websites in the form of web links to enable data sharing. In this chapter, you'll learn how to create menus and how to create menu items of different types so that they can be set to display articles, categories, contacts, web links, newsfeeds, login forms, and more.

■ **Note** In Joomla, the position of the menus is not fixed and is completely dependent on the template.

When you create a menu item, you assign a menu item type to it, which defines what it is supposed to display. The menu item types are broadly classified into the following categories:

- Articles
- Configuration Manager
- Contacts
- Newsfeeds
- Search
- Smart Search
- System Links
- Tags
- Users Manager
- Weblinks
- Wrapper

Though you can create menu items in any of the existing menus provided in the default Joomla web site, to keep the things separate and clean, you will create a new menu of your own for testing. So, let's start with creating a menu.

Creating a Menu

To add a new menu, you need to open the Menu Manager. Open the Administrator interface (by pointing the browser window to http://localhost/joomlasite/administrator). From the menu bar, select Menus ➤ Menu Manager. When the Menu Manager opens, click the New icon in the toolbar to create a new menu. You'll see a screen for entering information about the new menu, as shown in Figure 7-1. You want the menu title to be Electronic Products on the web site, so enter that text in the Title field.

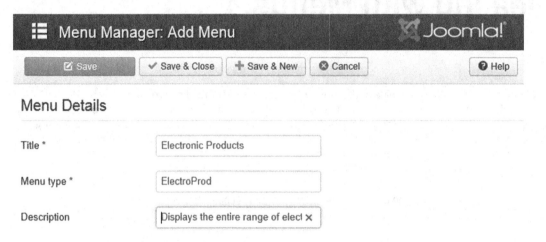

Figure 7-1. *Entering information for your new menu*

For reference, Table 7-1 gives a brief description of the fields on the Menu Manager: Add Menu screen.

Table 7-1. *Menu Manager: Add Menu Options*

Field	Description
Title	The name of the menu as displayed on the web page. In this exercise, it's specified as Electronic Products.
Menu Type	The name used by Joomla to identify the menu. It must be unique and must not include spaces. In this exercise, it's specified as ElectroProd (though it could be any name).
Description	Enter a brief description of the menu.

Table 7-2 gives a brief description of the icons on the Menu Manager: Add Menu screen's toolbar.

Table 7-2. *Icons in the Toolbar*

Icon	Description
Save	Saves the menu and remains on the Add Menu page
Save & Close	Saves the menu and returns to the Menu Manager page
Save & New	Saves the current menu and opens another Add Menu page for adding another menu
Cancel	Cancels any modifications made
Help	Opens the Joomla help web site

After entering the information for the new menu, click the Save & Close icon. Upon saving the menu, you'll find it listed in the Menu Manager, as shown in Figure 7-2.

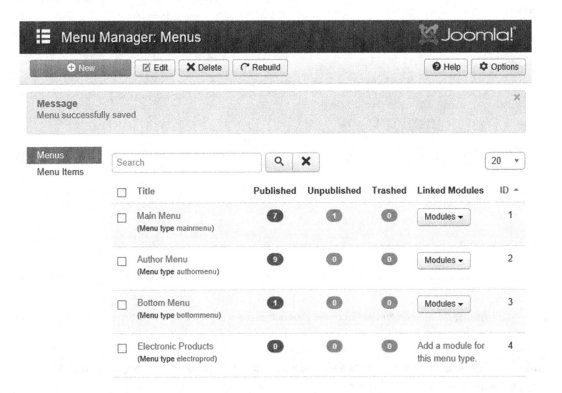

Figure 7-2. *The new menu, Electronic Products, displays in the Menu Manager*

To display the menu item from the front end, activate it via the Module Manager. Click the Add a Module for This Menu Type link shown under the Linked Modules column of the Electronic Products menu. The Module Manager opens as shown in Figure 7-3. In the Title field, enter the module title as Electronic Range. From the Select Menu drop-down list, select the menu that you want to display through this module (i.e., the Electronic Products menu). Let's display this menu to appear at the bottom of the site, so select the footer option from the Position drop-down list.

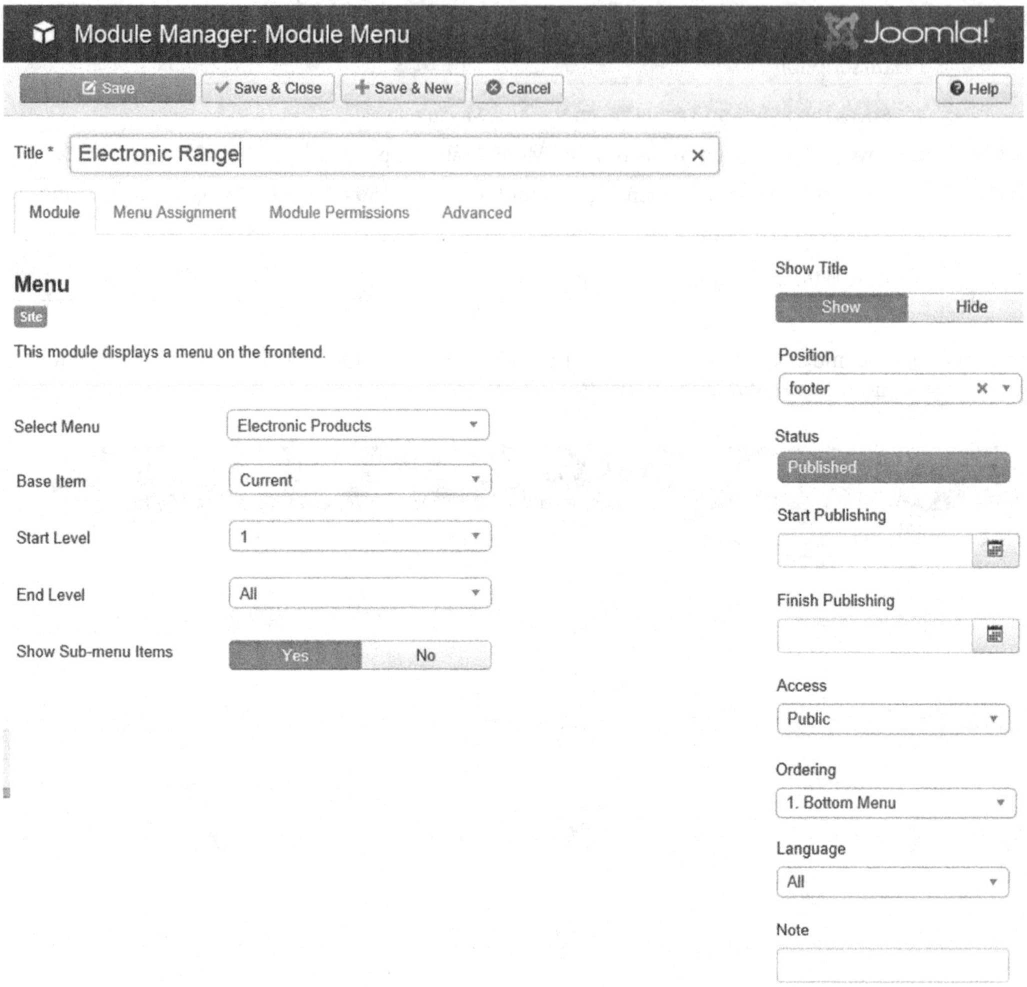

Figure 7-3. *Defining the module for the Electronic Products menu*

■ **Note**   The menu has to be activated via the Module Manager. The creation of the module confirms the appearance of the menu at the specified location.

Creating Menu Items

You can now add menu items to the Electronic Products menu. Click the Electronic Products menu title from the Menu Manager: Menus page to open it in edit mode. You can also check its checkbox and click Edit icon from the toolbar at the top. You'll see a Menu Manager: Menu Items page that will contain a listing of all the menu items created in this menu, as shown in Figure 7-4. At the moment, it is empty because you have not yet created any menu items in this menu.

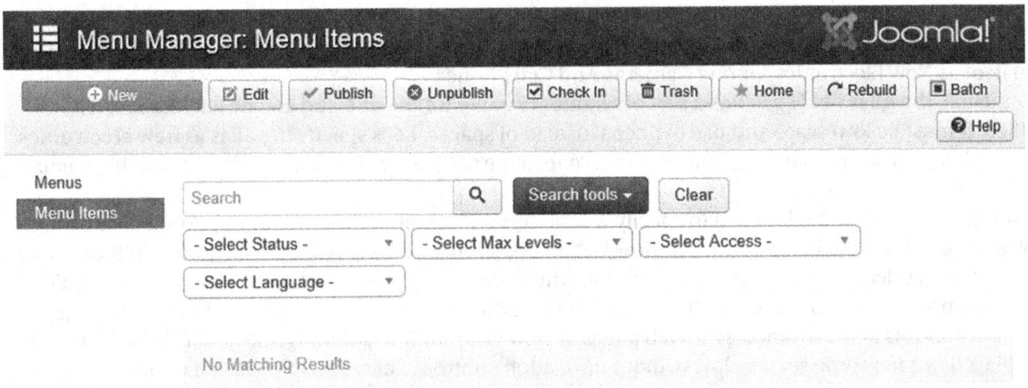

Figure 7-4. Menu Item Manager for the Electronic Products menu

Click the New icon to create menu items in this menu. You'll see a screen to enter information for the new menu item (see Figure 7-5).

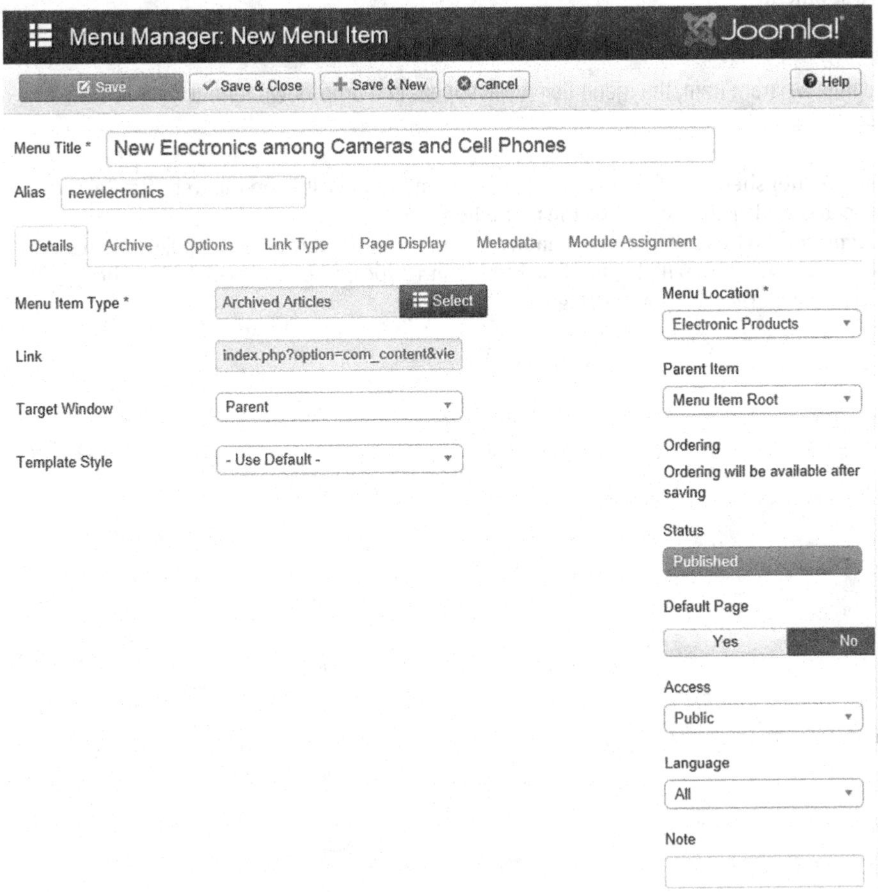

Figure 7-5. Creating a menu item of type Archived Articles

In the Title field, enter the title of the menu item. It can be any text. Because you will be creating one menu item and editing the same menu item to be used for different menu item types, specify the title of this menu item as New Electronics Among Cameras And Cell Phones.

As usual, the Alias field specifies a sort of secondary name for the title and can be left blank. If it is specified, it must be lowercase and use hyphens instead of spaces. Let's specify the alias as **new electronics**.

The Link field is automatically filled to point to the type of contents you want to display via this menu item. This field cannot be edited.

The Target Window field is used to specify where the contents of the articles are supposed to appear. The available options are Parent, New Window With Navigation, and New Without Navigation. If the Parent option is selected, the selected information will be displayed in the current window; if New Window With Navigation is selected, the desired contents will be displayed in a new browser window containing navigation controls to move among the web pages. If New Without Navigation is selected, the contents will be displayed in a new browser window without navigation controls. Let's select the Parent option.

The Menu Location field is used to specify the menu name under which this menu item will be displayed (the current menu name you are dealing with appears by default). Because you want the menu item to appear under the Electronic Products menu, set the Menu Location field to Electronic Products.

In the Parent Item field, you can specify whether the menu item is a top-level menu item or a submenu of an existing menu item. Because there is no other menu item present in this menu and it is the first menu item of this menu, there is only one option: Menu Item Root (the current menu item will appear at the top of the hierarchy, not as a submenu).

■ **Note**   When you define a parent item, the menu items will appear in a drop-down format.

Set the Status field to Published (the default) to make this menu item visible on the web site. Set the Access field to Public to allow all visitors to access the menu item.

The Menu Item Type combo box in Figure 7-5 enables you to select the menu item type, which decides the type of content that the menu item will display. The Menu Item Type combo box will display the available menu item type categories, as shown in Figure 7-6.

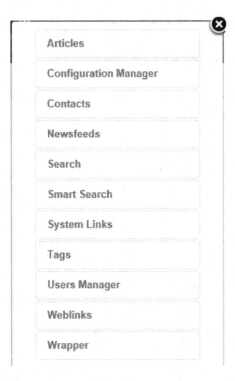

Figure 7-6. *Categories of menu item types*

A brief description of the menu item type categories follows:

- **Articles:** Designed to display article categories and articles that include featured articles and archived articles

- **Configuration Manager:** Designed to display site configuration and template parameter options

- **Contacts:** Designed to display contact categories and contact(s) that may be featured contacts or contacts of specific category

- **Newsfeeds:** Designed to display newsfeed categories and newsfeed(s) of a specific category.

- **Search:** Designed to display a search form and search results

- **Smart Search:** Designed to display a search form with extra options for precise search results

- **System Links:** Designed to display menu headings, link to external or internal URL, text separator and alias to another menu item

- **Tags:** Designed to display list of tags, items that are tagged and items with specific tags

- **Users Manager:** Designed to display forms that can be used to register a user, enable a user to login, display and edit a user's profile, reset a user's password and reminds username (if any user forgets the username)

- **Weblinks:** Designed to display web link categories, web links in a category, and submit a web link

- **Wrapper:** Designed to display a layout that displays an external web site inside the page of your web site

Let's start with the first option: Articles.

Articles

When the Articles link is selected, it expands to display the options shown in Figure 7-7.

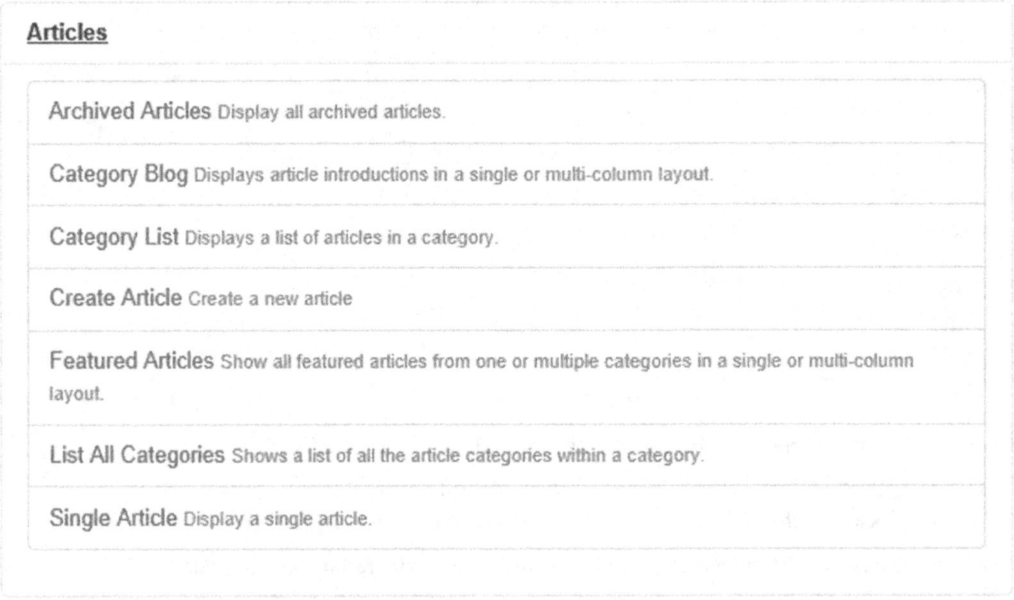

Articles

Archived Articles Display all archived articles.

Category Blog Displays article introductions in a single or multi-column layout.

Category List Displays a list of articles in a category.

Create Article Create a new article

Featured Articles Show all featured articles from one or multiple categories in a single or multi-column layout.

List All Categories Shows a list of all the article categories within a category.

Single Article Display a single article.

Figure 7-7. *Menu item types in the Articles node*

Table 7-3 briefly describes the options in the Articles node.

Table 7-3. *Articles Node Options*

Option	Description
Archived Articles	Displays a list of archived articles.
Category Blog	Displays an introduction to the articles from the specified category in different layouts.
Category List	Displays a list of the articles in the specified category.
Create Article	Used for creating articles from the front end of the site.
Featured Articles	Displays a list of articles that are marked as featured in different layouts.
List All Categories	Displays all article categories in a site.
Single Article	Displays the specified article.

Let's look at each option in detail. To see what each menu item type does, you don't have to create a new menu item for each one. Instead, you can create a menu item of one menu item type, observe its impact from the front end, edit it to set it to the next menu item type in the option list, and so on. Before creating a menu item of any type, however, you need to do a little groundwork.

For example, the Archived Articles menu item type is meant to display the articles that are archived (temporarily removed) from the web site. So, until you archive some articles from the web site, this menu item type will not show any effect. So click the Save & Close button from the toolbar to save whatever information you have entered for the new menu item (except the selection of the desired menu item type).

Archived Articles

This menu item type is used to show the list of articles that have been archived. "Archived" means that the contents are not currently required and are in a stored format. These articles can be searched by date. To try it out, open the Article Manager (Content ➤ Article Manager).

In the Article Manager, you see a list of articles, some provided by Joomla and others created by you. Select a few articles in the list and click the Archive icon in the toolbar to change the status of the articles from the published state to the archived state. Let's select the three articles that are marked in Figure 7-8 and archive them.

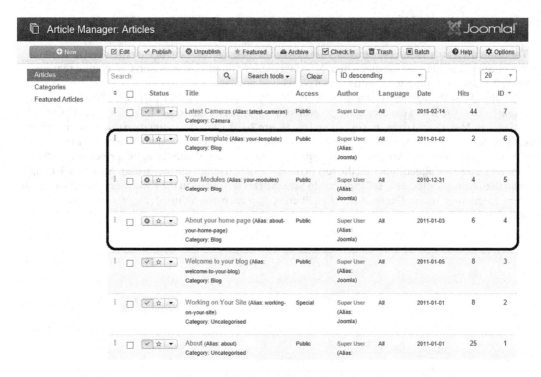

Figure 7-8. *Changing the state of three articles from published to archived*

The archived articles become invisible from the list of articles that are displayed in the Article Manager list (see Figure 7-9). It also means that the selected articles will not be displayed on the web site (by default) and are in the archived state.

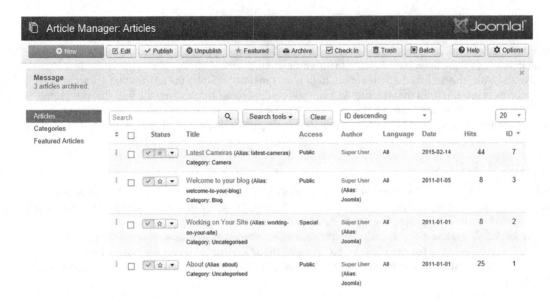

Figure 7-9. *Three archived articles are not visible on the Article Manager list*

These archived articles can be seen from the front end when a menu item of type Archived Articles is selected by the visitor. Let's set the menu item New Electronics Among Cameras And Cell Phones that you created in the Electronic Products menu to display archived articles.

Open the Menu Manager by selecting the Menu Manager option. Open the Electronic Products menu by clicking its title. You'll find the menu item, New Electronics Among Cameras And Cell Phones in the Menu Manager: Menu Items page that opens up (see Figure 7-10). Click the menu item title to open it in edit mode. Click the Menu Item Type combo box (refer to Figure 7-5) to select the menu item type. From the list of menu item types, select the Articles node to expand it and you'll see all the menu item types in it (refer to Figure 7-7). You have already entered the rest of the information about the menu item. So after selecting the menu item type, click the Save & Close icon to save the changes made in the menu item. Your new menu item, New Electronics Among Cameras And Cell Phones, appears in the Menu Manager: Menu Items list, as shown in Figure 7-10.

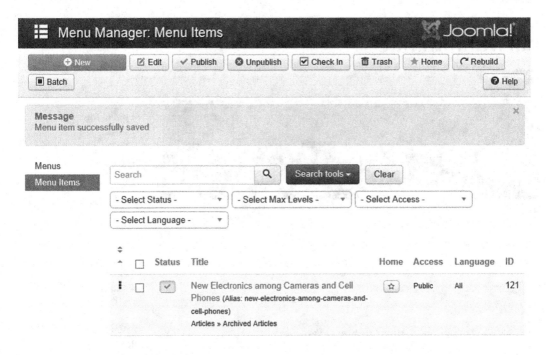

Figure 7-10. New menu item displays

After refreshing the front end of the site, you see the new menu item, New Electronics Among Cameras And Cell Phones, at the bottom of the site (because you have chosen the footer position for its module). When selected, the menu item will display a list of all the articles that have been archived (because the menu item type chosen was Archived Articles), as shown in Figure 7-11.

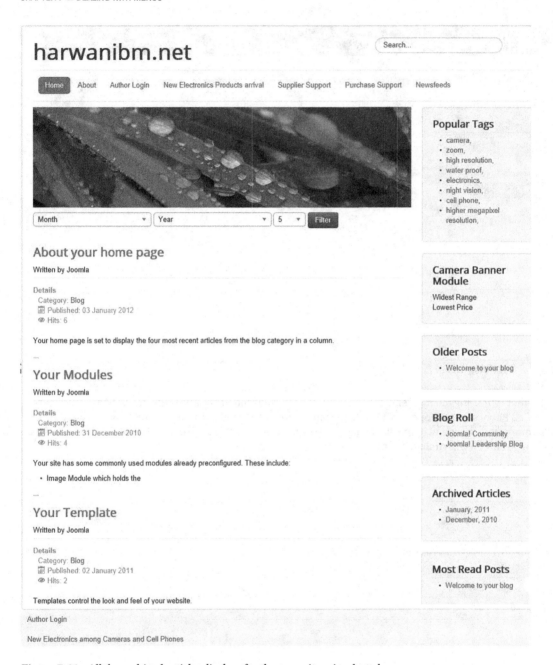

Figure 7-11. *All the archived articles displayafterthe menu item is selected*

You can also see all the archived articles from a particular date by using the drop-down boxes.

Moving Menu Items

Although the menu item that you just created is part of the Electronic Products menu, you can move it to another menu easily. Moving and copying menu items can be done by using the Batch button in the toolbar. Select the check box of the menu item to move (New Electronics Among Cameras And Cell Phones) and click the Batch button from the toolbar above (see Figure 7-12).

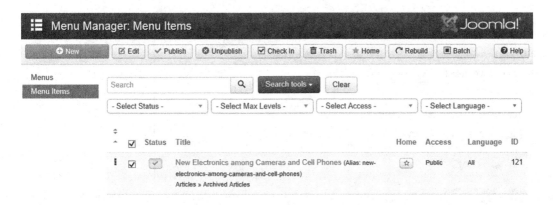

Figure 7-12. *Menu item New Electronics Among Cameras And Cell Phones is checked*

A batch process dialog box pops up, as shown in Figure 7-13. Select the Move radio button found at the bottom. From the Select Menu Or Parent For Move/Copy combo box, select the menu to which you want the selected menu item to be moved.

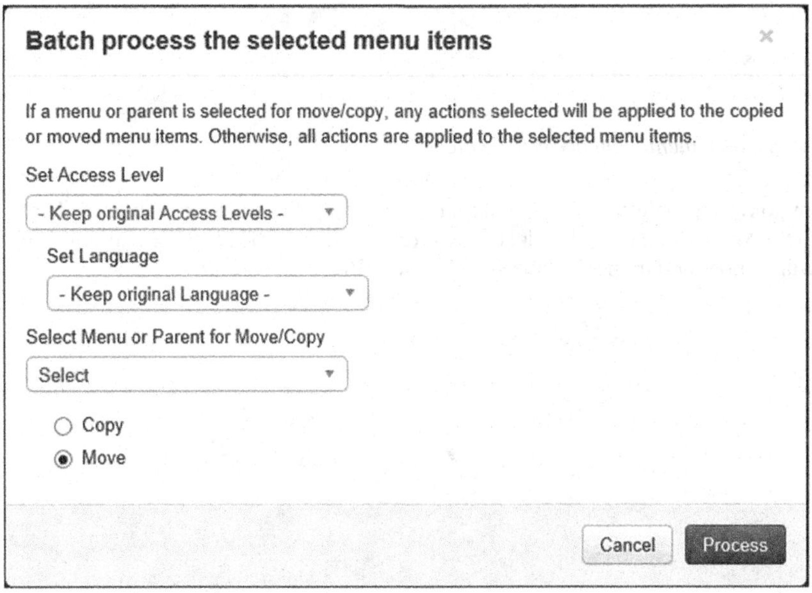

Batch process the selected menu items ×

If a menu or parent is selected for move/copy, any actions selected will be applied to the copied or moved menu items. Otherwise, all actions are applied to the selected menu items.

Set Access Level

- Keep original Access Levels - ▼

Set Language

- Keep original Language - ▼

Select Menu or Parent for Move/Copy

Select ▼

○ Copy
◉ Move

Cancel   Process

Figure 7-13. *Dialog box for batch processing tasks*

Assuming that you want to move the selected menu item to the Main Menu, select the option Add To This Menu, found below the Main Menu heading from the Select Menu Or Parent For Move/Copy combo box (see Figure 7-14).

Figure 7-14. *Selecting menu to which menu item needs to be moved*

After selecting the menu to which you want the menu item to be moved, click the Process button. The menu item will be moved to the Main Menu from the Electronic Products menu. The Electronics menu will become empty, and there will be no menu items in it now (see Figure 7-15).

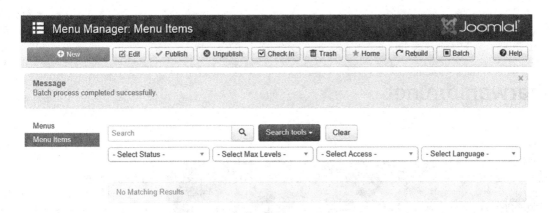

Figure 7-15. *Electronics menu has no menu items*

After opening the Main Menu, you will find the New Electronics Among Cameras And Cell Phones menu item (that was moved from the Electronics menu), confirming the successful move of the menu item, as shown marked in Figure 7-16.

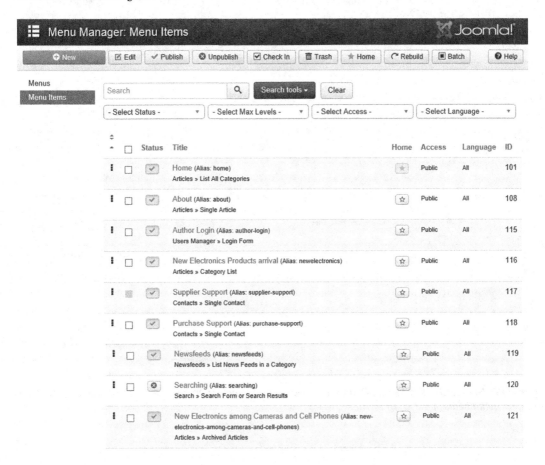

Figure 7-16. *New Electronics Among Cameras And Cell Phones menu item moved to the Main Menu*

From the front end of the web site, you can see that the menu item appears along with other menu items of the Main Menu (see Figure 7-17). It was previously found at the bottom of the site (refer to Figure 7-11).

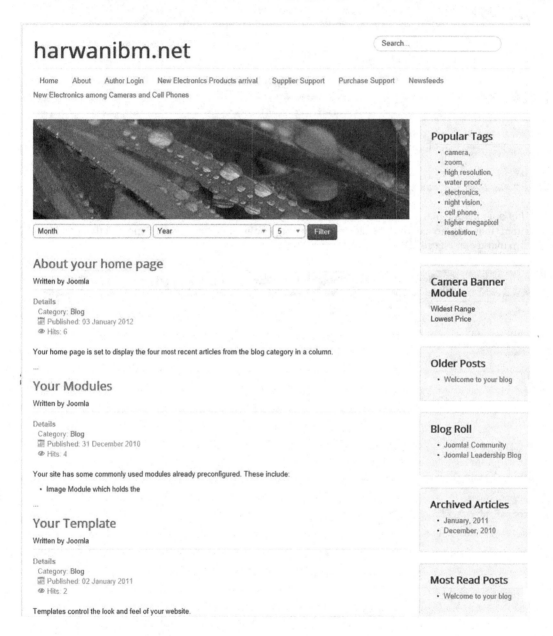

Figure 7-17. *New Electronics Among Cameras And Cell Phones menu item appears at the top of the site, along with other menu items of the Main Menu*

Doing the Groundwork for Other Menu Item Types

To understand how the other menu item types (Article, Category, and so on) work, it will help to do some preparation. Recall that you created a category named Electronics with a category called Camera in Chapter 3. You also created an article in that category called "Latest Cameras." For this exercise, you need to create one more subcategory in the Electronics category: Cell Phone. Also, you'll create the following three articles in the Camera subcategory:

- "Latest Cameras" (already created in Chapter 3)
- "Web Cams — Video Chatting"
- "Cameras for Safari"

Each article will contain some short text and an image (an example is shown in Figure 7-18).

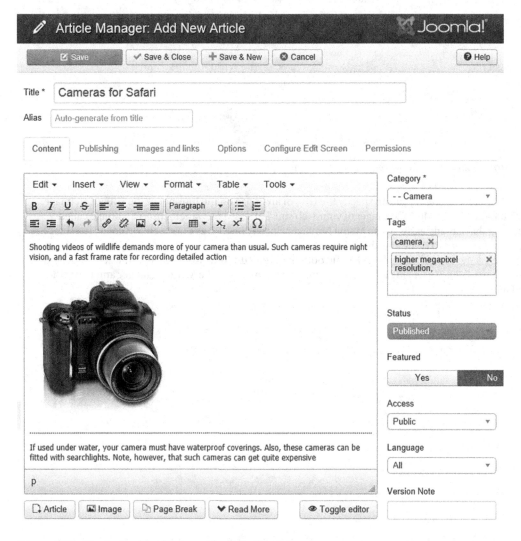

Figure 7-18. Contents of the "Cameras for Safari" article

■ **Note**   The dotted line in the article shown in Figure 7-18 designates the page break.

You can write any text and insert any image; just don't forget to load the images into the Media Manager first. There are two ways to insert images into the article: one way is using the Image icon in the tools provided at the top, and the other is using the Image button at the bottom left. The Image icon in the toolbar, when selected, displays the screen shown in Figure 7-19.

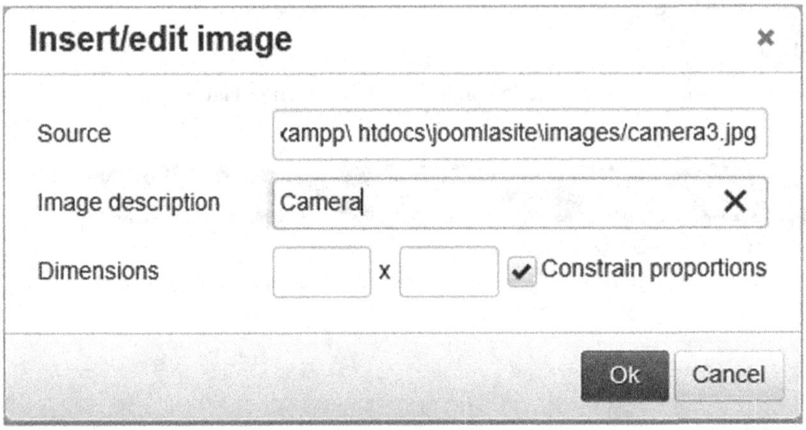

Figure 7-19. Dialog box to insert/edit image from a URL

In the Image URL field, you can specify the URL of an image on the Internet or the URL of an image already uploaded to the Media Manager of your web site. Let's say you want to insert an image called camera3.jpg that already exists in the Media Manager. Specify its URL as c:\xampp\ htdocs\joomlasite\ images/stories/camera3.jpg and then click the Insert button.

If you click the Image button found at the bottom of the Add New Article page, you'll see the screen shown in Figure 7-20. This dialog box helps to upload new images to the Media Manager and insert the selected image into the article.

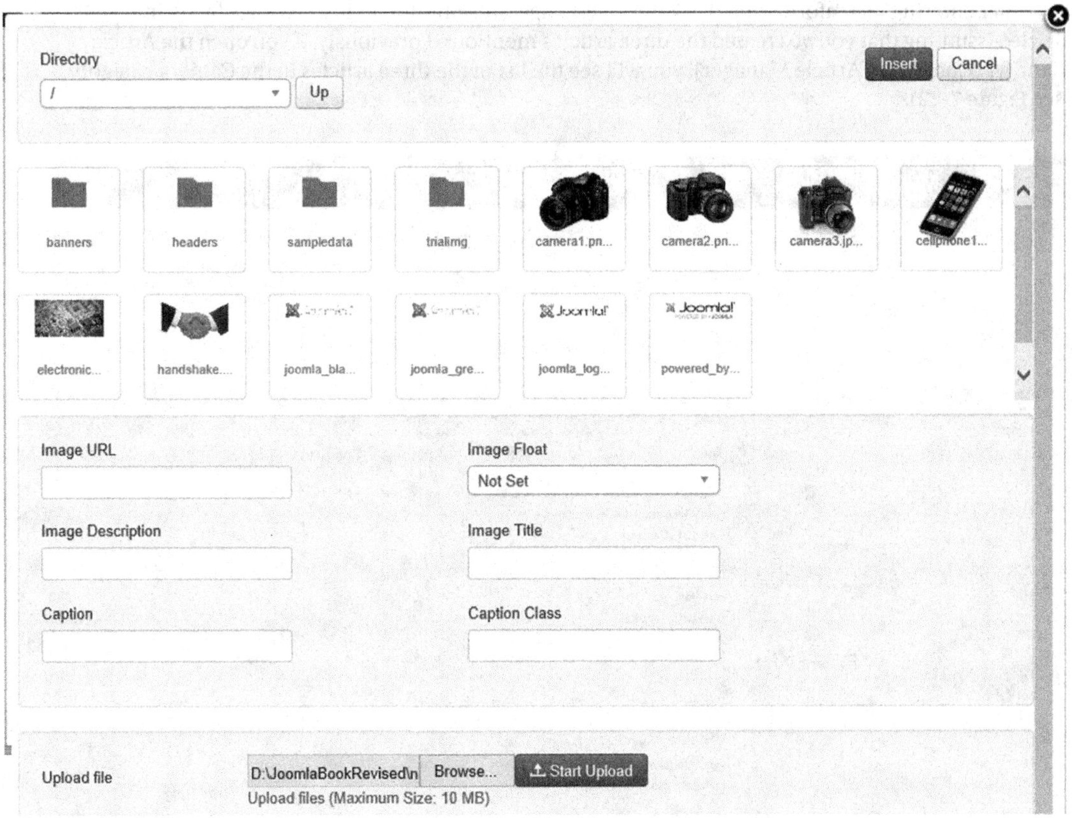

Figure 7-20. *Inserting an image from the Media Manager*

Select the camera3.jpg image and click the Insert link to insert the image into your article. You can also click the Browse button to select an image on your local disk drive and click Start Upload to upload the image to the Media Manager. Additionally, you can insert a page break by clicking the Insert Page Break icon at the bottom (refer to Figure 7-18). If you do this, you'll see a dialog box like the one shown in Figure 7-21. You can specify the page title for the second page and also the alias to be used for SEF URLs.

Figure 7-21. *Inserting a page break*

After entering this information, click the Insert Page Break button to insert a page break into your article. Assuming that you've created the three articles mentioned previously, if you open the Article Manager (Content ➤ Article Manager), you will see the list of the three articles in the Camera category (see Figure 7-22).

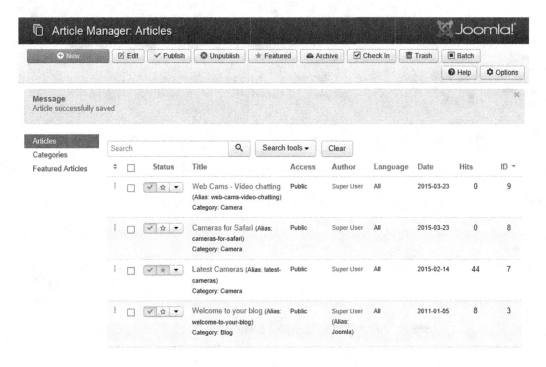

Figure 7-22. *Three articles of the Camera category*

Assuming that you have created one more subcategory called Cell Phone in the Electronics category, create three articles with the following titles in the Cell Phone category:

- "CDMA Cell Phones"
- "Java Supported Cell Phone"
- "Autotracking Cell Phones"

For example, the article "CDMA Cell Phones" might contain the information shown in Figure 7-23.

Figure 7-23. *The contents of the article "CDMA Cell Phones"*

If you open the Article Manager (Content Article Manager), you'll find that there are three articles in the Cell Phone category, as shown in Figure 7-24.

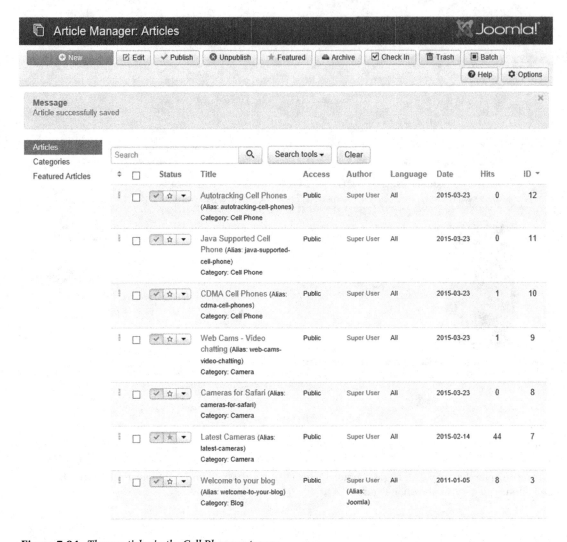

Figure 7-24. *Three articles in the Cell Phone category*

Now you have two article categories, Camera and Cell Phone, in the Electronics category, and each category has three articles in it. Let's go ahead and test the next menu item type: Single Article.

Single Article

This menu item type is used to display a single article. Upon selecting this menu item type, you'll see a form for specifying information, including the title, menu name, parent menu item, and so on. You can leave all the information the same as is shown in Figure 7-5.

The only thing you need to specify for this menu item type is the article name to be displayed. To do so, click the Select Article combo box, which will display a list of all available articles on your web site. Select the article "Latest Cameras" from the list, as shown in Figure 7-25. Then click the Save & Close icon to save the changes.

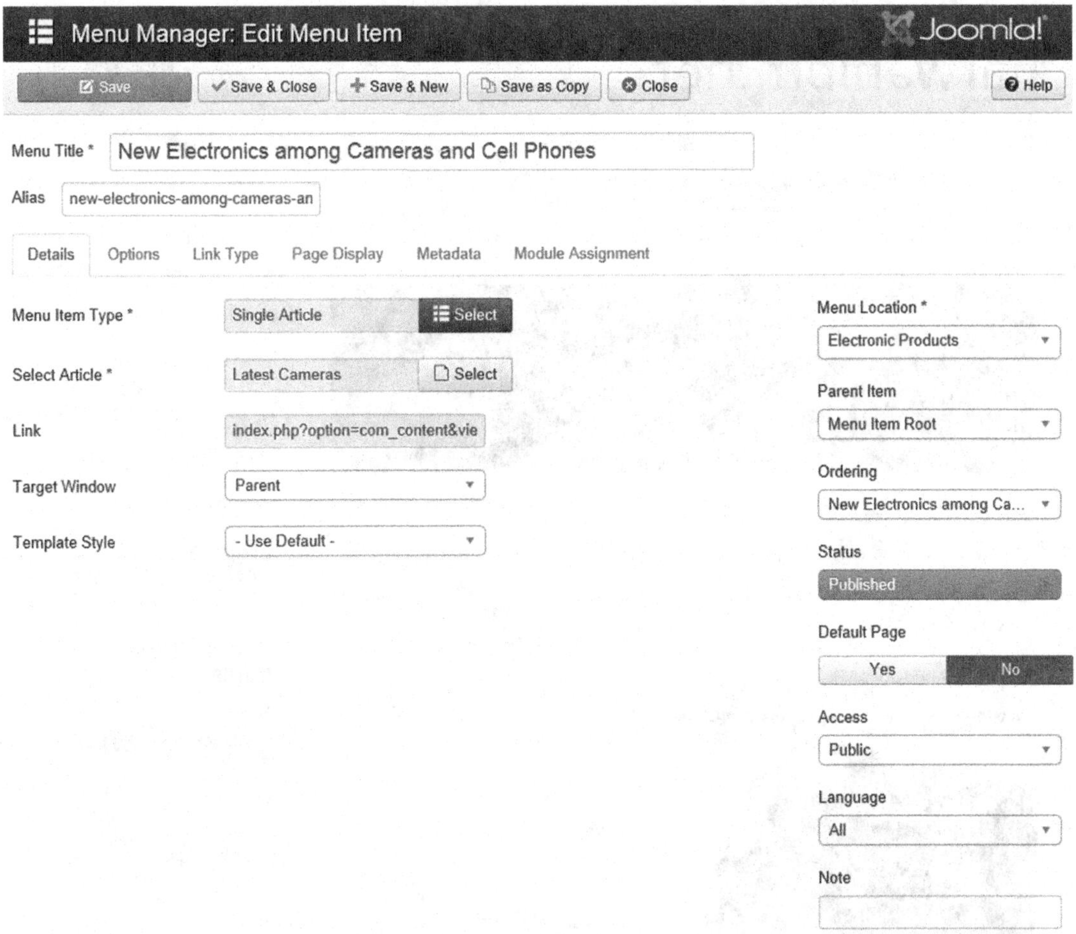

Figure 7-25. *Entering information for the menu item type Single Article*

Open the browser window pointing at your Joomla web site and click the Refresh button. This time, when you select the menu item New Electronics Among Cameras And Cell Phones, you'll see the contents of the article "Latest Cameras," as shown in Figure 7-26.

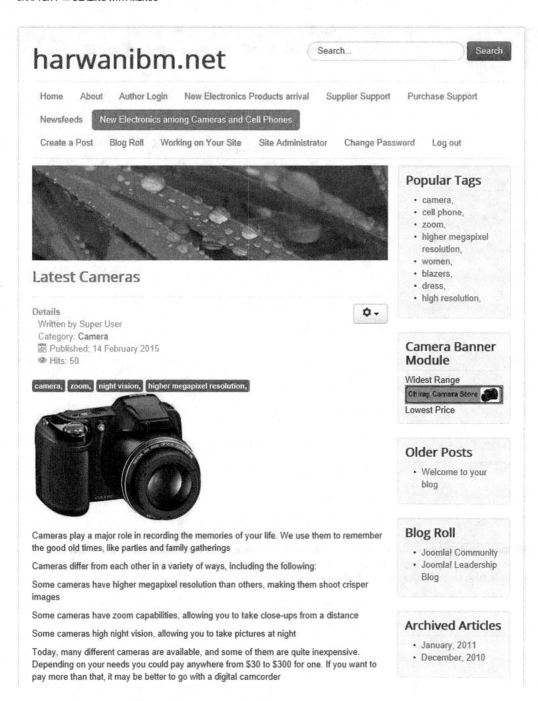

Figure 7-26. *Contents of the "Latest Cameras" article*

To see the usage of the different menu item types, you will be using the menu item just created: New Electronics Among Cameras And Cell Phones. After looking at the impact of each menu item type from the front end, you will open the same menu item (from the back end) in edit mode. That is, you will open the Menu Manager by selecting the Menu Manager option, click the Edit Menu Item(s) icon in the Menu Item(s) column in the Electronic Products row to open the Menu Manager: Edit Menu Item page, select the Electronics among Cameras and Cell Phones menu item to open it in Edit mode, click the Menu Item Type combo box to display the list of all menu item types available, and finally select the menu item type that you want to apply.

Create Article

This menu item type allows users in the Author, Publisher, and Editor groups to submit an article. Members of the Registered or Public groups will not be able to submit articles, and will see an error message when they select a menu item of this type.

To understand this better, let's create a user who belongs to the Author group with the help of the User Manager. The User Manager can be invoked by either selecting Users ➤ User Manager or clicking the User Manager icon from the control panel. In the User Manager, click the New icon from the toolbar to create a new user. You'll see a screen like the one shown in Figure 7-27.

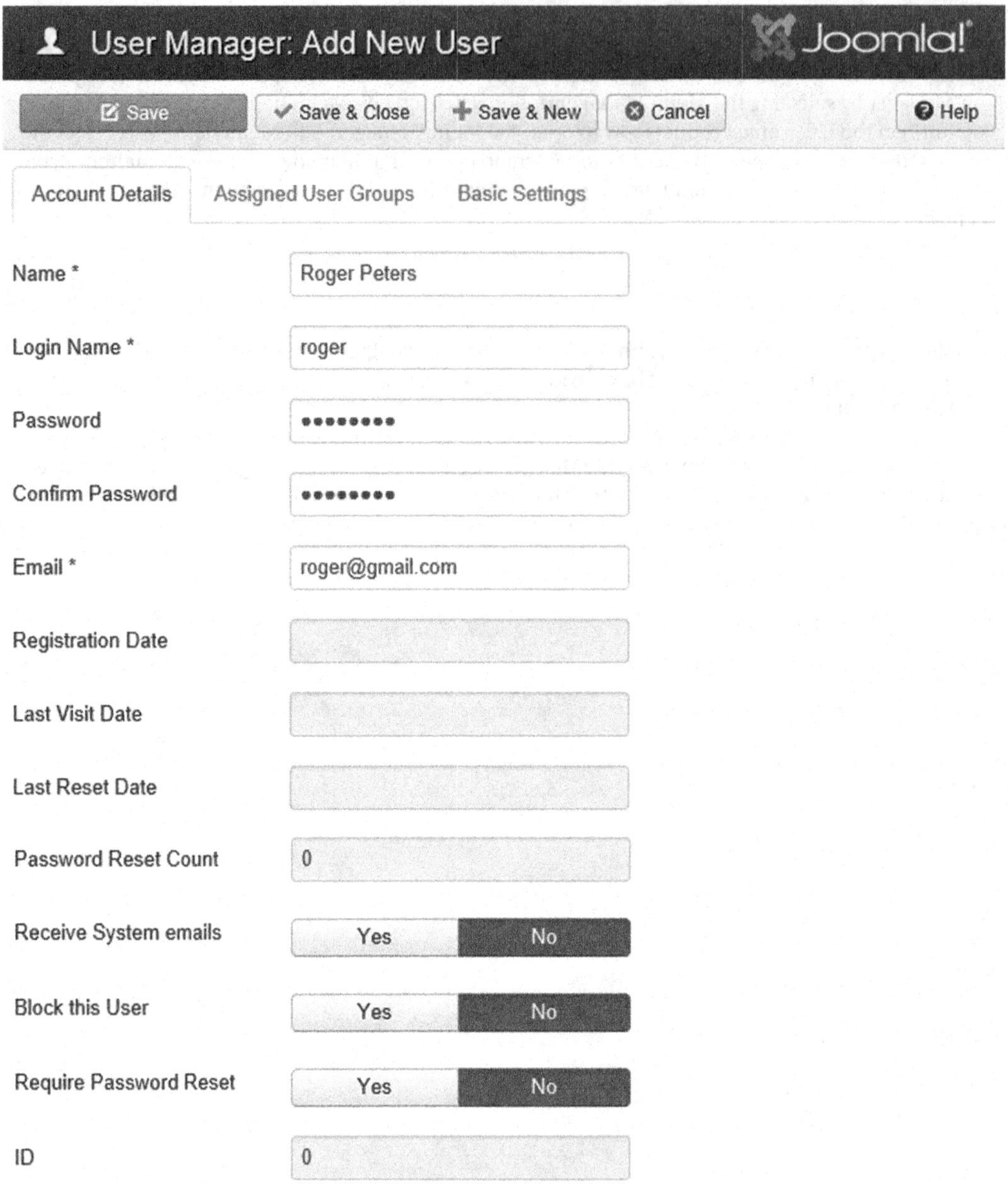

Figure 7-27. *Creating a new user*

For Name, enter **Roger Peters**, and for Login Name (with which your user will login to your web site), enter **roger**. Enter the passwords in Password and Confirm Password fields. Enter a valid e-mail address in the Email field. Open the Assigned User Groups tab and assign this user to the Author group. Keep the rest of the values at their defaults, and click the Save & Close icon on the toolbar to create this user.

The user Roger Peters will be created and will appear in the User Manager: Users page, as shown in Figure 7-28.

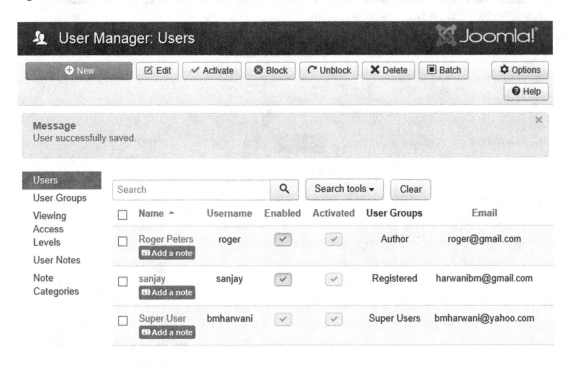

Figure 7-28. *Creating a new user: Roger Peters of the Author group*

Now open the New Electronics Among Cameras And Cell Phones menu item in edit mode. From the Select Article combo box (see Figure 7-29), select the Create Article menu item type option. Leave the values in the rest of the fields as is and click the Save & Close icon to save the changes.

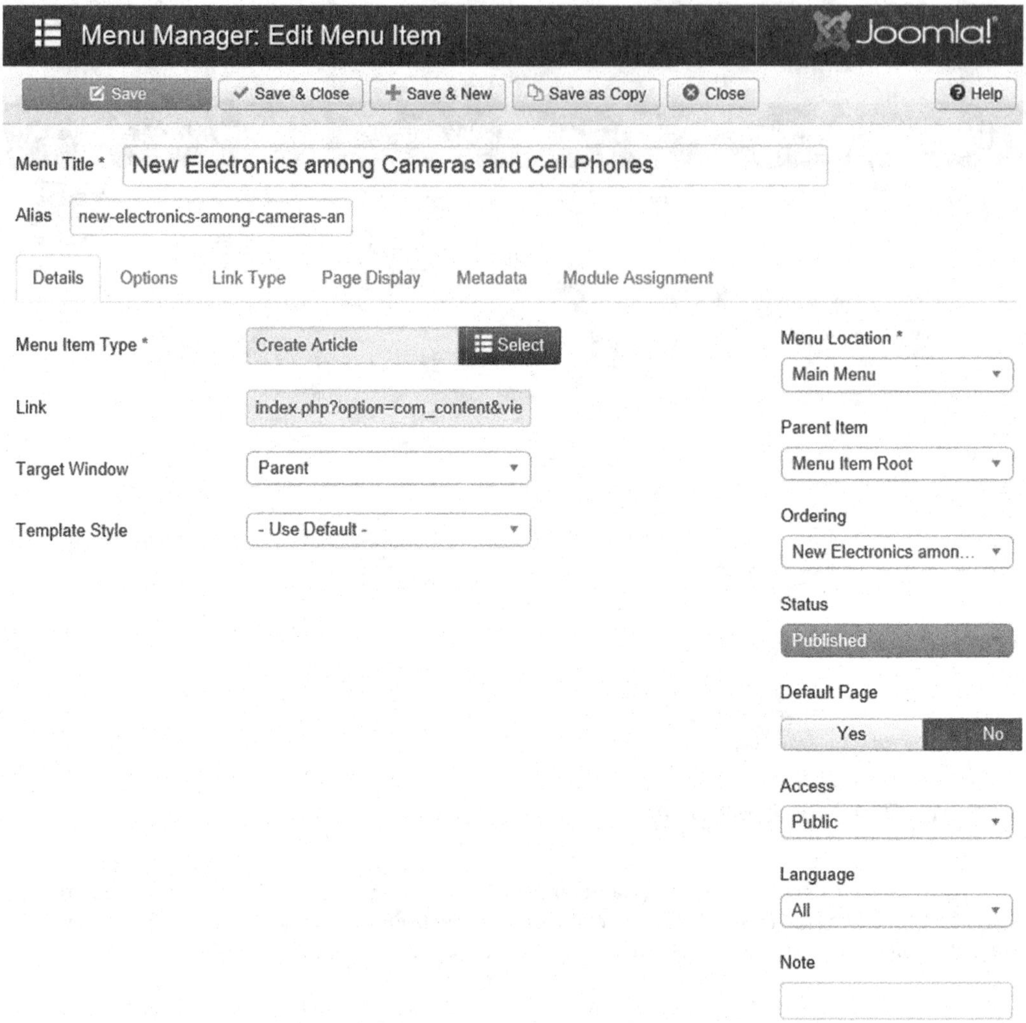

Figure 7-29. *Selecting the Create Article menu item type option*

From the front end of the web site, let new user roger log in your web site by entering the username and password, as shown in Figure 7-30.

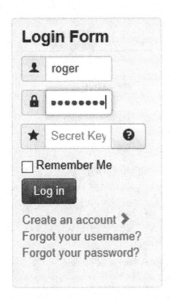

Figure 7-30. *User roger logging in to the web site*

After the user logs in, if the menu item New Electronics Among Cameras And Cell Phones is selected, you'll get an article submission form to fill in (as shown in Figure 7-31). You can specify the category and subcategory under which the article is to be published, as well as the category of users for the article, metadata, keywords, and other information.

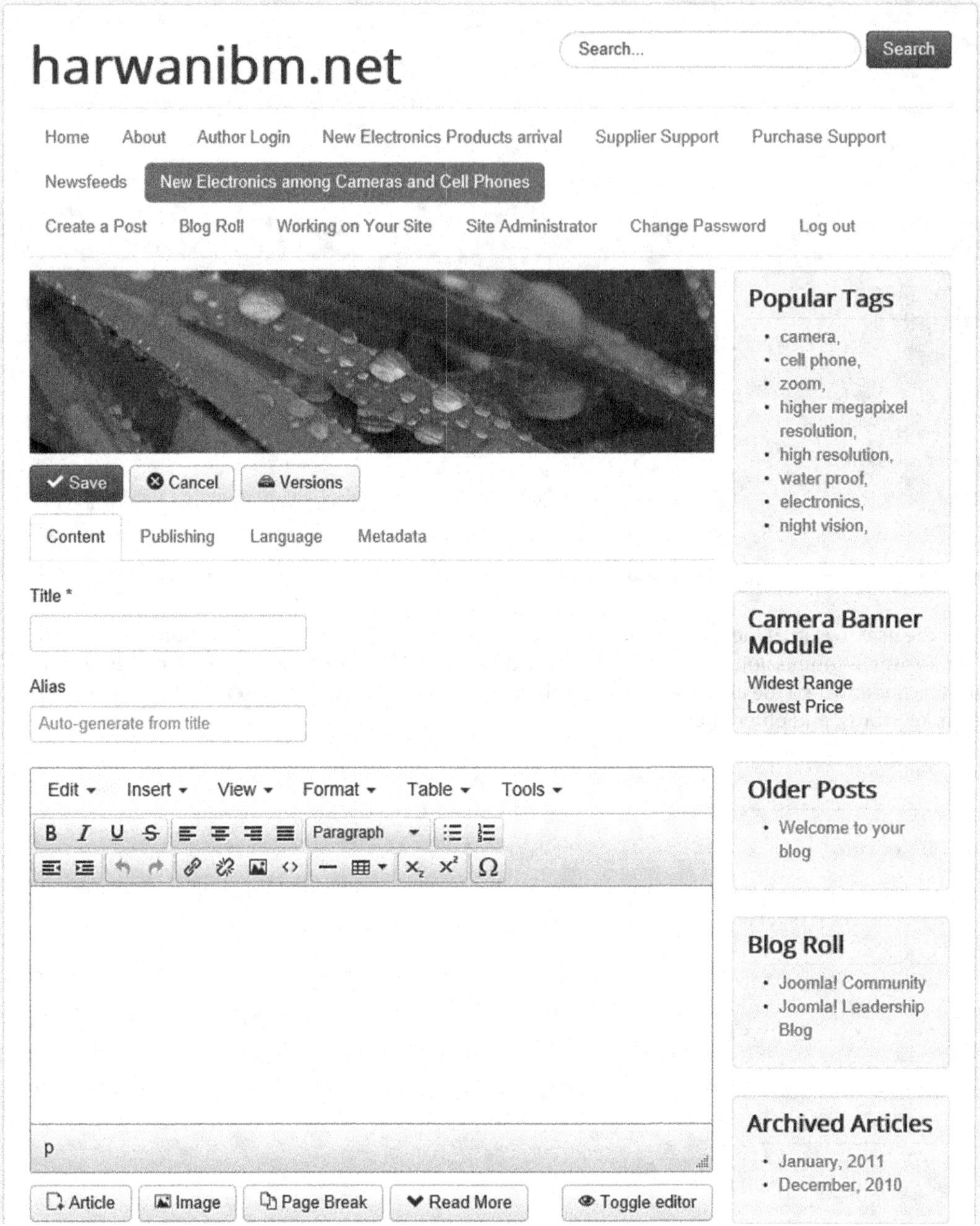

Figure 7-31. *Article submission form*

Category Blog

This menu item type is used for displaying articles of a particular category in blog layout. Blog layout consists of three main areas: the leading area, the intro area, and the links area, as illustrated in Figure 7-32.

Figure 7-32. *The three main areas of a blog layout: leading, intro, and links*

Articles displayed in the leading area use full display width and are shown in one column. Articles displayed in the intro area may appear in one, two, or three columns, depending on the value entered in the #Columns field of the Blog layout tab. The links area is used for displaying links to articles that couldn't be displayed on the first page.

Just open the New Electronics Among Cameras And Cell Phones menu item in edit mode; from the Select Article combo box, select the Category Blog menu item type option, as shown in Figure 7-33. From the Choose A Category combo box, select Camera to display the articles in the Camera subcategory of the Electronics category.

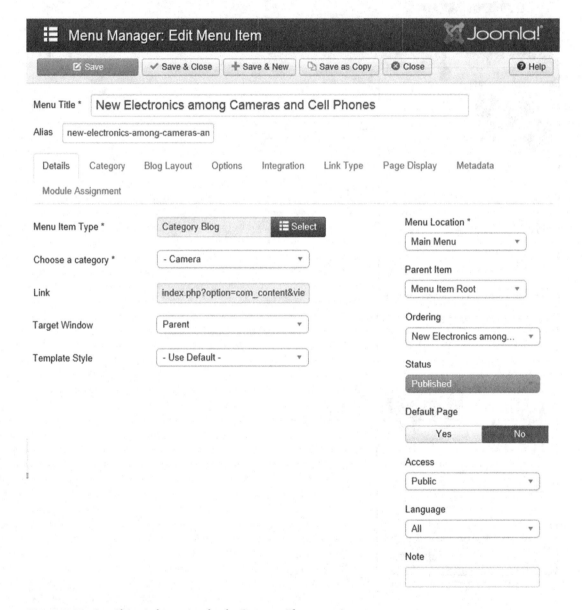

Figure 7-33. *Specifying information for the Category Blog menu item type*

To determine the number of articles to be displayed in the leading, intro, and links area, select the Blog Layout tab. You see the fields to determine the count of articles in different areas of the blog, as shown in Figure 7-34. The #Leading Articles field is for specifying the number of articles that you want to take up the full width of the main display area. Set it to **1** because you want one article to take up the full width. If you want all articles to appear in two or more columns, enter **0**. In the #Intro Articles field, specify the number of articles to be displayed after the leading article(s). Set its value to **4** because you want four articles to appear after the leading article.

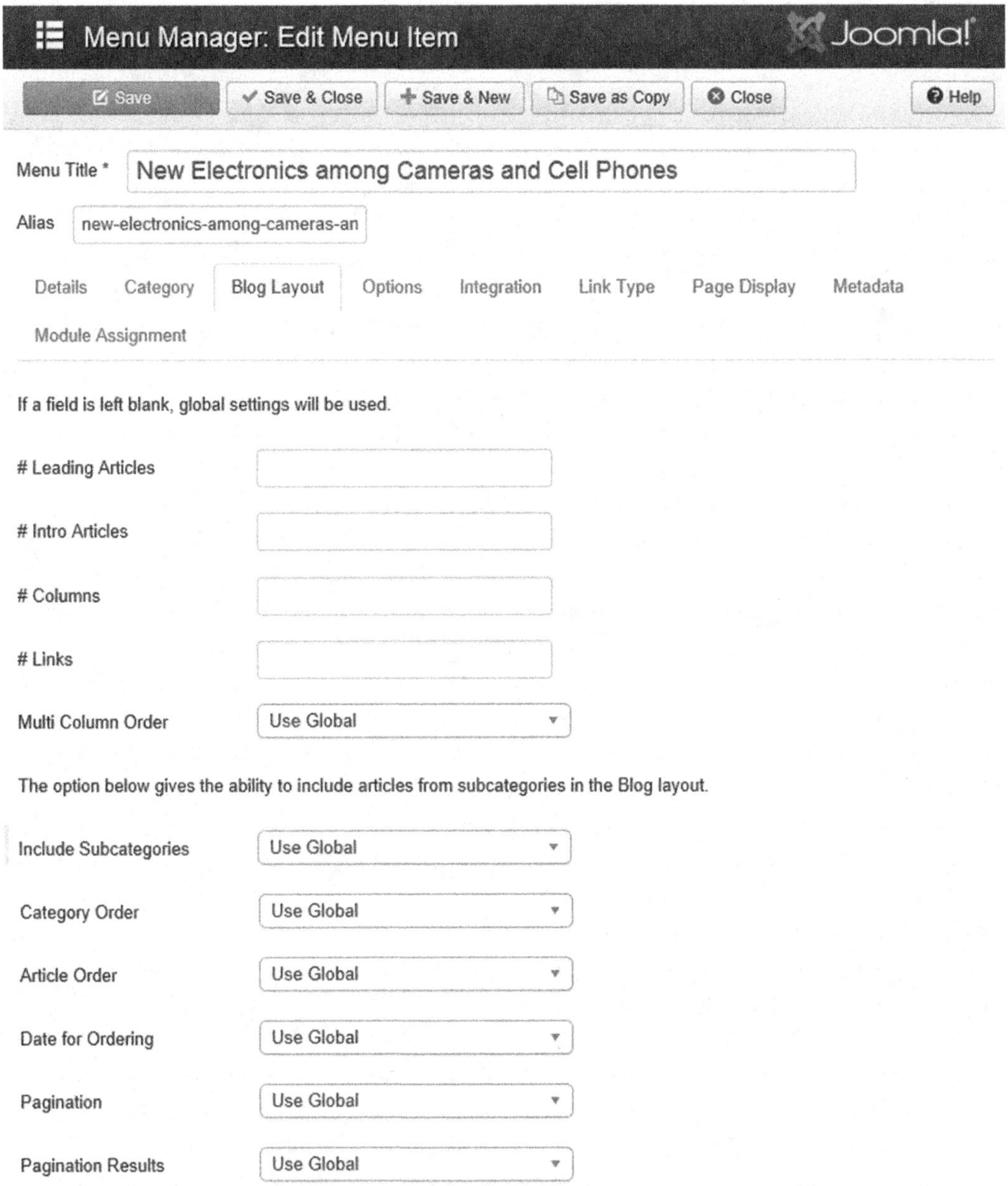

Figure 7-34. *Determining the number of articles to be displayed in different areas of the blog*

In the #Columns field, specify how many columns the number of articles specified in the #Intro field are to be displayed in. That is, if you enter 2 here, four articles will be displayed in two columns. In the #Links field, specify the number of links to be displayed in the links area of the page. This field is usually used when there are more articles than can fit on the first page of the blog layout. Set it to **4** so that if any of the four articles don't fit, they can appear as links.

After specifying the information, open your Joomla web site and refresh it. You should find that the articles in the Camera category are displayed in the Category Blog, as shown in Figure 7-35. In the figure, there are no entries in the links area because all three articles in the Camera category are visible in this layout (i.e., there are none that could not be displayed).

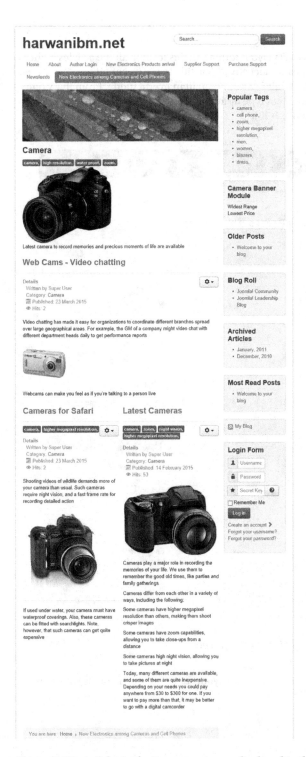

Figure 7-35. *Articles in the Camera category displayed in the Category Blog*

Category List

This menu item type is used for displaying articles in list layout format. In this format, all the articles in the category are displayed in a list from which a visitor can select any article title to see its contents.

Open the New Electronics Among Cameras And Cell Phones menu item in edit mode. From the Menu Item Type combo box, select the Category List menu item type option. From the Choose A Category combo box, select Cell Phone to display its articles (see Figure 7-36).

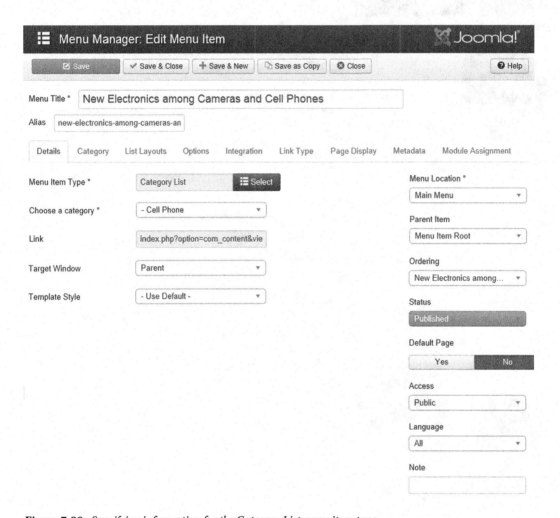

Figure 7-36. *Specifying information for the Category Listmenu item type*

To configure the Category List menu item type, click the List Layouts tab. You see the fields shown in Figure 7-37.

☰ Menu Manager: Edit Menu Item					✖ Joomla!

✏ Save	✔ Save & Close	➕ Save & New	❏ Save as Copy	✖ Close	❓ Help

Menu Title * **New Electronics among Cameras and Cell Phones**

Alias new-electronics-among-cameras-an

Details   Category   **List Layouts**   Options   Integration   Link Type   Page Display   Metadata

Module Assignment

Display Select   Use Global ▾

Filter Field   Use Global ▾

Table Headings   Use Global ▾

Show Date   Use Global ▾

Date Format   [   ]

Show Hits in List   Use Global ▾

Show Author in List   Use Global ▾

Category Order   Use Global ▾

Article Order   Use Global ▾

Date for Ordering   Use Global ▾

Pagination   Use Global ▾

Pagination Results   Use Global ▾

Articles to List   10 ▾

Figure 7-37. *Configuring the Category List menu item type*

Set Table Headings to Show to display the column headings in the article list table. The Show Date field determines whether to display the date on which the article was created. In the Date Format field, specify the format in which you want to see the creation date for articles. Usually this field is left blank because the default date format is taken from the language file.

In the Filter Field drop-down list, specify the field name you prefer to be used for filtering the articles. The options are Title, Author, and Hits. Set the value of this field to Title if you want the keyword entered in the Title Filter box to be searched among the titles of the articles (i.e., the articles with titles matching the keyword entered in the Title Filter box will be displayed). Leaving the values of other fields to their default, click the Save & Close icon to save the changes.

When you open your Joomla web site and click the menu item New Electronics Among Cameras And Cell Phones, the browser window will display the list of articles, as shown in Figure 7-38.

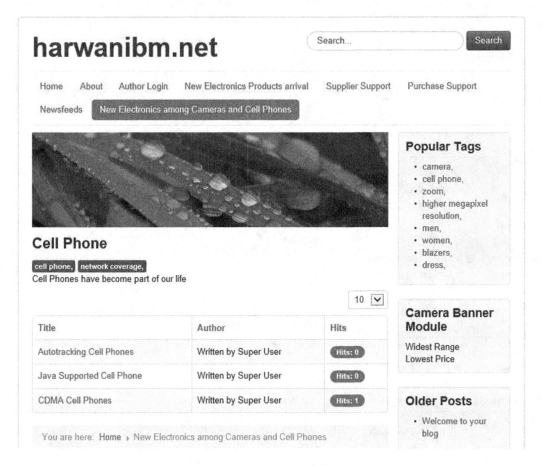

Figure 7-38. *Displaying the articles in the Cell Phone category in list layout*

You can see the contents of any article by selecting its title. For example, if you select "Autotracking Cell Phones," you'll see the contents shown in Figure 7-39.

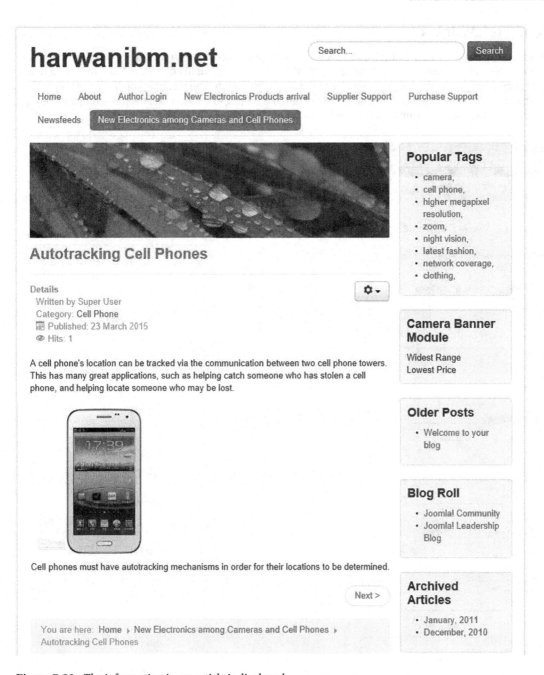

Figure 7-39. The information in an article is displayed

Featured Articles

This menu item type is used to display all articles set to be published on the front page in blog layout format. Open the New Electronics Among Cameras And Cell Phones menu item in edit mode. From the Menu Item Type combo box, select the Featured Articles menu item type option. The meanings of the rest of the fields are the same as earlier—and you also don't need to enter anything extra. Keep the default settings as they are and click the Save & Close icon to save the selected menu item type (see Figure 7-40).

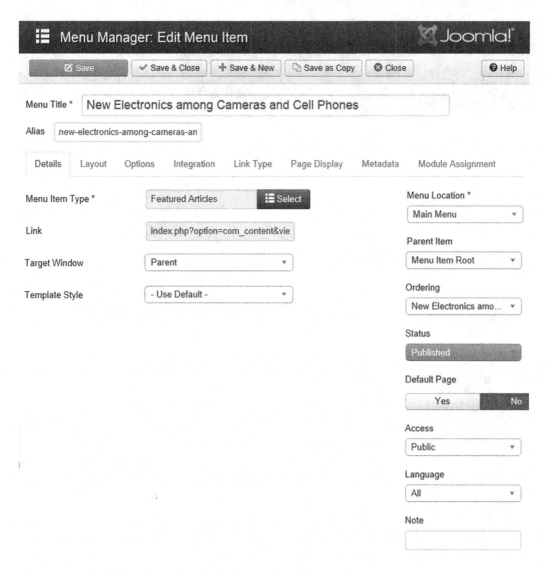

Figure 7-40. *Specifying information for the Featured Articles menu item type*

Before opening the Joomla web site to see the effect of this menu item type, you need to set the articles in both the Camera and Cell Phone categories to be published on the front page. Open the Article Manager by selecting Content ➤ Article Manager, and you'll find the articles in the Camera and Cell Phone categories, as shown in Figure 7-41. Because none of them is a featured article, none will be displayed on the front page.

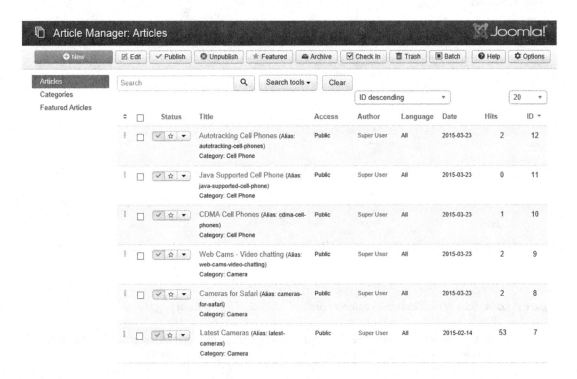

Figure 7-41. *Articles of the Electronics category*

To make these articles display on the front page, select the star icon of each article under the Status column. The white star will convert into a golden star to confirm that it is converted into a featured article, as shown in Figure 7-42.

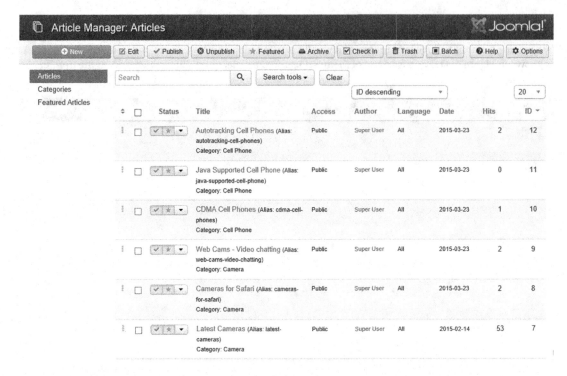

Figure 7-42. *Articles of the Electronics category are now published on the front page*

Now open the browser window to see the Joomla web site. You'll find that all the articles of the Camera and Cell Phone categories are displayed in blog layout format, as shown in Figure 7-43.

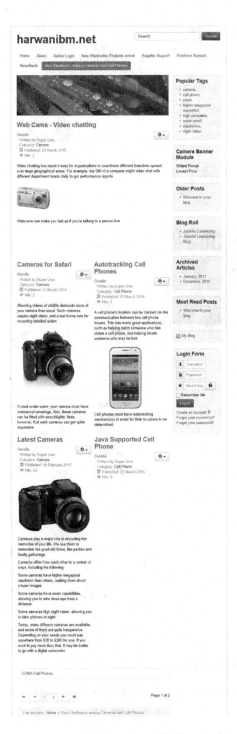

Figure 7-43. *Articles in the Cell Phone and Camera categories displayed on page 1 of the front page in blog layout format*

Because there are more articles than could be displayed on one page, links appear at the end, each pointing to an article that couldn't be displayed. Also, the links Start, Prev, 1, 2, 3, Next, and End appear at the bottom for navigating to the desired page. For example, if you select the 2 link, you'll see the articles on page 2, as shown in Figure 7-44.

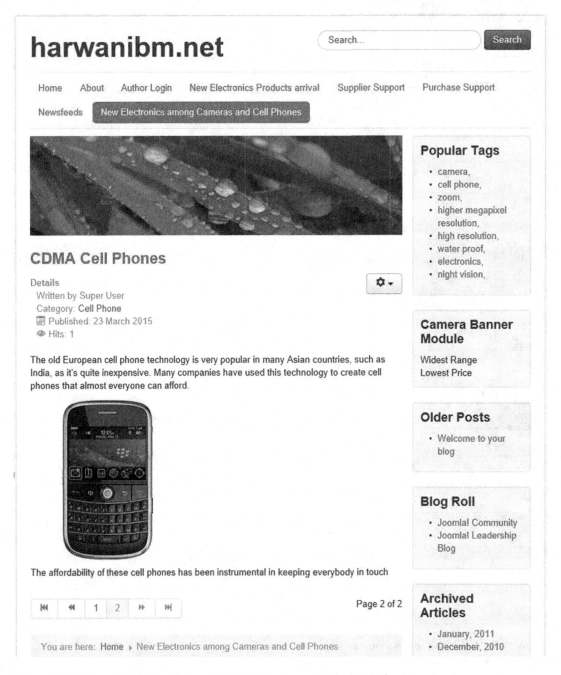

Figure 7-44. The article displayed on page 2 of the front page in blog layout format

List All Categories

Categories are used for structuring your content. You can group similar articles in one category, create a page that displays the intros of all the articles, and so on. This menu item type displays all the categories in the site. Each category, when selected, displays all the articles that belong to it in category list layout. Visitors can select any article title from the list to display its contents.

When you select this menu item type, you'll see a screen for entering information for the menu item. There is no need to make any changes except to select the category for which you want to see the subcategories. In this case, select the Electronics category, as shown in Figure 7-45.

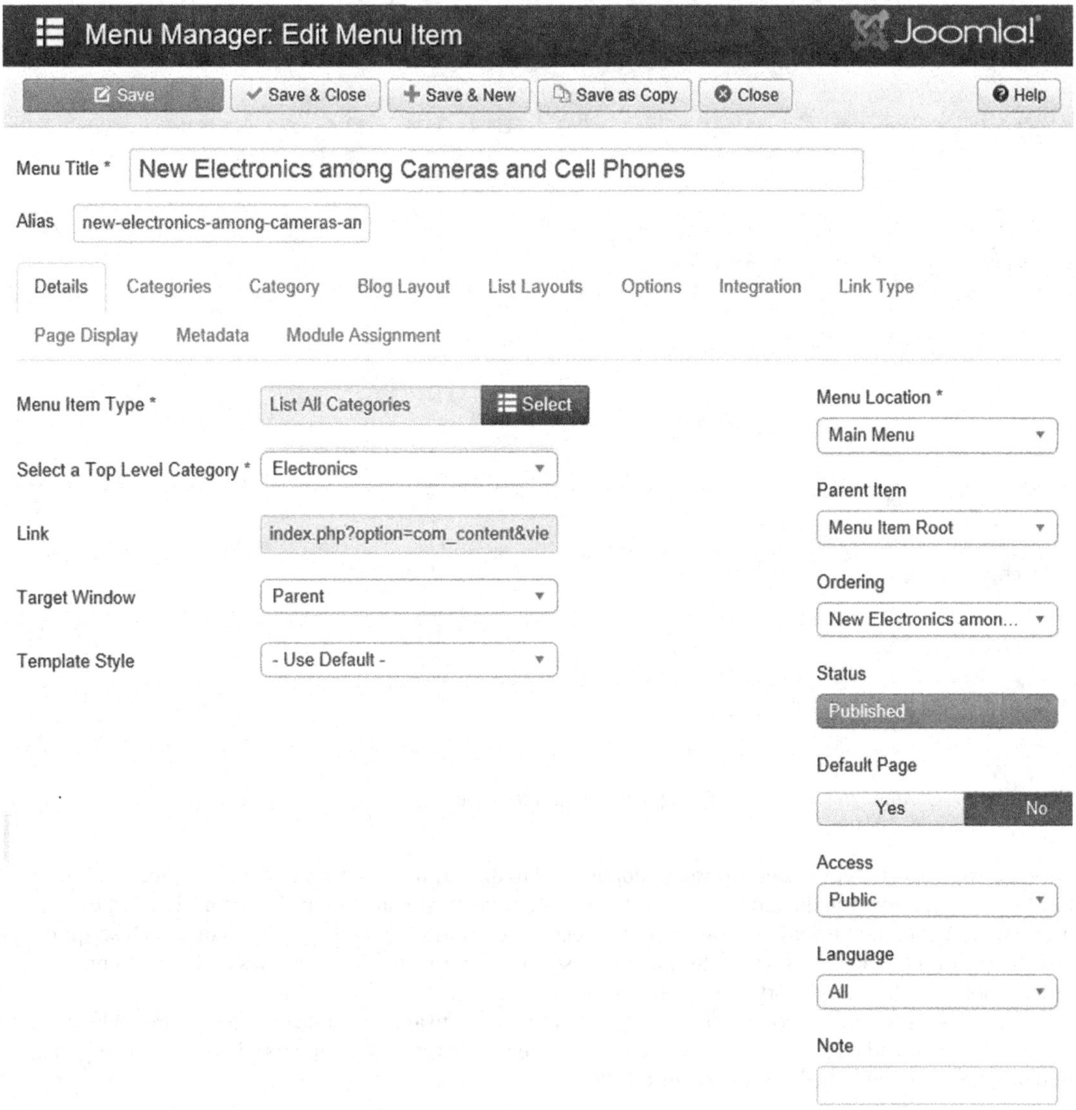

Figure 7-45. Entering information for the List All Categories menu item type

To configure the List All Categories menu item type, select the Categories tab. On selecting the Categories tab, you see the fields shown in Figure 7-46.

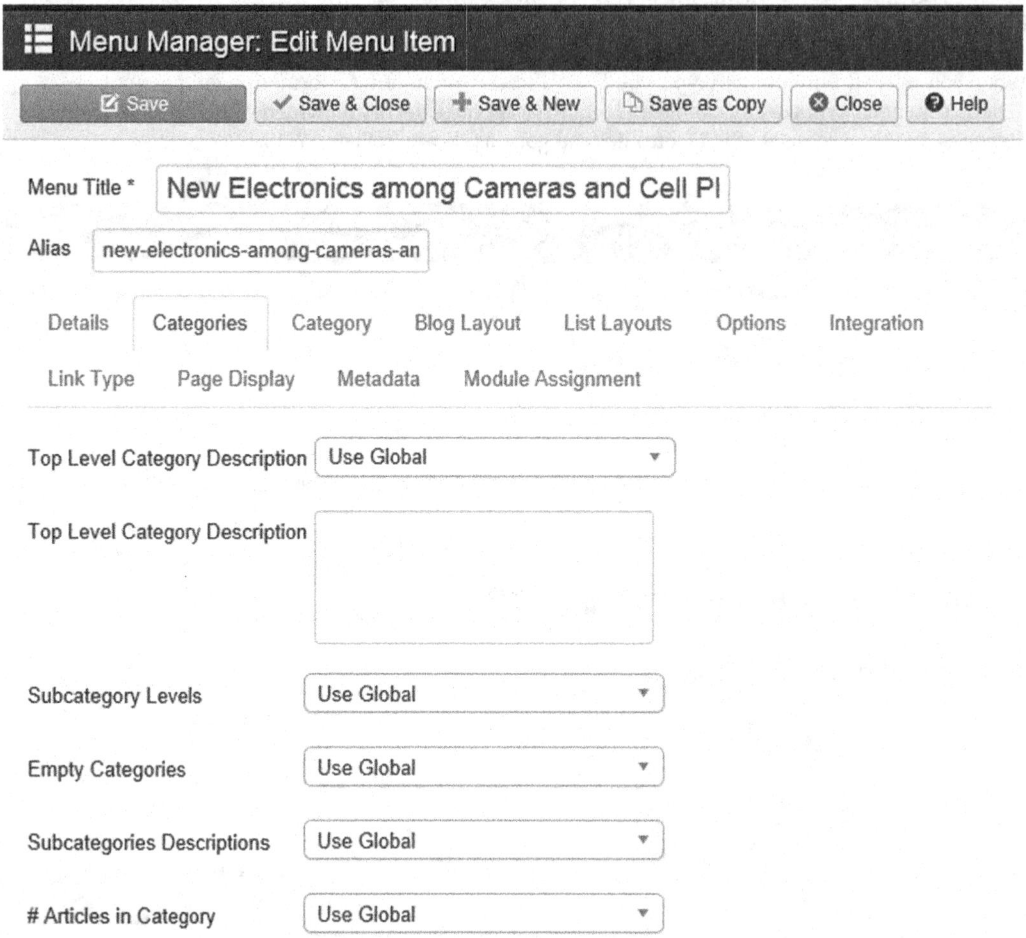

Figure 7-46. *Configuring the List All Categories menu item type*

The Top Level Category Description option is used to display the description of the category at the top of the page, under the title. In this case, set it to Hide because you are not interested in showing the description. If you set the field to Show, enter a category description in the Top Level Category Description box. Set the Empty Categories option to Hide because you want to hide the categories that contain no articles. Set #Articles In Category to Show to display the number of articles in each category.

In the browser window, when you open your Joomla web site and select the menu item New Electronics Among Cameras And Cell Phones, you'll find that the Electronics category appears with two subcategories under it: Camera and Cell Phone (see Figure 7-47).

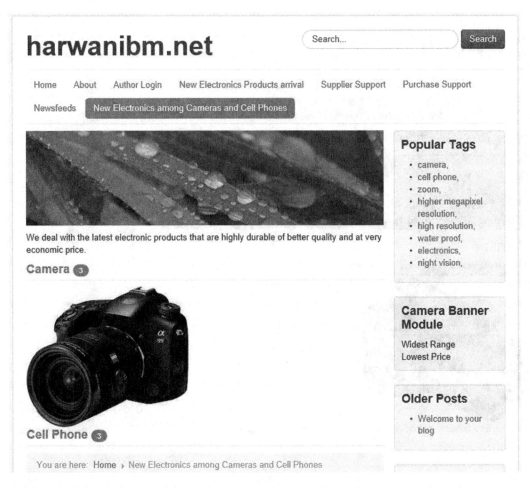

Figure 7-47. *The Electronics category with its two categories displayed*

If you select the Camera category, you'll see the list of articles under it, as shown in Figure 7-48.

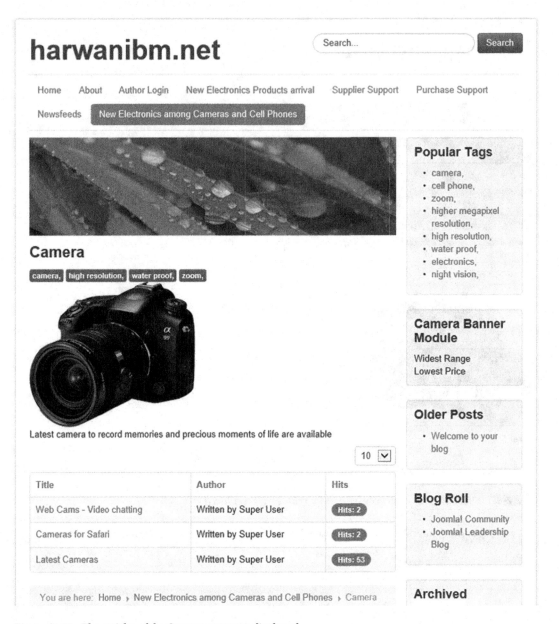

Figure 7-48. The articles of the Camera category displayed

If you select the Cell Phone category, you'll likewise see all the articles under it, as shown in Figure 7-49.

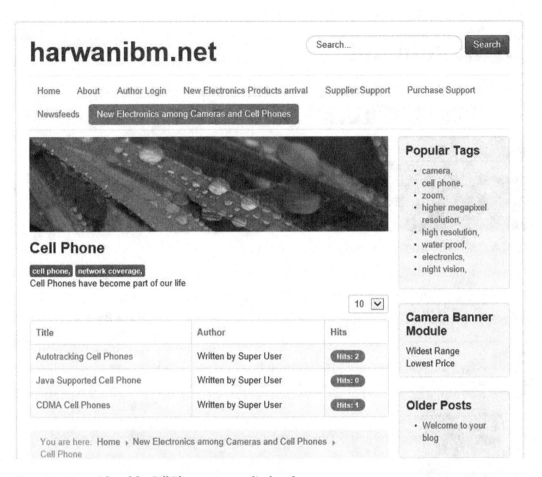

Figure 7-49. *Articles of the Cell Phone category displayed*

You can select the title of any article to see its contents. For example, if you select "CDMA Cell Phones," you'll see the contents displayed in Figure 7-50.

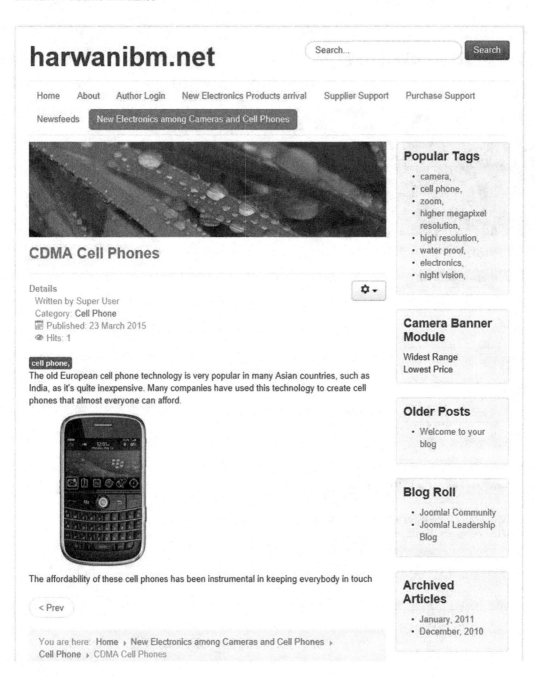

Figure 7-50. *Contents of the article displayed*

Configuration Manager

The Configuration Manager menu item type category displays the site global configuration option to the site administrator at the front end of the site. That is, a user can login and can modify or configure the site from the front end by using this menu item type category. This menu item type category has the following two menu item types (see Figure 7-51):

- **Display Site Configuration Options:** Shows fields to configure site settings
- **Display Template Options:** Shows fields to apply different templates to the site

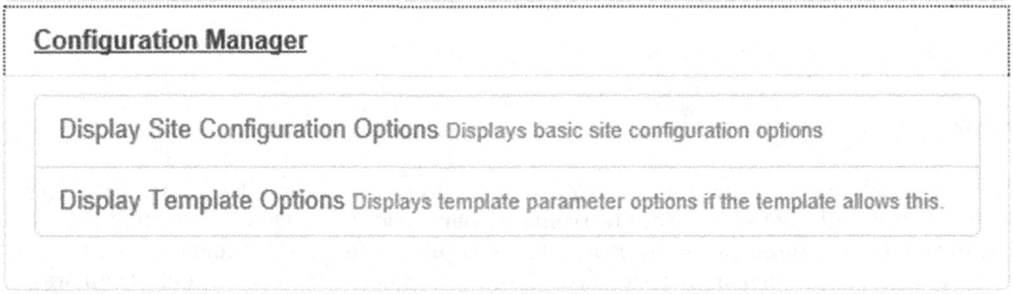

Configuration Manager

Display Site Configuration Options Displays basic site configuration options

Display Template Options Displays template parameter options if the template allows this.

Figure 7-51. *Menu item types in the Configuration Manager menu item type category*

Contacts

With this menu item type, you can display contact categories as well as contacts for submitting queries. This menu item type category has the following menu item types (see Figure 7-52):

- **Featured Contacts:** Displays all the contacts that are marked as featured in the Contact component
- **List All Contact Categories:** Displays all categories of contacts in the site
- **List Contacts in a Category:** Displays all the contacts from a specific category
- **Single Contact:** Displays only the specified contact

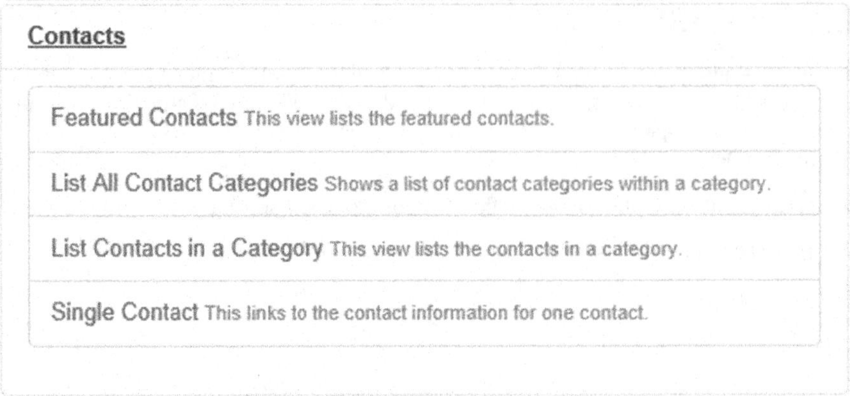

Contacts

Featured Contacts This view lists the featured contacts.

List All Contact Categories Shows a list of contact categories within a category.

List Contacts in a Category This view lists the contacts in a category.

Single Contact This links to the contact information for one contact.

Figure 7-52. *Contacts menu item type category*

The List Contacts In A Category menu item type is used to display all the published contacts of a given category. Recall that in Chapter 5 you created two contacts, John David and Purchases, under the Suppliers category. You saw that the Single Contact menu item type was linked to the specified contact and how a contact form was displayed when the menu item was selected. The query entered in the contact form was e-mailed to the linked contact.

Newsfeeds

Newsfeeds are used for receiving updates from certain web sites. If you regularly require access to information from certain web sites, it would be difficult to visit those web sites continually to look for updates. Newsfeeds help by merging the feeds from other pages into one page. This menu item type has three options in it, as shown in Figure 7-53:

- List All News Feed Categories
- List News Feeds in a Category
- Single News Feed

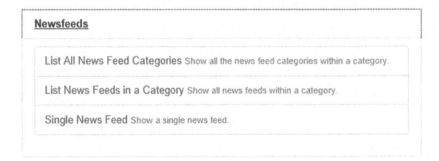

Newsfeeds

List All News Feed Categories Show all the news feed categories within a category.

List News Feeds in a Category Show all news feeds within a category.

Single News Feed Show a single news feed.

Figure 7-53. *Options in the News Feeds menu item type*

To understand these options, you need to create one more newsfeed inside the Cell Phones newsfeed category created in Chapter 6. Recall that in Chapter 6 you created a newsfeed category by the name of Cell Phones with one feed in it: "Cell Phones - fastest communication." Let's create a newsfeed with the name "Cell Phones - basic commodity" in the same Cell Phones newsfeed category. Select Components ➤ Newsfeeds ➤ Feeds; then click the New icon and enter the information shown in Figure 7-54 to create a newsfeed. In the Link field, enter the URL as `http://www.computerweekly.com/rss/Mobile-technology.xml`.

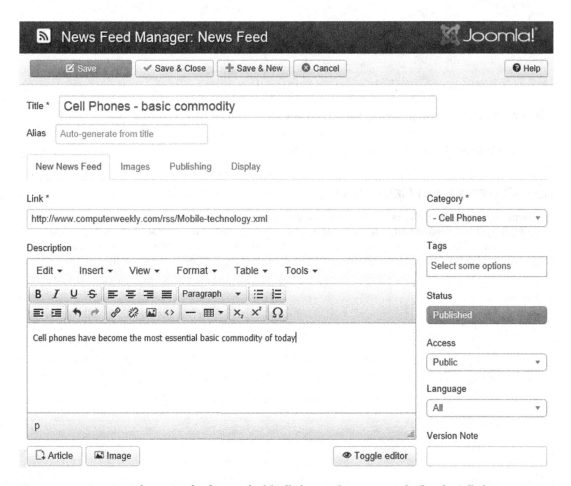

Figure 7-54. *Entering information for the newsfeed "Cell Phones – basic commodity" in the Cell Phones category*

After entering the information as shown in Figure 7-54, click the Save & Close icon to save the newsfeed. There will now be two newsfeeds in the Cell Phones category, as shown in Figure 7-55.

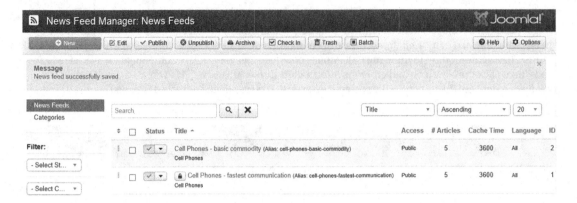

Figure 7-55. *Two newsfeeds in the Cell Phones category, as listed in the News Feed Manager*

Next, let's look at the impact of each menu item type.

List All News Feed Categories

The menu item type List All News Feed Categories displays a list of all newsfeed categories. Open the New Electronics Among Cameras And Cell Phones menu item in edit mode. From the Menu Item Type combo box, select List All News Feed Categories option under the Newsfeed menu item type category. Leaving the values of other fields to their default (see Figure 7-56), click the Save & Close icon to save the changes.

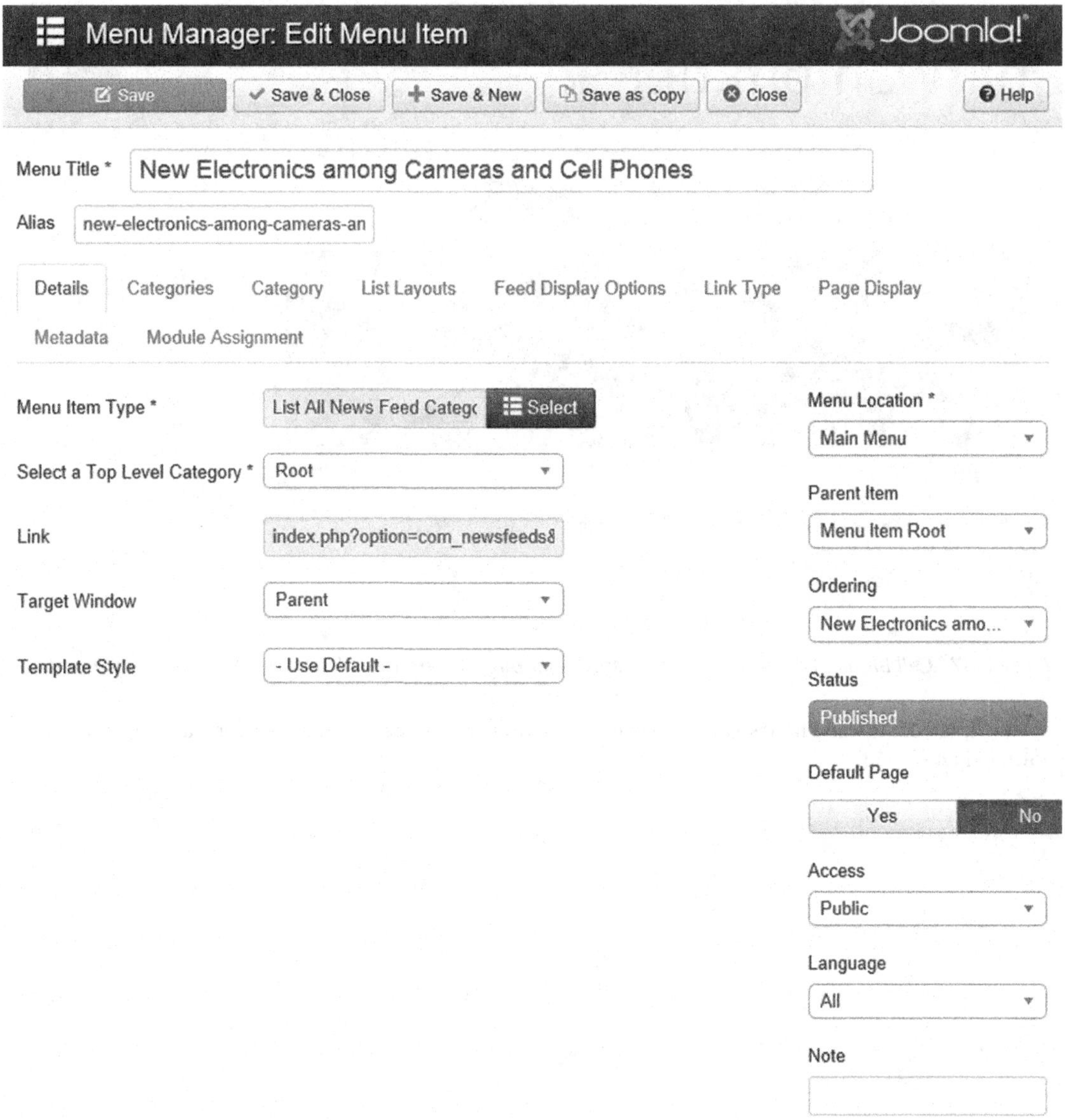

Figure 7-56. *List All News Feed Categories menu item type*

If you open the browser window pointing to your Joomla web site, you'll find that besides the default newsfeed categories provided by Joomla, there is a Cell Phones category, as shown in Figure 7-57. The number 2 in parentheses after Cell Phones indicates that it contains two newsfeeds.

Figure 7-57. *Cell Phones newsfeed category displayed along with the default categories provided by Joomla*

If you select the Cell Phones newsfeed category, both the newsfeeds in that category are displayed, as shown in Figure 7-58.

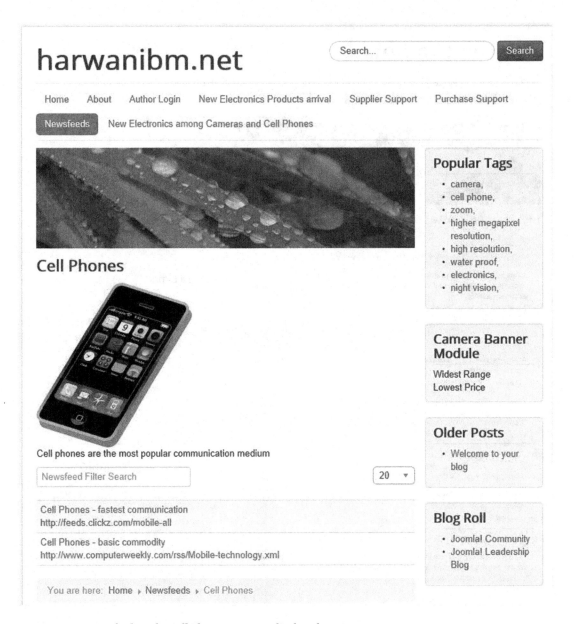

Figure 7-58. *Newsfeeds in the Cell Phones category displayed*

You can select either of the links shown in Figure 7-58 to get updates from the specified web site (the web site to which these newsfeeds are linked).

Select the newsfeed "Cell Phones - fastest communication" from the Cell Phone category to see the information supplied by that newsfeed. You will see the list of five articles shown in Figure 7-59.

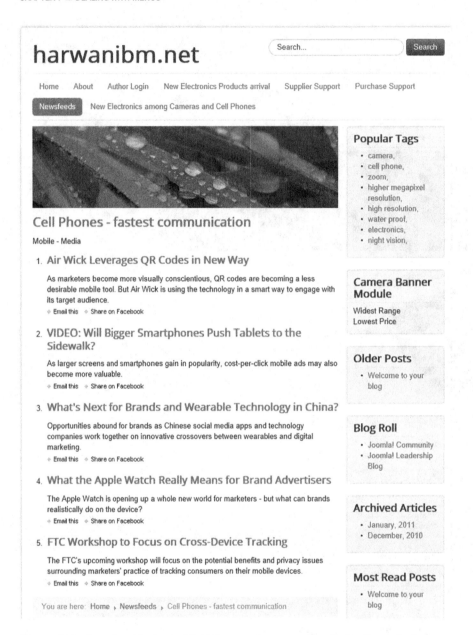

Figure 7-59. *List of articles in the "Cell Phones - fastest communication" newsfeed*

Similarly, the list of articles that will be displayed on selecting the "Cell Phones - basic commodity" newsfeed are as shown in Figure 7-60.

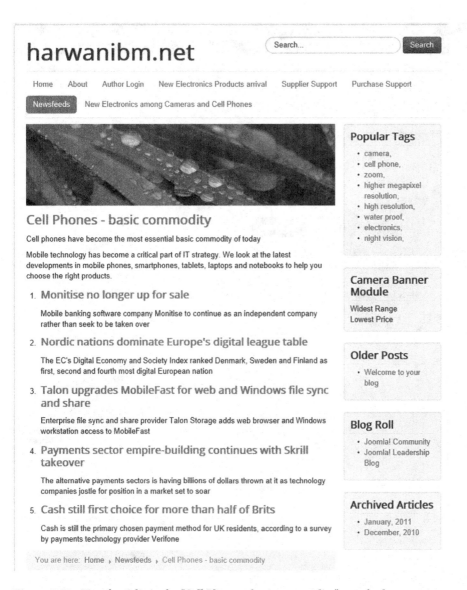

Figure 7-60. *List of articles in the "Cell Phones - basic commodity" newsfeed*

List News Feeds in a Category

This menu item type displays the list of all newsfeeds in the selected category. For this menu item type, you have to select only the newsfeed category whose newsfeeds you want to display. Let's select the Cell Phones newsfeed category, as shown in Figure 7-61.

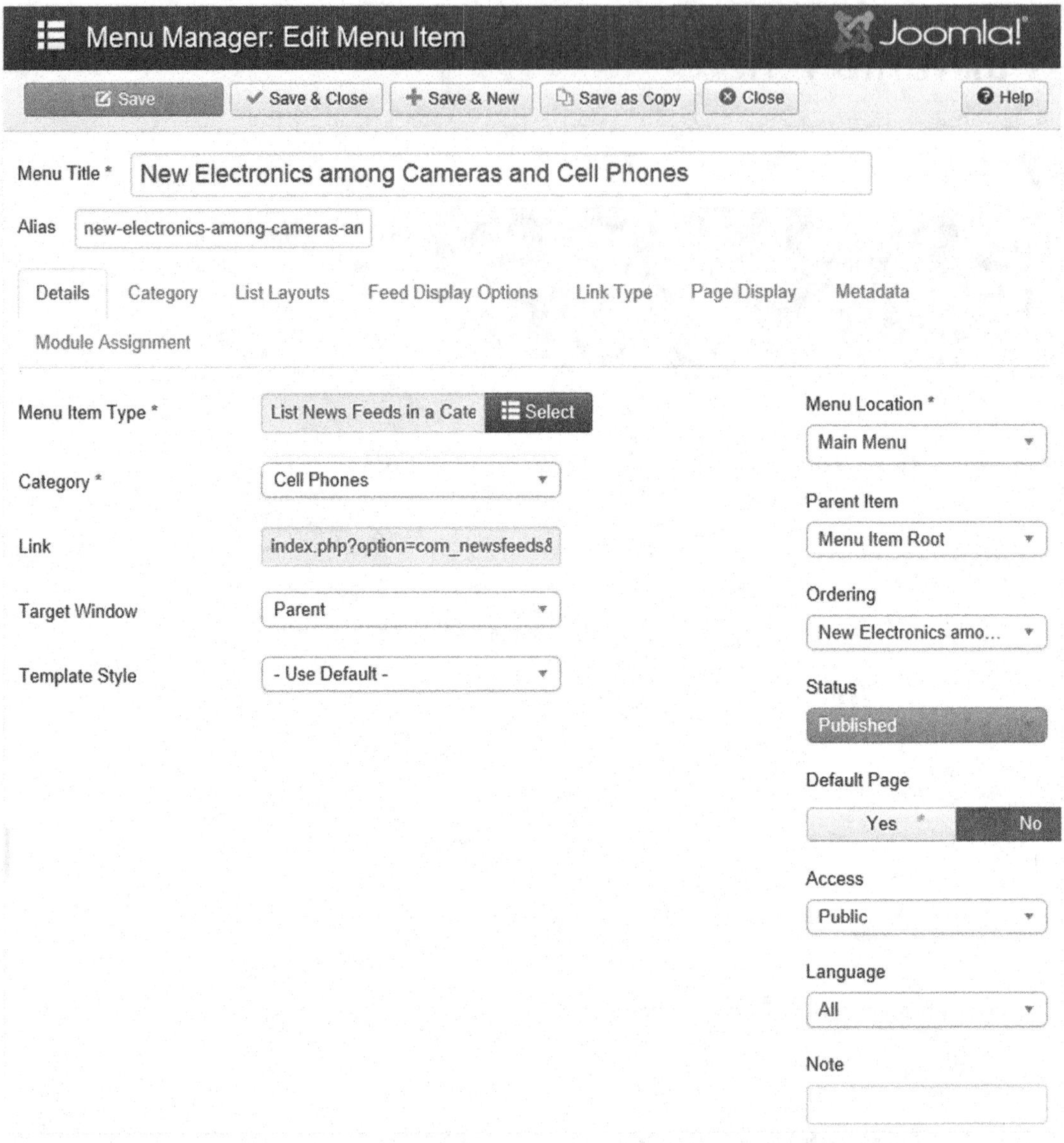

Menu Manager: Edit Menu Item

Save | Save & Close | Save & New | Save as Copy | Close | Help

Menu Title * | New Electronics among Cameras and Cell Phones

Alias | new-electronics-among-cameras-an

Details | Category | List Layouts | Feed Display Options | Link Type | Page Display | Metadata
Module Assignment

Menu Item Type * | List News Feeds in a Cate | Select

Category * | Cell Phones

Link | index.php?option=com_newsfeeds&

Target Window | Parent

Template Style | - Use Default -

Menu Location * | Main Menu

Parent Item | Menu Item Root

Ordering | New Electronics amo...

Status | Published

Default Page | Yes | No

Access | Public

Language | All

Note

Figure 7-61. *Selecting the List News Feeds In A Category menu item type to represent the Cell Phone category*

The Joomla web site will display the newsfeeds in the Cell Phone category, as shown previously in Figure 7-58.

Single Feed Layout

As the name suggests, this menu item type is used to show the articles from a single newsfeed. After selecting this menu item type, you need to select the newsfeed from which the updates have to be merged. You use the Feed drop-down list (see Figure 7-62) to specify the newsfeed from which you want to get updates upon selecting the menu item. Let's select the newsfeed "Cell Phones-basic commodity" from the drop-down list.

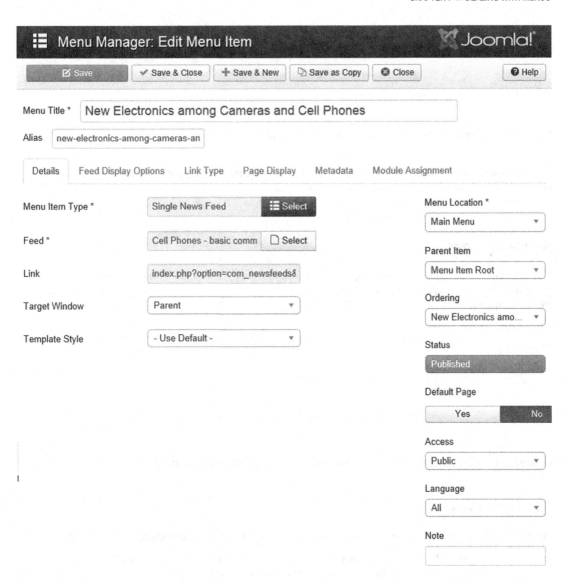

Figure 7-62. *Specifying the newsfeed from which the updates are to be merged*

Now this menu item will display the articles of the selected newsfeed, as shown previously in Figure 7-60.

Search

This menu item type has a search layout option, as shown in Figure 7-63.

Figure 7-63. *Menu item type under the Search menu item type category*

The search layout option is used for displaying a search form in which users can enter a keyword to be searched for in articles, contacts, categories, and so on. (You learned how to use this menu item type in Chapter 6.)

Smart Search

This menu item type category has one option, as shown in Figure 7-64. As the name suggests, this menu item type shows the search lists more precisely by applying advanced filters. (You learned to use this menu item type in Chapter 6.)

Figure 7-64. *Menu item type under the Smart Search menu item type category*

System Links

The System Links menu item type category has the following four options, as shown in Figure 7-65:

- **External URL:** This type is used to access web pages of an external web site. For example, you can use this type to access Google from the web site.

- **Menu Heading:** This type is used to separate links with images or text in a menu. It can also be used to display a short description before each link.

- **Menu Item Alias:** This type creates a link to an existing menu item. That is, it can access and display information that is already displayed in an existing menu item. Suppose you have a menu item by the name of Making Films that displays the information of the "Latest Cameras" article, and you want another menu item, Shooting Accessories, to display the same information. You can set the menu item type of Shooting Accessories to Menu Item Alias, which will make it refer to the same article.

- **Text Separator:** This type creates a separator (in the form of a horizontal line or a blank line) within a menu. It is used to break up long menus. Usually, you see a Text Separator in the form of a horizontal line in the File menu (in most word processing packages) between Save, Print, and other options.

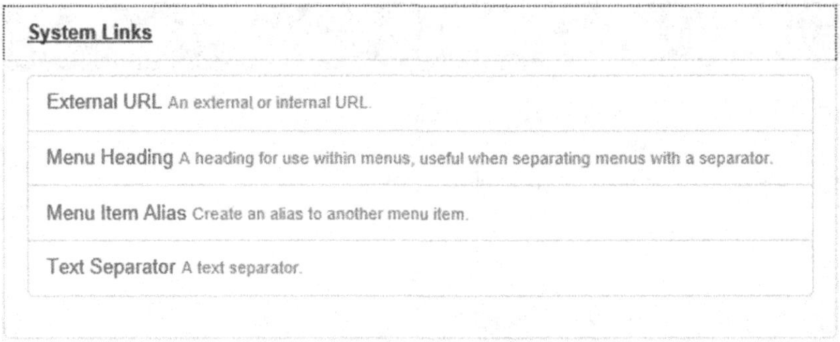

System Links

External URL An external or internal URL.

Menu Heading A heading for use within menus, useful when separating menus with a separator.

Menu Item Alias Create an alias to another menu item.

Text Separator A text separator.

Figure 7-65. *Menu item types under the System Links menu item type category*

External URL

This menu item type is used to create a menu item that links to an external web site or page. Open the New Electronics Among Cameras And Cell Phones menu item in edit mode. From the Menu Item Type combo box, select External URL option under the System Links menu item type category, as shown in Figure 7-66. For this example, you can leave all the settings as is, except for one field: Link.

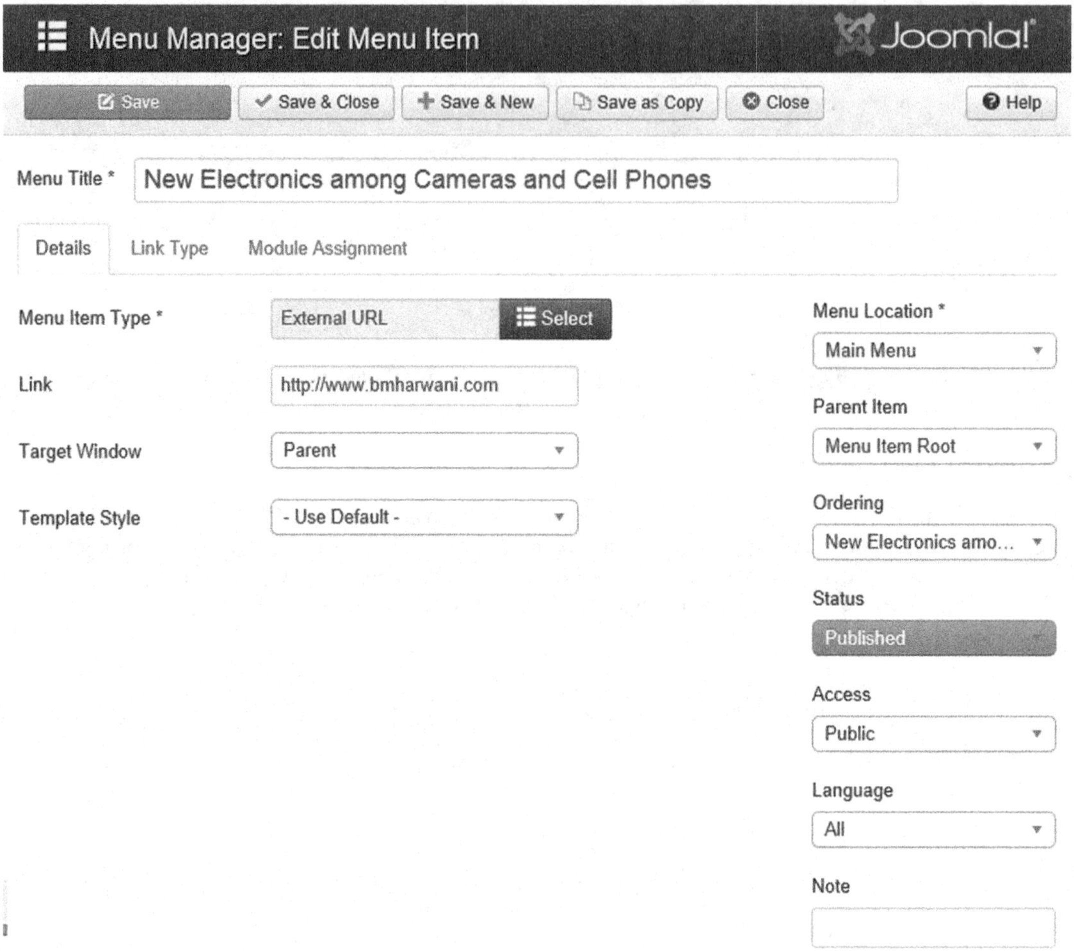

Figure 7-66. *Specifying the Link setting to link to an external web site*

For this field, specify the URL of the web page to which you want the visitor to navigate when the menu item of this type is selected. Let's specify **http://bmharwani.com**. After entering the URL of the web page or web site, click the Save & Close icon.

Menu Item Alias

This menu item type creates a link to an existing menu item. It enables you to have identical menu items in two or more menus without duplicating the settings. For example, suppose that you want the current menu item to point to the existing menu item Purchase Support. The idea is that you want the current menu item to display the same information to which the menu item Purchase Support is pointing.

When you select the Menu Item Alias menu item type, you'll see a screen for entering certain information. Keep all the settings as is, except for the Menu Item drop-down list, in which you can select the menu item to which the current menu item is to point. Select the menu item Purchase Support, as shown in Figure 7-67.

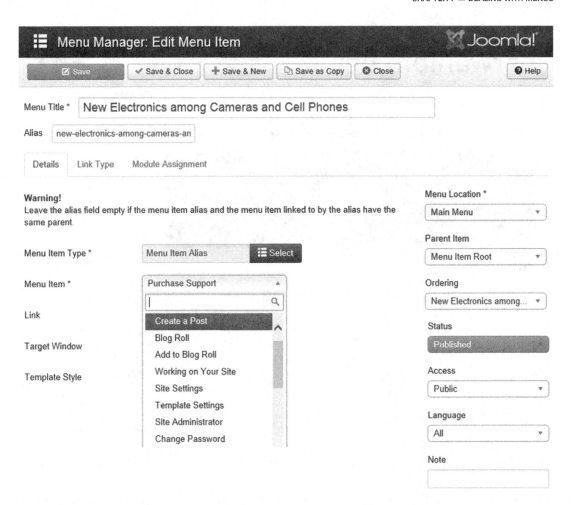

Figure 7-67. *Menu item New Electronics Among Cameras And Cell Phones set as an Menu Item Alias of Purchase Support*

Now when you select the menu item, it will display the same information that was attached to the Purchase Support menu item, as shown in Figure 7-68.

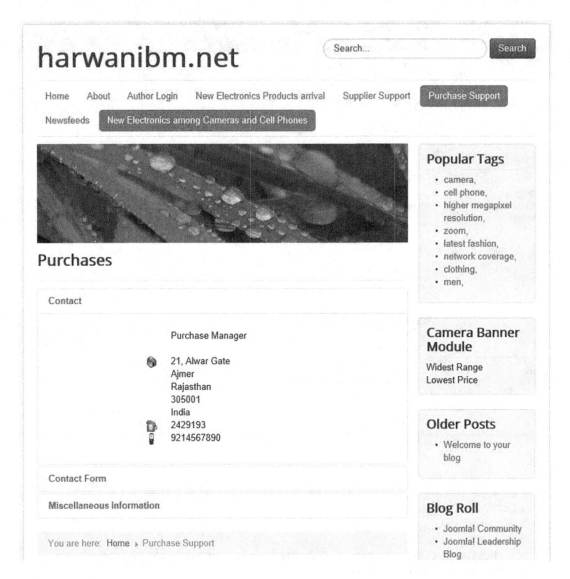

Figure 7-68. *Purchase Support information displayed*

Text Separator

This menu item type creates a menu placeholder, or Text Separator, within a menu and is used to break up a long menu. From the Menu Item Manager, select the New icon from the toolbar to make a blank separator. When you select the New icon, you'll see a screen to select the menu item type. On this screen, select Text Separator from the Menu Item Type combo box. That's it; you don't need to enter any information—just click the Save & Close icon to save this separator in the form of a blank line.

To see the effect of this separator, you can add one more menu item after this separator. Make a menu item of any type and save it. You should now have two menu items with a separator in between. When you open the browser window to open the Joomla web site, you'll find that the two menu items are displayed with a Text Separator in between.

Tags

The Tags menu item type category displays content on the basis of the specified tags. It has the following menu item types (see Figure 7-69):

- **Compact list of tagged items:** Displays a compact list of items that are tagged; a compact list for each selected tag

- **List of all tags:** Displays a list of all tags on the site

- **Tagged Items:** Displays a list of items that are tagged with the specified tags; a separate list for each selected tag

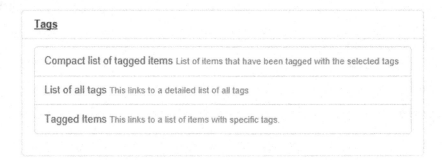

Figure 7-69. *Menu item types in the Tags menu item type cateogory*

Users Manager

Users Manager is accessed by clicking the User Manager listed on the right of the main "Site "Control Panel. You can also use the top menu bar, Users ➤ User Manager. The Users Manager menu item type has several options, as shown in Figure 7-70:

- **Edit User Profiles:** Displays the user's profile in edit mode

- **Login Form:** Displays the login form in the content area of the page

- **Password Reset:** Displays a password request form that can be used to reset user's password

- **Registration Form:** Displays user's registration form

- **User Profile:** Displays the user's profile

- **Username Reminder Request:** Displays a form that can be used to remind a user of a username

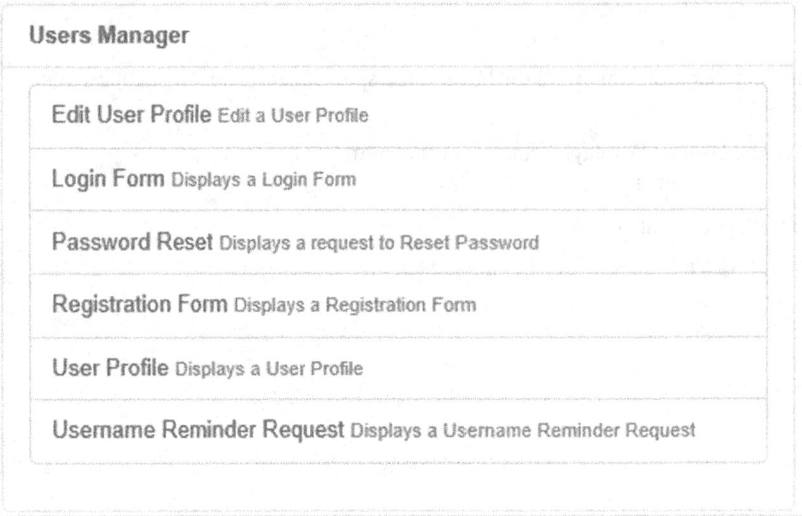

Users Manager

Edit User Profile Edit a User Profile

Login Form Displays a Login Form

Password Reset Displays a request to Reset Password

Registration Form Displays a Registration Form

User Profile Displays a User Profile

Username Reminder Request Displays a Username Reminder Request

Figure 7-70. *User menu item type*

Login Form

This menu item type displays a login form so that a visitor can log in to the site. Open the New Electronics Among Cameras And Cell Phones menu item in edit mode. From the Menu Item Type combo box, select the Login option under the Users Manager menu item type category (see Figure 7-71). Leaving the values of other fields to their default, click the Save & Close icon to save the changes.

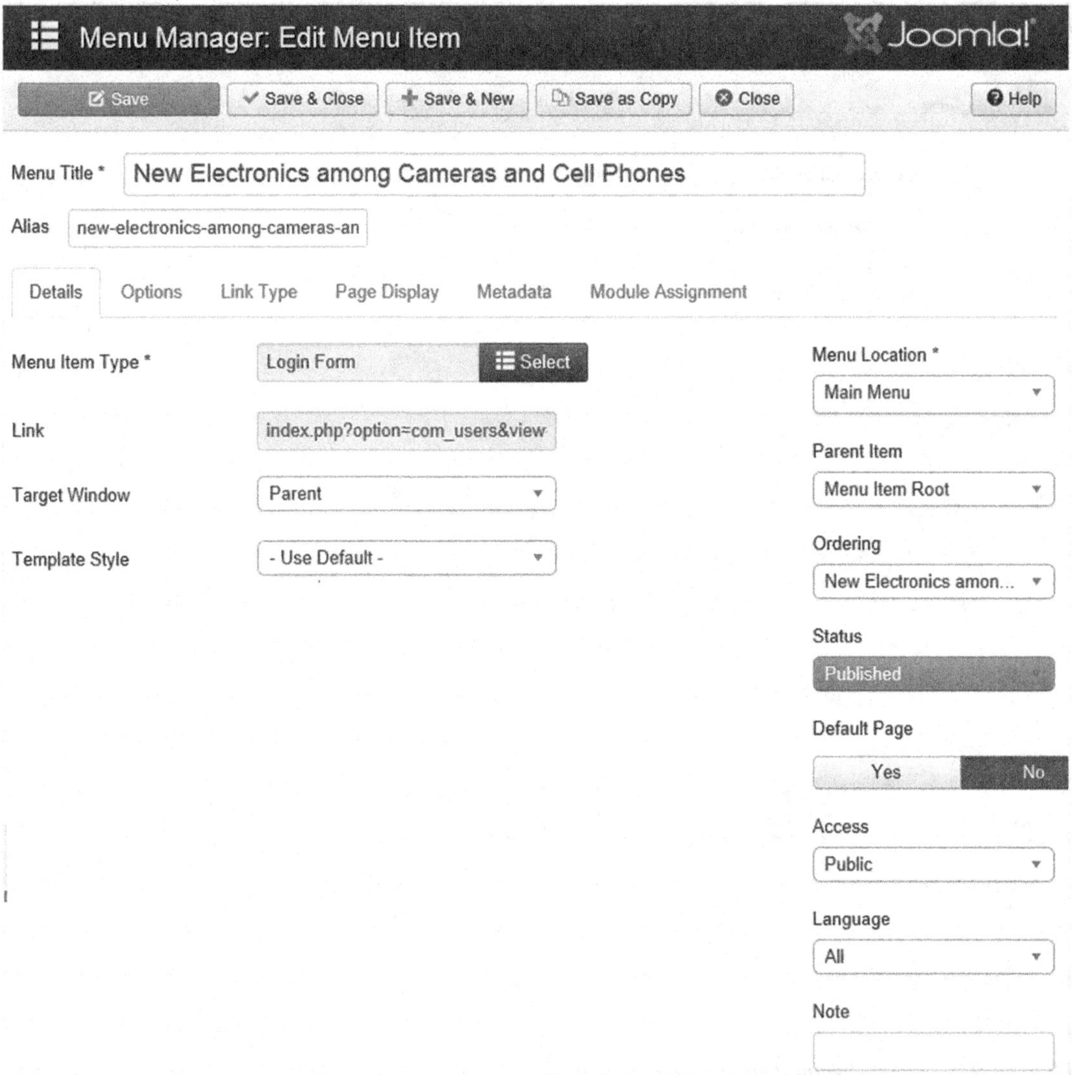

Figure 7-71. *Entering information for the login form*

To configure the login form, click the Options tab. The Options tab displays the fields for configuring the login form, as shown in Figure 7-72.

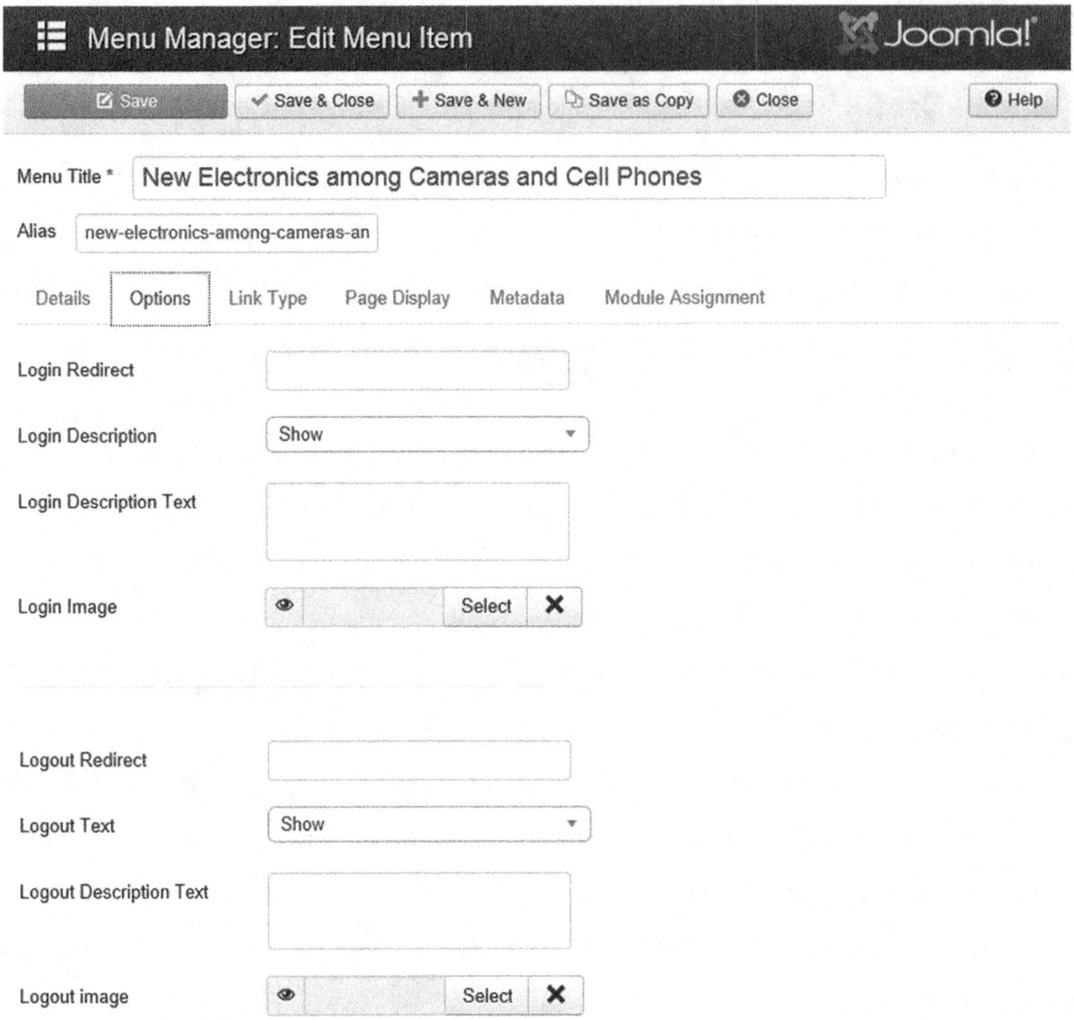

Figure 7-72. *Configuring the login form menu item type*

Table 7-4 gives a brief description of the Login Form options.

Table 7-4. *Default Login Layout Options*

Option	Description
Login Redirect	Specify the URL of the page to which the visitor is to be redirected after a successful login. If you leave this blank, the front page will be displayed.
Login Description	Select Show to display the login description text, which you enter in the following field.
Login Description Text	Enter the text to be displayed upon a successful login.
Login Image	Select the image from the images/stories folder to be displayed on the login page.
Logout Redirection	Specify the URL of the page to which the visitor is to be redirected after a successful logout. If you don't specify any URL, the front page will be displayed.
Logout Text	Select the Show option to display the logout description text, which you enter in the following field.
Logout Description Text	Enter the text to be displayed upon a successful logout.
Logout Image	Select the image from the images/stories folder to be displayed on the logout page.

On the front side of the website, you'll see a login form, as shown in Figure 7-73.

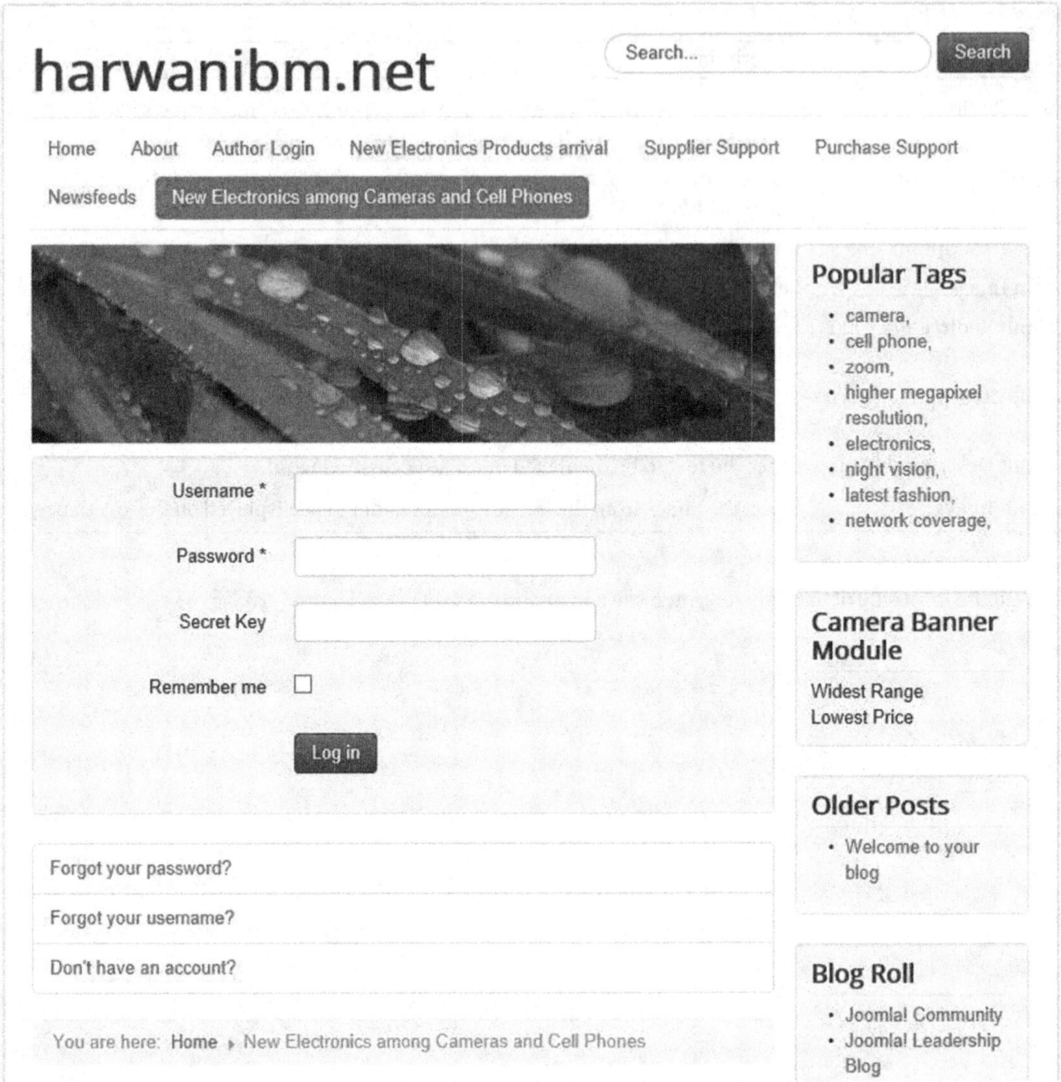

Figure 7-73. *The login form that displays after selecting the menu item*

Registration Form

This menu item type allows visitors to your web site to register, as shown in Figure 7-74.

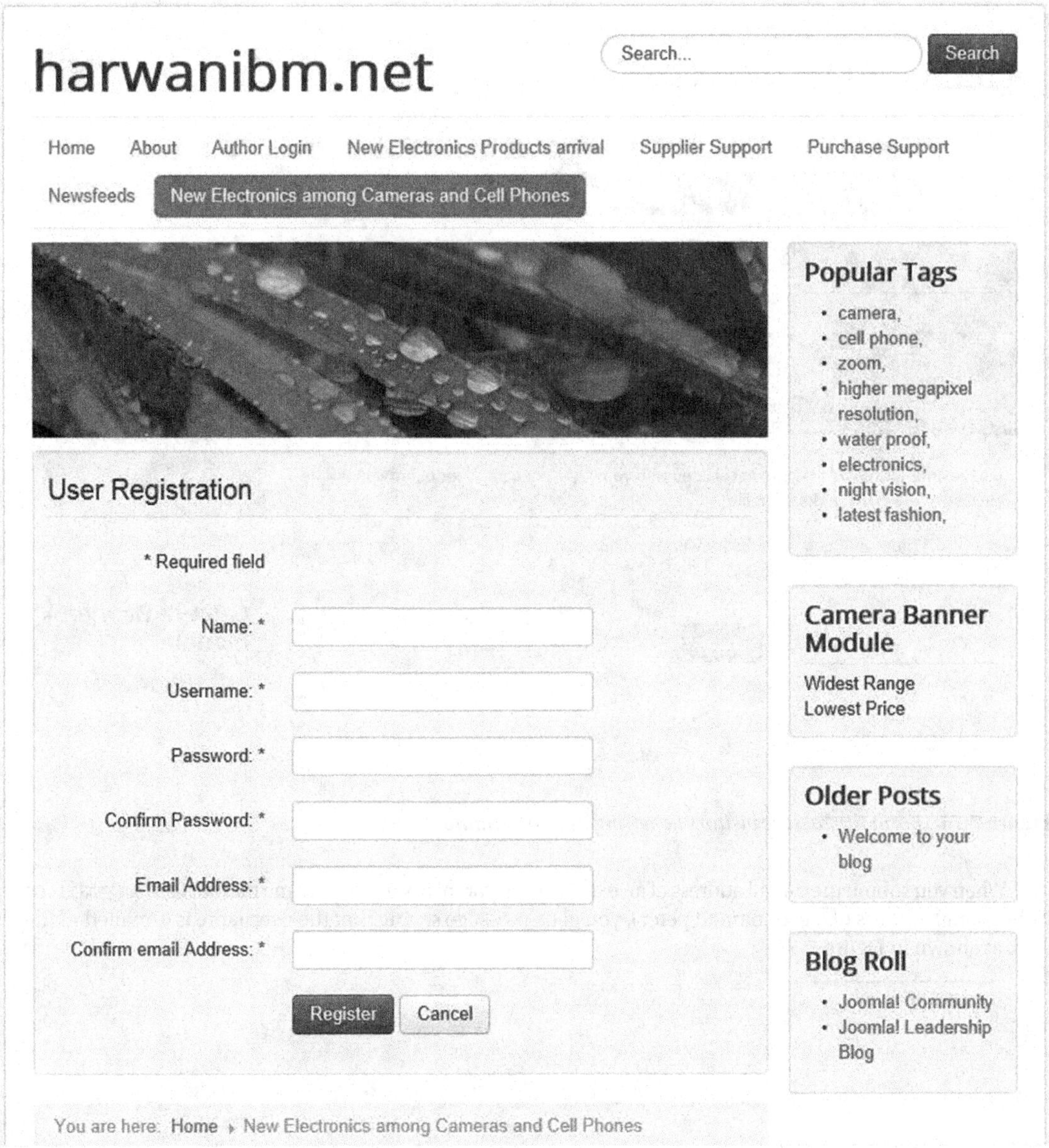

Figure 7-74. *Registration form displayed for the menu item type Registration Form*

Username Reminder Request

This menu item type is used to help visitors who have forgotten their username. It displays a layout asking the visitor to enter his or her e-mail address, as shown in Figure 7-75. The username will be e-mailed to the visitor.

Figure 7-75. *Form that assists visitors in getting their username*

When you submit the e-mail address of an existing user (for this example, assume that harwanibm@gmail.com is the e-mail address of a user named peter), you get a message saying that the username is e-mailed to the user, as shown in Figure 7-76.

Figure 7-76. *Message showing that the e-mail has been sent*

Open the e-mail and you'll find that the username is supplied as expected.

Password Reset

This menu item type displays a default layout form for visitors who have forgotten their password. The visitor is asked to enter his or her e-mail address, as shown in Figure 7-77. The user is sent a verification token and can then reset the password.

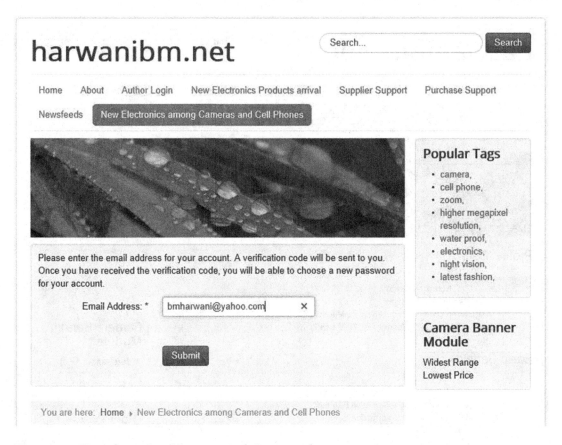

***Figure 7-77.** Form that assists visitors to reset their password*

On submitting the e-mail address, you get a dialog box to enter the verification token that is sent via e-mail. On opening the e-mail, you'll notice that the token is a long string of numbers and characters. You need to copy this verification token and paste it into the Token field; then click the Submit button.

On sending the verification token, you'll get a screen for entering a new password. Enter any password in the Password field, duplicate it in the Verify Password field, and then click the Submit button. The password will be reset, and a confirmation message will be displayed.

Registration Form

This menu item type displays a welcome message when the user enters the registered zone. The welcome message may look something like Figure 7-78.

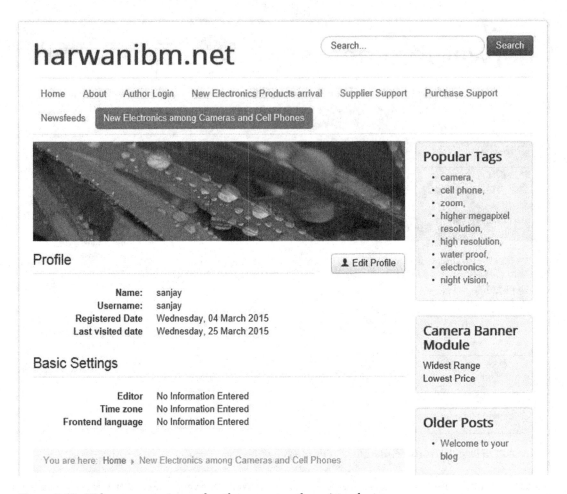

Figure 7-78. Welcome message seen when the user enters the registered zone

Edit User Profiles

This menu item type allows users to edit their account details, including the password, e-mail address, front-end language, and time zone (see Figure 7-79). Users with publishing permissions may choose a text editor, and those with administrator permissions may choose the help site they want to use on the back end.

Figure 7-79. *Form for editing user account details*

Web Links

This menu item type has following options, as shown in Figure 7-80:

- List All Web Link Categories
- List Web Links in a Category
- Submit a Web Link

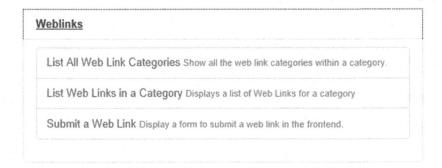

Figure 7-80. *Options in the Web Links menu item type*

To help you understand this menu item type, let's create a web link category called Camera and a web link called Camera Magazine belonging to the Camera category. Open the Web Links Category Manager by selecting the Components Web Links Categories. You'll see the default Web Links categories, as shown in Figure 7-81.

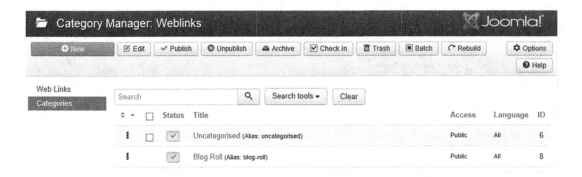

Figure 7-81. *Default Web Links categories*

Click the New button from the toolbar to create a new Web Links category. You'll see a screen similar to the one shown in Figure 7-82. Let's specify the title as **Camera** and the alias as **camera**. Enter a short description in the Description field, keep all the other settings at their defaults, and click the Save & Close icon to save it.

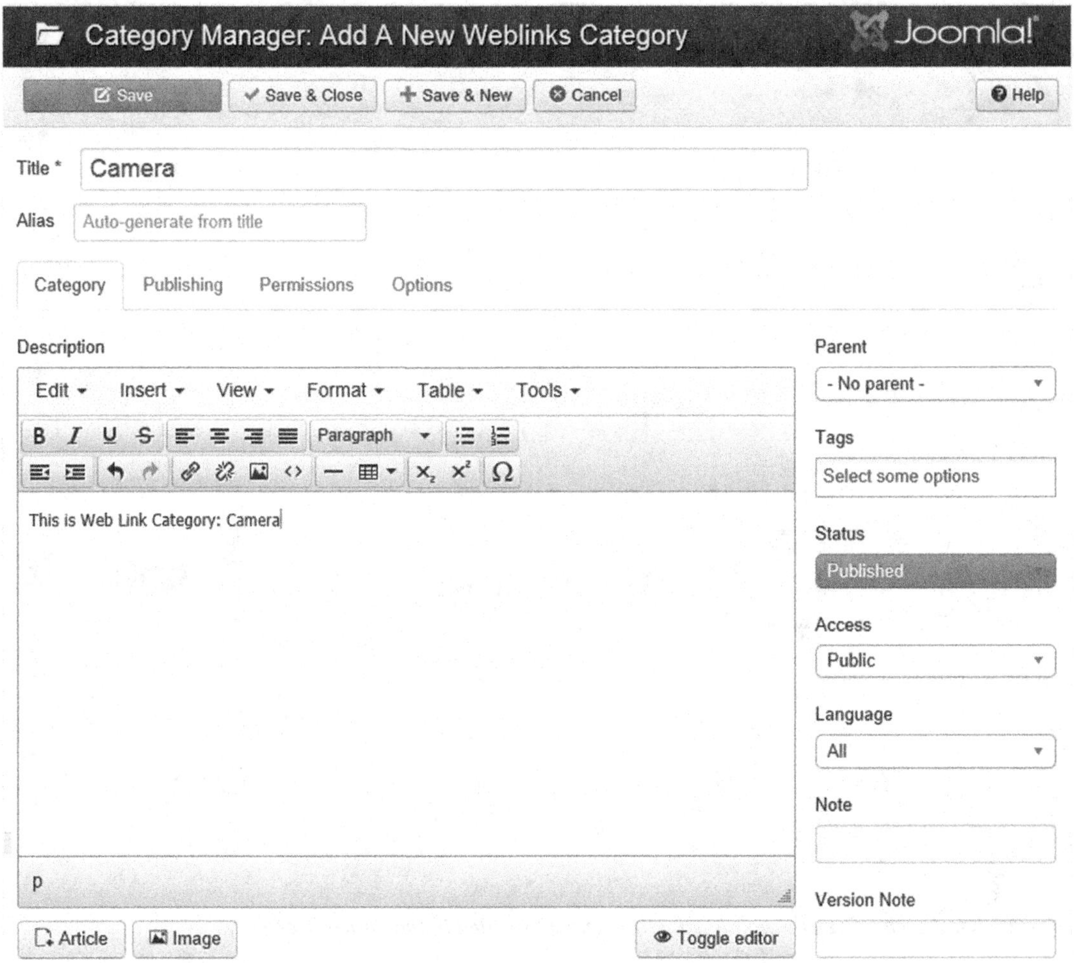

Figure 7-82. *Creating a web link category*

Next, you'll create a web link in this category. Let's select the Components ➤ Web Links ➤ Links option to open the Web Link Manager. In the Web Link Manager, click the New icon from the toolbar to create a new web link. Let's create a web link by the name Camera Magazine that will open the site www.digicamera.com when selected (as shown in Figure 7-83).

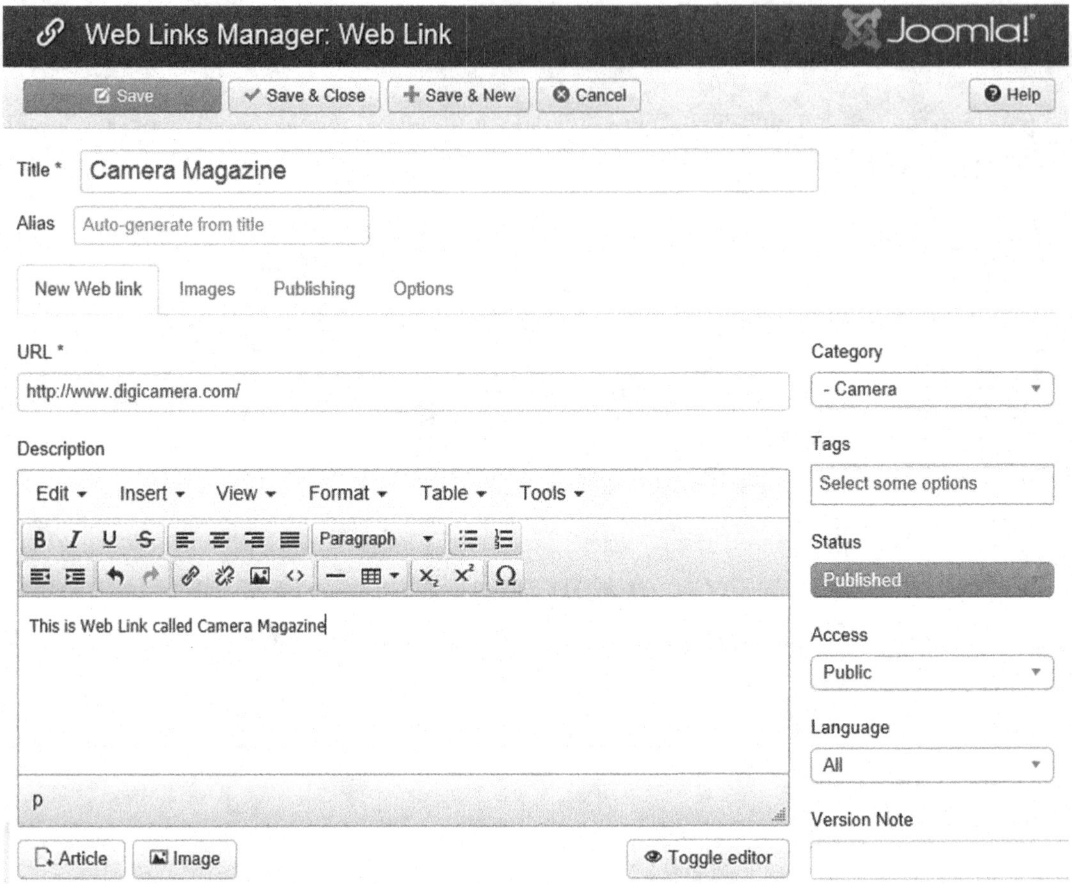

Figure 7-83. *A web link by the name Camera Magazine created in the Camera category*

In the Title field, enter the name **Camera Magazine**. In the Alias field (though it can be left blank), enter the alias as **camera-magazine**. Set the Status field to the Published option to make it visible. Set the Category of the web link to Camera, and in the URL field, specify any web site or web page location that you want to open when selecting the menu item. Enter http://www.digicamera.com in this field. Keeping the rest of the options at their defaults, click the Save & Close icon from the toolbar to save the web link.

Now that you have created a web link and a web link category, you are in a position to explore the Web Link menu item types.

List All Web Link Categories

This menu item type displays a list of all the web link categories. The user may click a category to see the links for that category. The web site will display output like that shown in Figure 7-84.

Figure 7-84. *List of all the web link categories, displayed when the menu item type is List All Web Link Categories*

Besides the default web link categories provided by Joomla, this menu item type displays the custom web link category, Camera. If you click the Camera link, you'll see the web links in it, as shown in Figure 7-85.

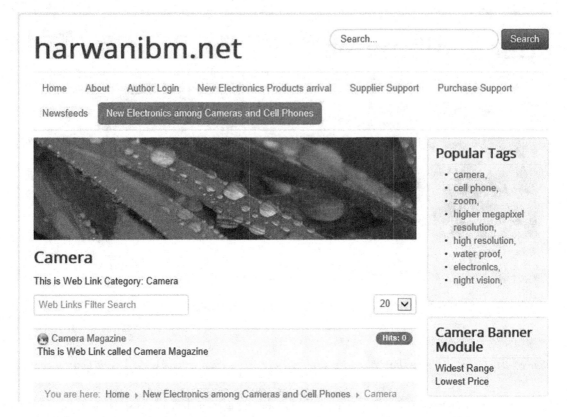

Figure 7-85. *Web links in the Camera category*

If you select the Camera Magazine web link, you will be navigated to the web site
http://www.digicamera.com because it is the URL that you specified in this web link (refer to Figure 7-83).

List Web Links in a Category

This menu item type displays a list of all the web links in the selected category. For example, if you select the
Camera category, as shown in Figure 7-86, it will display all the web links in that category.

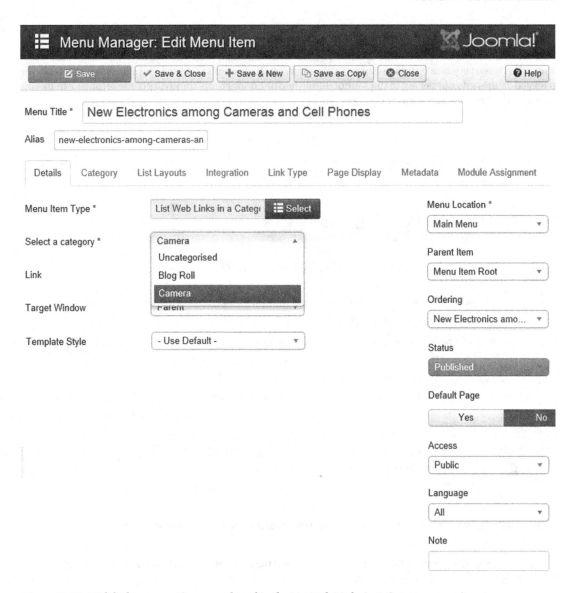

Figure 7-86. *Web link category Camera selected in the List Web Links In A Categorymenu item type*

■ **Note**   In case you create a category for weblinks with a few links within that category, you can create a weblinks module or menu item to display all weblink categories or all links within one weblink category.

Submit a Web Link

This menu item type displays a form that allows users in the Author, Publisher, and Editor groups to submit a web link. It is a very nice option because it allows users to also submit their web links from the front end. If logged-in users do not belong to the Author, Publisher, or Editor group, they will get the error shown in Figure 7-87 when they select this menu item type.

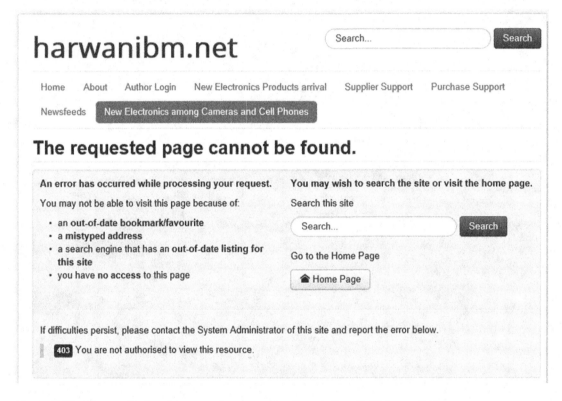

Figure 7-87. *Message displayed to users of a group other than Author, Publisher, or Editor*

If a user belonging to any of those groups logs in, and the menu item is selected, a web link submission form will appear, as shown in Figure 7-88.

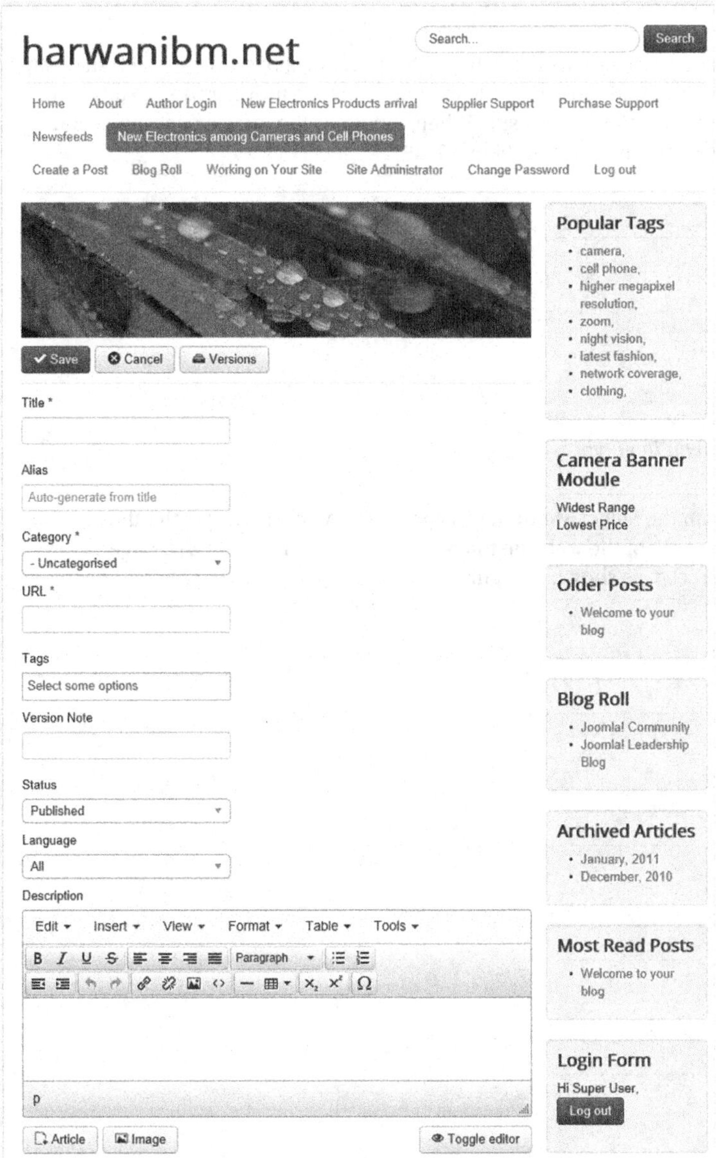

Figure 7-88. *Form that allows a web link submission*

The user has to specify the title of the web link, a category to which the web link will belong, the URL of the web page or web site to be displayed (on selecting the menu item), and a small description of the web link. After entering the information as shown in Figure 7-88, the user needs to click the Save button to submit the web link to the web site.

Wrapper

This menu item type provides a layout that displays an external web site inside a page of your web site using an HTML frame. The external web site is contained inside the wrapper. You can move around to any web page of the wrapped site, all inside the page of your web site. When you move the mouse over this menu item type, you'll see a message to this effect, as shown in Figure 7-89.

Figure 7-89. *Selecting the Wrapper menu item type*

If you select the Wrapper type from the Select Menu Item Type screen, you'll see, among other options, a field to specify the wrapper URL (the URL of the web site that you want to open in your web page). Let's enter the URL http://www.bmharwani.com, as shown in Figure 7-90.

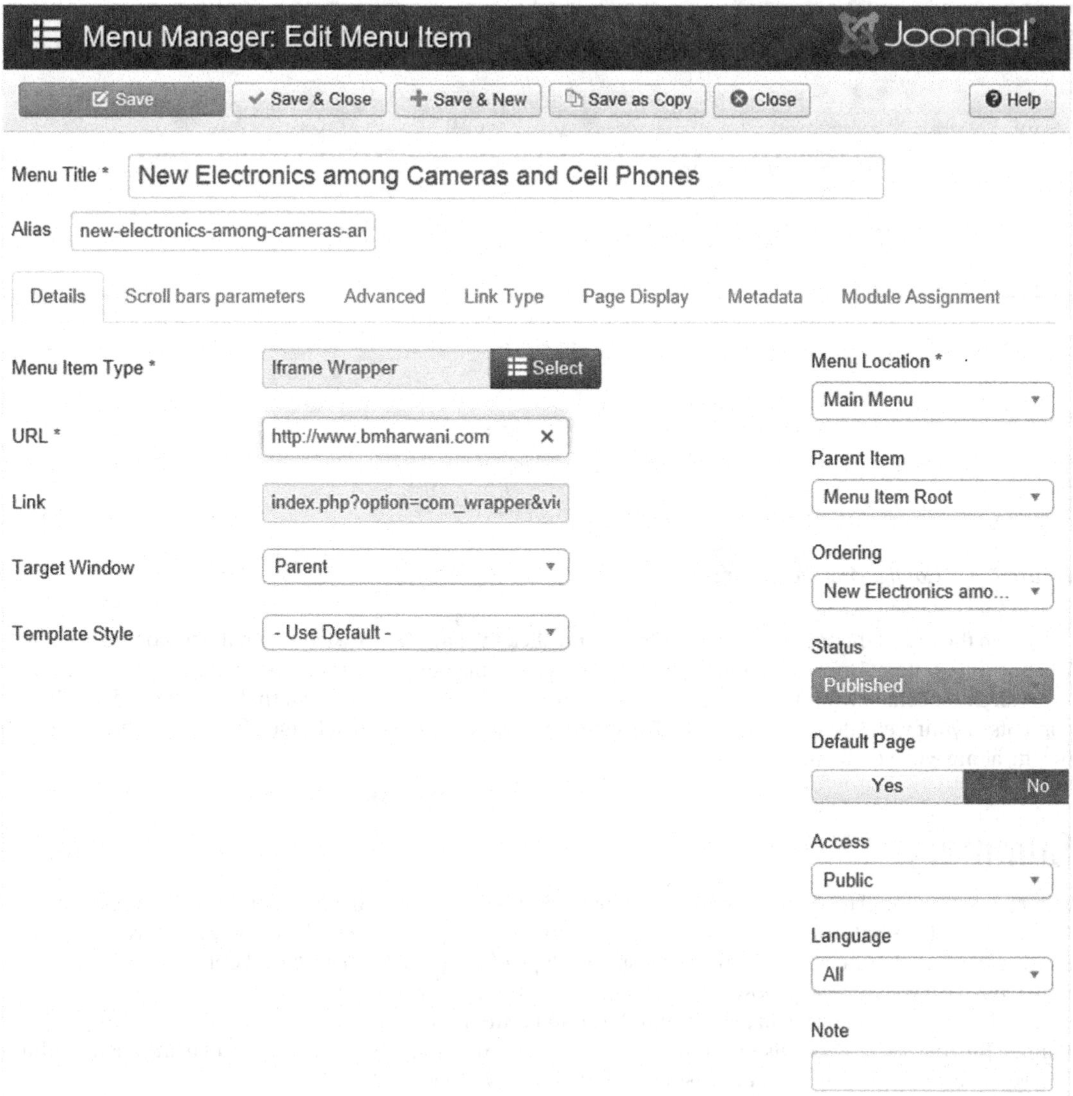

Figure 7-90. *Entering the wrapper URL*

Select the Scroll Bars Parameters tab to configure the wrapper. The tab displays the options shown in Figure 7-91. The Width and Height are for assigning the desired width and height to the web site that will be displayed. If the value of the Scroll Bars option is set to Auto, the scrollbars will appear only when some part of the web site is not visible. If you set the value of this option to Yes, scrollbars will always be displayed.

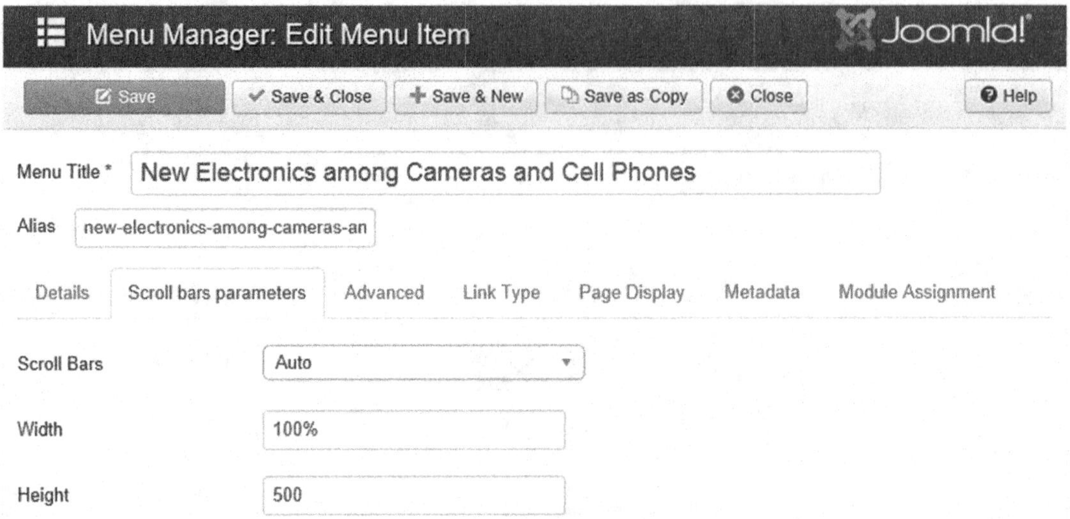

Figure 7-91. *Configuring the wrapper*

Keep the rest of the settings at their defaults and click the Save & Close icon from the toolbar to save the Wrapper menu item. Upon selecting the menu item type from your Joomla web site, you'll find that the web site with the specified wrapper URL opens. You can navigate the pages of the external web site and see the contents of your web site simultaneously. The external web site appears in a frame of the given width and height, along with scrollbars.

Summary

This chapter explored the four categories of menu item types that you can add to your Joomla menus: Internal Link, External URL, Text Separator, and Menu Item Alias. The Internal Link type has several subtypes, and each is meant for displaying a specific type of content. You have tested out the different menu item types, and you have seen how to create menus and the items within them.

In the next chapter, you will learn about the 20 standard modules provided by Joomla, including Banner, Breadcrumbs, Feed Display, RSS, Poll, and Search. You'll see the methodology of using each module and you'll discover their roles in increasing the functionality of a web site.

CHAPTER 8

■ ■ ■

Modules

In Chapter 7, you learned about menus and their menu item types. In this chapter, you'll learn about the different types of modules and their uses.

Module Manager

So what is a module? Simply put, it is a collection of several related items. For example, a module can be a collection of any of the following:

- Menus

- Popular articles or related articles

- Advertisements, banners, or random images

The main benefit of collecting several related items in a module is to gain better control. For example, you can make a module become invisible on the web site (which would be easier than unpublishing the individual items), apply a CSS style uniformly to all items in a module, change its access level or position, and so on.

Joomla provides the following front-end and back-end modules:

- **Site modules:** The modules for the front end of the system are called Site modules, and there are 24 different Site module types. These modules configure the site for the site visitors.

- **Administrator modules:** The modules for the back end are called Administrator modules, and there are 15 different Administrator module types. These modules enhance the administration interface and provides desired information to the administrator. The administrator can customize the site's admin interface using the administration modules.

You can always add more site modules by using the Module Manager. You can also use the Module Manager to customize the desired module(s). When you open the Module Manager (by selecting Extensions ➤ Module Manager), the list of Site modules in it is displayed, as shown in Figure 8-1.

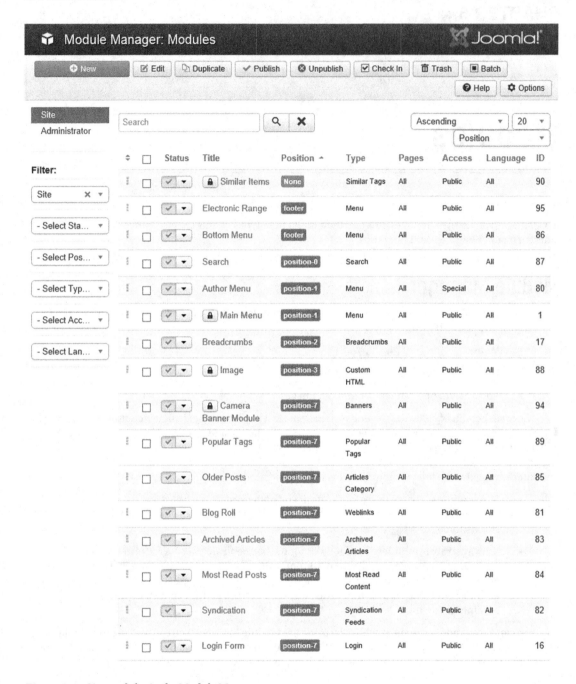

Figure 8-1. *Site modules in the Module Manager*

These modules are those visible on the Site link. After the Administrator link is selected, the Administrator modules will display, as shown in Figure 8-2.

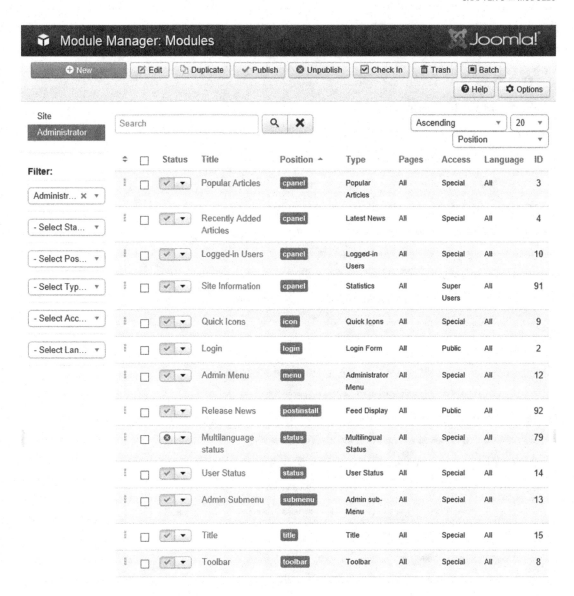

Figure 8-2. Administrator modules in the Module Manager

However, if you look at the Type column that displays the type of module to which the module belongs, you'll observe that several modules belong to the same type. Figure 8-3 shows the different Site module types provided by Joomla.

Select a Module Type:

Archived Articles This Module shows a list of the calendar months containing Archived Articles. After you...

Articles - Newsflash The Newsflash Module will display a fixed number of articles from a specific category.

Articles - Related Articles This Module displays other Articles that are related to the one currently being viewed....

Articles Categories This module displays a list of categories from one parent category.

Articles Category This module displays a list of articles from one or more categories.

Banners The Banner Module displays the active Banners from the Component.

Breadcrumbs This Module displays the Breadcrumbs

Custom HTML This Module allows you to create your own HTML Module using a WYSIWYG editor.

Feed Display This module allows the displaying of a syndicated feed

Footer This module shows the Joomla! copyright information.

Language Switcher This module displays a list of available Content Languages (as defined and published in...

Latest News This Module shows a list of the most recently published and current Articles. Some that...

Latest Users This module displays the latest registered users

Login This module displays a username and password login form. It also displays a link to...

Menu This module displays a menu on the frontend.

Most Read Content This Module shows a list of the currently published Articles which have the highest...

Popular Tags This Module displays tags used on the site in a list or a cloud layout. Tags can be...

Random Image This Module displays a random image from your chosen directory.

Search This module will display a search box.

Similar Tags The Similar Tags Module displays links to other items with similar tags. The closeness...

Smart Search Module This is a search module for the Smart Search system.

Statistics The Statistics Module shows information about your server installation together with...

Syndication Feeds Smart Syndication Module that creates a Syndicated Feed for the page where the Module is...

Weblinks This modules displays Web Links from a category defined in the Weblinks component.

Who's Online The Who's Online Module displays the number of Anonymous Users (e.g. Guests) and...

Wrapper This Module shows an iframe window to specified location.

Figure 8-3. Site module types in Joomla

Similarly, Figure 8-4 shows the Administrator module types provided by Joomla.

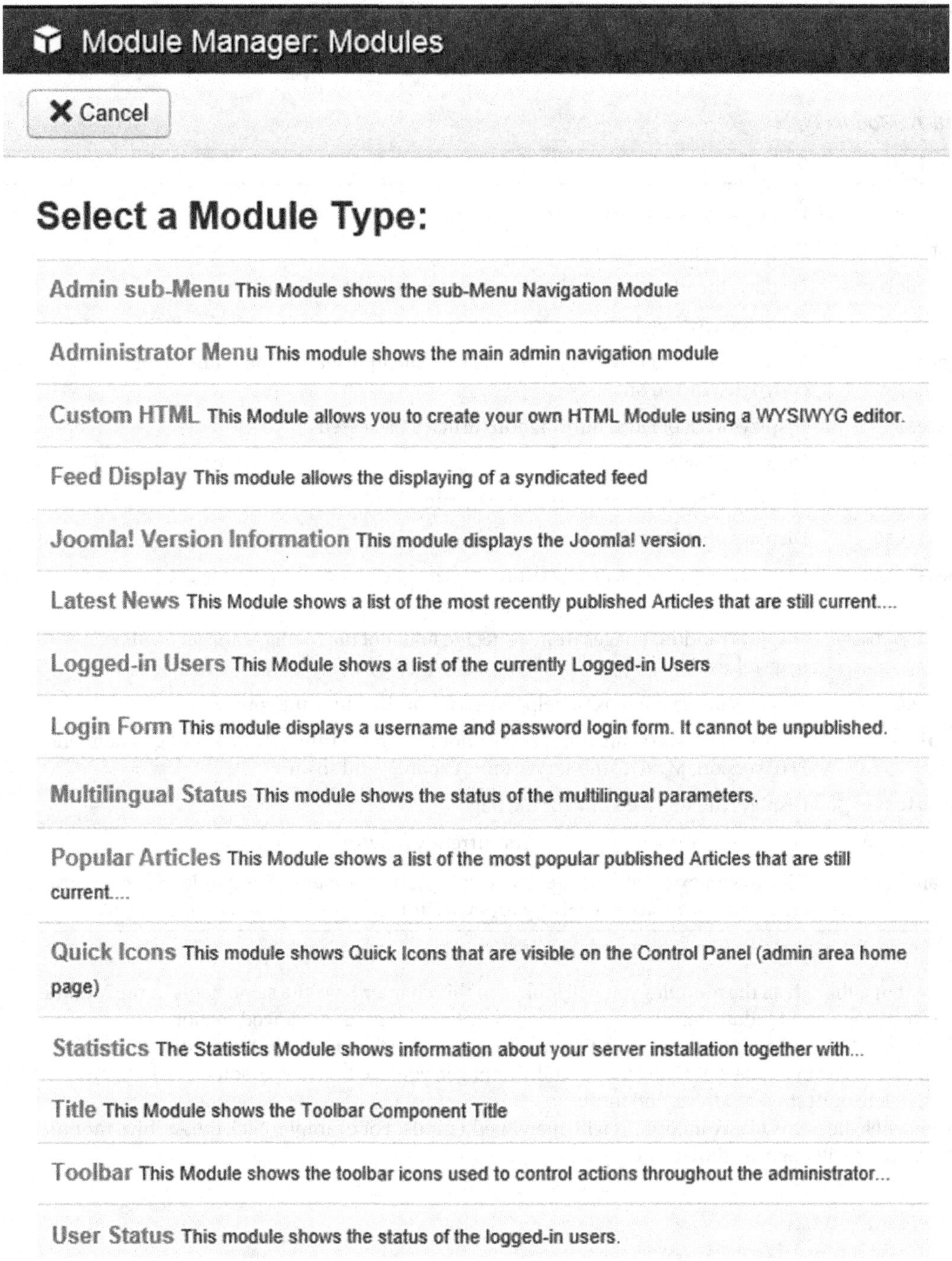

X Cancel

Select a Module Type:

Admin sub-Menu This Module shows the sub-Menu Navigation Module

Administrator Menu This module shows the main admin navigation module

Custom HTML This Module allows you to create your own HTML Module using a WYSIWYG editor.

Feed Display This module allows the displaying of a syndicated feed

Joomla! Version Information This module displays the Joomla! version.

Latest News This Module shows a list of the most recently published Articles that are still current....

Logged-in Users This Module shows a list of the currently Logged-in Users

Login Form This module displays a username and password login form. It cannot be unpublished.

Multilingual Status This module shows the status of the multilingual parameters.

Popular Articles This Module shows a list of the most popular published Articles that are still current....

Quick Icons This module shows Quick Icons that are visible on the Control Panel (admin area home page)

Statistics The Statistics Module shows information about your server installation together with...

Title This Module shows the Toolbar Component Title

Toolbar This Module shows the toolbar icons used to control actions throughout the administrator...

User Status This module shows the status of the logged-in users.

Figure 8-4. *Administrator module types in Joomla*

> ■ **Note**   You can also make your own modules that belong to an existing module type. A module type name is a sort of system name for the module. You cannot edit the module type name of any module.

Table 8-1 lists the different module types and their purposes.

Table 8-1. *Module Types*

Module Type	Purpose
mod_archive	Displays archived articles
mod_banners	Displays client banners
mod_breadcrumbs	Displays breadcrumbs to show your position in the web site
mod_feed	Displays news feeds
mod_footer	Displays the footer (often containing web site information including owner, copyright, and so on)
mod_latest	Displays a list of latest information (articles) accessed
mod_login	Displays a login form
mod_mainmenu	Displays different menus on your web site
mod_mostread	Displays popular articles
mod_newsflash	Displays one or more articles from the selected category each time the page is refreshed
mod_random_image	Displays random images from a specific folder of the Media Manager (with every page refresh)
mod_search	Displays the search box to help search for desired information
mod_stats	Displays web site statistics, such as information regarding the operating system, the PHP version, MySQL, the server time, caching, and so on
mod_syndicate	Displays the RSS feed link for the page
mod_whosonline	Displays information about users currently browsing the web site
mod_wrapper	Displays an external web site inside your web site (using this module, you can browse an external web site as well as your own site)

Note that although all the modules you will look at in this chapter have the same fields in the Module, Menu Assignment, and Module Permissions sections, they have different Advanced sections.

Open the Module Manager by selecting Extensions ➤ Module Manager. You'll see a list of modules, as shown previously in Figure 8-1. Using the Module Manager, you can add new modules, edit existing modules, delete undesired modules, and more.

If you click the name of any module, it will open in edit mode. For example, click the Archive module, and its edit page will open, as shown in Figure 8-5.

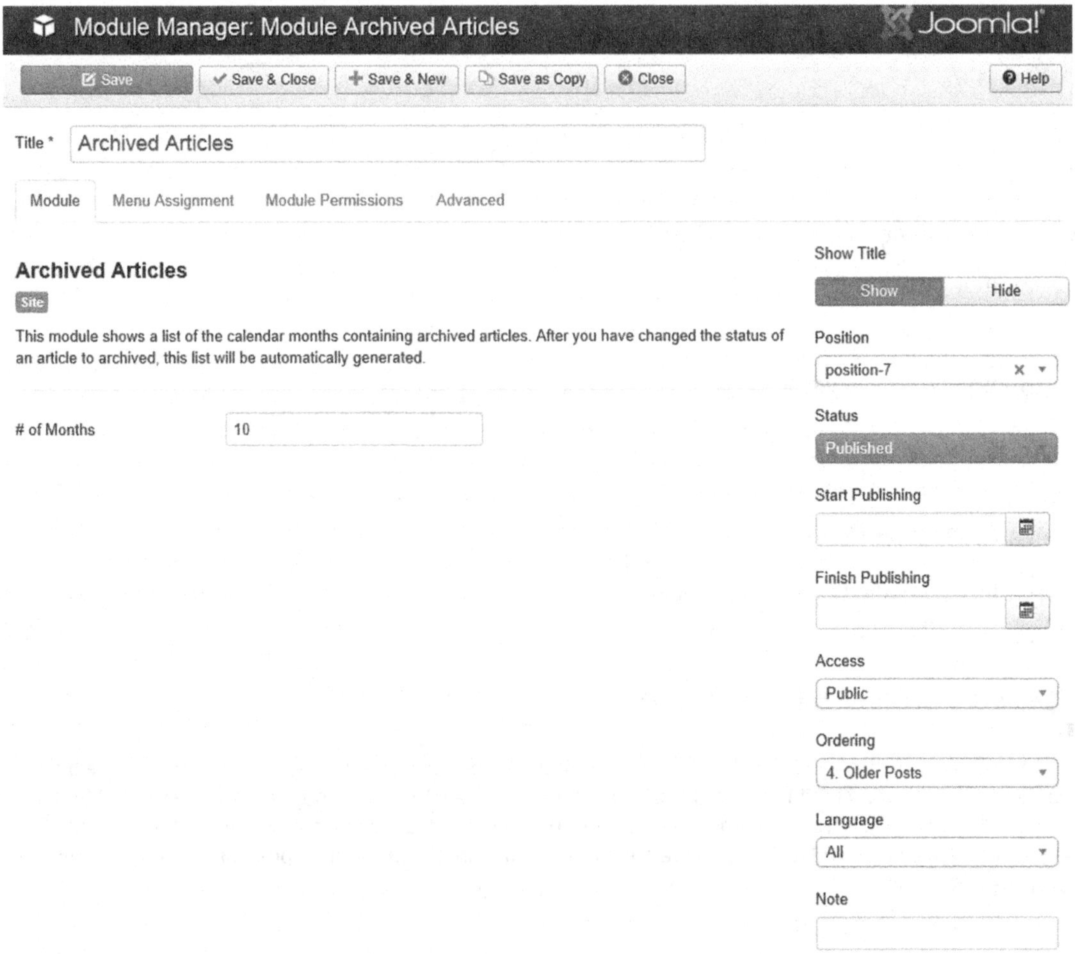

Figure 8-5. *Module information divided into four sections*

The settings displayed are divided into four sections: Module, Menu Assignment, Module Permissions, and Advanced. Again, all the module types have the same settings in the Module, Menu Assignment, and Module Permissions sections; the only difference is with the Advanced section options. The next section discusses Module section options.

Module Section

In the Title field, you enter the title of the module. For this example, enter **Archived Titles**, which is the name that will appear in the Module Manager. Set the Show Title option to Yes to see the title displayed on the front end. Set the Status option to Published to make the module visible on the web site. The Position drop-down list is used to specify the location of the module on the web page. The positions in the drop-down list are provided by the template you use and appear as shown in Figure 8-6. For this example, keep its default position: position-7.

Position

Figure 8-6. *Positions for displaying the module*

You can easily display all the default positions provided by the current template on the web page by simply adding the text ?tp=1 to the end of any front-end Joomla URL. For example, the web site URL is http://localhost/joomlasite/, so if you type the URL as http://localhost/joomlasite/?tp=1, you will see the web page displayed with labeled rectangles that indicate the predefined positions for the current template (see Figure 8-7).

harwanibm.net

Position: position-0 [Style: none outline] Search

Home position-1 [Style: none outline] New Electronics Products arrival   Supplier Support   Purchase Support   Newsfeeds
About   Author Login

New Electronics among Cameras and Cell Phones

Position: banner [Style: xhtml outline]
Position: position-8 [Style: xhtml outline] Position: position-3 [Style: xhtml outline]

Blog ①

Electronics ⓪

Position: position-2 [Style: none outline]

Position: position-7 [Style: well outline]
Most Read Posts
- Welcome to your blog

Position: position-7 [Style: well outline]
Popular Tags
- camera,
- cell phone,
- zoom,
- higher megapixel resolution,
- latest fashion,
- network coverage,
- clothing,
- men,

Position: position-7 [Style: well outline]
Blog Roll
- Joomla! Community
- Joomla! Leadership Blog

Position: position-7 [Style: well outline]
Login Form

👤 Username

🔒 Password

★ Secret Key   ❓

☐ Remember Me

Log in

Create an account ❯
Forgot your username?
Forgot your password?

Position: footer [Style: none outline]

Position: footer [Style: none outline]   Back to Top

Position: debug [Style: none outline]

Figure 8-7. *Rectangles indicatepredefined positions for the current template*

> ■ **Note** If the positions are not displayed, open the Template Manager. Click the Options icon from the toolbar and set the Preview Module Positions field to Enabled value. By default, its value is Disabled.

The Ordering drop-down list in the Module section (refer to Figure 8-5) is used to specify the display sequence if more than one module is assigned the same position. You can actually set the order of a module to appear in the ordering dialog box as well as the Module Manager main page just by clicking the up/down arrows. The module positions are decided by the template that you applied to your web site, and a template may specify the same position to several modules. For example, suppose that the Main Menu and Login Form modules have the same position (defined in the current template). In this case, the value in the Ordering drop-down list decides which will appear first on the front end. The drop-down list shows all modules being assigned the current position. You can select the module after which you want the current module to appear. The order can also be changed later from the Module Manager.

For this example, keep the default order (i.e., keep the value of this field unchanged so that the modules are displayed in the default sequence).

The Access Level field is used to specify the user level allowed to access this module. The access levels are as follows:

- **Public:** Everyone can access this module.

- **Registered:** Only registered users can access this module.

- **Special:** Only users with author status or higher can access this module.

For this example, set the Access Level to Public because you want the module to be publicly viewed.

Menu Assignment Section

The Menu Assignment section is used to determine the web pages on which the current module is to be displayed. You can make a module appear or disappear by selecting certain menu items. The Menus option is used to determine the menus in which you want to display the module. The options are as follows:

- **All:** Displays the current module on all menu items of the web page. Choose this option for this example.

- **None:** Makes the module invisible (not displayed on any menu items).

- **Select Menu Item(s) from the List:** Displays the module on only selected menu items.

The Menu Selection list is used when Select Menu Item(s) from the List is selected. It helps when selecting individual menu items on which you want to display the module. You can Ctrl+ click to select multiple menu items and Shift+ click to select a range of menu items.

> ■ **Note** Although the Menus option for a module is usually set to None by default, set it to All for all the modules that will be discussed in this chapter to make them appear on all menu items of the web page.

Now you'll look at each module in turn. Because all the module types have the same fields in the Module, Menu Assignment, and Module Permissions sections, only the fields of the Advanced section for each module will be discussed. Likewise, one example module per module type will be discussed because all the modules of a particular module type work according to the same concept.

Archive

The Archive module shows articles that have been archived (temporarily removed from active display and stored). This module displays nothing if no articles are archived. If an article is archived, it is stored by creation date, not by archive date, and the module displays the month and year of creation. This module and the menu item type Archived Article (discussed in Chapter 7) work in a similar fashion.

In the Module Manager, when you select the Archive module, it opens in edit mode. By default, the Module section opens up as shown in Figure 8-5. The # of Months is for specifying the number of calendar months containing archived articles to be displayed. The default value is 10, but you can set it to any value that you want. The fields in its Advanced section are as shown in Figure 8-8.

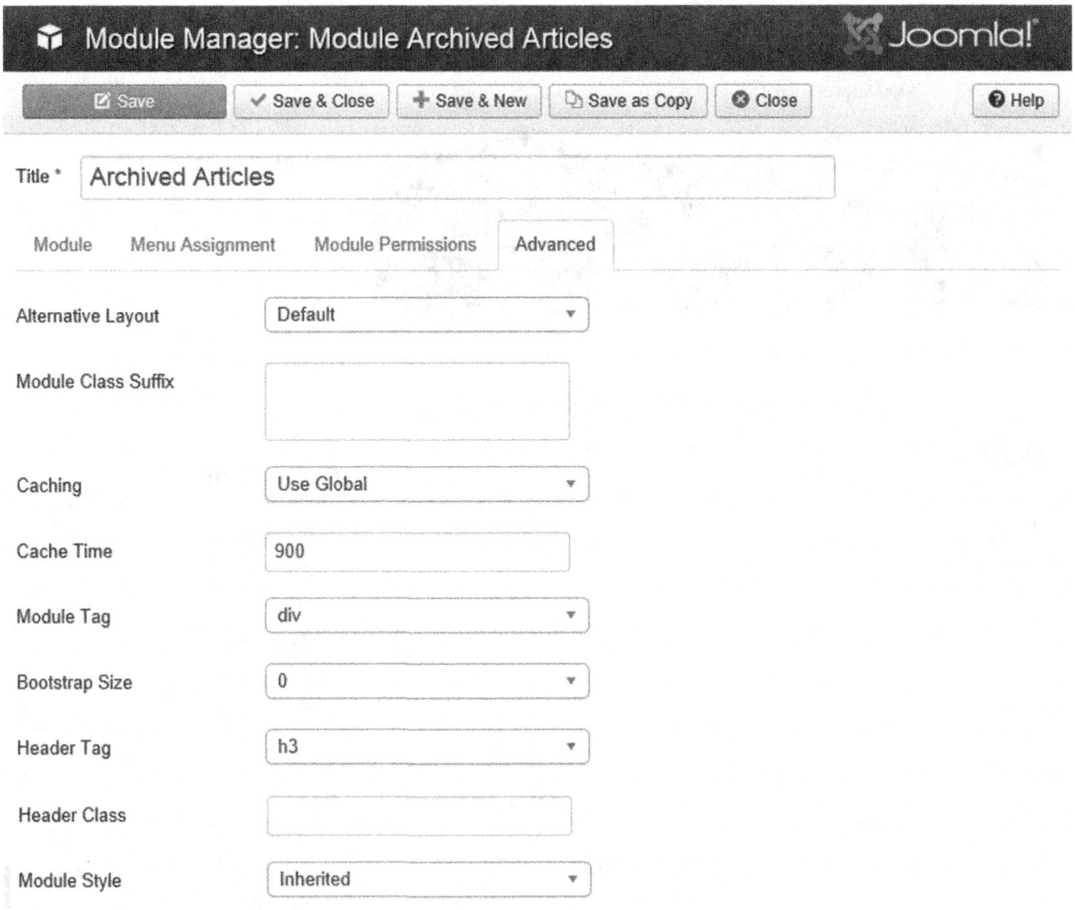

Figure 8-8. *Parameters of the Archive module*

The Module Class Suffix field allows you to specify a preset style that is defined by the template. Also, this field is used when you want to apply your own CSS class to certain modules, independent of the site's default template CSS classes. CSS classes are for applying your own styles (font, color, and so on) to the modules of your web site in a consistent manner. To do this, create CSS classes in the template CSS file and specify its name in this field. Suppose that the class name is module-archive; if you enter its suffix, -archive, in this field, its styles will be individually applied to the Archive module. Click the Save & Close icon from the toolbar to save the changes made in the module.

Upon opening the front end of your Joomla web site, you'll see a link with the title Archived Articles, indicating that some articles created in January 2011 and December 2010 have been archived. If you click the January 2011 link, you'll see all the archived articles that were created in that month and year, as shown in Figure 8-9.

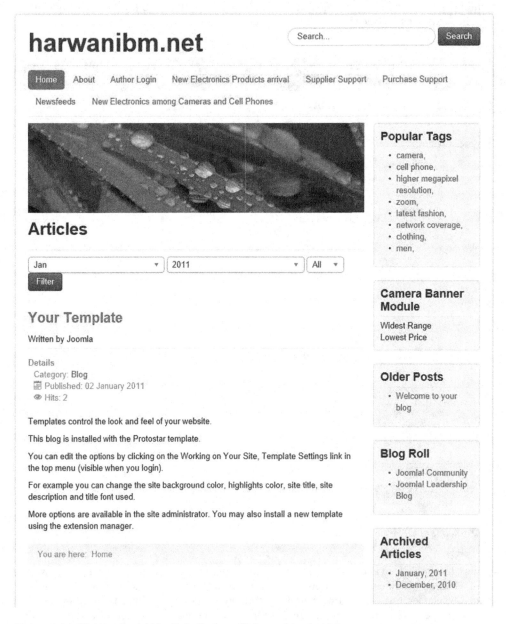

Figure 8-9. *Clicking the Archive link displays all the archived articles*

Banners

The Banners module is used to activate the banner(s) created through the Banner component (to display the banner on the web site). You learned how to use the Banner module, step by step, in Chapter 4.

Breadcrumbs

The Breadcrumbs module is helpful for quick navigation in a web site. It not only displays your current location in the web site but also the parent web pages through which you traveled to reach the current page. You can use the parent links to navigate back.

Select the Breadcrumbs module from the Module Manager to open it in edit mode. The options in the Parameters section will appear, as shown in Figure 8-10.

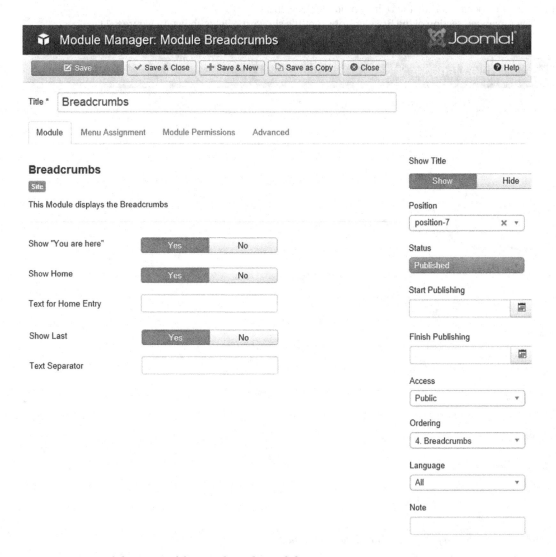

Figure 8-10. *Module section of the Breadcrumbs module*

The Show Home option is used to decide whether to display the home page in the breadcrumbs path. For this example, set it to Yes.

The Text for Home Entry field is for specifying the text to display for the home page in the breadcrumbs. Usually it is set to Home, but you can enter any text (e.g., Default or Index). Keep the default value Home in this field.

The Show Last option is used to deciding whether to display the current location of the web page. If you set this field to No, it will display the links up to the parent web page, but not the current page. For example, suppose that you select the Cell Phones category from the News Feeds menu. The breadcrumb will display Home ➤ News Feeds ➤ Cell Phones if the Show Last field is set to Yes. If you set this field to No, the breadcrumb will display Home ➤ News Feeds, which excludes the location of the current web page. Set this field to Yes.

The Text Separator field specifies the text to be used to separate the navigation elements. Usually the default, ➤, is used, but you can use any symbol. Keep this field blank to use the default. Let the Position of the module be position-7 (on the right-top side of the web site).

The Advanced section of the Breadcrumbs module shows the fields shown in Figure 8-11.

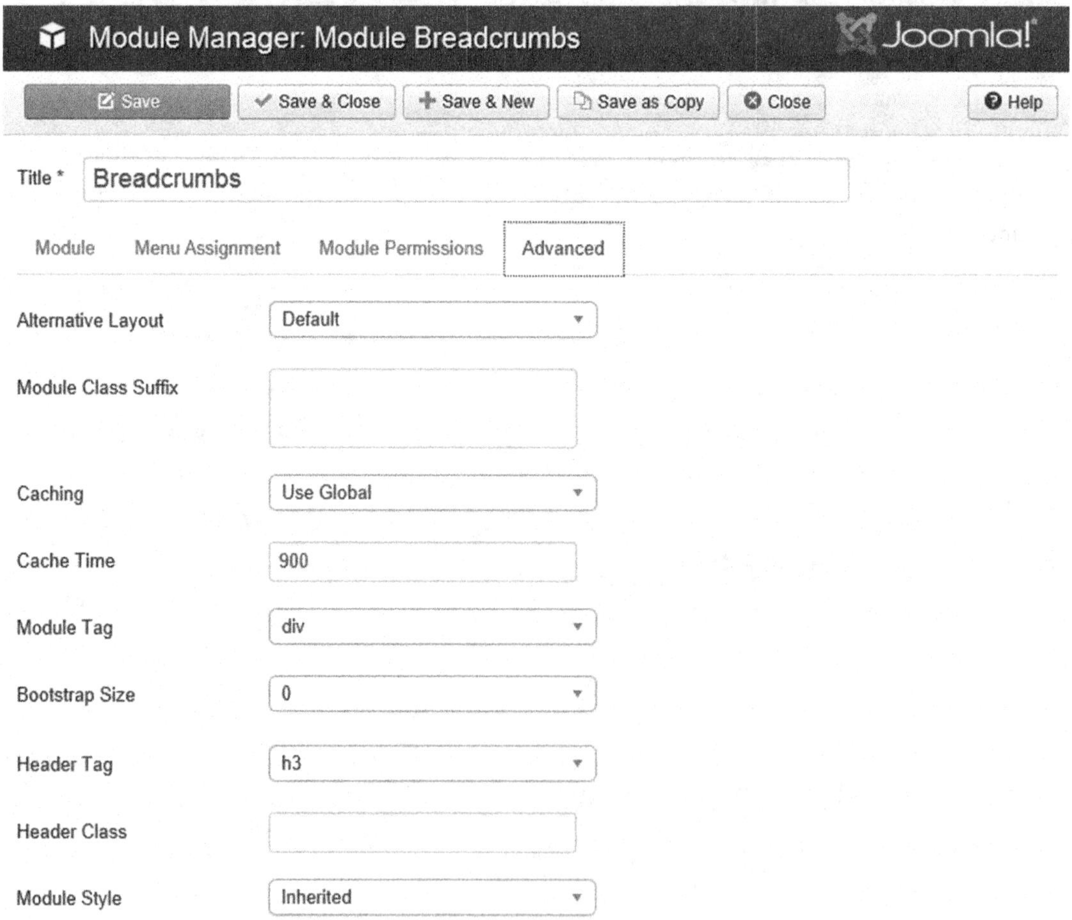

Figure 8-11. Advanced fields of the Breadcrumbs module

The Module Class Suffix field is used for applying individual styles to the module. In this field, you can specify the suffix of the style class created in the template CSS file. Keep this field blank and the rest of the fields at their default values. Click Save & Close button to save the module.

■ **Note**   Don't forget to set the value of the Menus option in the Menu Assignment section to All to keep the module visible when selecting any menu item of the web site. Remember that when you publish a module, it can be assigned to all pages or pages specified in the Pages/Items or Menu Assignment dialog box. You can assign modules only to pages that have menu items.

From the front side of the site, when you select the Web Cams - Video Chatting article of the Camera subcategory of the Electronics category, the Breadcrumbs module will display the breadcrumb as Home ➤ Electronics ➤ Camera ➤ Web Cams - Video chatting (see Figure 8-12).

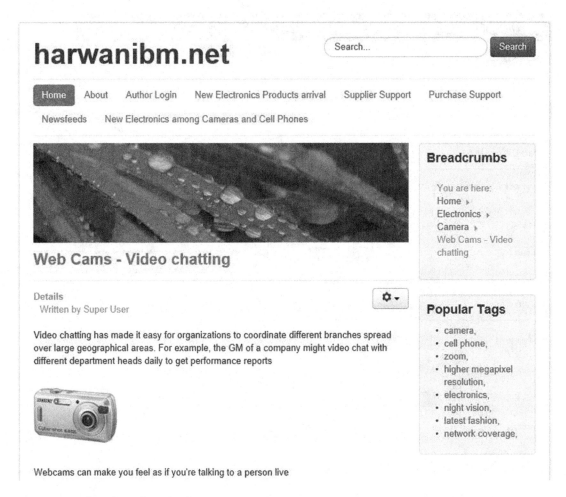

Figure 8-12. *Breadcrumb navigation upon execution*

Feed Display

The Feed Display module is used to display news feeds from other web sites. News feeds are generally used when you regularly want to access certain information from other web sites. So instead of visiting those web sites continually for the updated information, news feeds allow you to merge the updated content from the specific web sites into your pages. In other words, the Feed Display module is a facility that you can use to obtain new and updated content from the web site(s) that the feed is linked with.

The Feed Display module is of two types: the Site module type and the Administrator module type. If you want the module output on the front side, you can use the Site module type; choose the Administrator type if you want the output on the administrator interface. Choose the Administrator module type.

From the Module Manager page, click the Administrator link to display administrator type modules and click the New button to create a new module. You will be prompted to select the module type. From the list of displayed module types (refer to Figure 8-4), choose the Feed Display module type. Assign the title as News Feed Display to the new module (see Figure 8-13).

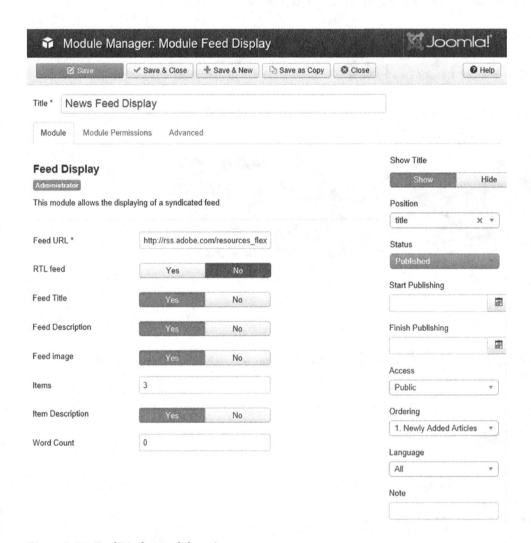

Figure 8-13. *Feed Display module options*

In the Feed URL field, you specify the URL of the RSS feed. Specify the URL `http://rss.adobe.com/resources_flex.rss?locale=en_US` in the Feed URL field. The RTL Feed option is used to specify whether the flow of information on your web site should go from right to left (RTL). You'll usually set it to Yes for Arabic languages and the like, in which the flow of information is in the right-to-left direction. For this example, leave it at No.

Set Feed Title to Yes to display the feed title, set Feed Description to Yes to display the feed description, and set Feed Image to Yes to display the feed image.

The Items field is used to specify the number of news feed items to display. The default value for the Items field is 3.

Set Item Description to Yes to display the description of individual items. The Word Count field is used to specify the maximum number of words to display in the item description (a value of 0 means that the entire item description will be displayed).

From the Position combo box, choose the location in which you want to display the module. Select the title position to display the module at the top of the site.

When clicked, the Advanced section will display the fields as shown in Figure 8-14. As discussed earlier for other modules, in the Module Class Suffix field, you specify the suffix of the style class created in the template CSS file. This option is used for applying individual styles to the module.

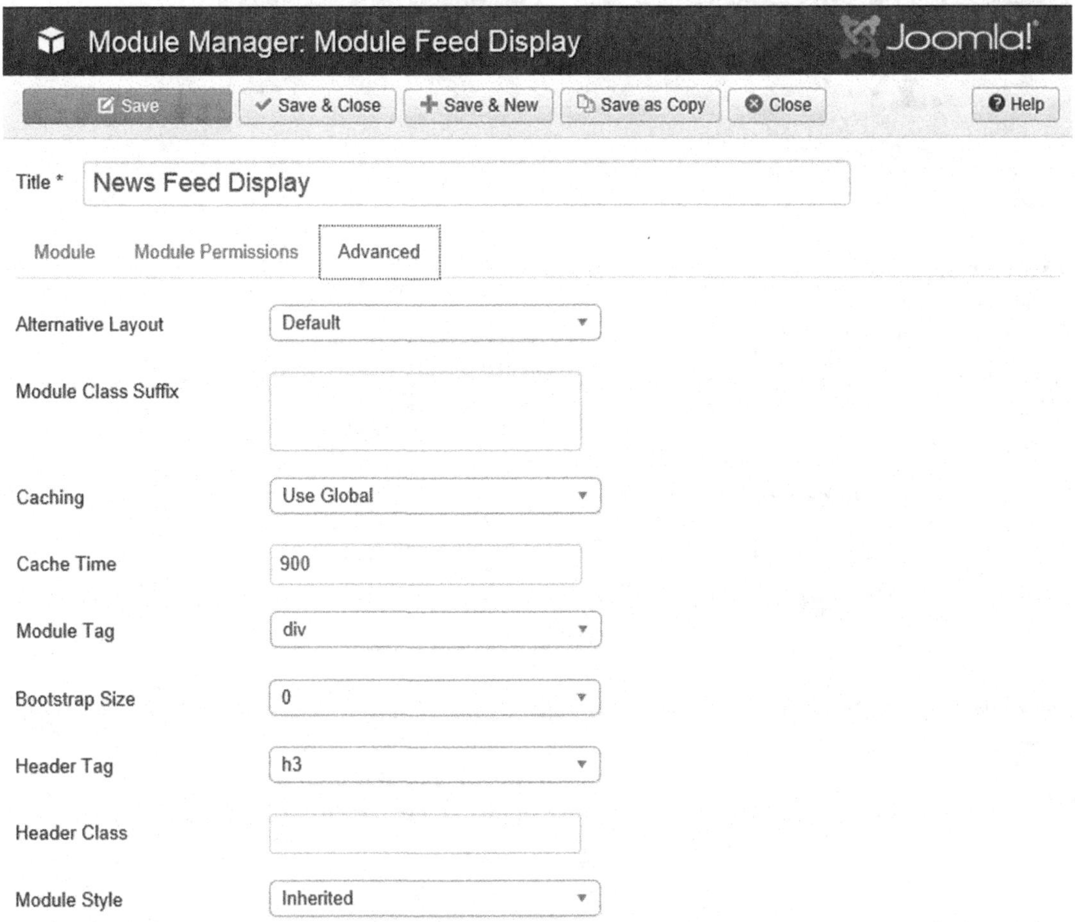

Figure 8-14. *Advanced fields of the Feed Display module*

After entering the information, click the Save & Close icon from the toolbar to save the module. Because this is the Administrator module, the impact of this module will appear at the back end (at the administrator interface). The moment you save the module, you'll immediately see the impact of the module (the news feed from the supplied web site), as shown in Figure 8-15. Notice that the web site displays links to certain articles. Any changes made by the source web site in the feed contents will be reflected in your Feed Display module.

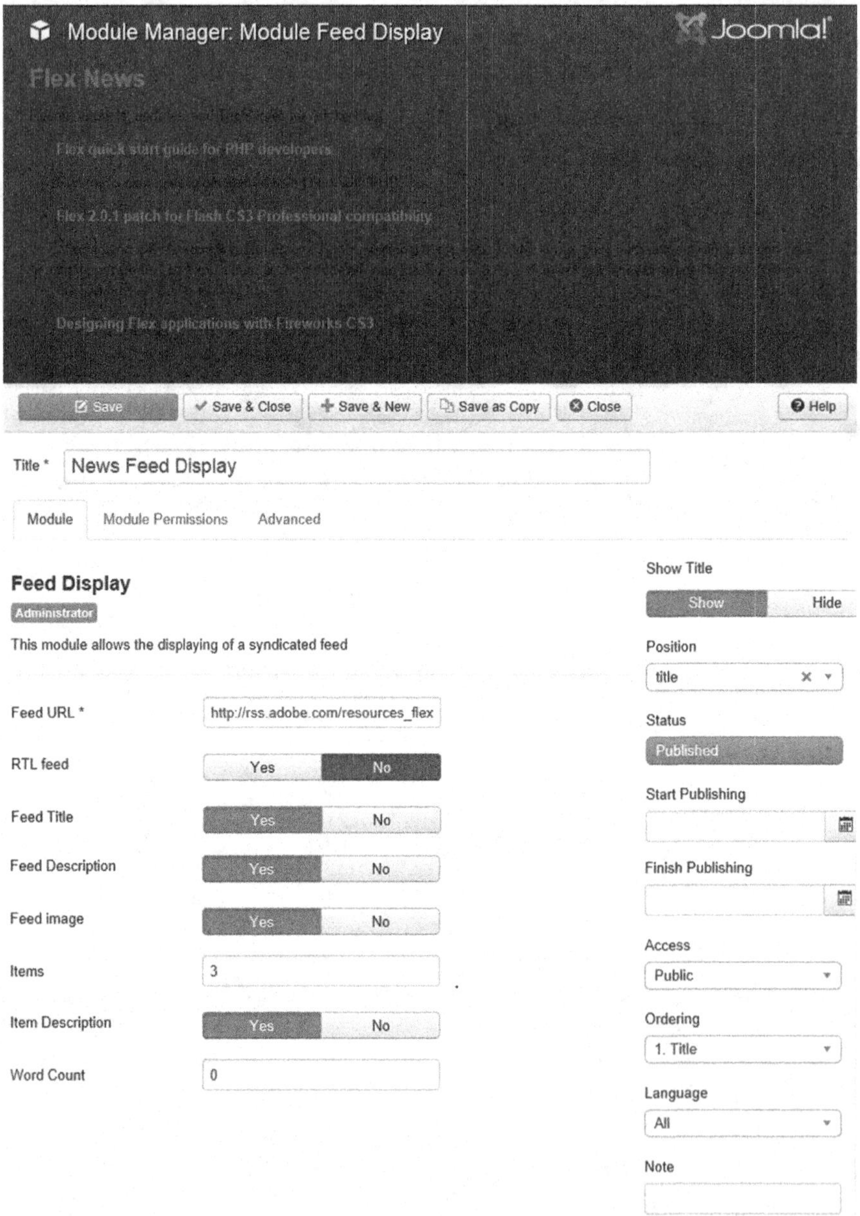

Figure 8-15. *Feed Display output upon execution*

Note   Because the news feed is regularly updated by the source web site, the list of items that you see may be entirely different from that shown in Figure 8-15.

Now let's supply the URL of another RSS feed location in the Feed URL field: http://feeds.joomla.org/JoomlaMagazine. In your Joomla web site, the Feed Display module shows links to certain articles supplied by the new RSS feed URL entered, as shown in Figure 8-16.

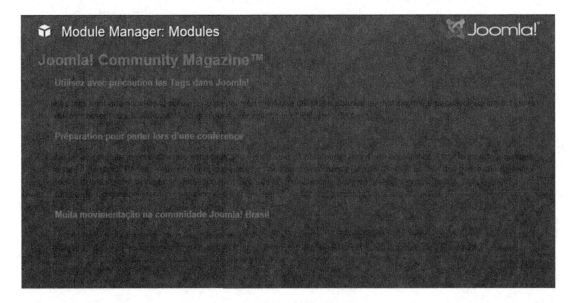

Figure 8-16. *Feed Display output upon execution for a different feed*

You can select any link shown in the Feed Display module to see the corresponding information.

Footer

The Footer module displays the web site copyright and Joomla license information. The module also works like the core menu module and allows you to split the menu across a number of columns. To create a Footer module, open the Module Manager, click the Site link to display Site type modules, and then click the New button to create a new module. You will be prompted to select the module type. From the list of displayed module types (refer to Figure 8-3), choose the Footer module type. You see a screen (shown in Figure 8-17) in which you enter information for the new module. Assign the title as Footer to the new module.

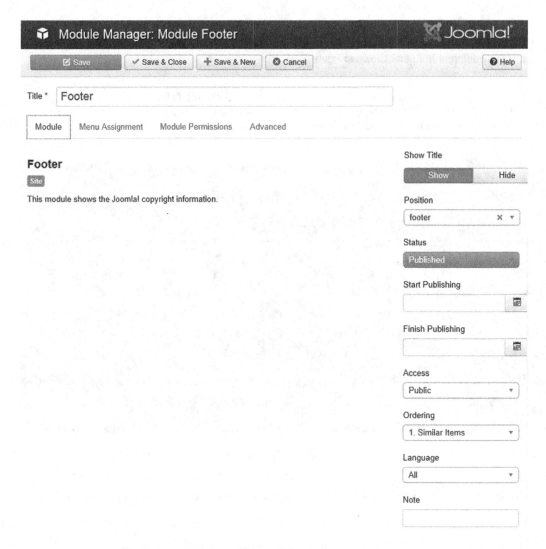

Figure 8-17. *Footer displaying copyright and license information*

There is nothing much to do in this module. Simply set the Position drop-down list to the footer value to display the result of this module at the bottom of the site. Leave the value of the rest of the fields to their defaults and click the Save & Close button to save the module.

The output of this module (copyright and other license information) will appear at the bottom of the site, as shown in Figure 8-18.

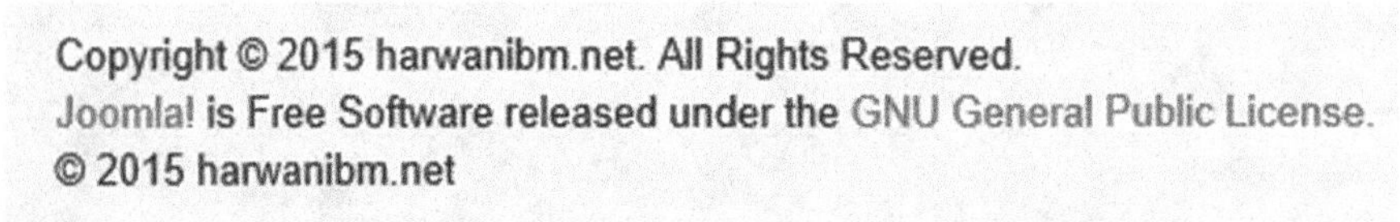

Copyright © 2015 harwanibm.net. All Rights Reserved.
Joomla! is Free Software released under the GNU General Public License.
© 2015 harwanibm.net

Figure 8-18. *Footer displaying copyright and license information*

Latest News

The Latest News module shows a list of the most recently published articles. From the Administrator's list of modules in the Module Manager, select the module with the title Recently Added Articles that is of the type Latest News. The module opens in edit mode, as shown in Figure 8-19.

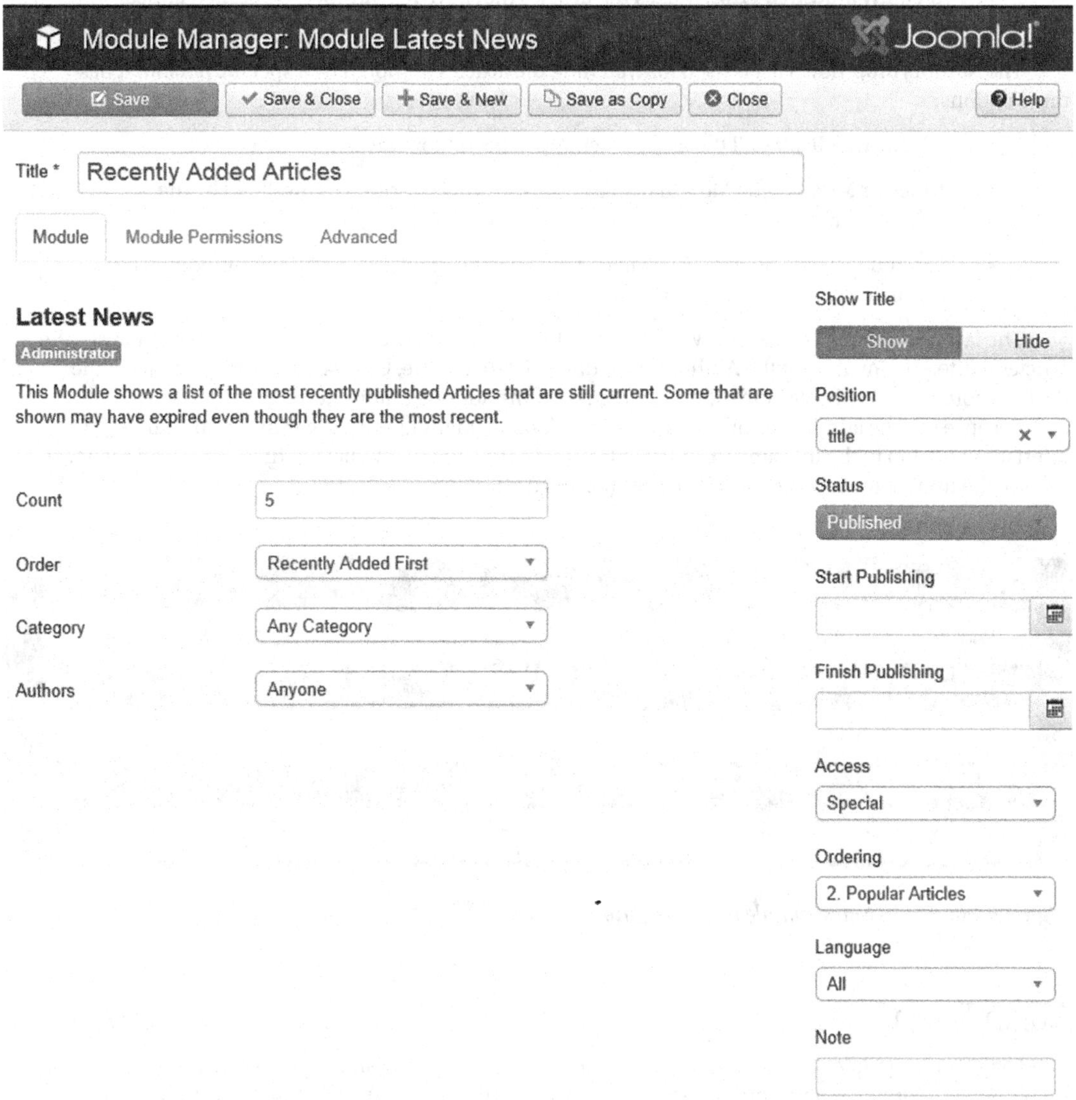

Figure 8-19. *Latest News module options*

The Count field specifies the number of articles to be displayed. The default value is 5. The Order drop-down list is used to specify the sequence in which the articles are to be displayed. The options are as follows:

- **Recently Added First:** Makes the articles that have recently been added appear first in sequence. Select this option.

- **Recently Modified First:** Makes the articles that have recently been modified appear first in sequence.

The Authors drop-down list is used for watching the articles authored by a specific person. It has three options:

- Anyone will display all the articles, whoever the author may be.

- Added or Modified By Me will display only the articles written or modified by the current user.

- Not Added or Modified By Me will display only the articles not written or modified by the current user.

The last two options are used only if the user is logged in to the web site. Because you want to see the articles written by anyone, set the Authors drop-down list to Anyone. Choose the Title option from the Position combo box to display the module at the top in the administrator interface.

Because it is the administrator module, the result of the module will appear in the administrator interface at the top in the title area the moment you save the module by clicking the Save & Close icon. You can see the titles of the recently added articles (see Figure 8-20).

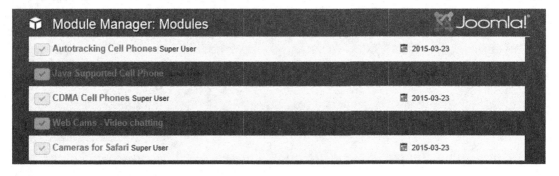

Figure 8-20. *Latest News module upon execution*

Login Form

The Login Form module displays a login form for entering a username and password. It also displays links for retrieving a forgotten password or username. A Create an Account link will also be displayed if user registration is enabled in the User Settings section of the Global Configuration file. This module functions in a similar way to the menu item of type Default Login Layout. When you select the Login Form module from the Site modules list in the Module Manager, it will open in edit mode, and the options should appear as shown in Figure 8-21.

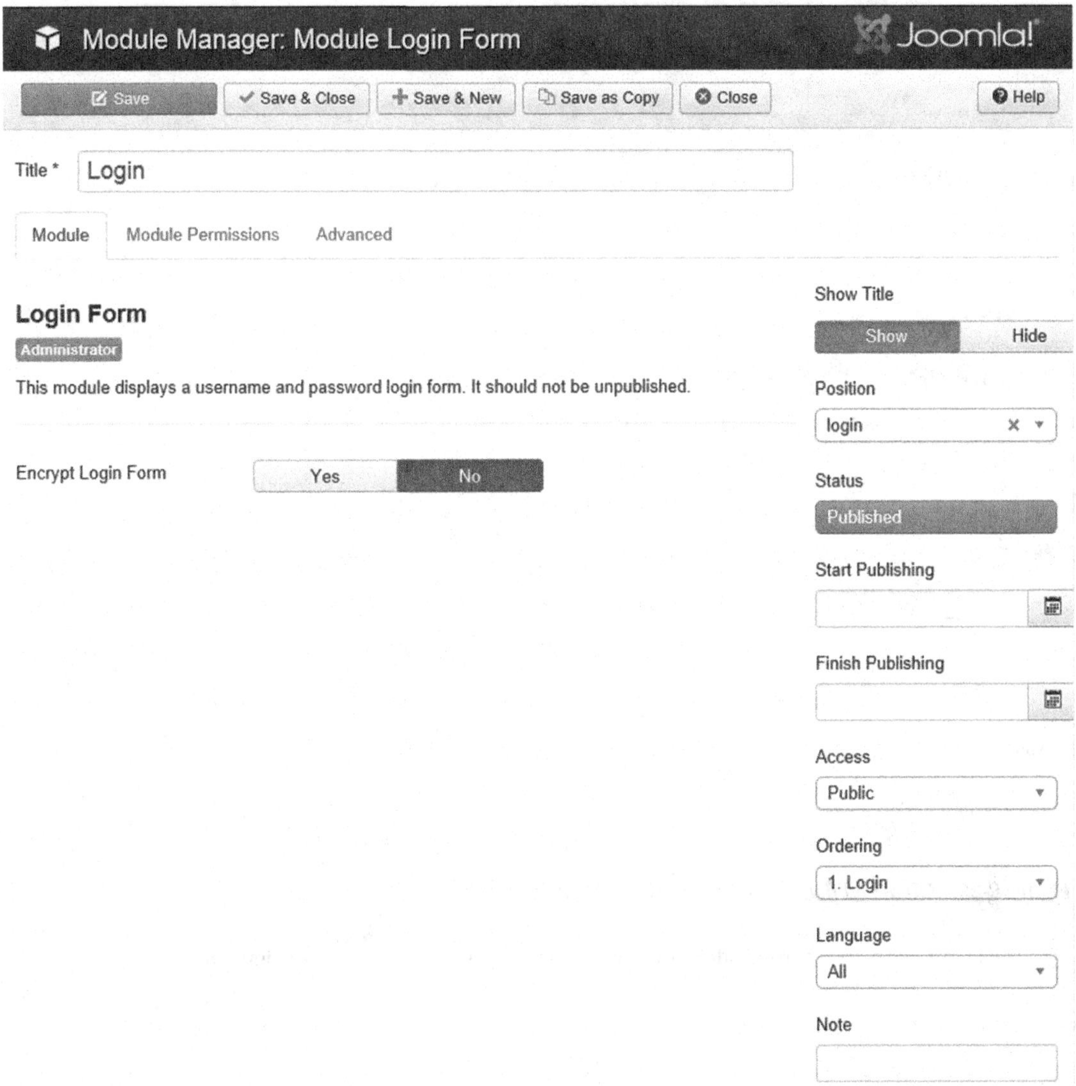

Figure 8-21. *Login module options*

The Encrypt Login Form option is set to Yes to encrypt the login form using SSL. It is used when Joomla is accessed using the https:// prefix. Set it to No. The rest of the fields are the same, as discussed earlier.

The Advanced section will display the fields as shown in Figure 8-22. The Caching drop-down list allows you to control the speed of the loading process of a module by keeping the module in server memory. It takes less time to load the module from memory than it does to retrieve it from the disk drive. Caching is usually applied for modules that are frequently used but not frequently updated, such as the Footer module that displays copyright and other static information. In this case, set the Caching option to No Caching because you're not interested in caching. The Module Class Suffix field is used to apply individual module styling.

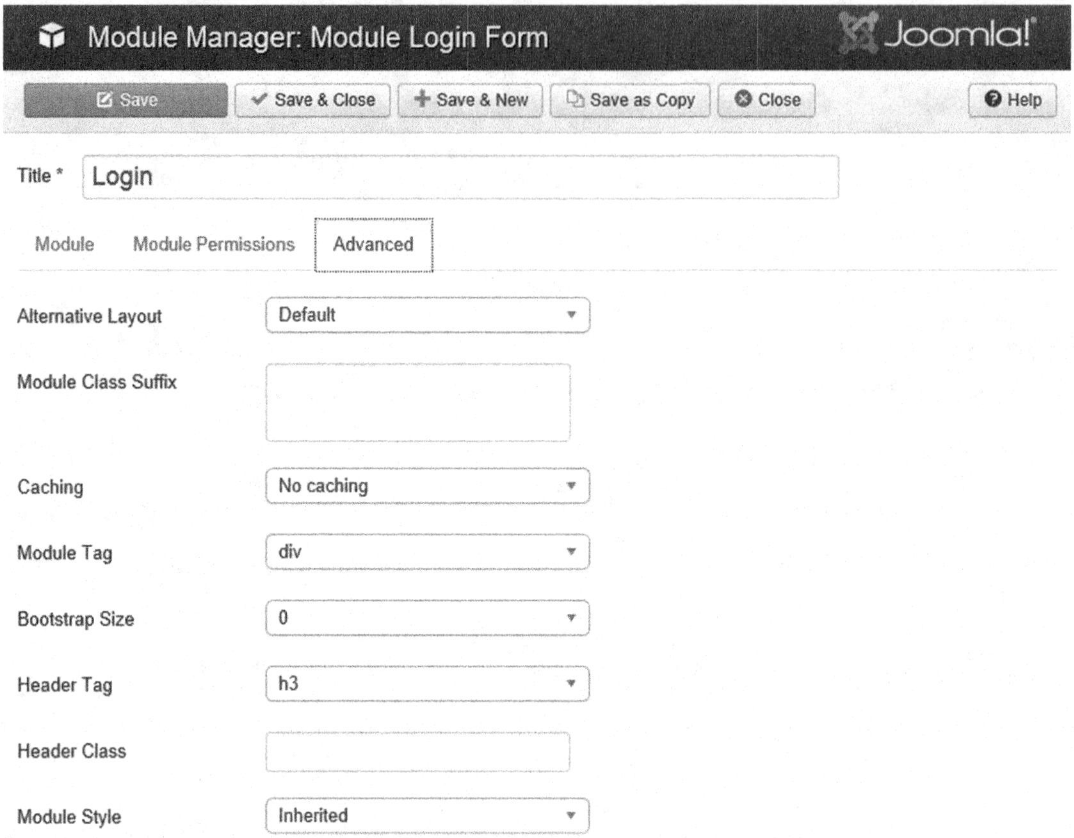

Figure 8-22. *Advanced fields of the Login Form module*

The Login Form on the front side of the web site should appear as shown in Figure 8-23.

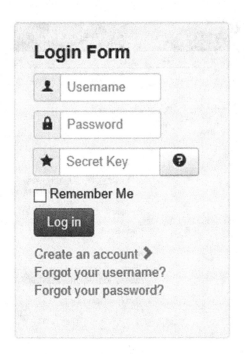

Figure 8-23. *Login Form module upon execution*

Main Menu

The Main Menu module can be used to create your own menus and edit existing ones. You can also define the pages in which you want the specific menus to appear and the location in which you want the menus to appear on the desired web pages. When you select the Main Menu module from the Module Manager, it opens in edit mode, as shown in Figure 8-24.

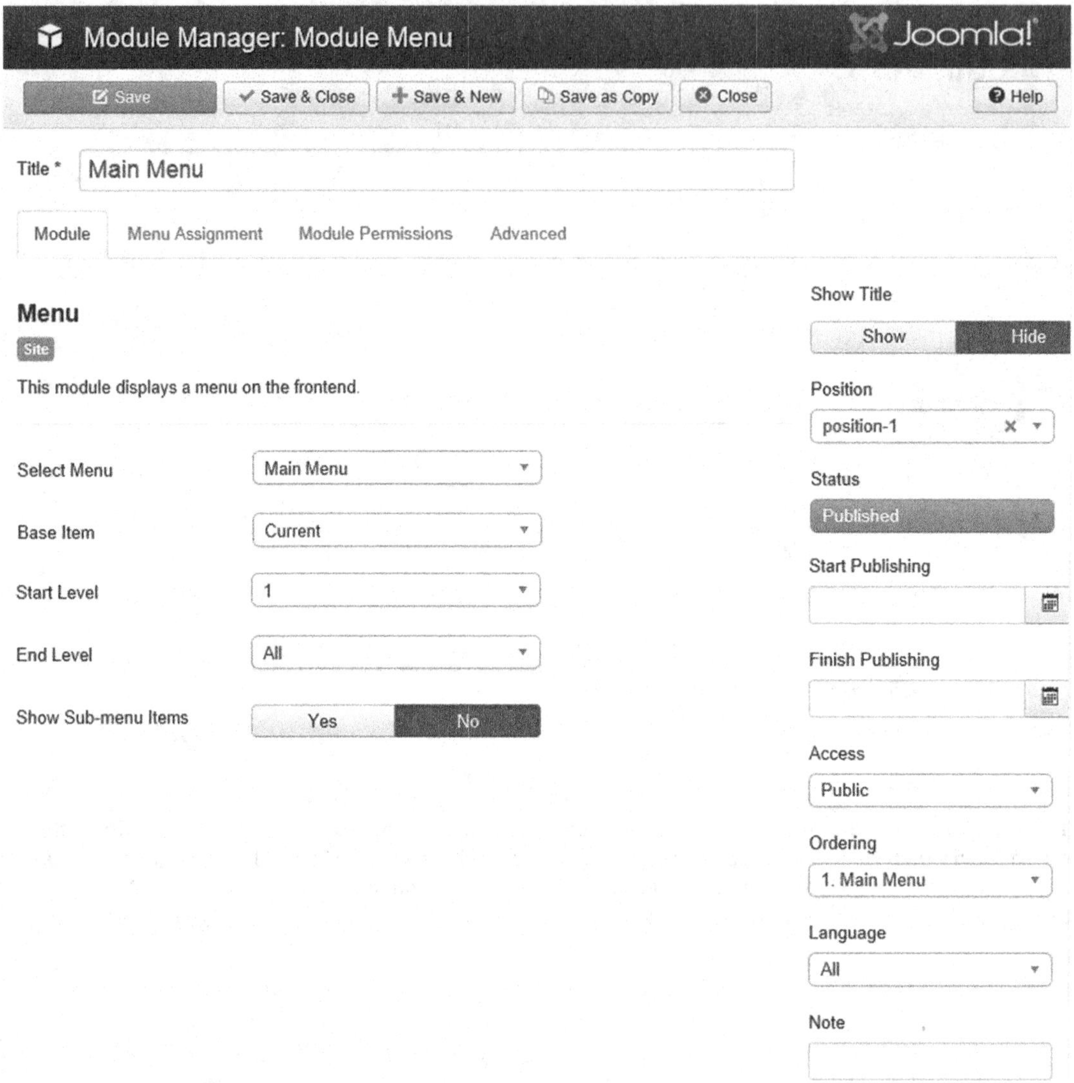

Figure 8-24. *Module section of the Main Menu module*

In the Start Level and End Level fields, you specify the level of depth of the menus. The top level is numbered 1. For example, if you set the Start Level to 1 and the End Level to 2, all the top-level menus will be displayed, along with all the menus at level 2. However, menus at level 3 or deeper will not be displayed. As you might expect, the Start Level is the highest level of menu to be displayed; the default is 1 (top level). For this example, keep the default value here. The End Level is the lowest level in the menu hierarchy to be displayed; the default, All, will display all menu levels. Again, for this example, keep the default value here.

The Show Sub-menu Items option is used for deciding whether to display submenu items when the parent is not active. If No, a submenu item will be displayed only when the parent item is clicked. If Yes, submenu items will always be displayed in the menu.

The Position field is used to specify the location of the menu in pixels. If you don't specify any position here, it is supplied by the template being used.

■ **Note**   For precise positioning, you can even download the Modules Anywhere extension and use it to put a module anywhere on your site. That is, you can place a module inside an article or inside another module by using the Modules Anywhere extension.

You learned to work with menu items in Chapter 3 and later chapters. The main menu on the front side may appear as shown in Figure 8-25.

Figure 8-25. *Main menu on the front side of the web site*

Most Read Content

This module displays a list of the articles with the highest hit counts—the most popular articles among all visitors. From the Site module type list, select the module with the title Most Read Posts of the Most Read Content module type. The module will open in edit mode, as shown in Figure 8-26.

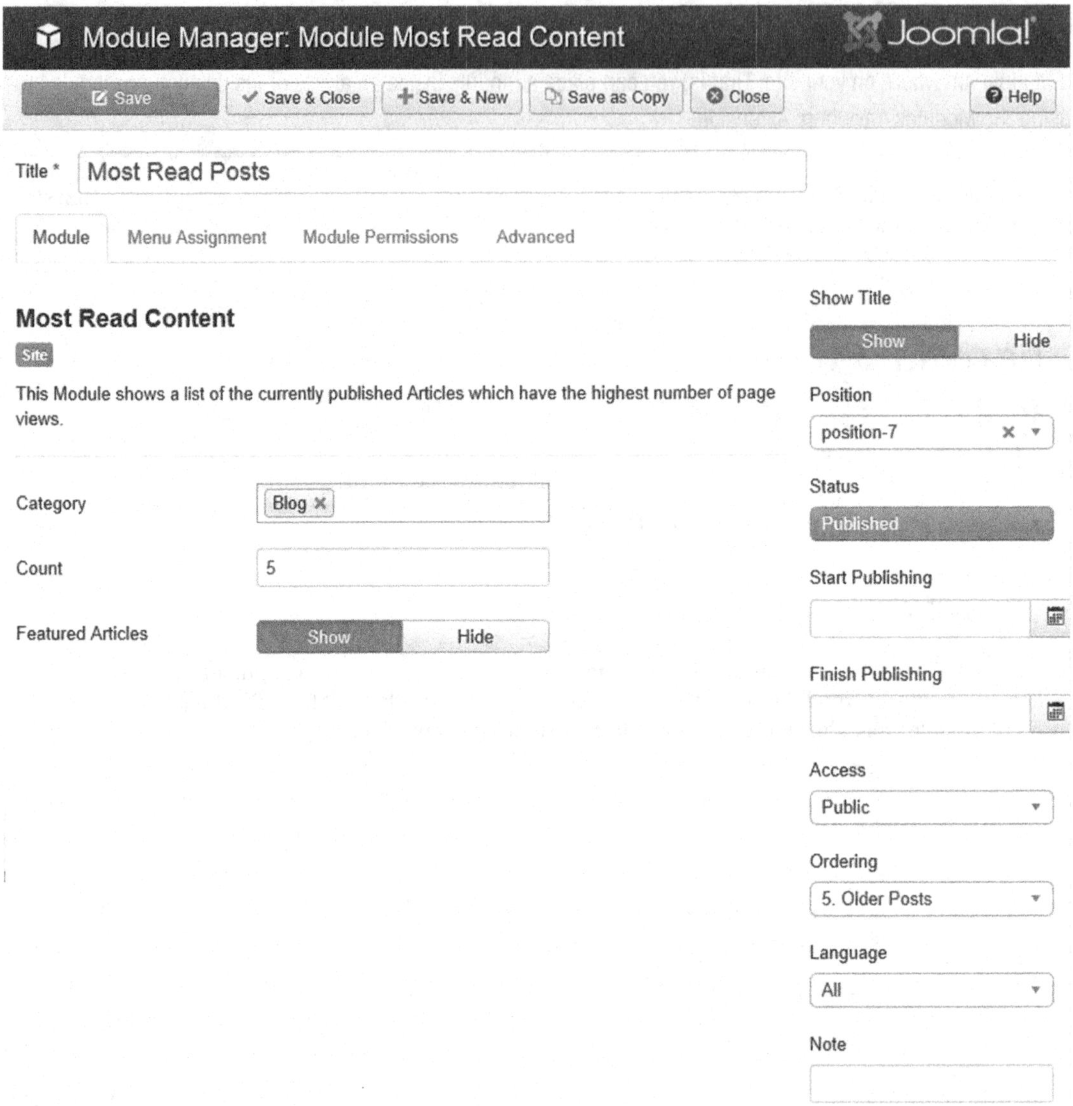

Figure 8-26. *Most Read Content module options*

The title of this module is Most Read Posts (on the front side of the site, the result of this module will be headed with this title). The Category field is used for displaying articles only from specific categories. You specify the category(ies) for the articles you want to see. To specify more than one category, separate them with a comma. The default value for this field is Blog, so keep the default value because you don't want to see any particular articles.

The Count field is used to specify the number of articles to display in the list. The default value is 5. Keep the default value. The Featured Articles option is used to decide whether to display the featured articles in the list. For this example, set this field to Show.

Output of the Most Read Content module on the web site should appear as shown in Figure 8-27. The title of the module is Most Read Posts, the one that was specified in the module.

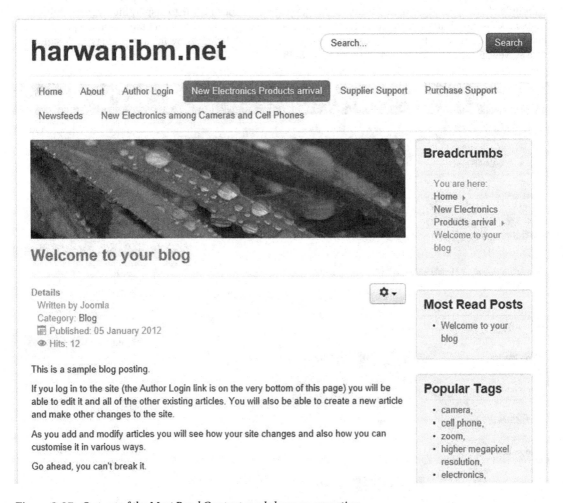

Figure 8-27. *Output of the Most Read Content module upon execution*

Articles - Newsflash

This module displays one or more articles from the selected category each time the page is refreshed. This is a module of Site type, so from the Module Manager page, click the Site link to display Site type modules and then click the New button to create a new module. You will be prompted to select the module type. From the list of displayed module types (refer to Figure 8-3), choose the Articles - Newsflash module type. Assign the title as NewsFlash to the new module (see Figure 8-28).

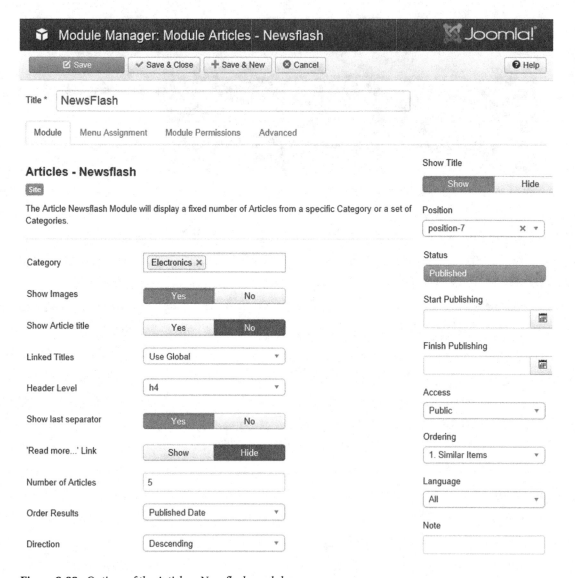

Figure 8-28. *Options of the Articles - Newsflash module*

In the Category drop-down list, you can select a category whose articles you want to display. Select Electronics because you want to see the articles of the Electronics category and of the Camera and Cell Phone subcategory.

Set the Show Images option to Yes because you also want to display the images of the article.

The Show Article title field allows you to set whether the title of the article will be displayed. In this case, set it to No because you don't want the title to be displayed.

The Linked Titles drop-down list is for deciding whether you want the title of the article to act as a hyperlink to the article—that is, whether the contents of the article will be displayed upon clicking its title. Set this field to Use Global to get its value from the Global Configuration file.

Set the Show Last Separator option to Yes to display a separator after the last article.

The Read More... Link option is for deciding whether to show a Read more link (used in large articles to display the next portion of the article). In this case, set it to Hide.

The Number of Articles field is used to specify the number of the articles to be displayed. The default is 5. You can leave this field blank to keep the default value.

From the Position drop-down list, choose the position-7 option to display the newsflash on the right-top side of the screen.

The output of Articles-Newsflash should appear as shown in Figure 8-29. You can see that the content of an article from the Electronics category. On refreshing the site, you'll get some other article displayed from the same category.

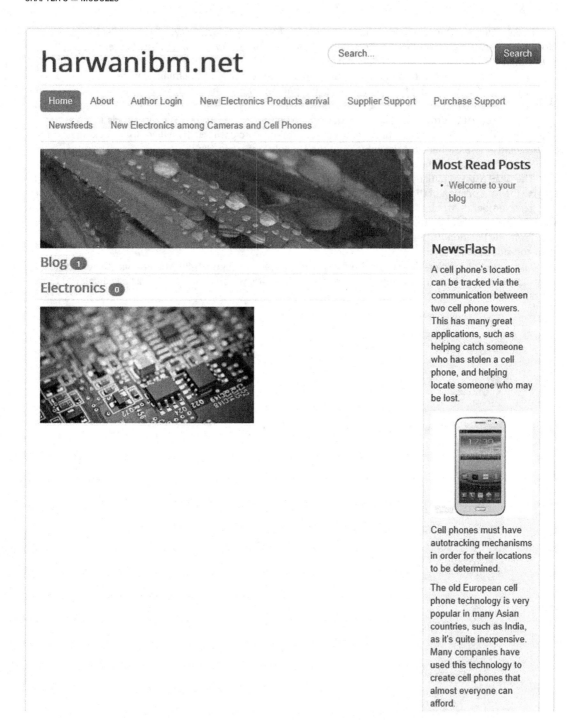

Figure 8-29. Output of the Newsflash module upon execution

■ **Note**   If you find that too many modules are enabled, and the screen appears cluttered, you can disable certain modules to make the front end appear neat and tidy.

Random Image

This module displays a random image from the selected directory. Specifically, every time someone visits the site, Joomla randomly pulls a different image from the images folder that you have created. From the Site type module, from the Module Manager page, click the Site link to display Site type modules and then click the New button to create a new module. You will be prompted to select the module type. From the list of displayed module types (refer to Figure 8-3), choose Random Image module type. Let's assign the title as Images Flash to the new module (see Figure 8-30).

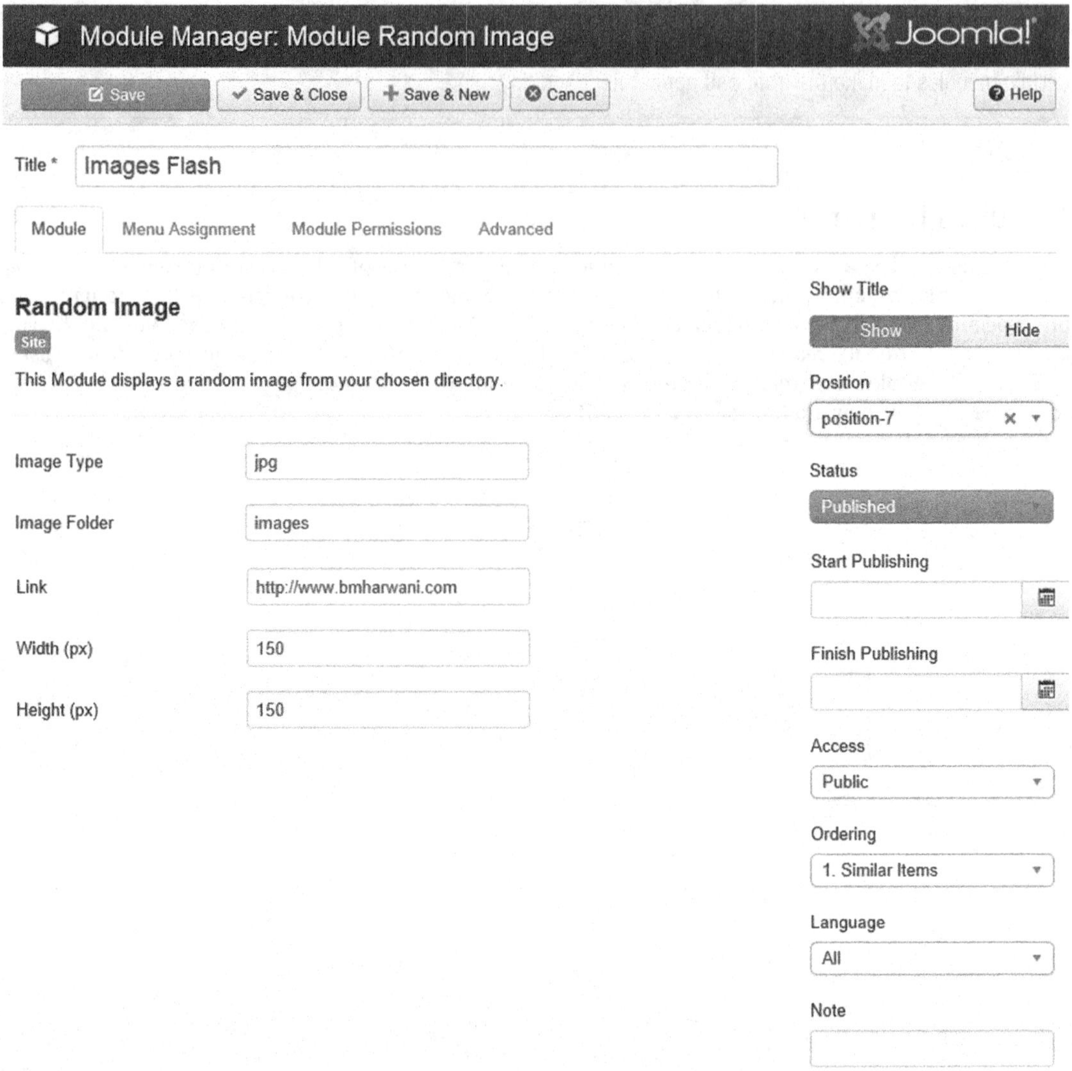

Figure 8-30. *Options of the Random Image module*

The Image Type field is used to specify the type of image to be displayed (JPG, PNG, GIF, and so on). The default is JPG.

In the Image Folder field, select the folder from which the images are to be displayed. The path specified is relative to the web site URL. Enter the folder name **images**, which is where you uploaded a few images during the creation of new articles.

The Link field is used to specify the URL of the web site to which you want the visitor to navigate if the image is clicked. You can enter www.bmharwani.com (although it can be any URL). In the Width (px) field, you specify the width of the image in pixels. The image will be resized to this width. In the Height (px) field, you specify the height of the image in pixels. The image will be scaled to the given height. Specify the width and height of the image to be 150 px. Let the Position to display the module be position-7 (right-top side of the web site). After entering the information, click the Save & Close button to save the module.

Output on the web site should appear as shown in Figure 8-31. It displays a random image picked from the images folder under the title Images Flash.

Figure 8-31. *Output of the Random Image module upon execution*

If you click the Refresh button, the picture should change, as shown in Figure 8-32.

Figure 8-32. Image changes in the Random Image module afterthe Refresh button is clicked

Search

This module displays a search box in which the user can enter a keyword for the information being sought on the web site. You learned how to use this module in detail in Chapter 6.

Statistics

This module shows a list of web site statistics, including which operating system you're working on, which versions of PHP and MySQL you're using, your server time, and whether caching is enabled or disabled (see Figure 8-33).

Figure 8-33. Sample output of the Statistics module

To use this module, open the Module Manager page, and from the Administrator module type list, select the module with title Site Information of the module type Statistics. The module will open in edit mode, as shown in Figure 8-34.

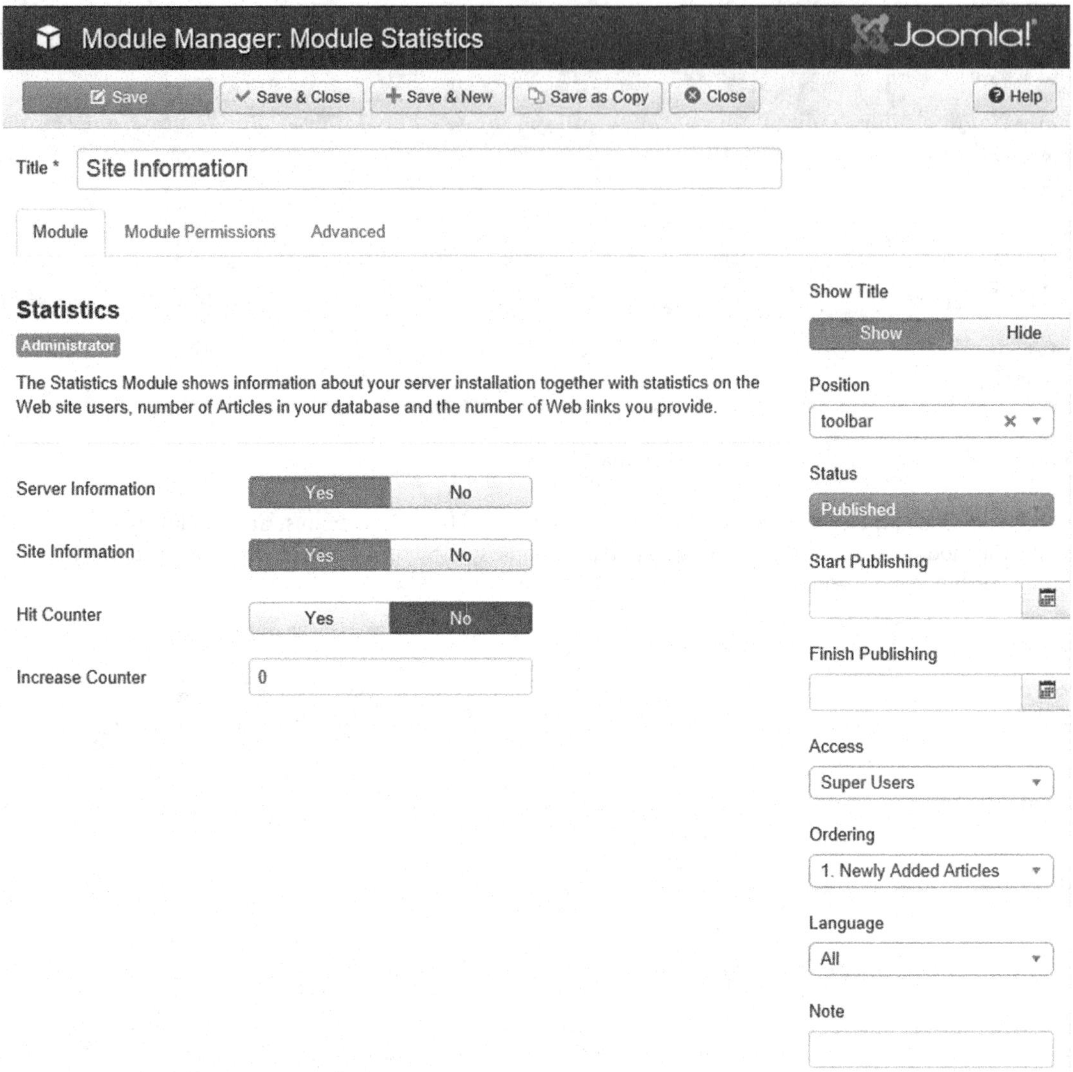

Module Manager: Module Statistics

Joomla!

☑ Save   ✔ Save & Close   ✚ Save & New   ⎙ Save as Copy   ✖ Close   ❓ Help

Title * Site Information

Module   Module Permissions   Advanced

Statistics

`Administrator`

The Statistics Module shows information about your server installation together with statistics on the Web site users, number of Articles in your database and the number of Web links you provide.

Server Information   **Yes** | No

Site Information   **Yes** | No

Hit Counter   Yes | **No**

Increase Counter   0

Show Title

Show | Hide

Position

toolbar   ✖ ▾

Status

Published

Start Publishing

📅

Finish Publishing

📅

Access

Super Users ▾

Ordering

1. Newly Added Articles ▾

Language

All ▾

Note

Figure 8-34. Statistics module opened in edit mode

Set the value of the Server Information field to Yes to show server information. Set the Site Information field to Yes to show site information. Set the value of Hit Counter to Yes to show hit counter information.

In the Increase Counter field, enter a number to be added to the actual number of hits. The Increase Counter field is usually used when you want the hit counter to begin from a value other than the default of 0. From the Position drop-down list, choose toolbar to display the result at the top of the administrator interface.

After entering the information, click the Save & Close button to save the module.

Being the Administrator module, the moment you save the module, the result of the module (i.e., information about the server and other site information) will appear on the back end at the top of the administrator interface (refer to Figure 8-33).

Syndication

This module creates an RSS Feed link for the page, which enables a user to create a news feed for the current page. The module is very frequently used because the moment you add a news feed, the visitors will receive a link to display content from your site on their site. From the Site module types list, select the module with the title Syndication of the Syndication Feedsmodule type. The module will open in edit mode, as shown in Figure 8-35.

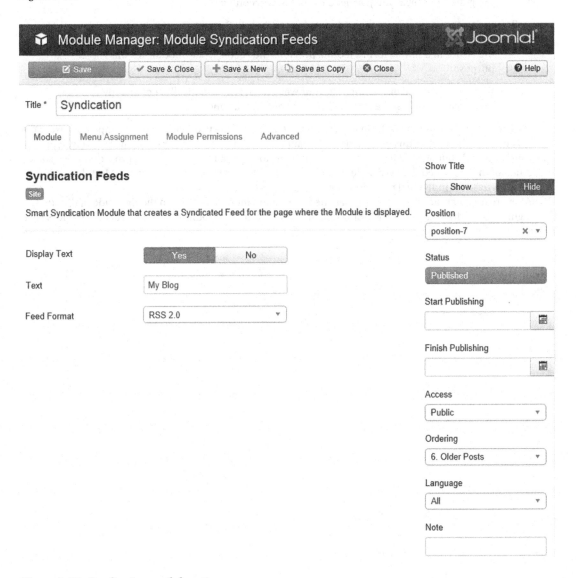

Figure 8-35. *Syndication module options*

Before I describe the fields that are used to configure this module, it is helpful to have a bit of background on RSS feeds. RSS, which stands for Really Simple Syndication, is a technique by which visitors to your web site can receive information about new and updated content on your web site. It is the simplest way to have your information syndicated for others to read.

The procedure to syndicate your information is as follows:

1. Create an RSS feed for the information that you want to syndicate. Joomla has an integrated RSS feed; you just need to enable and configure it.

2. Visitors to your web site then add this feed to their RSS reader (known as an aggregator, which collects new content from your web site and provides it to the visitor in a simple form). Joomla provides the Feed Display module for this purpose.

3. Whenever you add new content to your web site, it is automatically sent directly to the readers—it can be accessed via the Feed Display module.

Back to the Syndication module, in the Text field, you specify the text that you want to appear next to the RSS Link button. If you leave this field blank, the default text Feed Entries will appear. Alternatively, type a space inside double quotes (" ") if you don't want any text to appear. From the Format drop-down list, select the format of the news feed. The available options are RSS 2.0 and Atom 1.0. As usual, the Module Class Suffix field is used for individual module styling.

After creating new article(s), you will see the Syndication module appear on the right side of the site (see Figure 8-36). After clicking the My Blog link in the Syndication module, the user can access the RSS Feed of your site.

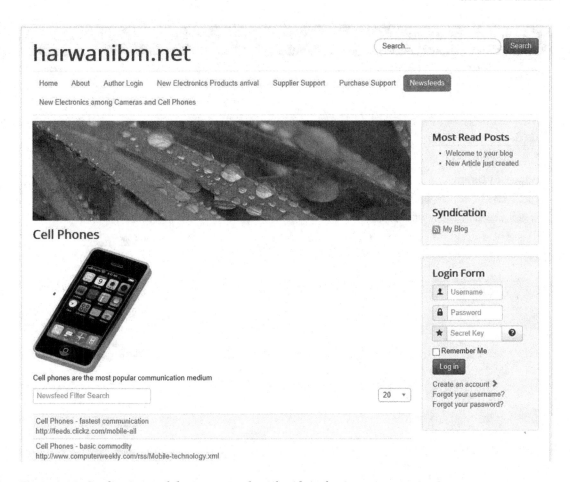

Figure 8-36. Syndication module appears on the right side in the site

Who's Online

This module displays information about users currently browsing the web site. It is a module of administrator type. So from the Administrator module type list in Module Manager, select the module with the title Logged-in Users. The module will open in edit mode, as shown in Figure 8-37.

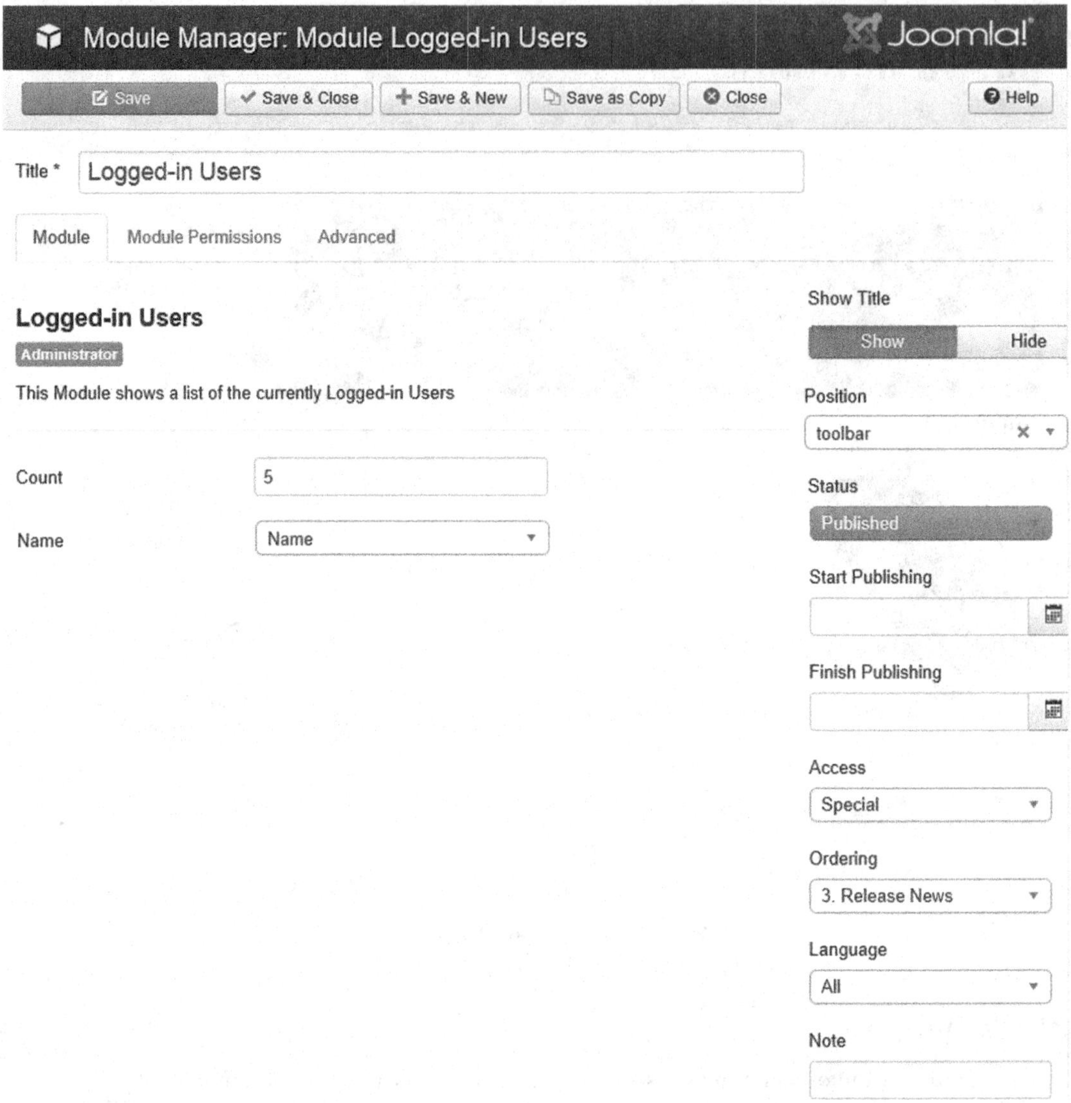

Module Manager: Module Logged-in Users 🔷 Joomla!®

Save | Save & Close | Save & New | Save as Copy | Close | Help

Title * Logged-in Users

Module | Module Permissions | Advanced

Logged-in Users

Administrator

This Module shows a list of the currently Logged-in Users

| Count | 5 |
| Name | Name ▾ |

Show Title: Show | Hide

Position: toolbar ✕ ▾

Status: Published

Start Publishing: 📅

Finish Publishing: 📅

Access: Special ▾

Ordering: 3. Release News ▾

Language: All ▾

Note:

Figure 8-37. *Options of the Who's Online module*

The Count field determines the number of names to be displayed that are logged in. The default value is 5. The Name field is used to specify what is to be displayed, whether it is the name of the user or his/her username.

From the Position combo box, choose the toolbar option to display the module at the top in the administrator interface. From the Access combo box, choose the Special option to make the output of the module visible to only authorized persons of the site, not every viewer.

After the Save & Close button is clicked, the list of logged-in member names will appear as shown in Figure 8-38.

Figure 8-38. *Names of online members displayed*

Wrapper

This module is used to insert an external web site into an iframe at the module position. An iframe (inline frame) is used to insert frames (windows) into your web page, in which you can view another page inside your site. In other words, the Wrapper module enables you to visit an external web site while remaining inside your web site (both web sites can be simultaneously accessed). If the external web page is bigger than the module, scrollbars will appear.

To create the Wrapper module, open the Module Manager, click the Site link to display Site type modules and then click the New button to create a new module. You will be prompted to select the module type. From the list of displayed module types (refer to Figure 8-3), choose the Wrapper module type. You see a screen (shown in Figure 8-39) to enter information for the new module. Assign the title as External Site to the new module.

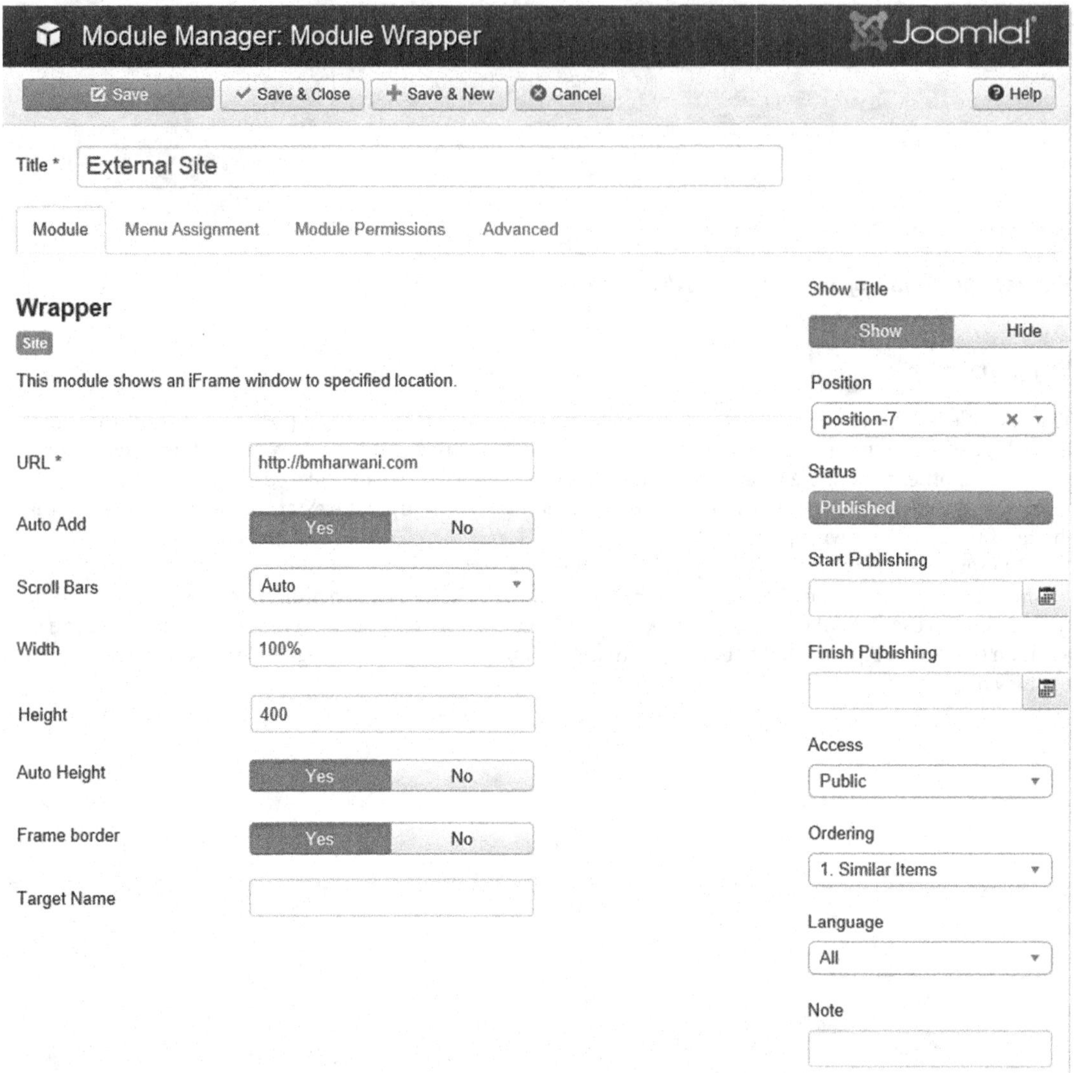

Figure 8-39. *Creating the Wrapper module*

In the URL field, you specify the URL of the web site that you want to open in your web page. Specify the URL as http://bmharwani.com. The Auto Add option determines whether http: or https: is to be added to the beginning of the URL if it is missing. Set this field to Yes.

The Scroll Bars option is used to decide whether to provide scrollbars for the iframe. If the setting is Auto, scrollbars will be provided automatically if required.

In the Width field, you enter the width of the iframe in pixels or as a percentage. Leave it at its default value: 100%. The Height field is used for specifying the height of the iframe in pixels. Set it to 400 pixels to have a better view of the external web site. Set the Auto Height option to Yes because you want the height to automatically be set to the size of the external page.

In the Target Name field, you specify the name of the iframe (it is optional). The name that you specify here can be used to display dynamic contents (contents of different web sites) in the same iframe. In this case, let's leave it blank.

After setting the values as just discussed, click the Save & Close button to save the module. The output of the Wrapper module will appear as shown in Figure 8-40.

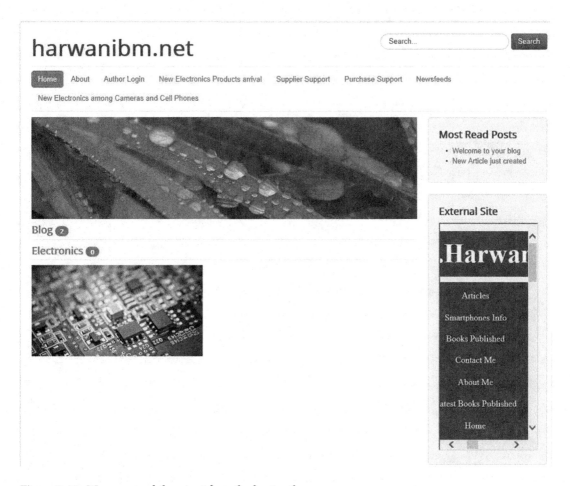

Figure 8-40. *Wrapper module output from the front end*

The conclusion of this chapter is that Joomla provides many different types of modules, enabling you to create a fully functional web site. As an administrator, you can enable or disable a module from the Module Manager, and you can make it display the desired information by setting its parameters.

Summary

This chapter showed you different built-in modules provided by Joomla and the roles they play in a web site. You also saw how to set the parameters to get desired results.

In Chapter 9, you will learn how to add more features to your web site by installing different extensions. You will learn to download and install several extensions, including templates (to make your Joomla web site appear more dynamic), e-commerce extensions (to create an online store and sell products via your web site), an RSS feed reader (to get RSS feeds from the selected web sites), and a chatting extension (to allow visitors of your web site to communicate).

CHAPTER 9

■ ■ ■

Adding Extensions

This chapter shows you how to add more features to your Joomla web site. To add a particular feature, you need to install the respective extension. Extensions are packages that can be downloaded from the Internet at no cost and are easily installed on your Joomla web site. Some examples of extensions are shopping carts, forums, social networking profiles, job boards, and estate listings. Extensions are like add-ons to your Joomla web site for features that are not provided in the default Joomla package.

You'll learn how to download, install, and use the following extensions:

- Templates to make your web site appear more dynamic

- E-commerce extensions to maintain an online store and sell products via your web site

- RSS feed readers to receive RSS feeds periodically from the selected web sites

- Chatting to allow visitors to your web site to converse with one another

Extension Manager

As the name suggests, *extensions* are packages meant for extending features of a Joomla web site. There are many extensions available on the Internet, ranging from large complex components to small lightweight modules and plug-ins. You can add features such as a chatting functionality, discussion forum, and shopping cart to your web site by installing the respective extension.

As described in the following list, all types of extensions can be installed or uninstalled with the help of the Extension Manager:

- *Components*: A component is an independent application with its own functionality, database, and presentation. Installing a component in your web site is just like adding an application to your web site. For example, forums, shopping carts, newsletters, and guest books are all examples of components. A component can consist of one or more modules.

- *Modules*: Modules add functions (features) to an existing component (application) of your web site—for example, a login module, a sign-in module of a guest book component, a subscription module of a newsletter component, or a digital counter module of a guest book component. A module is one running unit of an application and cannot be a stand-alone component.

- *Plug-ins*: Plug-ins were called *mambots* in Joomla 1.0.x, but have been called plug-ins since Joomla 1.5.x. A plug-in is a function that can be applied to a particular component or an entire web site—for example, a search plug-in that can be used by visitors to search the forum or a bookmark plug-in to place bookmarks on desired contents of the web site.

■ **Note**　To understand the differences among components, modules, and plug-ins, consider this example: the shopping cart is a component that has several modules, including modules for maintaining inventory, storing payment information, and printing bills. Plug-ins can be added to the shopping cart component, including a plug-in to change the price of a particular product or a search plug-in to enable searching for a desired product from the shopping cart. You can also use external companies that can install any Joomla extension for you.

- *Languages*: This type of extension provides a facility for presenting the front end and back end of Joomla in any desired language. That is, you can present your Joomla web site in different languages without much effort.

- *Templates*: The purpose of a template is to give a dynamic appearance to your web site. A template contains the style sheets, locations, and layout of the web contents being displayed. It separates the appearance of the web site from its content.

Let's open the Extension Manager by selecting Extensions ➤ Extension Manager. You'll see a screen like the one shown in Figure 9-1.

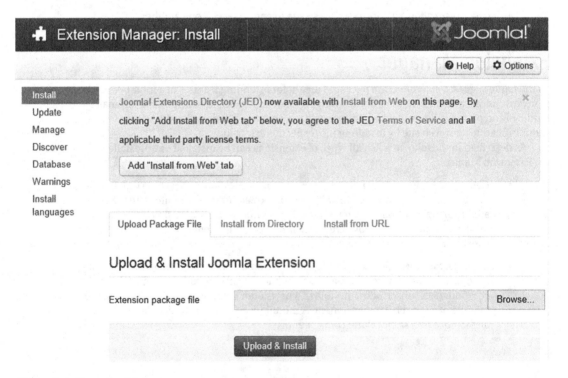

Figure 9-1. Extension Manager

The Install tab enables you to install all types of extensions. The remaining tabs are for updating and managing the respective extensions.

■ **Note** In Joomla, you can install an extension from any location on the Internet by providing the URL of the extension's installation package. That is, you can install an extension without downloading it to your local disk drive.

Installing Extensions

There are many types of Joomla extensions that you can add to the site, such as components, modules, plugins, and so on. Joomla extensions can be installed by using any of these methods:

- Upload Package File

- Install from Directory

- Install from URL

Let's take a quick look through the advantages and disadvantages of each method.

Upload Package File

You use this method when you prefer installing the extension without unpacking the archive file. However, it takes a long time to install the extension to a hosted web site (on a remote server).
Follow these steps:

1. Download one or more archive files (normally in .zip or tar.gz format) from the extension provider's web site to your local disk drive.

2. Click the Browse button to specify the location to which the extension's archive file is to be downloaded.

3. Click the Upload File & Install button. Joomla will read the contents of the archive file and install the extension.

Install from Directory

Using this method, you unpack the archive file into a directory and upload that directory onto the server.
Follow these steps:

1. Download the extension's archive file to your local disk drive.

2. Create a temporary directory on the local disk drive and unpack the extension's archive file into this temporary directory.

3. Using FTP, upload the contents of this directory (including files and subdirectories) to a directory on the server.

4. In the Install Directory field, specify the directory to which you uploaded the files and subdirectories of the package.

5. Click the Install button. Joomla will install the contents of the given directory.

Install from URL

Using this method, you don't download the archive file to your local computer; you instead just specify the URL of the target archive file. Then click the Install button and Joomla will automatically install the extension directly from this URL. This method is preferred when installing the extension on a hosted web site (remote server). The archive file of the extension (to be installed on the web site) is first uploaded to the remote domain; then its URL is specified in the Install URL box.

When installation is done, the screen displays the message Install Component Success. If the installation is not successful, an error message is displayed.

By default, the newly installed extension is in unpublished mode, so you need to enable it from the respective manager, such as the Module Manager or Plugin Manager.

Installing New Templates

You can download any of hundreds of attractive templates that are available on the Internet. Let's download the Purity_III template, which is a free Joomla template. Its archive file is named purity_iii.v1.1.2.zip. Download it from www.joomlart.com/joomla/templates/purity-iii to a folder on your local disk drive.

Open the Extension Manager by selecting Extensions ➤ Extension Manager. Click the Install tab and, in the Extension package file field, click the Browse button to locate the archive file of the Purity_III template, as shown in Figure 9-2.

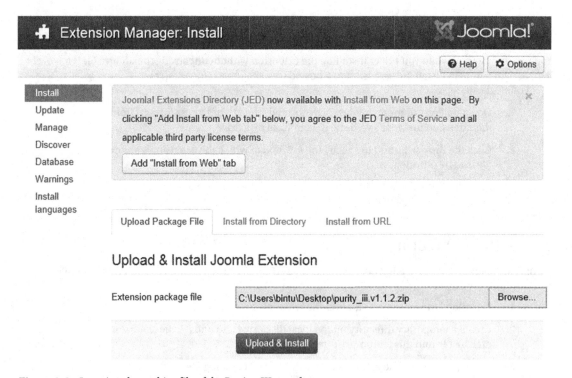

Figure 9-2. *Locating the archive file of the Purity_III template*

After specifying the template archive file, `purity_iii.v1.1.2.zip`, click the Upload & Install button to install the template. If the template is successfully installed, you'll see the message Installing Template Was Successful, as shown in Figure 9-3. Besides the successful template installation message, the figure also tells you that the Purity III template requires a T3 plug-in to be installed and enabled.

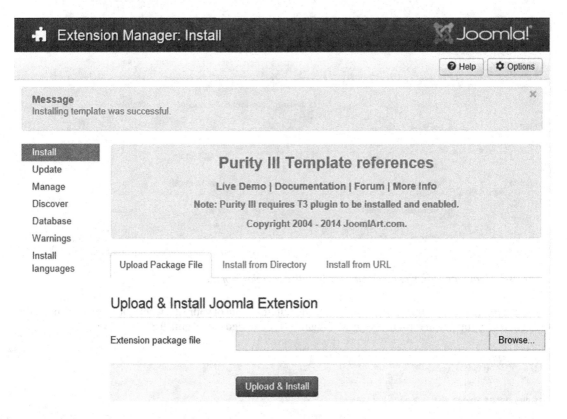

Figure 9-3. *Message after successful installation of the template*

To apply the newly installed template to your web site, use the Template Manager, which displays after you select Extensions ➤ Template Manager. The Template Manager opens; you'll see that besides the four default templates provided by Joomla (Beez3, Hathor, isis, and protostar), a new template named `Purity_III` also appears in the list. Let's select `Purity_III` from the list and click the Default icon (star) from the Default column to make it the default template, as shown in Figure 9-4.

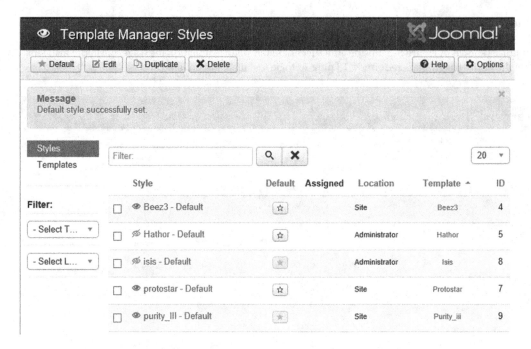

Figure 9-4. *Template Manager displaying the installed templates of the site*

After you make the Purity_III template the default template of your site, when you open the front side of the web site, you get an error message: T3 Plugin Is Not Enabled (see Figure 9-5).

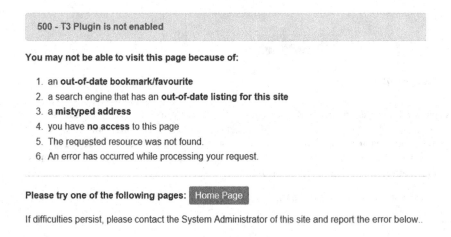

Figure 9-5. *Error message indicating that the T3 plug-in is not enabled*

Download the T3 plug-in from `https://github.com/t3framework/t3/releases/tag/v2.4.8` into any local drive. The downloaded archive file is `t3-2.4.8.zip`. Install the plug-in using the Extension Manager, the way you installed the `Purity_III` template (see Figure 9-6).

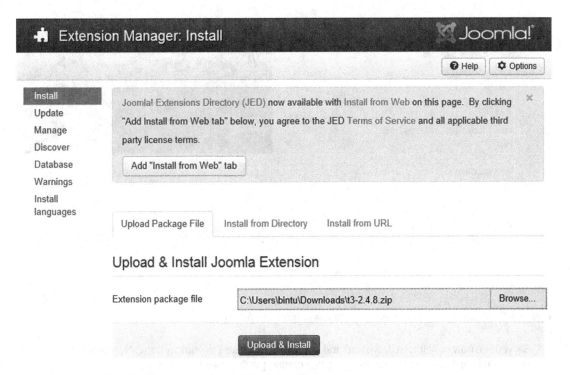

Figure 9-6. Installing the T3 plug-in using the Extension Manager

The `Purity_III` template works perfectly after the T3 plug-in is installed. Now you're ready to see the impact of the newly applied template from the front end. Open the browser and point it to the address `http://localhost/joomlasite` to open the Joomla site's front end (alternatively, you can use the Preview button at the top right). Notice that the Joomla web site's front end has changed, and the positions of all the web site contents (menus and other components) are set according to the layout specified in the `Purity_III` template (see Figure 9-7).

HARWANIBM.NET

Home

About

Author Login

New Electronics
Products arrival

Supplier Support

Purchase Support

Newsfeeds

New Electronics
among Cameras
and Cell Phones

Figure 9-7. *Impact of applying the Purity_III template on the front end*

So, you see how easy it is to download and apply new templates to your web site. Now let's make the web site capable of doing some business by selling certain products and services.

Adding E-commerce

Most of the web sites that you see on the Internet do some type of e-commerce—they publicize their products and services through the Internet and eventually do some business. E-commerce is a heavily desired feature in almost all web sites. To add an e-commerce system to the web site, you can download one of hundreds of components available on the Internet. I downloaded one named VirtueMart. Its archive file is available on the Internet at `http://virtuemart.net/downloads`, and the one I used in this book is named `com_virtuemart.3.0.6.2.zip`.

The VirtueMart component provides a complete store system. Using its features, you can do the following:

- Have access to an unlimited hierarchy of products (a category within a category, and so on)

- Specify attributes of products, such as width, height, and color

- Use different currencies

- Specify different shipment methods

- See that the components use SSL encryption

- Perform complete inventory administration

You'll see how the VirtueMart component can be installed on a hosted web site rather than on a web site located on a local server. You can use the package file method to specify the location of VirtueMart's archive file, but it can take a long time to install.

A better option is to upload the archive file to the web site. Assuming that the domain name of the web site is bmharwani.net, upload the archive file to this domain. To install the component, you need to specify its location (www.bmharwani.net/com_virtuemart.3.0.6.2.zip) in the Install URL field and click the Install button, as shown in Figure 9-8.

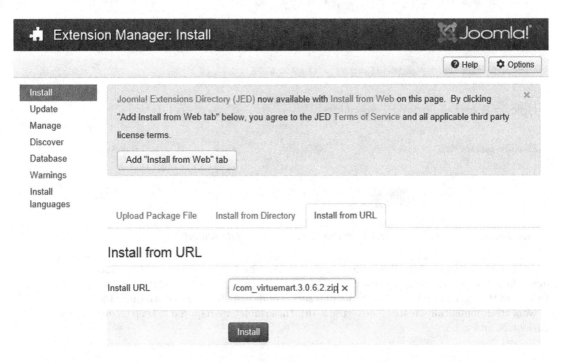

Figure 9-8. *Specifying the location of the archive file for the VirtueMart component*

The VirtueMart component is installed, and you'll see the message Installation Was Successful (see Figure 9-9). The figure shows the links for the documentation of the VirtueMart. Besides the links, the figure tells you that you also have to install the AIO component for successful installation of VirtueMart.

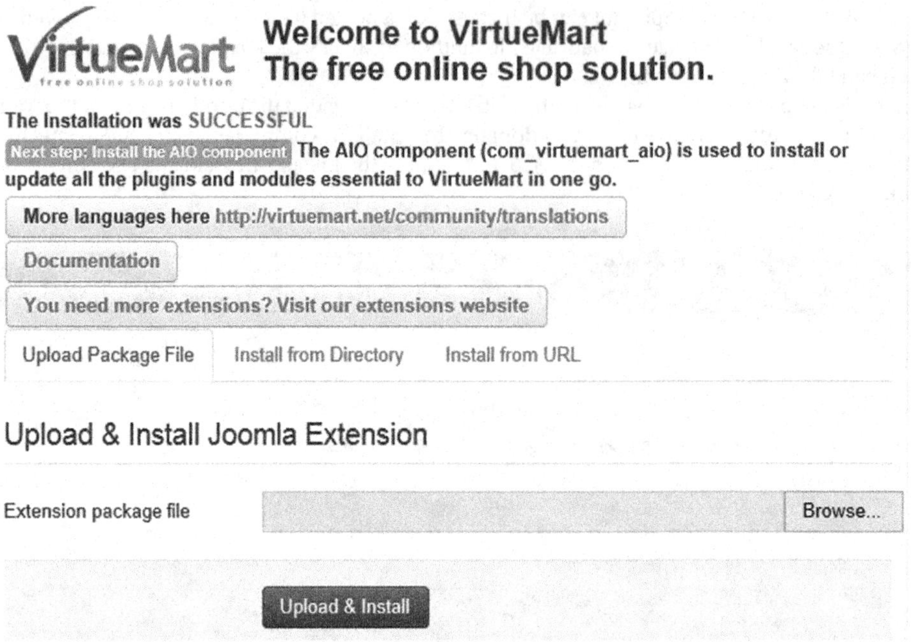

Welcome to VirtueMart
The free online shop solution.

VirtueMart
free online shop solution

The Installation was SUCCESSFUL

Next step: Install the AIO component The AIO component (com_virtuemart_aio) is used to install or
update all the plugins and modules essential to VirtueMart in one go.

More languages here http://virtuemart.net/community/translations

Documentation

You need more extensions? Visit our extensions website

Upload Package File   Install from Directory   Install from URL

Upload & Install Joomla Extension

Extension package file   [   ] Browse...

Upload & Install

Figure 9-9. Welcome screen of VirtueMart displays after successful installation

The AIO component is available from the same URL:http://virtuemart.net/downloads. The
downloaded archive file is com_virtuemart.3.0.6.2_ext_aio.zip. Install the AIO component using the
Extension Manager. After the AIO component is successfully installed, the tables required for VirtueMart
to work are automatically created (see Figure 9-10). These tables are required to keep records of products,
customers, and so on.

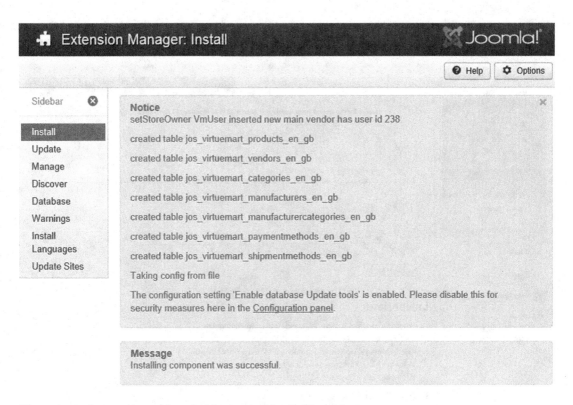

Figure 9-10. *Automatic creation of tables required by the VirtueMart component*

■ **Note** VirtueMart is accessible from the Components menu in the Administrator interface. There are still some minor vulnerabilities for nonpersistent XSS that are not yet solved with VirtueMart, but they are expected to be solved in the future.

When all the tables and other configuration files required for e-commerce are created, you'll see the Control Panel for your store, as shown in Figure 9-11.

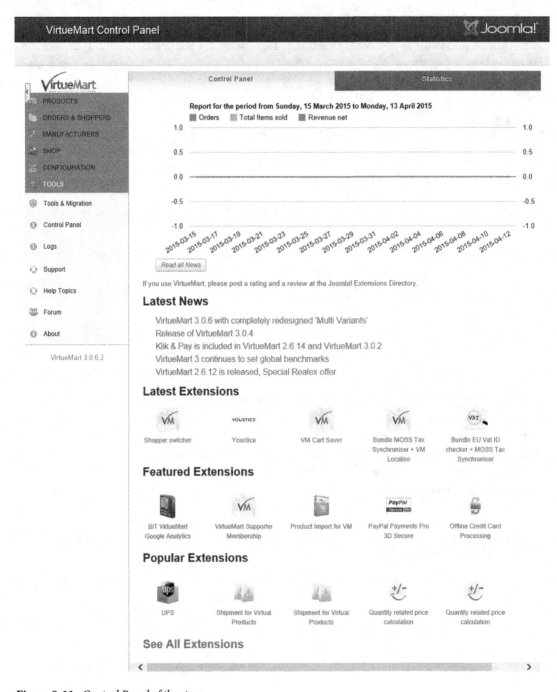

Figure 9-11. *Control Panel of the store*

The Control Panel contains icons for viewing and managing a product list, categories of products, orders placed, different payment methods, vendors, users, and so on. All the e-commerce maintenance tasks are performed here.

Click the Products menu on the left side to expand it and display the menu items under this menu. The menu items that appear under the Products menu are Product Categories, Products, Custom Fields, and so on. After clicking Product Categories, you should see a screen like the one shown in Figure 9-12.

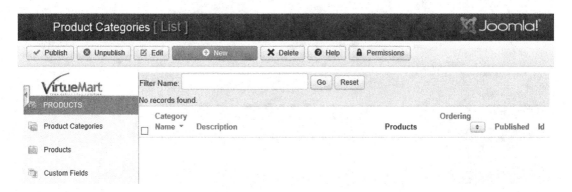

Figure 9-12. *Product Categories [List] page, currently blank*

Notice that there are currently no categories in the category tree. You can create a new category by clicking the New icon in the toolbar. The remaining icons in the toolbar — Publish, Unpublish, Edit, and Delete— are for publishing (displaying the products of the selected category); unpublishing (making the products of the selected category invisible); and editing the category and removing the selected category, respectively.

Upon clicking the New icon, you'll see a screen for creating a new product category, as shown in Figure 9-13.

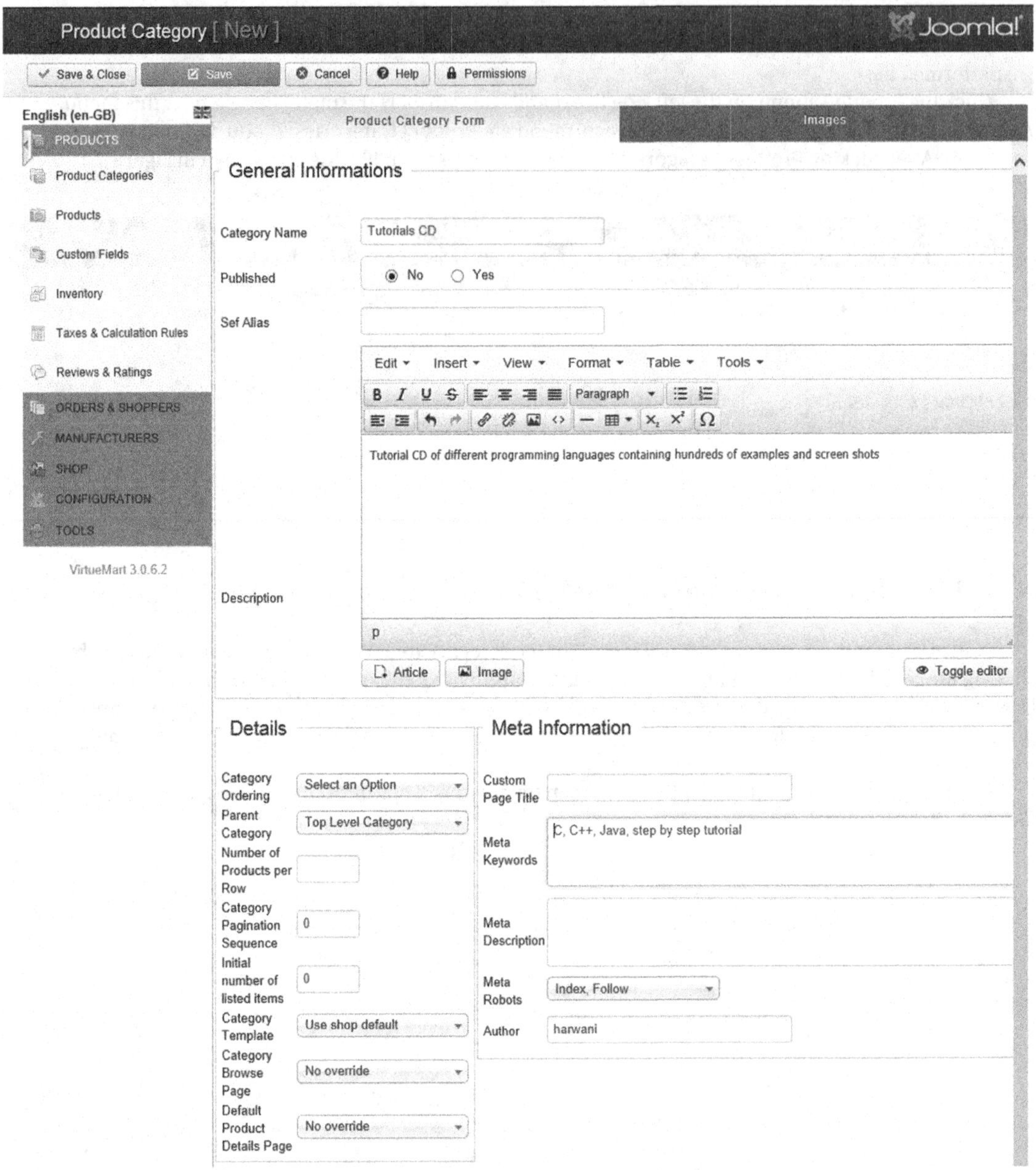

Figure 9-13. *Creation of a new product category: Tutorials CD*

The screen prompts for a category name and description. Usually, the newly added category appears last in the category tree, but you can easily change its order later if desired. You don't have any other categories, so you don't have to worry about ordering.

Let's assume that you want to sell products belonging to two categories: Tutorials CD and Computer Books. You create the first category by specifying the Category Name as **Tutorials CD**. In the Category Description column, enter a brief description of the category. Also mention some meta keywords for the category to make it appear on the front side of the site if visitor searches for the categories via keywords.

After entering the information for Tutorials CD, save it by clicking the Save & Close icon in the toolbar. Using the same technique, create another category named Computer Books. The category tree now contains two categories, as shown in Figure 9-14.

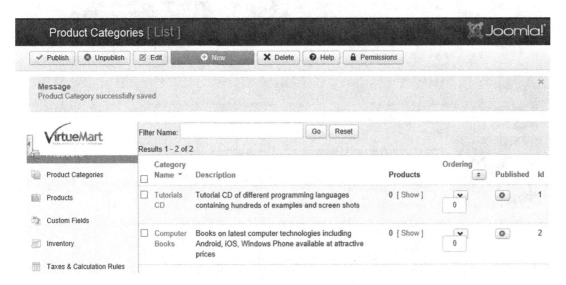

Figure 9-14. *Two product categories displayed on the Product Categories [List] page*

To add products to these two newly created categories, click Products in the menu on the left. The Products menu will expand. From the expanded menu, select the menu item Products; the Product [List] screen will display. The product list is currently blank because no product is present in the store.

Notice in Figure 9-15 that this screen enables you to search for products with a particular keyword (if the volume of products is large). You can also look for products that have been added/modified before or after a particular date. These facilities are not applicable here, so click the New icon to add a new product.

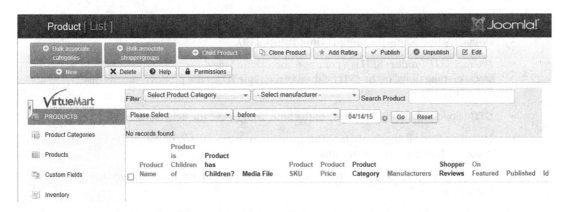

Figure 9-15. *Product list is currently blank*

You'll see a screen for specifying product information. By default, the Product Information tab is opened (see Figure 9-16).

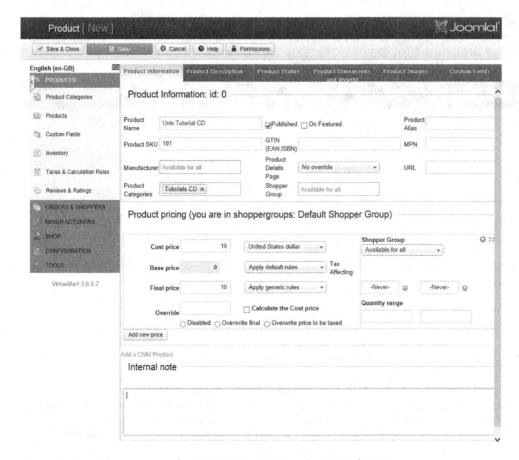

Figure 9-16. *Adding a new product, Unix Tutorial CD, in the Tutorials CD category*

The Product Information tab shows the fields as follows:

- *Product Name*: Name the product **Unix Tutorial CD**.

- *Product SKU*: Product SKU is a common abbreviation used in catalog systems for stock-keeping units. In the SKU field, enter a unique ID for the product—in this case, enter **101**.

- *GTIN*: Specify the GTIN number. For the time being, leave the field blank.

- *URL*: This field allows the visitor to navigate to a web page to see details of the products. In this case, leave it blank.

- *Manufacturer*: This field is the name of the manufacturer of the product. Keep it blank (the default).

- *Product Categories*: In this box, you specify the category to which this product belongs. Select the category Tutorials CD.

- *Cost price*: Enter the price as **10**, and the currency for all of the prices for the product as United States dollar.

- *Final price*: Specify the gross product price as **10** (dollars).

The Product Description tab (see Figure 9-17) displays fields for entering a description of the new product.

Figure 9-17. *Supplying a description of the product*

The fields are as follows:

- *Short Description*: In this box, you can include a short introduction of the product (it doesn't include images).

- *Product Description*: Here you enter a product description. This is a detailed description that can also include images of the product.

- *Meta Keywords*: Here you specify the keywords that make this product appear in the front when a visitor searches for the respective keywords.

Notice the other tabs at the top of the New Product window: Product Status, Product Dimensions and Weight, Product Images, and so on. These tabs can be used to supply a lot more information about the product.

To define the product image, select the Product Images tab. You see the fields shown in Figure 9-18. Assuming that there is an image called dsimage.png on your local drive, click the Browse button in the Upload File field and select the dsimage.png image file.

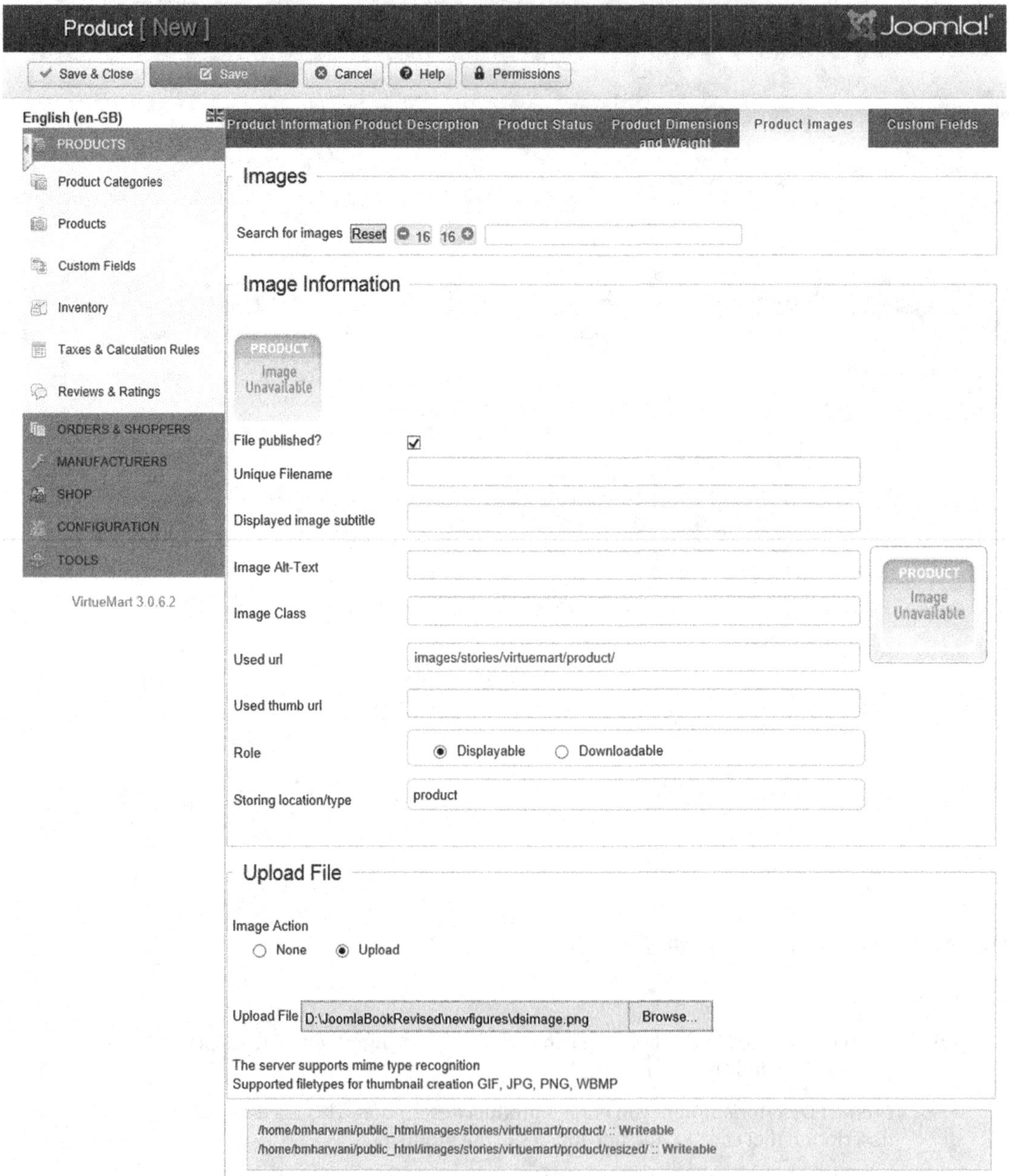

Figure 9-18. Screen for specifying the product image

After entering the information about the product, click the Save & Close button from the toolbar to save the newly created product. After the product is saved, you'll see a message confirming that the new product is successfully saved (see Figure 9-15). The Product [List] page indicates that the first new product has been added: Unix Tutorial CD in the Tutorials CD category, as shown in Figure 9-19.

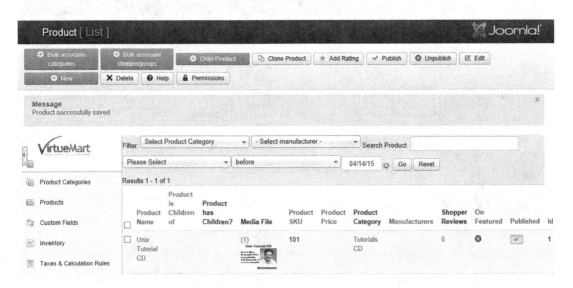

Figure 9-19. *Unix Tutorial CD displayed in the product list*

Let's enter information for another product, Data Structures Tutorial CD, by selecting the New button in the toolbar (see Figure 9-20).

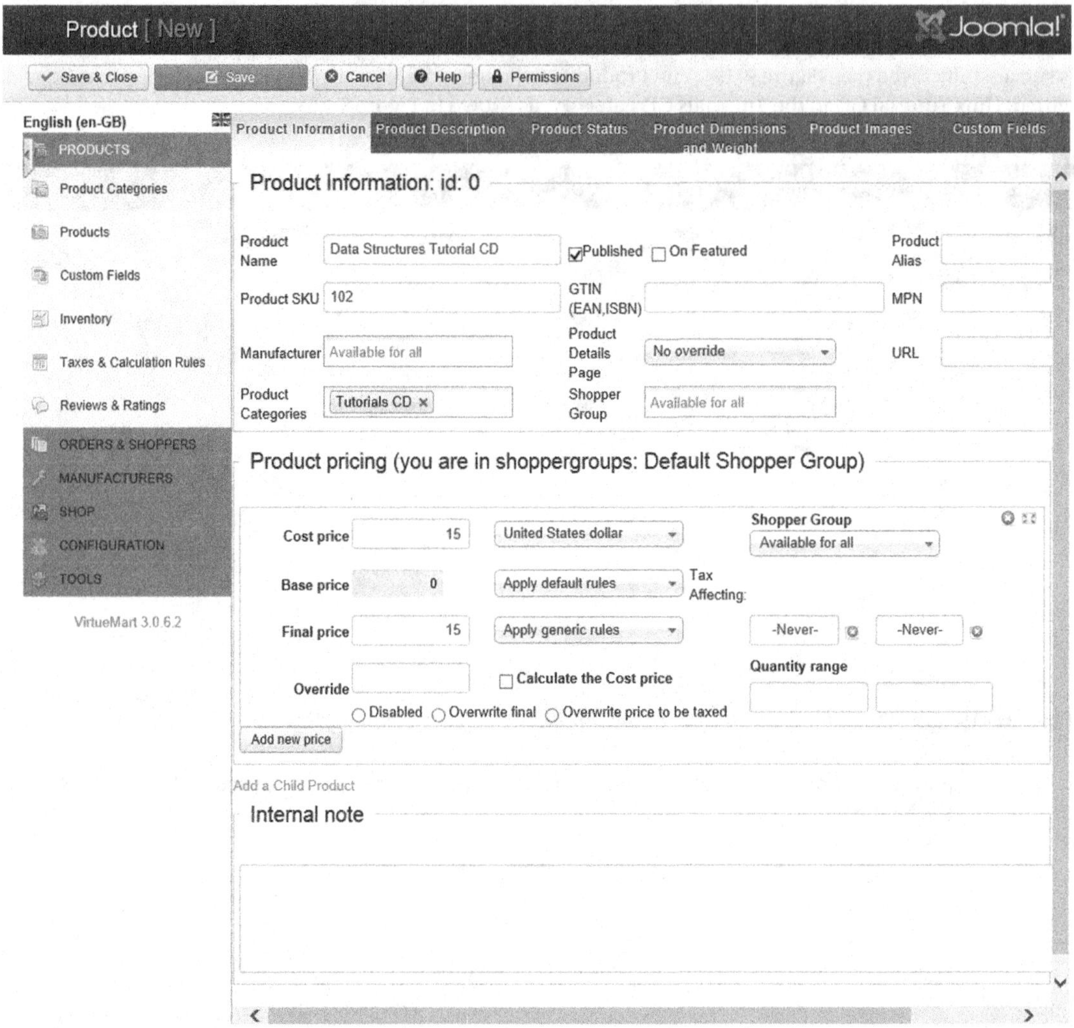

Figure 9-20. *Creation of the Data Structures Tutorial CD product in the Tutorial CD category*

Enter the following information about the new product as follows:

- *Product Name*: Enter **Data Structures Tutorial CD**.

- *Product SKU*: As a unique ID for this product, enter **102**.

- *GTIN*: Enter the GTIN number or other taxation ID. For the time being, leave this field blank.

- *URL*: Because you're not allowing the user to navigate to a web page to see details for this product, leave this field blank.

- *Manufacturer*: Leave the manufacturer of the product at the default.

- *Product Categories*: Select Tutorials CD for the category for the product.

- *Cost Price*: Enter **15** and set the currency to US dollar.

- *Final Price*: Enter **15**.

Click the Product Description tab and enter a short description and product description of the product. Click the Product Images tab and provide the image of the new product. After providing the information for the new product, save it by clicking the Close & Save button. You'll see a message confirming that the new product is successfully saved, along with the other product information that has been added in the products list (see Figure 9-21).

Figure 9-21. *Message confirming the creation of the Data Structures Tutorial CD product*

Until now, you've been adding products to the Tutorials CD category. Now you'll add two products to the Computer Books category. Figure 9-22 shows the information entered to define a book product titled Android Programming.

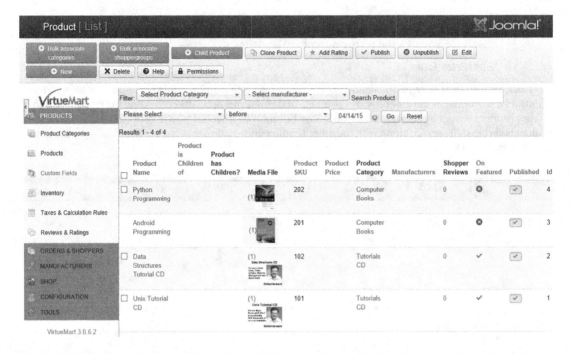

Figure 9-22. *Products list after adding the Android Programming and Python Programming products to the Computer Books category*

Using the same technique, define another product, Python Programming, in the Computer Books category with an SKU of 202 and a price of $7. Now you have two categories defined in the online store (Tutorials CD and Computer Books), and each category has two products: Unix Tutorial CD and Data Structures Tutorial CD in the Tutorials CD category, and Android Programming and Python Programming in the Computer Books category.

To make the products appear on the front side of the site, declare them as featured products. To make any product a featured product, in the On Featured column, click the red cross icon to convert it into a right check sign.

Now it's time to access this VirtueMart component from the front end (the web site). The Module Manager (see Figure 9-23) shows the following VirtueMart modules: VM - Shopping cart, VM - Search in Shop, VM - Featured products, VM - Category, VM – Currencies, and VM - Manufacturer. Each module does its respective job in implementing e-commerce.

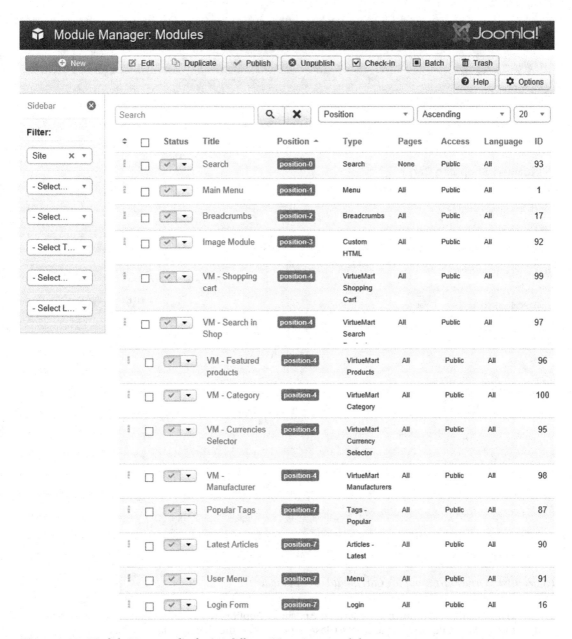

Figure 9-23. Module Manager displaying different VirtueMart modules

But one step is still left. The VirtueMart modules are in unpublished mode; although they're installed on the web site, they don't display onscreen. To display the modules on the front side of the site, you need to publish the component's modules at desired positions in the site.

As expected, the VM - Shopping cart module will display all the products that are selected by the visitor in the cart. Let's publish VM - Shopping cart at position-7 of the template (on the right side of the site). To do so, click the VM-Shopping cart module, which will open it in edit mode (see Figure 9-24).

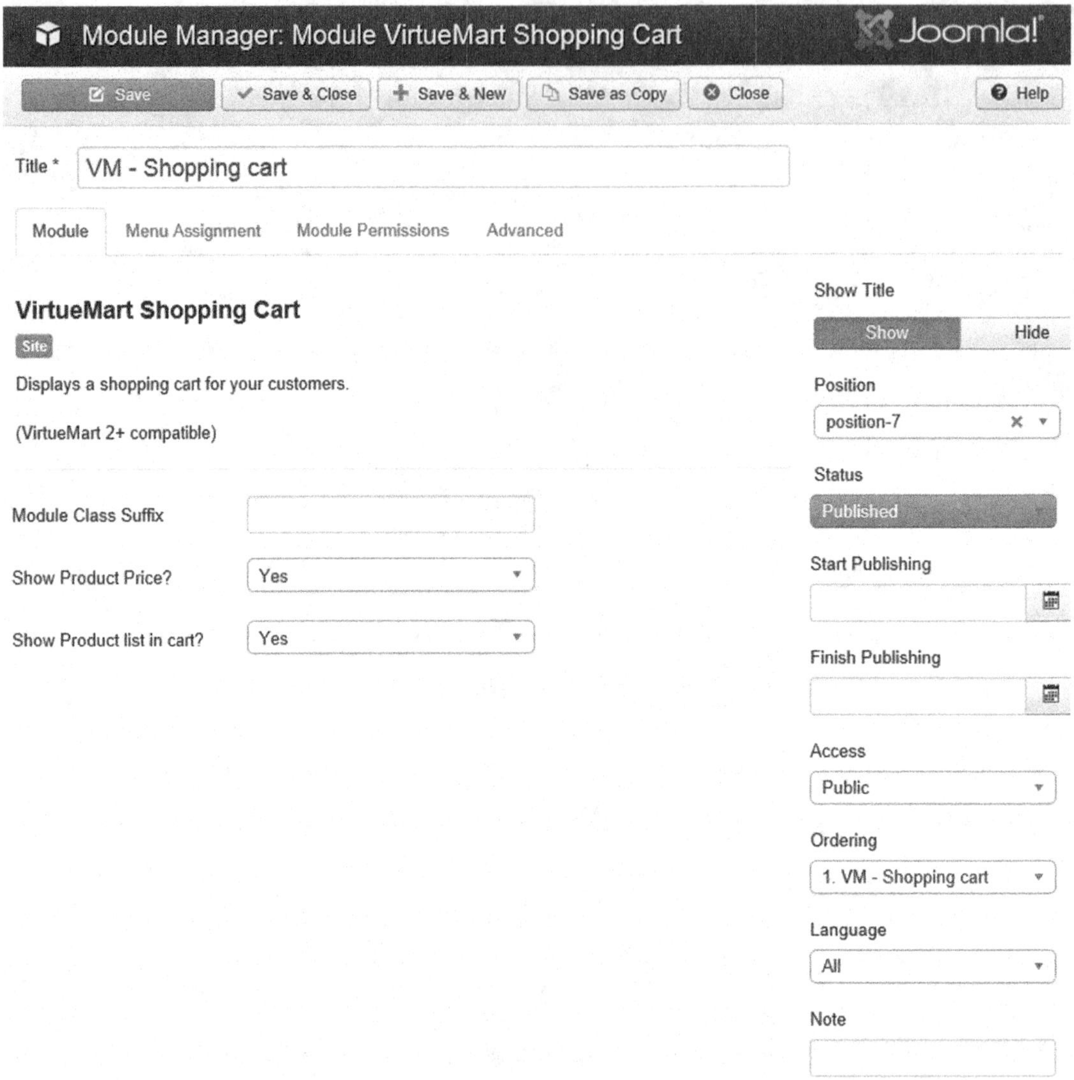

Figure 9-24. *VirtueMart Shopping Cart module in edit mode*

From the Position drop-down list, choose the position-7 option. Keeping the values of the rest of the fields to their default values, click the Save & Close button to save the changes made to the module.

Similarly, publish the VM - Featured products module on position-7 of the site. As expected, the VM-Featured products module will display all the featured products on the site. For successful implementation and for visitors' convenience, you need to define two important factors of e-commerce: shipment method and payment method.

Let's begin with the shipment method. Select the Component ➤ VirtueMart ➤ Shipment Methods option. The Shipment Method [List] page opens up, but is initially empty because no shipment method exists (see Figure 9-25).

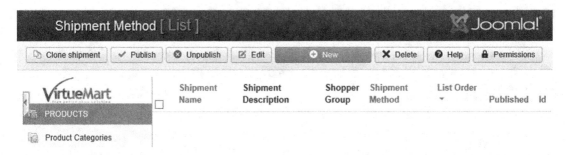

Figure 9-25. *Shipment Method [List] page is currently empty*

■ **Note** There is a security issue that you should be aware of when using VirtueMart. Visit this link for more details:http://extensions.joomla.org/extension/virtuemart.

Click the New button to create a new shipment method. You see the screen shown in Figure 9-26.

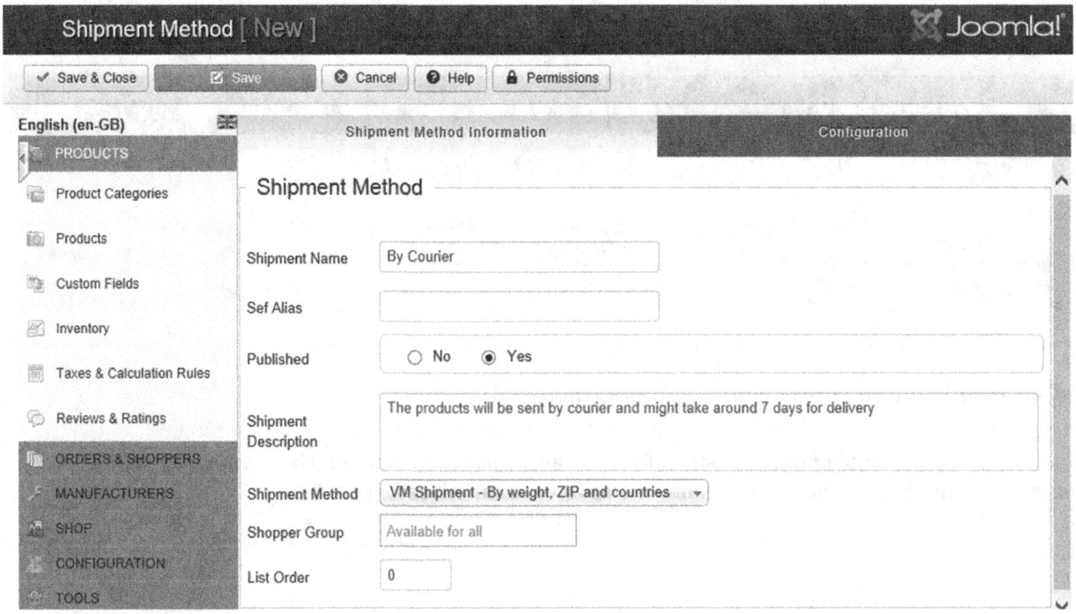

Figure 9-26. *Defining the new shipment method*

In the Shipment Name field, enter **By Courier** to specify that the shipment will be usually sent by courier. In the Shipment Description field, enter a small description about the method. Leave the values of the rest of the fields to their default and click the Save & Close button to save the shipment method.

A Shipment Method Successfully Saved message appears on the screen, and the Shipment Method [List] page shows the newly created shipment method: By Courier (see Figure 9-27).

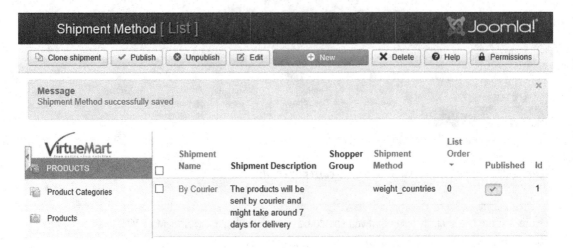

Figure 9-27. *Shipment Method [List] page showing the By Courier shipment method*

Similarly, for defining the payment method, select the Component ➤ VirtueMart ➤ Payment Methods option. The Payment Method [List] page opens up, which initially is empty because no payment method exists by default (see Figure 9-28).

Figure 9-28. *Payment Method [List] page is currently empty*

Click the New button from the toolbar to create a new payment method. The Payment Method [New] page opens up, showing the fields to define the payment method (see Figure 9-29).

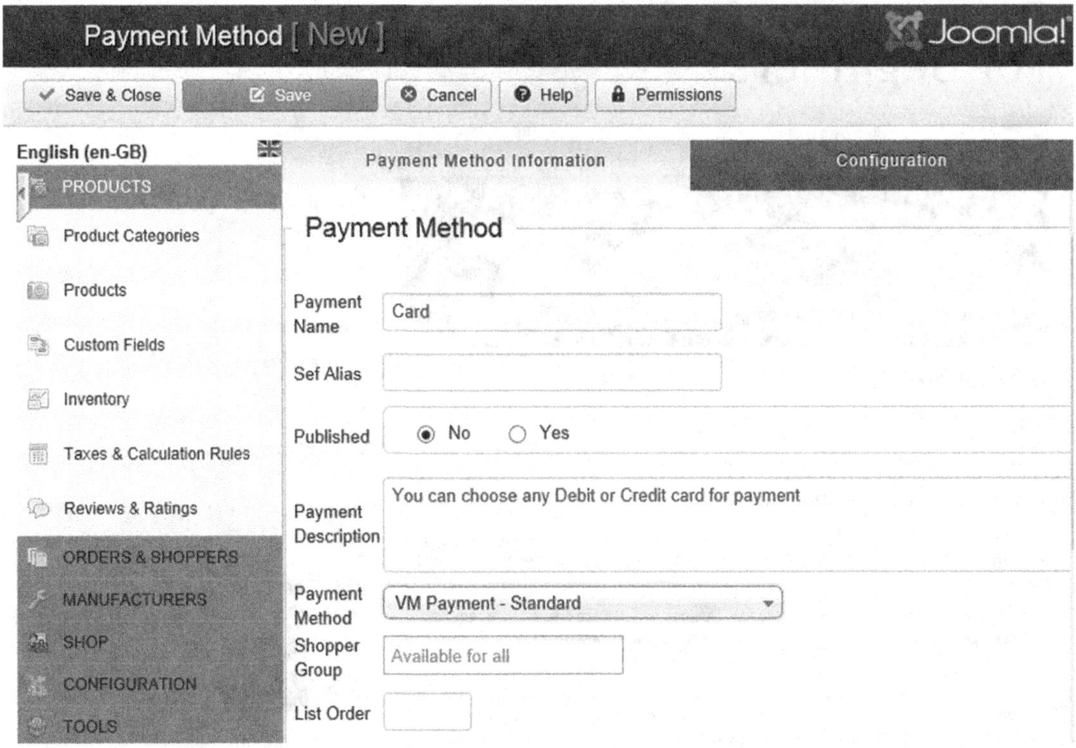

Figure 9-29. *Defining a new payment method*

In the Payment Name field, enter **Card** to indicate that this payment method will require a credit or debit card for payment. In the Payment Description field, enter a small description of this payment method. Leaving the values of the rest of the fields to their default, click the Save & Close button to save the newly defined payment method.

Now, you are ready to access the VirtueMart component from the front side of the site. The VM-Featured products module displays the featured products, as shown in Figure 9-30.

For Beginners

Home   VirtueMart Shopping Cart

Getting Started

Joomla

It's easy to get started creating your website. Knowing some of the basics will help.

What is a Content Management System?

A content management system is software that allows you to create and manage webpages easily by separating the creation of your content from the mechanics required to present it on the web.

In this site, the content is stored in a *database*. The look and feel are created by a *template*. Joomla! brings together the template and your content to create web pages.

Logging in

To login to your site use the user name and password that were created as part of the installation process. Once logged-in you will be able to create and edit articles and modify some settings.

Creating an article

Once you are logged-in, a new menu will be visible. To create a new article, click on the "Submit Article" link on that menu.

The new article interface gives you a lot of options, but all you need to do is add a title and put something in the content area. To make it easy to find, set the state to published.

You can edit an existing article by clicking on the edit icon (this only displays to users who have the right to edit).

Template, site settings, and modules

The look and feel of your site is controlled by a template. You can change the site name, background colour, highlights colour and more by editing the template settings. Click the "Template Settings" in the user menu.

The boxes around the main content of the site are called modules. You can modify modules on the current page by moving your cursor to the module and clicking the edit link. Always be sure to save and close any module you edit.

You can change some site settings such as the site name and description by clicking on the "Site Settings" link.

More advanced options for templates, site settings, modules, and more are available in the site administrator.

Popular Tags
- Joomla

Latest Articles
- Getting Started

VM - Shopping cart
Cart empty

VM - Featured products

Python Programming

Add to Cart

Unix Tutorial CD

Bintu Harwani
Unix Tutorial CD

Add to Cart

Login Form

Figure 9-30. *VirtueMart module visible on the front end*

Each of the featured products is accompanied by a quantity text field and the Add to Cart button. The product names are in the form of links that can be clicked to show detailed information for the product.

After the Unix Tutorial CD name from the featured products column is clicked, the details of the products will be displayed, along with the image and description (see Figure 9-31).

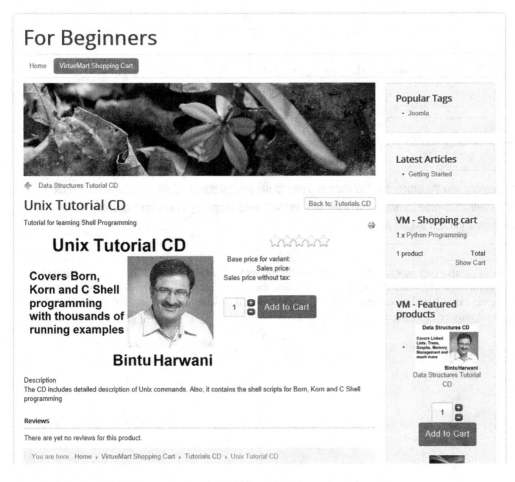

Figure 9-31. *Detailed information for the Unix Tutorial CD product*

The quantity text field has a default value of 1. You can specify the desired quantity of a product in the quantity field and click the Add to Cart button to add the product to the cart.

Keeping the default quantity value at 1, click the Add to Cart button on the Unix Tutorial CD to add it to the cart. You get a message indicating that Unix Tutorial CD is added to the cart (see Figure 9-32).

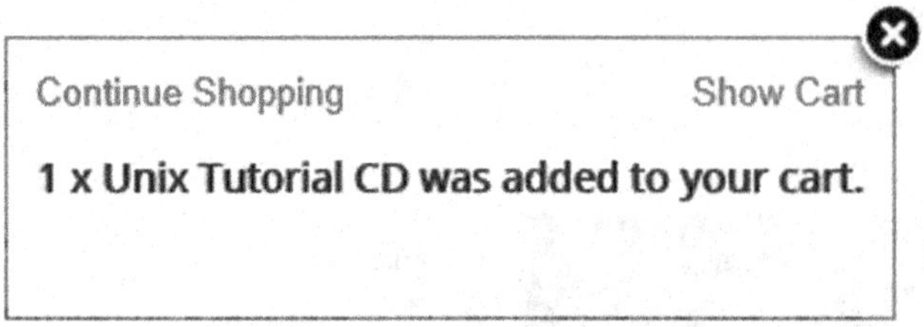

Figure 9-32. Message that the product has been added to the shopping cart

---

■ **Note** You can add the product to the shopping cart at the time of product listing as well as when the details of an individual product are being displayed. You just need to specify the desired quantity of the selected product and click the Add to Cart button.

The message also contains two links: Continue Shopping and Show Cart. The Continue Shopping link is for viewing more products for shopping purposes, and the Show Cart button is for displaying the products in the shopping cart. Click the Continue Shopping link to continue watching the featured products and selecting those required (see Figure 9-33).

Figure 9-33. *Front side showing featured products to continue shopping*

This time, keeping the default quantity as 1, select the Add to Cart button for the Android Programming book. Again, you see a message indicating that the Android Programming book is added to the cart. The message also contains two links: Continue Shopping and Show Cart. This time, click the Show Cart link to see the products that are selected in the cart. You see the page shown in Figure 9-34.

Figure 9-34. *Showing the number of products in the cart*

The page shows the items that are chosen in the cart, along with their SKU and the quantity. You can update the quantity of a selected product (increase or decrease its quantity in the cart) or remove any product from the cart by clicking the Remove icon for that product. The page contains the buttons that can be clicked to supply billing and shipping information. The page also prompts to select the shipment and payment method. You can choose the shipment and payment method that you have already defined (see Figures 9-26 and 9-29) or supply new information.

Don't forget to select the Terms of Service check box. You can always click the link below to read terms of service before selecting the checkbox.

The page shows the Continue Shopping link to see more products and continue with the shopping. Click the Add/Edit Billing Address Information button to supply the billing address. You see the page that contains fields to add or edit the billing address information, as shown in Figure 9-35.

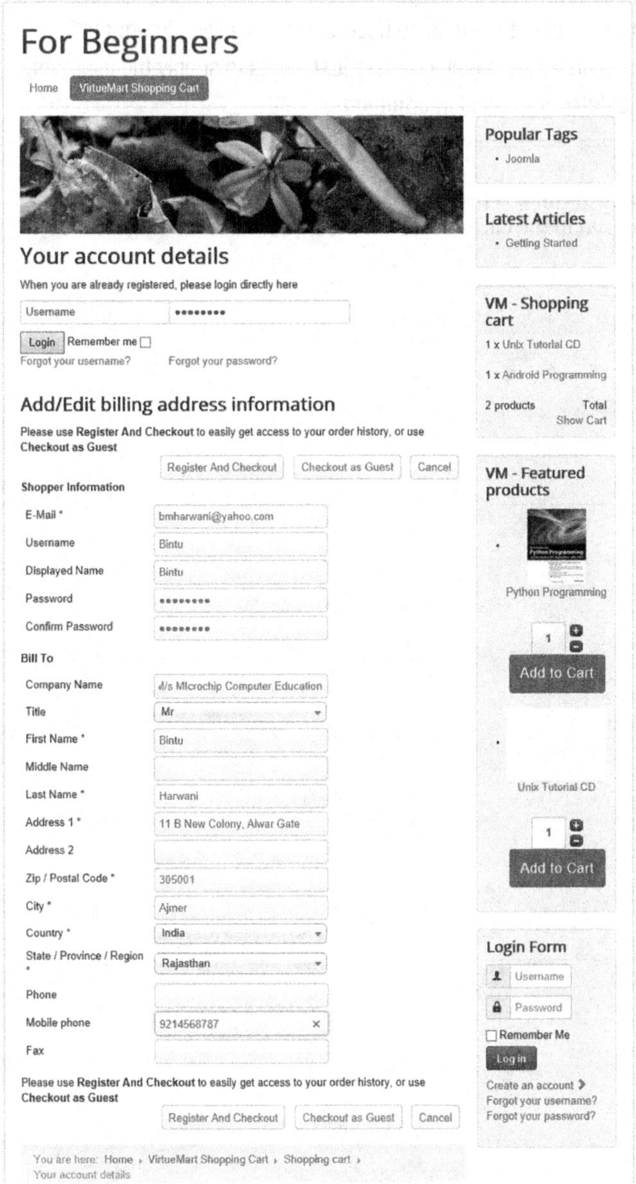

Figure 9-35. *Page for adding/editing billing address information*

Enter the e-mail address, name, password, name on which billing has to be done, and address; along with city, country, and zip code. The checkout can be done either as a registered user or as a guest. The benefit of being a registered user is that shipping and billing information will be saved for future use.

After entering the billing address information, click the Register and Checkout button. This button will register the user and subsequently initiate the checkout procedure. If you don't want to register with the site and simply want to checkout, click the Checkout as Guest button.

■ **Note** If the user has already created his or her account, there is no need to provide billing information because this information is picked up from the account. The registered user just needs to supply the username and password, and then click the Login button to fetch the saved information.

The next page confirms that the checkout procedure is performed. The page displays the billing and shipping information, and shows the items chosen in the cart along with their quantities (see Figure 9-36).

Figure 9-36. *Page for confirming purchase*

The cart items are also displayed to enable the customer to make any amendments to the cart (edit the quantity and even delete any item from the cart). If the user is confirmed with the items chosen in the cart, he/she can click the Confirm Purchase button to confirm the purchase and finally place the order.

The VirtueMart module will display a thank you message to ensure that the transaction was successful (see Figure 9-37). The order number is shown for future correspondence.

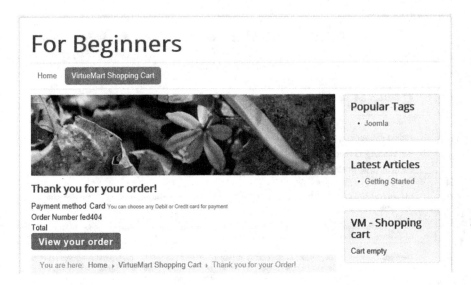

Figure 9-37. *Customer and billing information entered on the registration form, creating a new account*

Installing an RSS Feed Reader

Joomla provides a feed reader for reading RSS feeds, but if you need more flexibility, you can install any of the RSS feed reader modules available on the Internet. In this section, you'll learn how to install an RSS feed reader module named Simple RSS Feed Reader, which was developed by JoomlaWorks (`www.joomlaworks.net`). Simple RSS Feed Reader, which is based on the SimplePie PHP class, supports both RSS and Atom formats. With an efficient caching system, it displays feeds quite quickly.

After you select this module on the Internet, you'll see an introductory description, as shown in Figure 9-38.

Figure 9-38. Introductory screen for the Simple RSS Feed Reader module

■ **Note** If you use the FeedWind RSS feed to display in a Joomla site, you need a module extension because FeedWind RSS contains JavaScript (to run JavaScript, you need a module extension).

The module's archive file, as I downloaded it from the Internet, is mod_jw_srfr-v3.3_j2.5-3.x.zip. You can download it from www.joomlaworks.net/extensions/free/simple-rss-feed-reader to a folder on the local disk drive. To install the module, open the Extension Manager and select Extensions ➤ Extension Manager. The Extension Manager will open, and you can specify the location of the Simple RSS Feed Reader archive file by clicking the Browse button of the package file option. After selecting the archive file on the local disk drive, click the Upload & Install button to install the module. The Simple RSS Feed Reader module is installed and can be seen listed in the Module Manager.

To open the Module Manager, select Extensions ➤ Module Manager, and you'll find the newly installed Simple RSS Feed Reader module, as shown marked in Figure 9-39. The module is in unpublished mode because it is the default for every newly installed module.

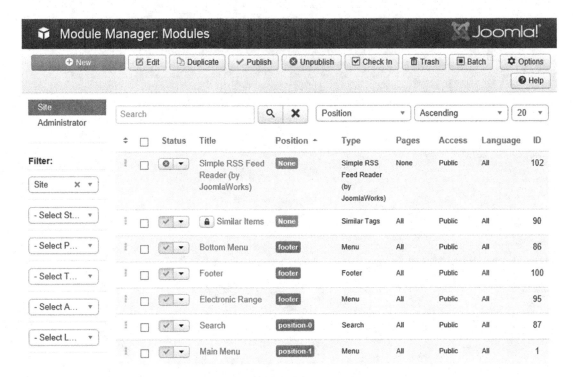

Figure 9-39. *Simple RSS Feed Reader module listed in the Module Manager*

To convert the Simple RSS Feed Reader to published mode, just select its check box in the Status column. The module will be changed to published mode and will be visible on the front end. Click the module title to edit it. You'll see a screen like the one shown in Figure 9-40, displaying the module type and a description.

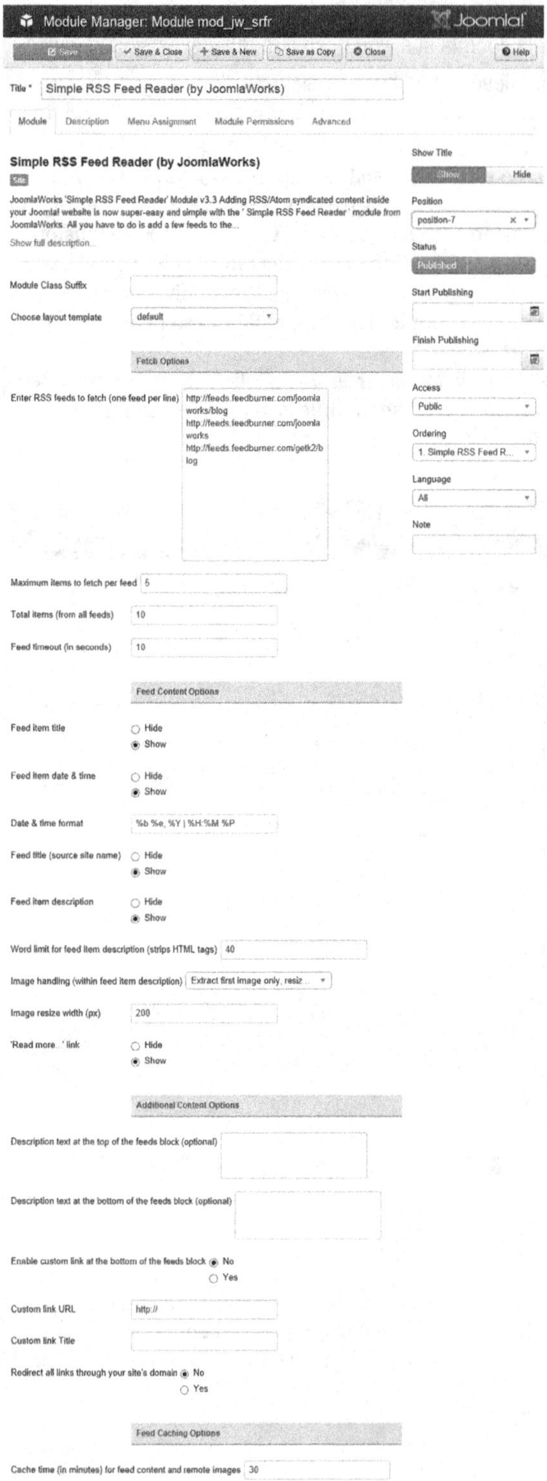

Figure 9-40. *Module editing screen showing RSS module attributes*

On this screen, you specify the position at which the module is to be displayed on the front end. From the Position combo box, choose position-7 to make the module appear on the right top of the site. You can also specify the access level: whether the module can be used by any visitor of the web site (Public), or is meant only for registered or special user groups. The module also displays certain parameters to configure the module. In the Enter RSS Feeds to Fetch field, you can specify the feed (RSS) URLs of the web sites that you want to syndicate (from which you want to receive RSS feeds). By default, the field contains three URLs: `http://feeds.feedburner.com/joomlaworks/blog`, `http://feeds.feedburner.com/joomlaworks`, and `http://feeds.feedburner.com/getk2/blog`.

The Maximum Items to Fetch Per Feed field is set to 5 by default to show only 5 syndicated feed items at a time. The Feed Item Title and Feed Item Date & Time fields are set to Show to display the title of the feed item as well as the time it was last modified at the source. You can leave the remaining parameters at their default values.

■ **Note**　You can add feed URLs of any encoding. The Simple RSS Feed Reader module will detect your web site's encoding and adjust all feeds to that specific encoding.

When you invoke the front end of your Joomla web site by going to `http://localhost/joomlasite`, you'll see that the Simple RSS Feed Reader module lists the feed items from the specified feed URL, as shown in Figure 9-41. You can select any feed title from the list to navigate to that web site to view details.

Figure 9-41. *Output of the RSS module on the front end of the Joomla web site*

Adding a Chat Feature to a Joomla Web Site

Chatting develops social networking among visitors to your web site. Several chat components are available on the Internet, and you can download any of them. A few of the popular chat components include JoomlaLiveChat (www.joomlalivechat.com), MyLiveChat, and so on. I downloaded the MyLiveChat component, which is available at http://extensions.joomla.org/profile/extension/communication/live-support-hosted/my-live-chat. Its archive file is mod_mylivechat_3.0.zip. Download it to the local disk drive.

After you download the file, open the Extension Manager by selecting Extensions ➤ Extension Manager. In the Extension Package File box, specify the location of the archive file and click the Upload & Install button, as shown in Figure 9-42.

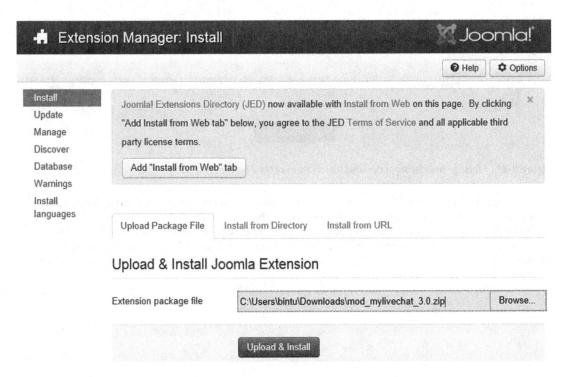

Figure 9-42. *Specifying the location of the archive file for the MyLiveChat component*

The MyLiveChat module will install, and you'll see the message Installing Module Was Successful, as shown in Figure 9-43.

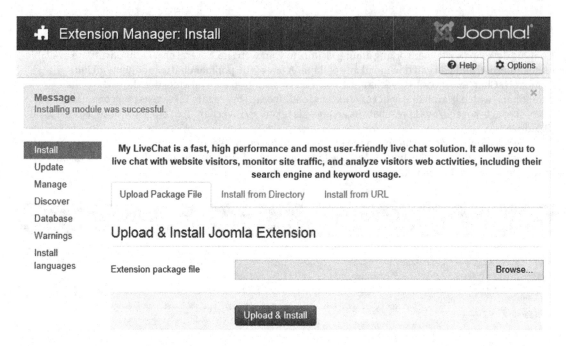

Figure 9-43. *Message indicating successful installation of the MyLiveChat component*

You'll also find the module included in the Module Manager, but in unpublished mode. To publish the module, click the red cross icon in the Status column. The icon will toggle to a green check sign, which means the module is converted to published mode. A message appears at the top of the Module Manager that says 1 Module Successfully Published (see Figure 9-44) to confirm that the chat module is enabled.

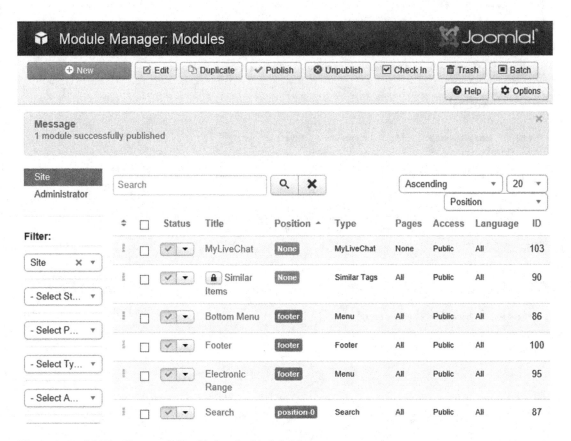

Figure 9-44. *MyLiveChat module added to the Module Manager page*

After MyLiveChat is selected from the Module Manager page, it will open in edit mode, in which you can specify certain settings, as shown in Figure 9-45.

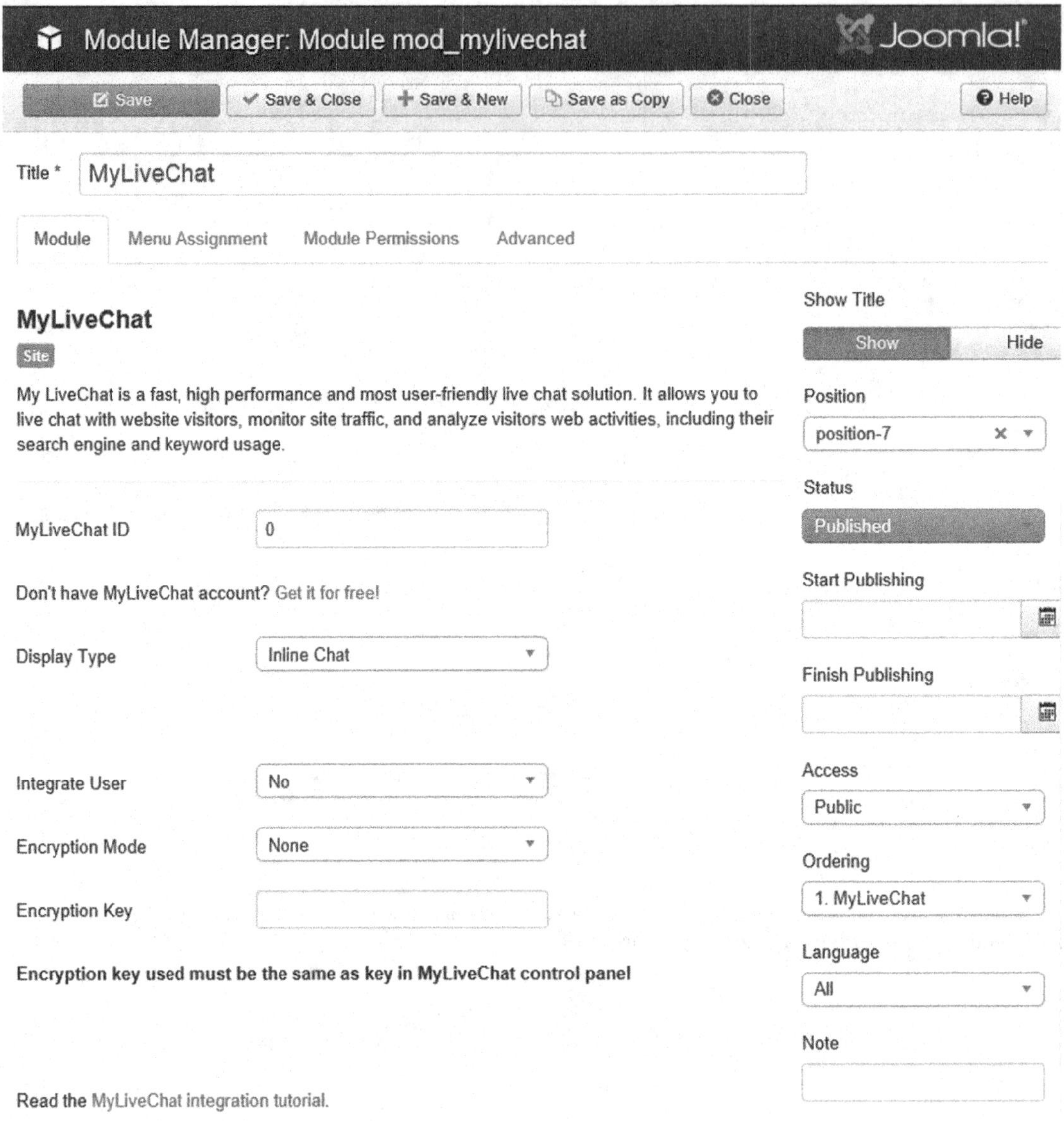

Module Manager: Module mod_mylivechat   Joomla!

| Save | Save & Close | Save & New | Save as Copy | Close | Help |

Title *   MyLiveChat

Module   Menu Assignment   Module Permissions   Advanced

MyLiveChat

`Site`

My LiveChat is a fast, high performance and most user-friendly live chat solution. It allows you to live chat with website visitors, monitor site traffic, and analyze visitors web activities, including their search engine and keyword usage.

MyLiveChat ID   `0`

Don't have MyLiveChat account? Get it for free!

Display Type   `Inline Chat ▼`

Integrate User   `No ▼`

Encryption Mode   `None ▼`

Encryption Key   `_____`

Encryption key used must be the same as key in MyLiveChat control panel

Read the MyLiveChat integration tutorial.

Show Title   `Show`   `Hide`

Position   `position-7 ✕ ▼`

Status   `Published`

Start Publishing   `📅`

Finish Publishing   `📅`

Access   `Public ▼`

Ordering   `1. MyLiveChat ▼`

Language   `All ▼`

Note   `_____`

Figure 9-45. *MyLiveChat module in edit mode*

You can specify settings such as the type of user who can access the chat module (i.e., whether everyone or only users of a specific group can access it), the chat language, display type, and so on. You also have to specify the position in which the chat module has to appear on the site. From the Position combo box, select the position-7 option that makes the module appear on the right top of the site.

To make the module appear on all the pages of the site, open the Menu Assignment tab. From the Module Assignment combo box, select the On All Pages option to make the chat module appear on all pages of the site (see Figure 9-46).

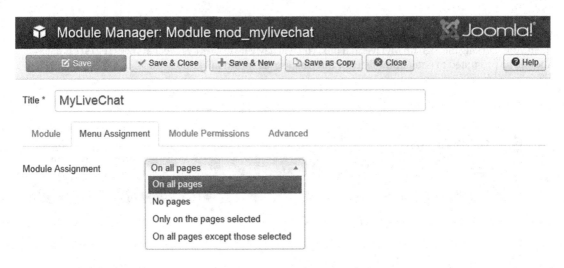

Figure 9-46. Making the MyLiveChat module appear on every page of the site

Now it's time to access the chat module from the front end. Let's access the Joomla web site by pointing the browser to http://localhost/joomlasite. You'll find a new module on the right side of the site with the title MyLiveChat. The module contains a link, Sign up MyLiveChat (see Figure 9-47).

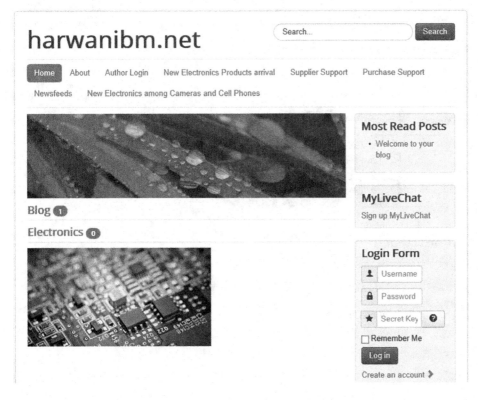

Figure 9-47. MyLiveChat module appears on the front side of the site

The MyLiveChat module wants the site administrator to sign up and register at www.mylivechat.com. Why? Because after registering at the site, the administrator can login, monitor site visitors, and even chat with them. After clicking the Sign up MyLiveChat link, you will navigate to www.mylivechat.com/register.aspx and will be prompted to enter administrator information, as shown in Figure 9-48.

Figure 9-48. *Registering at the MyLiveChat.com site*

You need to supply the administrator's e-mail address, password, first and last name, and so on. Enter the displayed captcha, check the Terms of Service check box, and click the Create Account Now button at the bottom.

If everything goes well, your account is created, and a dialog box pops up and displays Your Account Has Been Created Successfully. Click the OK button to close the dialog box and move on. You will be supplied with a chat code that you can paste on your site to enable visitors to chat with you (i.e., the administrator), as shown in Figure 9-49.

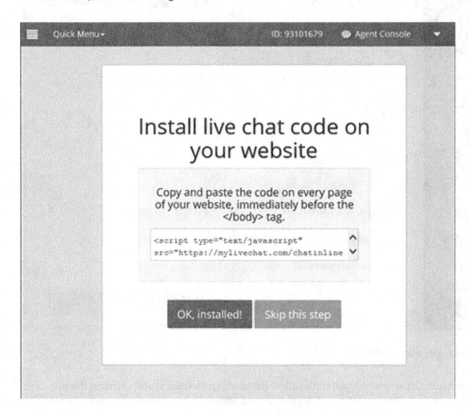

Figure 9.49. Code for displaying chat window on the front side of the site

You will learn later in this chapter how to display a chat window on your site using the supplied chat code by making use of the Custom HTML module. Just copy the code, paste it into Notepad for future use, and click the Skip This Step button to move on.

You will be navigated to the Dashboard that displays several menus on the left side that can be used to manage the account (see Figure 9-50). The page also displays a congratulations message for the successful creation of the account, and the administrator's LiveChat ID and Agent Console link at the top of the page.

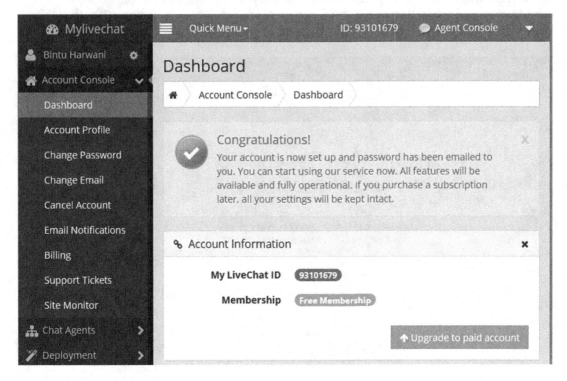

Figure 9-50. *Page showing the Dashboard*

It is through the Agent Console window that the administrator can monitor visitors visiting the site and can accept or decline their chat invitations. After the Agent Console link is clicked, the Agent Console window opens up as shown in Figure 9-51.

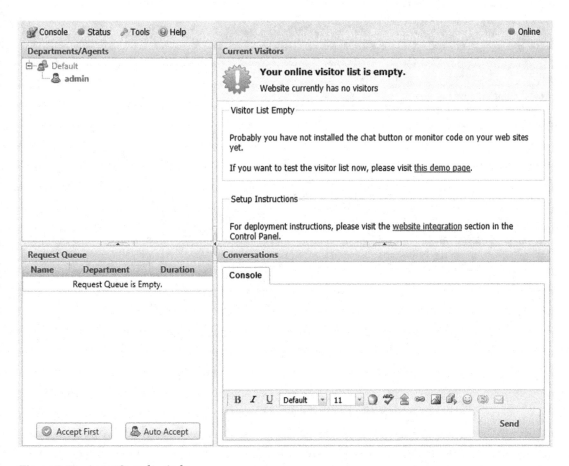

Figure 9-51. *Agent Console window*

The window is divided into four panes. The top-left pane shows the agents (the number of administrators of the site who are logged in). The top-right pane shows the list of visitors who are trying to chat with the administrator. Users can chat with any of the visitors and can even ban any undesired visitors from chatting. The bottom-left pane shows the request queue (i.e., the list of customers who are waiting for the administrator's response). The bottom-right pane displays the chat messages of the selected visitors and enable the administrator to chat with them. Whenever the administrator selects any visitor from the top-right pane, the chat messages will appear in the bottom-right pane, hence enabling the administrator to chat with many visitors simultaneously.

As discussed, the MyLiveChat module on the front side allows only the administrator to access the Dashboard and Agent Console to chat and monitor visitors. To allow the visitors of your site to chat with the administrator, you need to create a separate module and paste the code that was supplied by the MyLiveChat site (refer to Figure 9-49).

Open the Module Manager and click the New button from the toolbar to create a new module. Select Custom HTML when prompted to select the module type. You see the fields to enter information of the new module, as shown in Figure 9-52.

Figure 9-52. *Creating a new module of Custom HTML type*

In the Title field, enter the title of the module as **Chat With Us**. From the Position combo box, select the position-7 option to display the chat window on the top-right side of the site.

To paste the HTML and JavaScript code of the chat window, select the Tools ➤ <> Source code option from the menus of the TinyMCE editor window to open the Source code box. Paste the code supplied by the MyLiveChat site in the Source code box (see Figure 9-53).

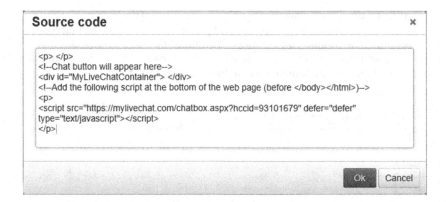

Figure 9-53. *Source code box for pasting the HTML/JavaScript code*

Click the OK button after pasting the code to go back to the new module page. Click the Save & Close button to save the module. Now visitors of your site can request and chat with the site administrator. Open the front end of the site and refresh it. You will see the Chat With Us module below the MyLiveChat module, as shown in Figure 9-54.

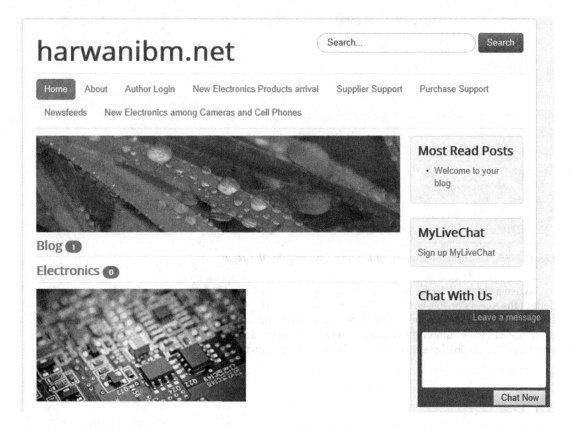

Figure 9-54. *Chat With Us module appears on the front side of the site*

415

The Chat With Us module shows a small chat window with a Chat Now button at the bottom.

When a visitor clicks the Chat Now button, a window appears and prompts the user to leave a message for the administrator/agent to respond. The window (see Figure 9-55) prompts the visitor to enter the following information: name, e-mail address, subject of chatting, and a small message. After entering the required information, the visitor needs to click the Send button for the agent to respond.

Figure 9-55. *Live Chat dialog box for leaving a message for the agent*

When a visitor clicks the Send button, the administrator finds the visitor's name listed in the top-right pane of the Agent Console window. After the visitor's name is clicked, her information pops up that includes her location, time, subject, browser that she is accessing, and so on. Below the visitor's information appear the buttons that the administrator can use to invite the visitor for chat, ban her, and view her location on the map (see Figure 9-56). Let's click the Invite button to chat with the visitor.

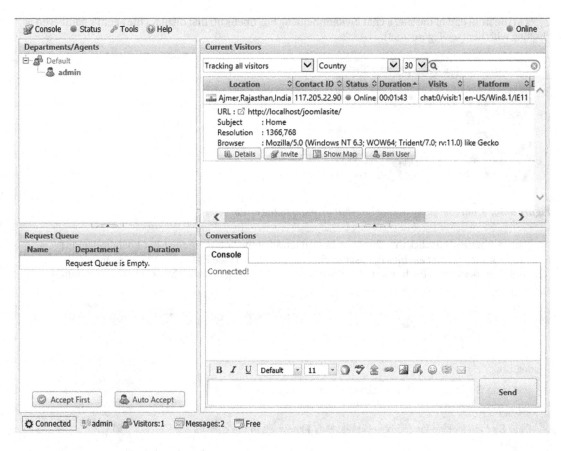

Figure 9-56. *Agent Console window showing the visitor's information*

A Chat Invitation dialog box pops up to greet the visitor and display the agent's name. In the default text, replace the text *Agent* with the agent's name who is chatting with the visitor; then click the OK button (see Figure 9-57).

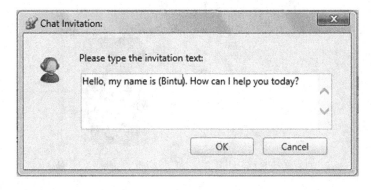

Figure 9-57. *Chat Invitation dialog box*

417

On the front end of the site, a chat invitation dialog box opens up that displays the agent's name who is chatting with her (see Figure 9-58).

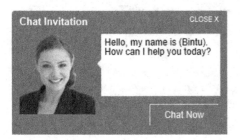

Figure 9-58. *Chat Invitation dialog box that displays to the visitor*

The visitor needs to click the Chat Now button found at the bottom in the Chat Invitation window. A dialog box pops up that enables the user to chat with the agent (see Figure 9-59). The user can type the required chat message in the box found at the bottom of the dialog box and then click the Send button.

Figure 9-59. *Box for chatting with the agent or administrator of the site*

The chat message typed by the visitor can be seen by the agent/administrator in the Agent Console's bottom-right pane, as shown in Figure 9-60. The agent can type a responding chat message and click the Send button.

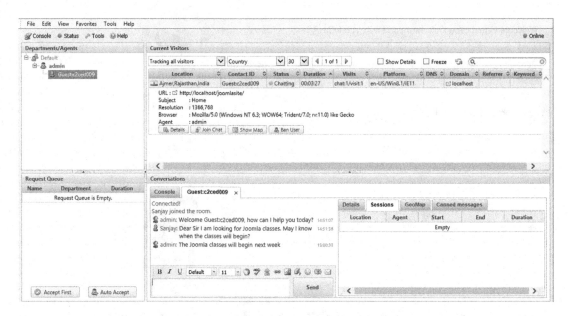

Figure 9-60. *Agent chatting with the visitor through the Agent Console page*

The conclusion is that the visitor chats with the administrator through the chat window found at the front end of the site, and the administrator responds to the visitor through the Agent Console window.

Figure 9-61 shows the text message sent by the administrator in the Agent Console window that is visible to the site visitor. Although MyLiveChat works well, you can also use eAssistance Pro live chat.

Figure 9-61. *Visitor seeing the chat messages of the agent*

Uninstalling Extensions

Following are the steps to uninstall extensions:

- From the administrative interface, open the Extension Manager by clicking Extensions ➤ Extension Manager.

- In the Extension Manager page, click the Manage link in the left column.

- You see a list of the installed extensions. Select the check box of the extension that you want to uninstall and then click the Uninstall icon from the toolbar at the top (see Figure 9-62).

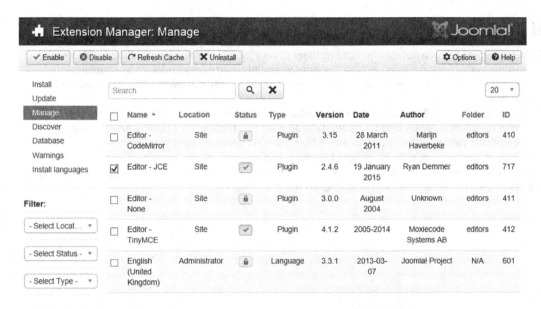

Figure 9-62. *Manage tab showing the installed extensions in Extension Manager*

■ **Note** You can use the Filter field to quickly search for the extension if you can't locate it.

- The selected extension will be uninstalled, and a message will display at the top to confirm it (see Figure 9-63).

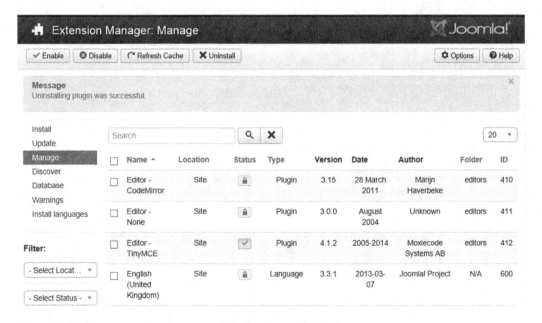

Figure 9-63. *Message confirming successful extension uninstallation*

Summary

In this chapter, you learned how to add extra facilities to your Joomla web site by installing a wide variety of extensions available on the Internet. You saw how commonly used extensions such as templates, e-commerce extensions, RSS feed readers, and chatting extensions can be downloaded, installed, and used in a Joomla web site.

In Chapter 10, you will learn the techniques of configuring the Joomla global settings. Also, you will see the steps of installing an editor and how to make search engine–friendly (SEF) URLs. Additionally, you will see how activation links can be sent to visitors who register on your web site (to activate their accounts). You'll also see how to change the language of the front end of your web site and provide a multilingual facility to your visitors (the ability to translate the contents of a web site into different languages). Finally, you will learn how to make your own local help server.

CHAPTER 10

■ ■ ■

Making it Global

In the previous chapter, you learned how to add extra features to a Joomla web site by installing various extensions. You saw how the most commonly required extensions, such as templates, e-commerce extensions, RSS feed readers, and chatting extensions can be downloaded, installed, and used in a Joomla web site.

In this chapter, you'll learn how to do these tasks:

- Configure global settings for Joomla

- Install an editor

- Make search engine–friendly (SEF) URLs

- Allow visitors to register at your web site and send them an activation link to activate their account

- Change the language of the front end of your web site

- Provide a multilingual facility to your visitors (the ability to translate the contents of the web site into different languages)

Global Configuration Settings

Global settings, chosen by using the Global Configuration menu, enable you to apply global features to your web site. These settings play a major role in the following processes:

- Enabling visitors to create an account by registering on your web site

- Making SEF URLs

- Highlighting the description of your web site in the form of metadata to be caught by search engines

- Getting help screens from a local or remote help server

- Setting the upper limit of the size of MIME files and verifying whether they are valid

---

■ **Note**   MIME, which stands for Multipurpose Internet Mail Extensions (an extension done by the IETF of the SMTP), is a specification for formatting non-ASCII messages, including graphics, audio, and video files to be sent over the Internet. Verification of MIME files means ensuring that the MIME file uploaded to your web site is a valid MIME file.

- Setting the session lifetime and caching time

- Configuring mail settings and database settings

- Selecting the local time zone

- Applying compression techniques to increase site performance

Global Configuration can be invoked by either selecting its icon from the Control Panel or choosing Site Global Configuration. It contains five tabs: Site, System, Server, Permissions, and Text Filters.

Site Tab (Global Configuration)

Using the Site tab, you can set a message that your web site is offline, select an editor for managing site contents, set the size of the lists and feeds, specify metadata information for search engines, make SEF URLs, and so on (see Figure 10-1). As shown in the figure, there are four sections within the Global Configuration Site tab (each is described in the sections that follow).

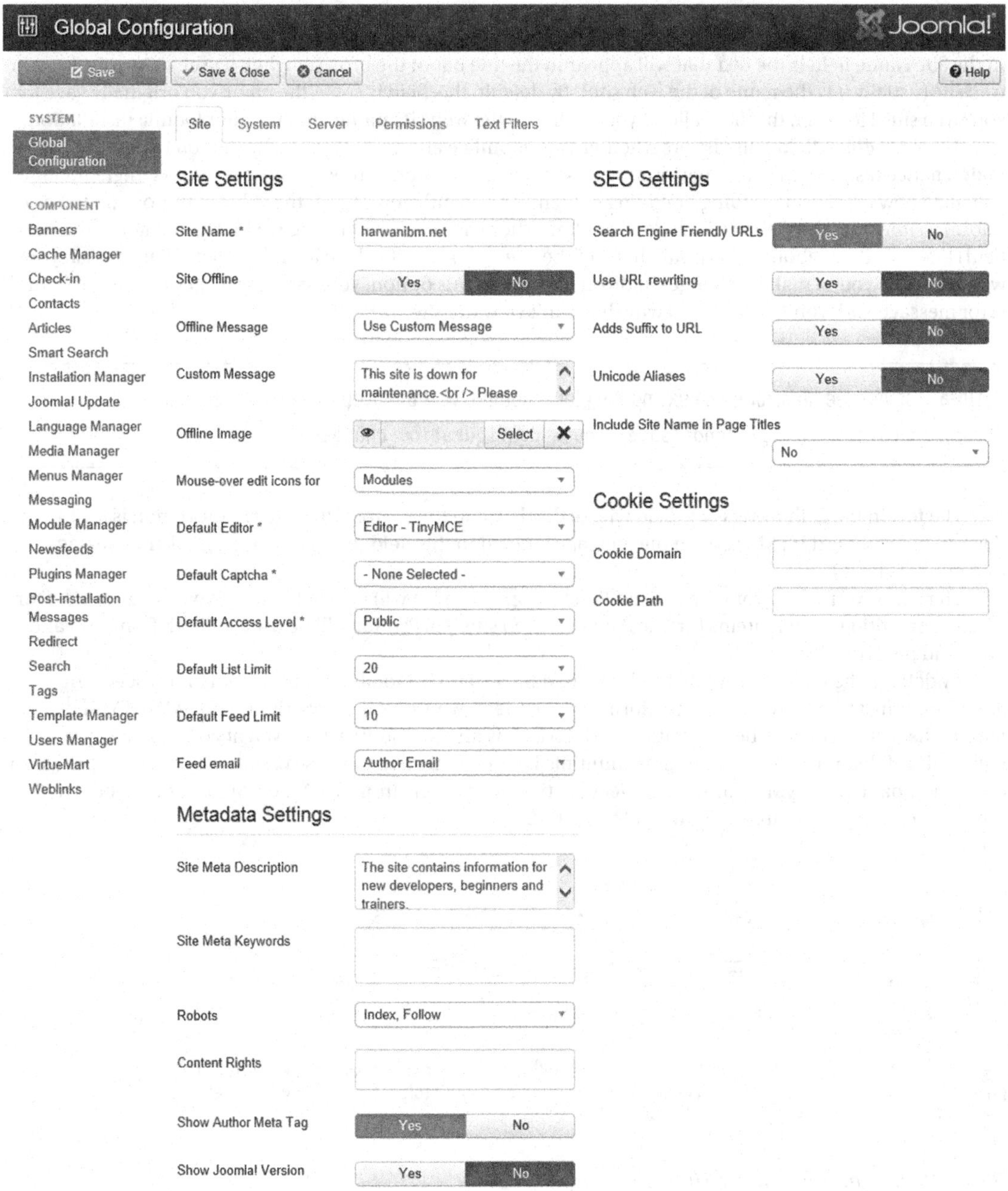

Figure 10-1. *Global ConfigurationSite tab*

Site Settings (Site Tab)

In the Site Name field is the text that will appear in the title bar of the browser when a user visits your Joomla web site (usually it is the name of the web site). By default, this field is set to the name you originally gave for your web site. However, this field allows you to change the web site name anytime after Joomla installation.

The Site Offline field tells visitors whether your Joomla web site is temporarily shut off for a maintenance task. When you're performing a maintenance task on your web site (these tasks might include installing new extensions, adding or editing content, and so on), you can set the value of this option to Yes to inform visitors that the web site is currently offline. They will receive a message (which you enter in the next field) that tells them about the unavailability of the site and when it will be available again. If users visit your web site while you're making changes and you haven't set this option, your visitors will get a Page Not Found error message and won't understand why they can't view the site.

■ **Note**   If you see an error while saving the global setting, visit this web page for the solution:
`https://docs.joomla.org/Cannot_save_Global_Configuration_changes`.

The text in the Offline Message field will be displayed to the visitor if the Site Offline option is set to Yes. You can use standard HTML code in the message entered in this field (e.g., `<br />`) to break the message into multiple lines).

The editor you select from the Default Editor drop-down list will be used as the global default editor for creating or editing content items (articles) on your web site. This editor will be used for both front-end and back-end purposes.

By default, the editor is TinyMCE, which provides a standard toolbar that's helpful for most editing and formatting tasks. TinyMCE is a platform-independent, web-based, JavaScript HTML WYSIWYG editor control that can very easily be integrated into a CMS. It is an open source, lightweight editor that's Ajax-compatible. It loads quickly and supports multiple languages through the use of different language packs. To see the toolbar that TinyMCE provides, select the title of an article from the Article Manager to open it in the TinyMCE editor; an example is shown in Figure 10-2.

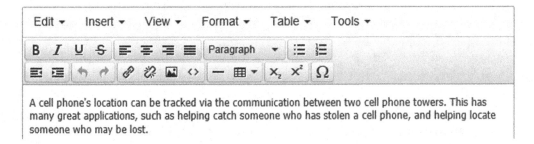

Figure 10-2. *Article open in the TinyMCE editor*

Keep in mind that you can always install more editors, so let's do that now. From among the many editors that are freely available on the Internet, I downloaded JCE Editor, a lightweight, fast, advanced, feature-rich editor. This editor has the same sophisticated interface as Microsoft Word, making the content management task much easier. The editor has image and document management capabilities that assist in uploading and administering files within the editor's GUI. Its archive file name is com_jce:246.zip. You can download it from the following address to your local disk drive: www.joomlacontenteditor.net/downloads.

To install the editor, invoke the Extension Manager by selecting Extensions ➤ Extension Manager. You'll see a page like the one shown in Figure 10-3. In the Extension Package File section, click the Browse button to locate the archive file and then click the Upload File & Install button.

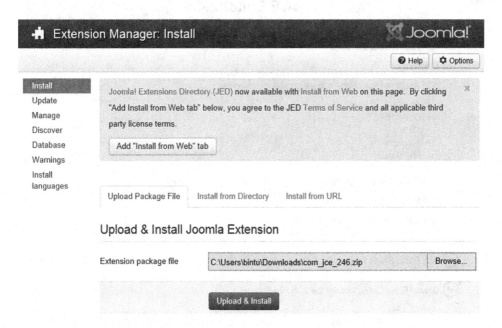

Figure 10-3. *Using the Extension Manager to install the JCE Editor*

Once the editor is installed, you'll see this message: Installing Component Was Successful (see Figure 10-4).

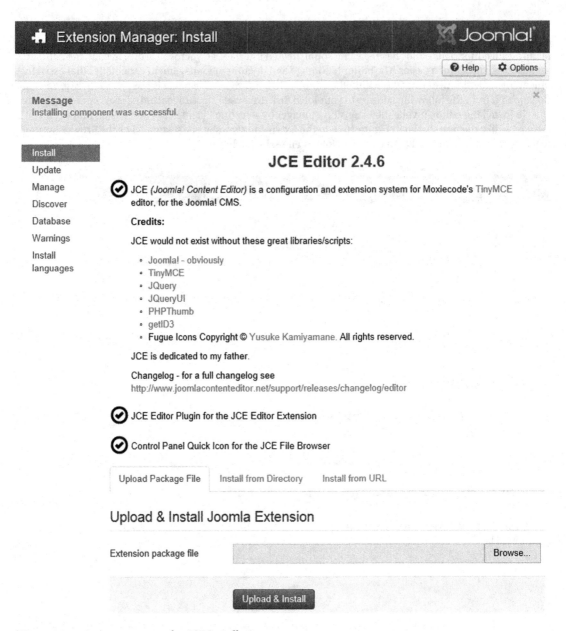

Figure 10-4. *Success message after JCE installation*

In the Site Settings section of the Site tab of Global Configuration, you can see an extra option in the Default Editor list: Editor - JCE, as shown in Figure 10-5. Let's select it to see what facility it provides.

Figure 10-5. *Default Editor drop-down list showing the Editor - JCE option*

If you now edit an article by selecting its title in the Article Manager, the article will open in the JCE Editor and you'll see its toolbar, as shown in Figure 10-6. This toolbar looks quite a bit more advanced than that of the TinyMCE editor.

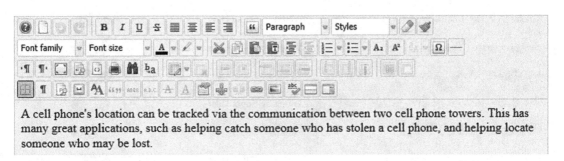

Figure 10-6. *JCE tools*

Here are some advantages of using JCE:

- It makes adding and editing jobs very easy.

- It has familiar Office-like buttons for formatting content and performing common editing tasks: cutting, pasting, deleting, inserting, and so on.

- You can easily create links to other Sections, Categories, and Articles in your site using the Link Browser.

- It implements integrated spellchecking using your browser's Spellchecker (or PSpell and ASpell).

Now, let's return to the rest of the settings in the Site tab of Global Configuration.

The Default List Limit drop-down list determines how many items can appear in a list. By default, its value is 20, which means that if you're looking at the articles list on your web site (from the front end), you'll see the articles in a group of 20. If you have more than 20 articles, they'll appear on the next page (or pages). You can change the value of this option to any value from 5 to 100, in increments of 5.

For example, suppose that there is a category named Electronics that displays a list of all articles under the Electronics category. Assuming that there are seven articles in the Electronics category, and the length of the list is the default (20), all the titles of the articles will appear on the first page (see Figure 10-7). The list length is also displayed in the drop-down list that appears on the extreme right above the list. You can even change it from the front end to set the desired number of articles to be displayed at one time, but this setting is temporary and vanishes when you select another menu item.

Electronics

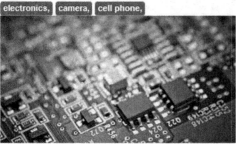

We deal with the latest electronic products that are highly durable of better quality and at very economic price.

20 ⌄

Title	Author	Hits
Autotracking Cell Phones	Written by Super User	Hits: 3
Java Supported Cell Phone	Written by Super User	Hits: 1
CDMA Cell Phones	Written by Super User	Hits: 2
Web Cams - Video chatting	Written by Super User	Hits: 7
Cameras for Safari	Written by Super User	Hits: 2
Latest Cameras	Written by Super User	Hits: 55
Welcome to your blog	Written by Joomla	Hits: 14

Figure 10-7. List of seven articles when the list length is 20

If you set the list length to 5 in the Global Configuration settings, you'll see that only 5article titles appear in a list at one time, and again the, pagination occurs if there are more articles. The links are displayed as 1, 2, Next, and End to navigate to any page, as shown in Figure 10-8.

Electronics

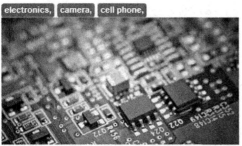

electronics, | camera, | cell phone,

We deal with the latest electronic products that are highly durable of better quality and at very economic price.

5 ⌄

Title	Author	Hits
Autotracking Cell Phones	Written by Super User	Hits: 3
Java Supported Cell Phone	Written by Super User	Hits: 1
CDMA Cell Phones	Written by Super User	Hits: 2
Web Cams - Video chatting	Written by Super User	Hits: 7
Cameras for Safari	Written by Super User	Hits: 2

|◀◀ ◀◀ 1 2 ▶▶ ▶▶| Page 1 of 2

Figure 10-8. *List of articles is paginated when the list length is 5*

Upon clicking the 2 link to see the second page, you'll see the titles of the articles, as shown in Figure 10-9.

Electronics

electronics, camera, cell phone,

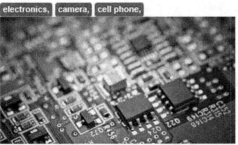

We deal with the latest electronic products that are highly durable of better quality and at very economic price.

5 ∨

Title	Author	Hits
Latest Cameras	Written by Super User	Hits: 55
Welcome to your blog	Written by Joomla	Hits: 14

| ◄◄ | ◄ | 1 | 2 | ►► | ►►| | Page 2 of 2

Figure 10-9. *Second page of articles list*

Back to the Site Settings tab; the Default Feed Limit drop-down list determines the number of content items to be shown in the specific feed. By default, its value is 10. You'll create a Feed Display module for checking this setting. First, open the Module Manager by selecting Extensions ➤ Module Manager. From the toolbar, click the New icon to create a new module based on the Feed Display module type. From the list of module types, select the Feed Display module type. The new module page appears, as shown in Figure 10-10.

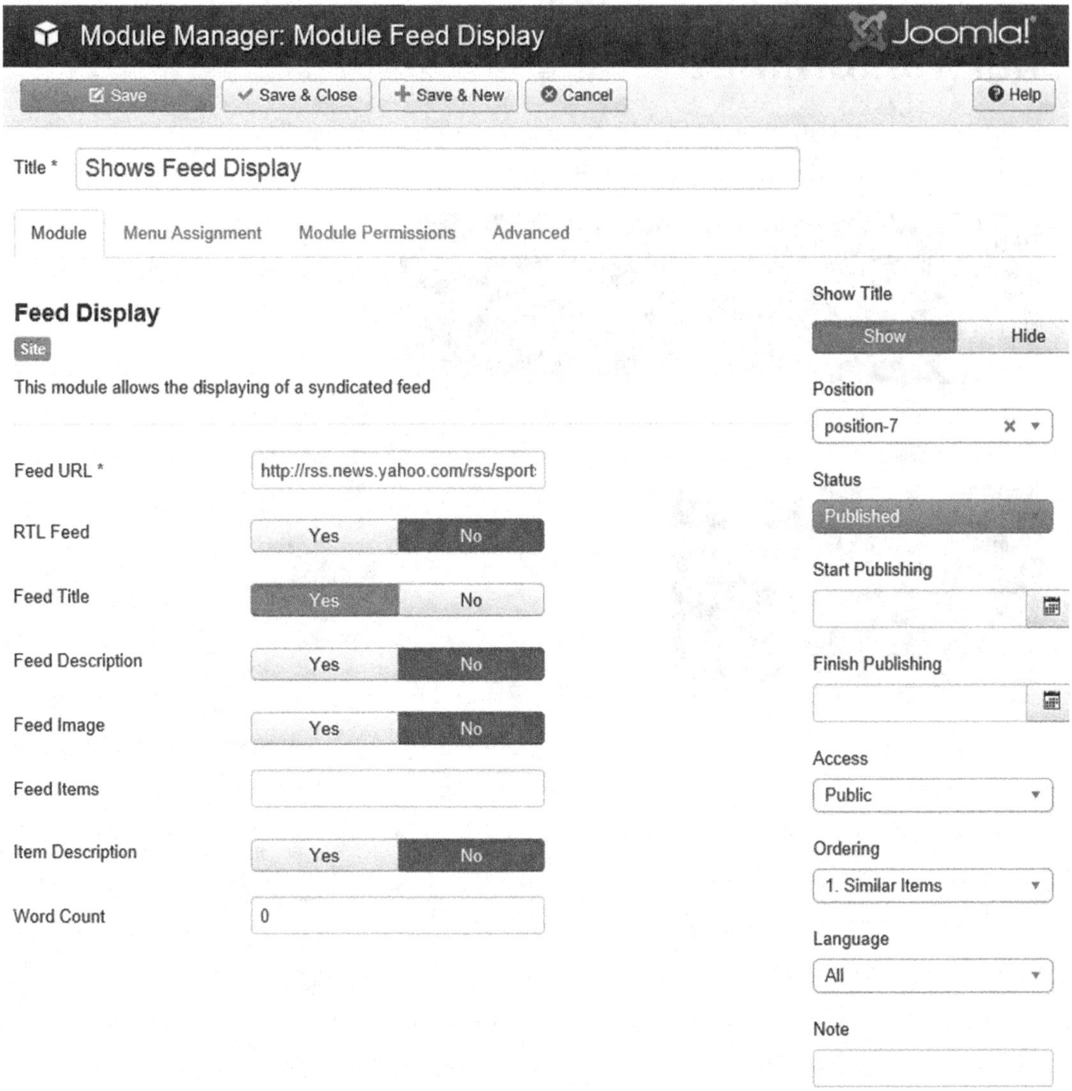

Figure 10-10. *Creating a module of the Feed Display type*

In the Title field, specify the title of the module as Show Feed Display. In the Feed URL field, specify the URL of the RSS feed as `http://rss.news.yahoo.com/rss/sports`. Note that the Feed Items field must be blank (no values showing), or else the value will override the Global Configuration settings. For example, if the value in this field is 3, the number of items displayed by the RSS feed will always be 3, no matter what value you specify in the Feed length drop-down list of the Global Configuration settings. Because you want to display only the feed titles and not their descriptions, set the Feed Title field value to Yes and set the Feed Description and Feed Image field values to No.

Because the default value of the Default Feed Limit (in the Site Settings tab) field is 10, a total of 10 Items are displayed in the RSS feed from the front side of the site, as shown in Figure 10-11.

Figure 10-11. *Ten items are displayed in the RSS feed when the feed length is 10*

If you set Default Feed Limit to 5, the front end of the Joomla web site will show 5 items of the RSS feed, as shown in Figure 10-12.

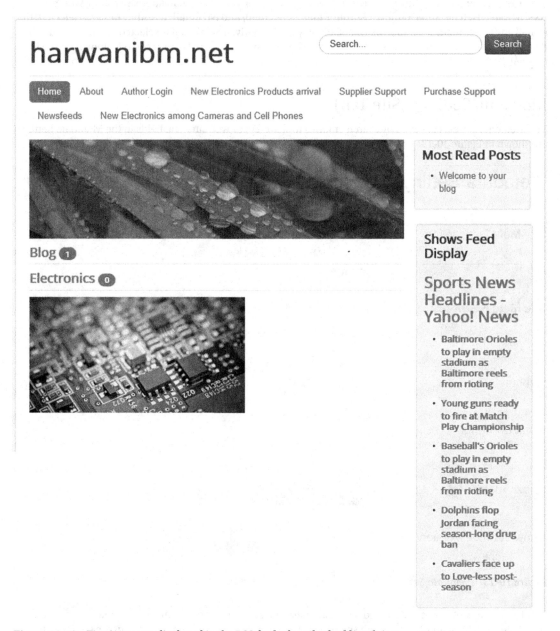

Figure 10-12. *Five items are displayed in the RSS feed when the feed length is 5*

Again, let's go back to see the rest of the settings in the Site tab of Global Configuration (by selecting its icon from the Control Panel or choosing the System ➤ Global Configuration option).

The Feed Email drop-down list determines whether to display the e-mail addresses along with the RSS/newsfeeds. It has three options: Author Email, Site Email, and No Email. If Author Email is selected, the e-mail addresses of the feed authors will be displayed. Similarly, if Site Email is selected, the front end will display the web site e-mail address (if any) of the site from which the feeds are accessed, along with the feed contents.

Metadata Settings (Site Tab)

The Metadata settings are used by search engines to search your web site. The fields in the Metadata Settings are shown in Figure 10-13.

Metadata Settings

Site Meta Description	The site contains information for new developers, beginners and trainers.
Site Meta Keywords	
Robots	Index, Follow ▼
Content Rights	
Show Author Meta Tag	Yes / No
Show Joomla! Version	Yes / No

Figure 10-13. Metadata Settings fields

In the Site Meta Description field, you can enter a brief description of your web site that will be used by search engines for searching your web site (the description will be indexed by search engine spiders). This information will be displayed with your web site name when users perform a search via any search engine, as shown in Figure 10-14. The description should be to the point and explanatory because the user will decide whether to visit the site depending on the description given. It is best to limit the description to 20 words because any extra words will be ignored by the search engines.

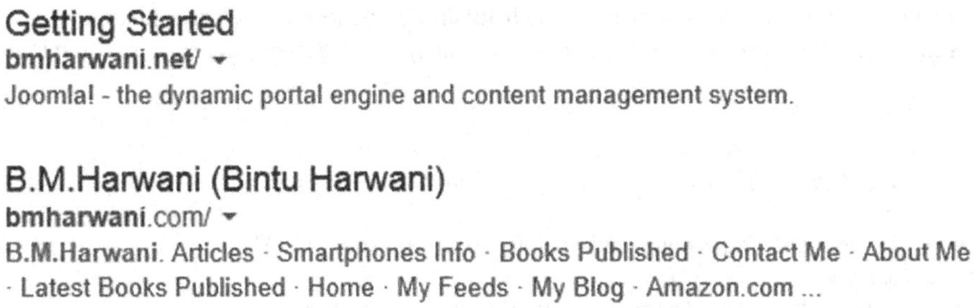

Getting Started
bmharwani.net/ ▾
Joomla! - the dynamic portal engine and content management system.

B.M.Harwani (Bintu Harwani)
bmharwani.com/ ▾
B.M.Harwani. Articles · Smartphones Info · Books Published · Contact Me · About Me
· Latest Books Published · Home · My Feeds · My Blog · Amazon.com ...

Figure 10-14. *Brief description of web siteand theweb site link*

In the Site Meta Keywords field, you can enter the keywords that best describe your web site to improve the capability of search engine spiders to index the site. You should enter keywords that briefly and precisely explain the products, services, facilities, and so on provided by your organization. The keywords should be limited to a total of 1,000 characters because the search engines will not read more than that. Separate the keywords with a comma. Think about the keywords that are likely to be searched from the visitor's point of view and include them in the keywords list.

▓ **Note**   Search engines such as Google do not currently use any content in the Meta Keywords section when indexing.

Let's specify a meta description and some keywords for the web site. Assuming that the site sells computer books and tutorial CDs, publishes computer-related articles, and offers virtual classes, let's set the Global Site Meta Description and Global Site Meta Keywords as shown in Figure 10-15.

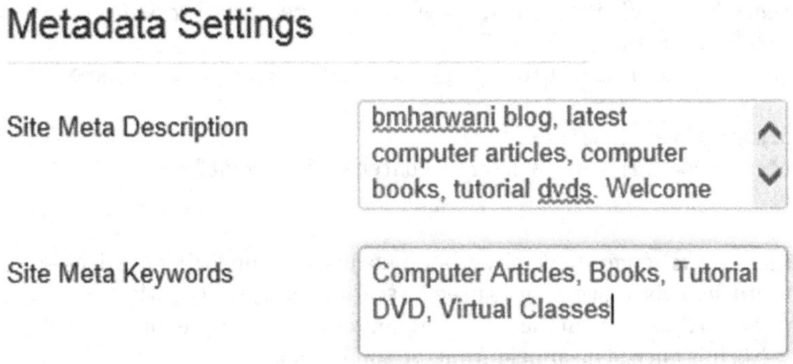

Metadata Settings

Site Meta Description | bmharwani blog, latest computer articles, computer books, tutorial dvds. Welcome |

Site Meta Keywords | Computer Articles, Books, Tutorial DVD, Virtual Classes |

Figure 10-15. *Metadata settings*

You can see the meta description and keywords from the front end of the Joomla web site. Just right-click the web site and select View Source from the shortcut menu that appears. You might see something like the following:

```
<!DOCTYPE html>
<html xmlns="http://www.w3.org/1999/xhtml" xml:lang="en-gb" lang="en-gb" dir="ltr">
  <head>
    <meta name="viewport" content="width=device-width, initial-scale=1.0" />
    <base href="http://bmharwani.net/" />
    <meta http-equiv="content-type" content="text/html; charset=utf-8" />
    <meta name="keywords" content="Computer Articles, Books, Tutorial DVD, Virtual Classes" />
    <meta name="description" content="bmharwani blog, latest computer articles, computer
    books, tutorial
       dvds. Welcome to B.M. Harwani's web site" />
    <meta name="generator" content="Joomla! - Open Source Content Management" />
  <title>Home</title>
```

Notice that the `<meta name="keywords">` and `<meta name="description">` tags display what you specified in these fields in the Global Configuration settings.

Each article on your web site can have its own meta information. Let's open the "Latest Cameras" article that you created in Chapter 3. When the article is displayed, view the source code, which should look something like the following. Notice that the `<title>` tag shows the title of the article as Latest Cameras, which may be used by search engines.

```
<!DOCTYPE html>
<html xmlns="http://www.w3.org/1999/xhtml" xml:lang="en-gb" lang="en-gb" dir="ltr">
  <head>
    <meta name="viewport" content="width=device-width, initial-scale=1.0" />
    <base href="http://bmharwani.net/index.php/en/newelectronics/12-camera/7-latest-cameras" />
    <meta http-equiv="content-type" content="text/html; charset=utf-8" />
    <meta name="keywords" content="night vision, zoom, camera, high megapixel resolution" />
    <meta name="author" content="Super User" />
    <meta name="description" content="bmharwani blog, latest computer articles, computer
    books, tutorial
       dvds. Welcome to B.M. Harwani's web site" />
    <meta name="generator" content="Joomla! - Open Source Content Management" />
  <title>Latest Cameras</title>
```

The Show Author Meta Tag option allows you to show the author meta information for each article—information about the creator of the article. This information is used by search engine spiders when indexing the site. Note the `<meta name="author">` tag in the preceding source code. If you set the value of the Show Author Meta Tag option to No, this tag will disappear from the source code.

SEO Settings (Site Tab)

Joomla has built-in search engine optimization (SEO) functionality. The SEO Settings section of the Site tab handles global SEO settings for your Joomla site.

SEF URLs change the way site links are presented and optimize them so that search engines can access more of your web site. The SEF URLs option is available only to sites hosted on Apache servers. Select Yes to enable Joomla to create SEF URLs instead of normal database-generated URLs.

When the SEF URLs option is set to No, the URL of an item selected on a web site is usually difficult to remember. For example, if you click the Virtue Mark link on the web site, the URL will appear as shown in Figure 10-16.

Figure 10-16. *URL when SEF URLs is set to No*

You can see that the URL contains symbols and numbers. After you enable SEF URLs, the symbols and numbers will disappear, and the URL will appear as shown in Figure 10-17.

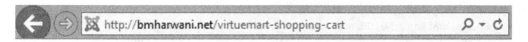

Figure 10-17. *Friendly URL that appears when SEF URLs is set to Yes*

■ **Note**   The alias text auto generated by Joomla (or specified by you) is set as the SEF URL.

When the SEF URLs option is set to Yes, the URL that appears in your browser is friendly and easy to remember by the search engines.

When the Add Suffix to URL option is set to Yes, Joomla will add .html to the end of the URLs. The default setting is No. For example, after this option is enabled, the URL for Virtue Mart will appear as shown in Figure 10-18.

Figure 10-18. *Suffix .html added to URL*

To support SEO, use general SEO best practices with your Joomla site. A few of them are listed here:

- Create the Title tag because it shows up in the search engines as headlines for your page.

- Use limited and required keywords in your pages.

- Use the Meta tags for a Joomla web site because some search engines still use them while searching sites.

- Get lots of internal and external links from relevant sites.

- Create a sitemap of your site, which is an .xml file that contains links to every page on your site. Then submit your site and your sitemap to Google. Google will crawl the sitemap, so it can read and search your web site's content more quickly.

Besides these best practices, you can also use Joomla SEO plug-in extensions to optimize your content for search engines. There are several popular plug-ins that support SEO in Joomla: SEO Glossary, SEO Generator, Easy Frontend SEO (EFSEO), SEF Translate, and so on.

Cookie Settings

Cookies are used to keep track of user activities on the browser. For example, they can be used to remember sites that are frequently visited by users, data entered in sites, options selected on different sites, and so on. The Cookie Settings tab shows the following fields to configure cookies:

- *Cookie Domain*: Enter the domain name for which the site's cookies will be valid. To make cookies valid for just the primary domain, enter `www.your domain.com`. The cookie must be set for the primary domain. Leave this field blank to make the full domain of the document set the cookie.

- *Cookie Path*: Enter the URL path for which the site's cookies will be valid. Other pages cannot read or use the cookie. To make the cookie valid for the entire site, simply enter /. The default value has the current directory set the cookie.

System Tab (Global Configuration)

The System tab (see Figure 10-19) is used for various configurations, including setting the path of the log folder; specifying the location of the help server; and enabling, disabling, or setting the time for caching and sessions.

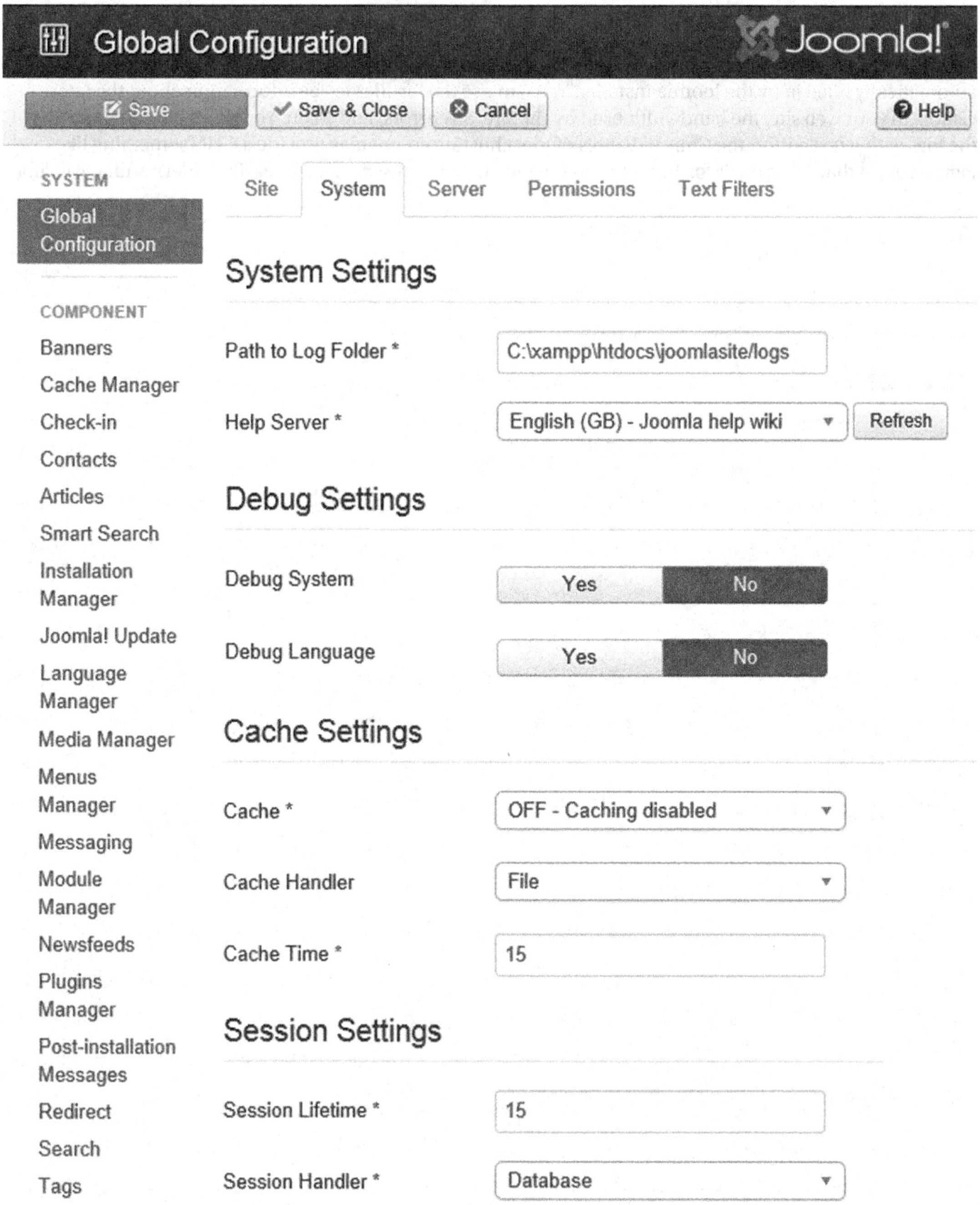

⊞ Global Configuration ✖ Joomla!

| ☑ Save | ✔ Save & Close | ⊗ Cancel | ❷ Help |

SYSTEM

Global Configuration

COMPONENT

Banners

Cache Manager

Check-in

Contacts

Articles

Smart Search

Installation Manager

Joomla! Update

Language Manager

Media Manager

Menus Manager

Messaging

Module Manager

Newsfeeds

Plugins Manager

Post-installation Messages

Redirect

Search

Tags

Site   System   Server   Permissions   Text Filters

System Settings

Path to Log Folder *   C:\xampp\htdocs\joomlasite/logs

Help Server *   English (GB) - Joomla help wiki ▾   Refresh

Debug Settings

Debug System   Yes   No

Debug Language   Yes   No

Cache Settings

Cache *   OFF - Caching disabled ▾

Cache Handler   File ▾

Cache Time *   15

Session Settings

Session Lifetime *   15

Session Handler *   Database ▾

Figure 10-19. Global Configuration System tab

441

System Settings (System Tab)

In the Path to Log Folder field, you specify the location in which the logs will be stored. This path is automatically filled in by the Joomla installer. You can use the log files to see information about the latest visitors to your web site, the bandwidth used by the site, any errors, and so on. You don't have to open the logs with a text editor; the Control Panels of most hosting companies provide a GUI (something like Figure 10-20) that reads the information from the log files and presents it in an easily understandable format.

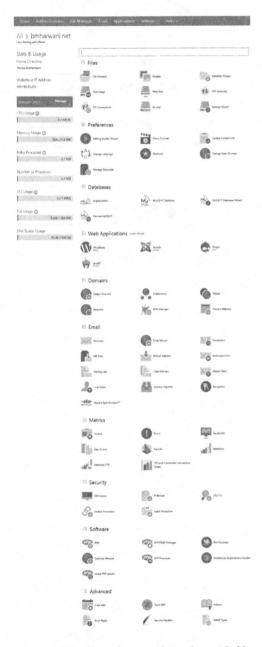

Figure 10-20. *Sample Control Panel provided by a web hosting company*

Some web hosting companies provide icons, as shown in Figure 10-21, to extract information from the log files and present a report in the desired format.

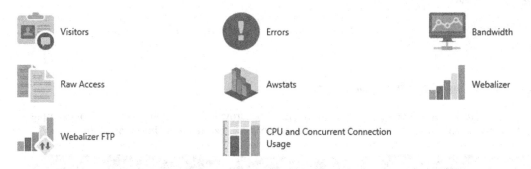

Figure 10-21. *Analysis and log file tools*

Back to System Settings; the Help Server field is used to display help screens when the user clicks the Help icon. By default, the server that's specified in the Help Server drop-down list is a remote server, `help.joomla.org`, but you can also set up your own local help sever.

Debug Settings (System Tab)

With the debug settings, you can decide whether to apply the debug system on your Joomla web site and whether to display debug indicators in case of bugs.

The Debug System option is used to detect any bugs that may occur during an operation performed on the front-or back end of your Joomla web site. If you set this option to Yes, it will activate Joomla's debug system, and you will start getting diagnostic information, language translations, and SQL errors. That is, you will start getting debugging information at the end of each page of your web site that includes the following:

- Profile information (the amount of time it takes to execute code up to various points in the code)

- Memory usage (the amount of RAM used)

- SQL queries executed for building the page

- Language files loaded (all the language files loaded for building the page, along with their full path and the number of times the file was referenced)

- Untranslated string diagnostics (list of all the untranslated strings found)

- Untranslated string designer (list of all the untranslated strings found in a key = value format).

After you set the Debug System option to Yes, the debug information may look something like that shown in Figure 10-22.

Figure 10-22. *Debug console appears on every page*

You get more detailed information after clicking the links provided in the debug console. For example, you get the profile information shown in Figure 10-23 when you click the Profile Information link.

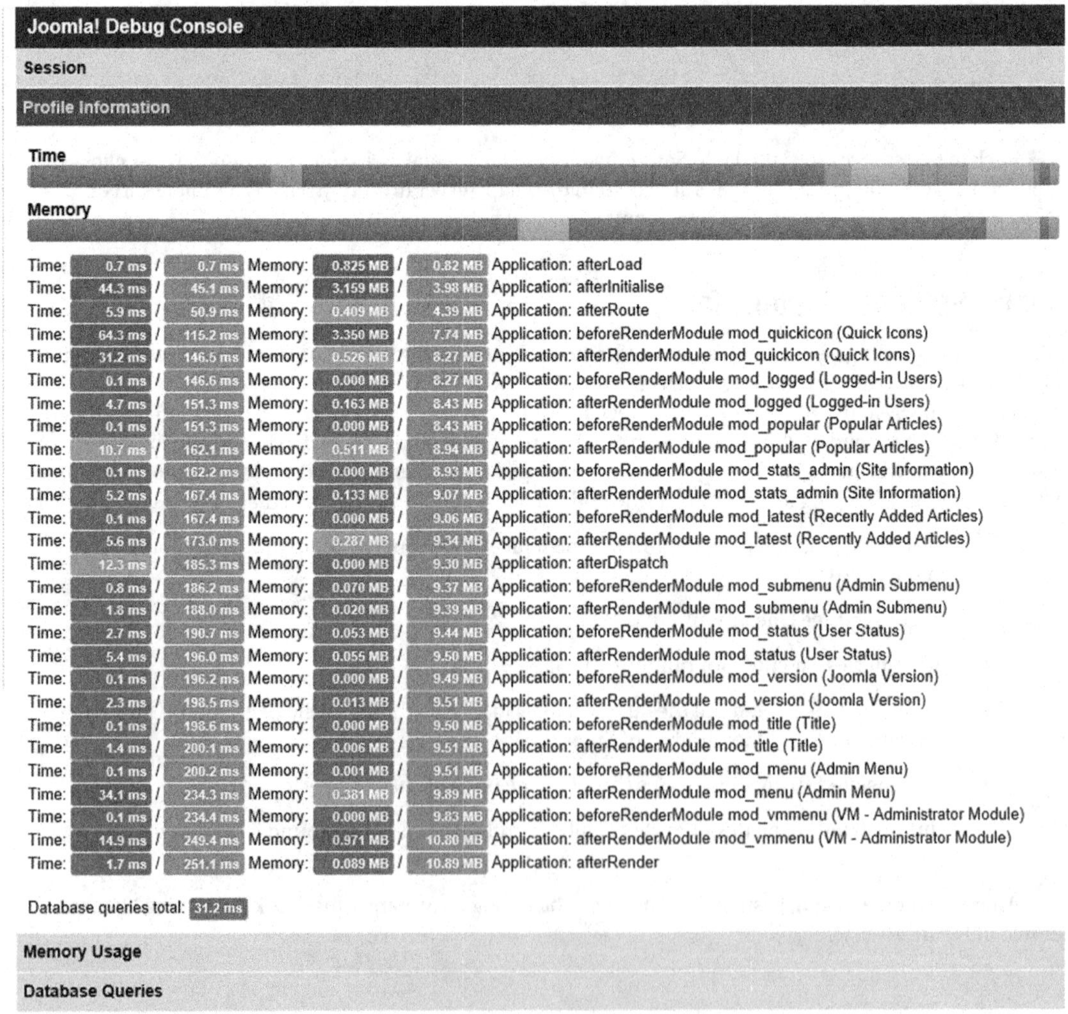

Figure 10-23. *Debug information is displayed at the end of each web page*

Back to Debug Settings; the Debug Language option is used for switching on the debugging indicators for the Joomla language files. That is, all translatable text is enclosed in special characters that reflect their status. Any text enclosed in bullets indicates that a match has been found in the language definition file, and the text has been translated. Any text enclosed in pairs of asterisks (**) indicates that the string is translatable, but no match was found in the language definition file. Text with no surrounding characters indicates that the string is not translatable. You can use language debugging without enabling the Debug System option, but if you do, you won't get additional detailed information about the bugs to help you correct them.

An example of the use of the Debug Language option on the front end of a Joomla web site (displaying text enclosed in asterisks) is shown in Figure 10-24.

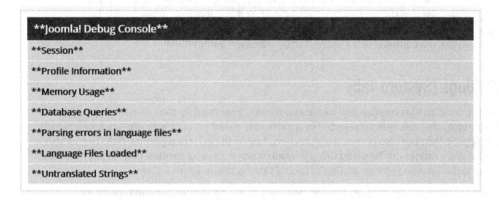

Joomla! Debug Console

Session

Profile Information

Memory Usage

Database Queries

Parsing errors in language files

Language Files Loaded

Untranslated Strings

Figure 10-24. *Text enclosed in asterisks when the Debug Language option is set to Yes*

Cache Settings (System Tab)

The cache is a small, temporary storage area on the hard drive in which browsers keep web site contents that have been repeatedly viewed by visitors. In this way, caching is a technique to improve the speed of displaying web site contents. Recall that because the web site is a CMS, whatever contents you see on it are accessed from the MySQL database. Using caching, Joomla creates a local copy of the contents being viewed (a cache) on the server's hard disk, so the next time the contents are requested by the visitor, Joomla can access them from there.

The options in the Cache Settings section of Global Configuration are as follows:

- *Cache*: You can set the value of this option to any of the following values, depending on your requirement:

  - *ON — Conservative caching*: Enables basic caching of your web pages and content

  - *ON — Progressive caching*: Enables caching for the site that either does not change often or is a bulky site

  - *OFF - Caching disabled*: Disables caching on your site

- *Cache Handler*: Displays how the caching is performed. There are two caching mechanisms:

  - *File*: In file-based caching, reading and writing operations are performed using the file cache. That is, the read operations read from an area in system memory known as the system file cache instead of the physical disk. Similarly, for write operations, the data is written to the system file cache rather than to the disk.

  - *Cache_Lite*: A faster caching system that focuses on enhancing PHP performance.

- *Cache Time*: The amount of time to keep the local copy of the contents before refreshing it. When the time specified in this field expires, Joomla updates the local copy maintained in the cache with that of the MySQL database contents (to display the latest updated information). The default value is 15 minutes (after every 15 minutes, the contents of the cache will be refreshed automatically).

Session Settings (System Tab)

Sessions allow your system to recognize that requests are being generated by the same client (visitor). This not only helps to remember the options selected by a particular visitor on your web site (such as products selected in a shopping cart) but also prevents visitors from having to perform repetitive tasks (e.g., a visitor who has logged in once should not be asked to log in again when accessing another page of your web site).

The options in the Session Settings section of Global Configuration are as follows:

- *Session Lifetime*: This field determines how long a session should last and how long a user can remain signed in after being inactive. The default value is 15 minutes, which means that a visitor who logs into your web site and doesn't perform any action for more than 15 minutes will be prompted to log in again.

- *Session Handler*: This drop-down list determines how the session should be handled after a user connects and logs into the site. The default setting is Database, which means that all the actions taken by the visitor on the webpage are temporarily stored in a database until the visitor either logs out or closes the browser window. If you set the value of this option to None, your Joomla web site won't be able to maintain the session (i.e., it won't be able to recognize whether the requests have been made by the same user).

Server Tab (Global Configuration)

The Server tab of Global Configuration (see Figure 10-25) is used for configuring several servers, including FTP, database, and mail. You can use this tab to apply a compression technique to enhance your web site performance; set the local time zone to display the time to your visitors; specify the FTP host, username, and password; specify the type and name of the database in which your Joomla web site is stored; specify the mailer to be used for sending e-mail; and so on.

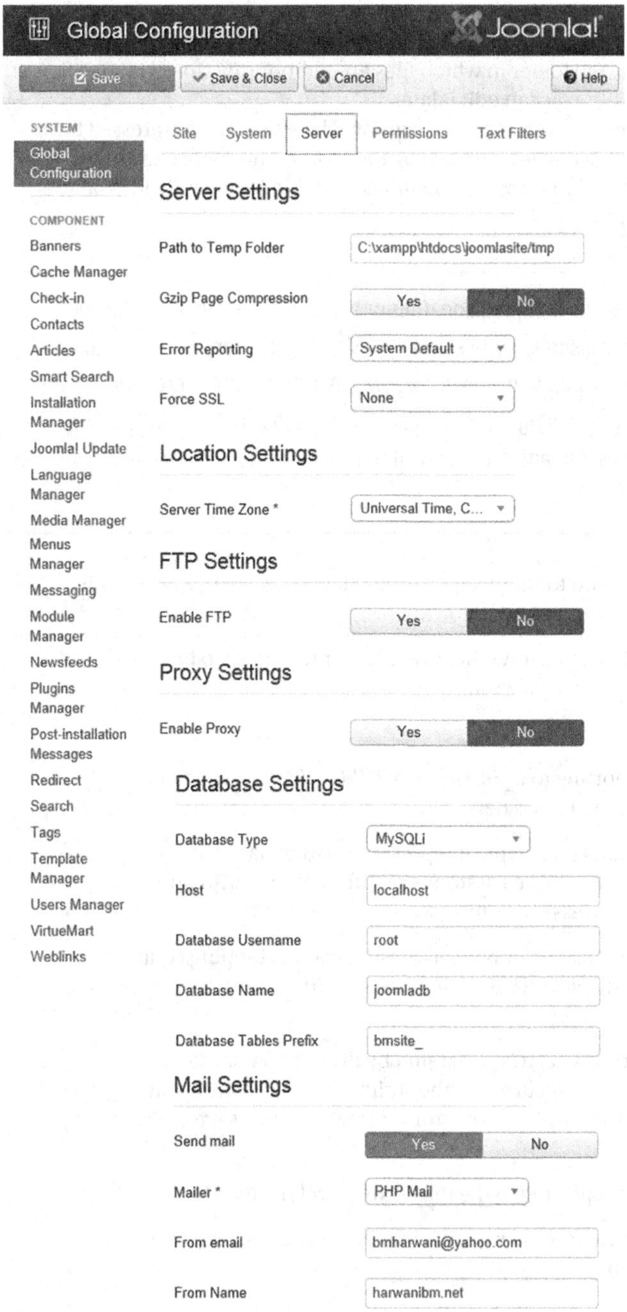

Figure 10-25. *Global Configuration Server tab*

Server Settings (Server Tab)

In the Path to Temp Folder field, the location of the folder in which files are temporarily stored is specified. It is filled in by default when Joomla is installed, but you can edit it later.

If you set the GZIP Page Compression option to Yes, the web pages will be stored in compressed form when in an inactive state and will be uncompressed when invoked by the visitor. This increases your web site's speed. The only drawback of GZIP compression is that it consumes valuable CPU bandwidth on the web servers. Hence, the default value of this option is No.

■ **Note**   GZIP is a software application used for file compression. Compression is a simple and effective way to save bandwidth and speed up a site. The reason is quite simple: HTML files are very bulky because every <html>, <table>, and <div> tag has a corresponding closing tag (words are repeated throughout the document). Compression reduces the file size by removing the repetitions without loss of information. The browser can easily download the zipped file, extract it, and then show it to the user. This compression results in quick page loading.

The Error Reporting drop-down list allows you to set the appropriate level of reporting. The error-reporting options are shown in Figure 10-26 and described following.

- *System Default*: This option (the default) allows the level of error reporting to be determined by the php.ini file on the web server.

- *None*: This option turns error reporting off.

- *Simple*: This option turns error reporting to E_ERROR|E_WARNING|E_PARSE, which are the standard error types in PHP, as explained here:

  - E_ERROR: This is the most serious error type; it represents errors that PHP cannot recover from. The error handler in this case stops execution of the script and displays the error number and message to the user.

  - E_WARNING: This is the intermediate error type; it doesn't lead to stopping script execution. The error handler displays a warning message with the error number to the user.

  - E-PARSE: This is the lowest error type; it is generated by the PHP parser to denote that some syntax error has occurred in the script. The error handler also stops execution of the script and displays the error number and message to the user.

- *Maximum*: This option turns error reporting to the maximum level (E_ALL).

- *Development*: This option returns the feedback displaying the error cause with technical details. It is mostly used by developers.

Error Reporting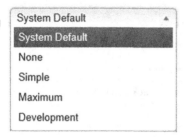

Figure 10-26. *Error-reporting options*

■ **Note** The output from the error reports is displayed at the bottom of every page of the web site.

The Force SSL setting makes the web site more secure. Secure Sockets Layer (SSL) is a protocol developed by Netscape and a security technology used to establish an encrypted link between a web server and a browser. The encryption in the link ensures that all data passed between the web server and browser remains private and is not visible to unauthorized persons. To encrypt data, two cryptographic keys are used: a private key and a public key. The public key is known to everyone, but the private key is known only to the recipient of the message.

To establish an SSL connection, a web server requires an SSL certificate. To get an SSL certificate, follow these steps:

1. Choose to activate SSL on your web server.

2. Provide information about your web site and your company.

3. On the basis of the information provided, the web server creates two cryptographic keys: a private key and a public key. The public key is placed in a certificate signing request (CSR): a data file containing information about you and your web site. Then the CSR is submitted to the web server.

4. Upon submission of the CSR, the certification authority (CA) validates your details and issues an SSL certificate, which allows you to use SSL.

5. The web server matches the issued SSL certificate with your private key and then establishes an encrypted link.

■ **Note** URLs that require an SSL connection start with `https:` instead of `http:`.

The next step is to configure the `configuration.php` file. Open the `configuration.php` file (found in the `C:\xampp\htdocs\joomlasite` directory).Find the following line:

```
var $live_site ='';
```

Replace the line with this one:

```
var $live_site = 'https://www.your-domain.com';
```

Save the file.

The options in the Force SSL drop-down list are as follows:

- *None*: SSL is not activated

- *Administrator Only*: SSL is valid only for the back end

- *Entire Site*: SSL is valid for the whole site (front and back end)

Location Settings (Server Tab)

The only option in the Location Settings section is Server Time Zone, which identifies the time zone in which the web site is to operate. You can set the time zone so that your web site displays local times to your visitors. The time should reflect where the site's server is located. The default setting is (Universal Time, Coordinated (UTC))

FTP Settings (Server Tab)

The FTP settings in this section play an important role in the way files are uploaded to the web server. The options in this section are as follows:

- *Enable FTP*: You can set the value of this field to Yes to enable Joomla to use its built-in FTP function instead of the normal upload process used by PHP.

    - *FTP Host*: In this field, you specify the URL of the host server with which you will be performing FTP.

    - *FTP Port*: In this field, you specify the port that is used by FTP. The default setting is 21.

    - *FTP Username*: In this field, you specify the name of the user who is allowed to access the FTP server.

    - *FTP Password*: The password that Joomla will use when accessing the FTP server is specified in this field.

    - *FTP Root*: In this field, you specify the root directory in which you want the uploaded files to be kept initially.

Proxy Settings (Server Tab)

The Proxy settings help when configuring the proxy server, if any. If set to Yes, the Enable Proxy field in this section will display the fields that prompt for information about the proxy host, proxy port, proxy username, and proxy password.

Database Settings (Server Tab)

The database settings include information about the database used for your Joomla web site, including the type of database, the location of the database server, the name of the database, and the users who have permission to access the database. The options in the Database Settings section are as follows:

- *Database Type*: The type of database to be used. The default setting is MySQLi, but it can be changed during Joomla installation.

- *Host*: The server in which the database exists. The server IP address is entered here. It is typically set to local host by default.

- *Database Username*: The username with which you access the database is entered in this field.

- *Database Name*: The name of the database in which the Joomla web site is stored is specified here.

- *Database Tables Prefix*: The term to be used before every table in the selected database is specified, which enables you to have multiple Joomla installations in the same database. The default setting is jos_, but it can be changed. There is a warning attached to this setting that reads as follows: "Do not change unless you have a database built using tables with the prefix you are setting." So you should change the database prefix only if you have already created a database with tables having the prefix that you will specify here.

Mail Settings (Server Tab)

The mail settings are set during the initial setup of Joomla, but they can be changed whenever necessary. The following are the options in the Mail Settings section of Global Configuration:

- *Send mail*: Set this field to Yes if you want to send mail from your site.

- *Mailer*: This setting determines which mailer to use to deliver e-mail from the site. The default setting is PHP Mail Function, but it can also be changed during the initial setup of Joomla. Figure 10-27 shows the different mailer options, and they're described following.

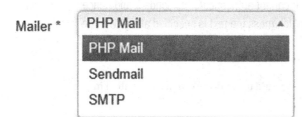

Figure 10-27. *Mailer options*

- *PHP Mail*: This option uses the mail function that is built into PHP.

- *Sendmail*: This option uses the Sendmail program, which is typically used when creating HTML e-mail forms. Sendmail is a widely used mail transport agent (MTA). MTAs are meant for sending mail from one machine to another: they work internally to move e-mail over networks or the Internet to their destinations. Sendmail supports a variety of mail transfer protocols, including SMTP, ESMTP, HylaFAX, QuickPage, and UUCP. Most of the mail servers on the Internet today run Sendmail.

- *SMTP Server*: This option uses the site's SMTP (Simple Mail Transfer Protocol) server. SMTP is a network protocol used to send messages from the mail client to the mail server. Messages can only be pushed with this protocol, meaning that they can only be sent to the server, not retrieved from it. The protocols POP and IMAP are used to retrieve the message from the server.

  - *SMTP Authentication*: If the SMTP server requires authentication to send mail, set this to Yes; otherwise, leave it at No. This option is used only if Mailer is set to SMTP.

  - *SMTP Security*: Choose the desired SMTP security protocol used by your mail server.

  - *SMTP Port*: Specify the port number of your SMTP server. The default port value is 25.

  - *SMTP Username*: This is the username to use for access to the SMTP host. It is used only if Mailer is set to SMTP.

  - *SMTP Password*: This is the password to use for access to the SMTP host. It's used only if Mailer is set to SMTP.

  - *SMTP Host*: This is the SMTP address to use when sending mail. It's used only if Mailer is set to SMTP.

■ **Note**   After verifying the configuration, an SMTP server gives permission to the sending machine to send an e-mail message. The message is sent to the specified destination, and a validation that it has been delivered successfully is performed. If the message has not been delivered successfully, an error message is sent to the sending machine. There are two limitations of SMTP: it cannot authenticate the senders and hence cannot stop e-mail spamming, and it is a text-based protocol in which message text is specified along with the recipients of the message.

- *From Email*: The e-mail address used by Joomla to send site e-mail is specified in this field.

- *From Name*: This is the name that Joomla uses when sending site e-mail messages. By default, Joomla uses the site name specified during the initial setup.

Users, visitors, and administrators play a major role in the success of any web site. Let's have a quick look at how configuration can be set for the users of your site. Open the Global Configuration page and from the list of components shows on the left, click the Users Manager to open the Users Configuration page. You learn more in the following section.

Users Configuration

Users Configuration settings determine whether visitors to your web site can register themselves, whether an activation link will be sent for e-mail verification, what the default user group for a new user should be, and so on. The Users Configuration page shows the fields shown in Figure 10-28.

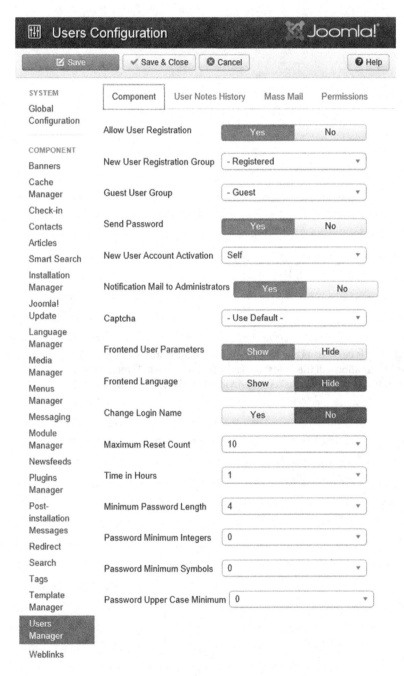

Figure 10-28. *Users Configuration page*

Set the Allow User Registration option to Yes if you want to enable a visitor to your web site to create an account. If this option is enabled, you'll see a Create an Account link in the Login module, as shown in Figure 10-29. If you set this field to No, the Create an Account link disappears; no visitor can create an account from the front end, and only existing users can log in and access the member areas of the web site. The administrator can still create new users from the back end.

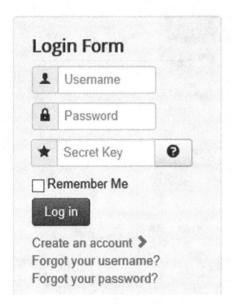

Figure 10-29. *Login module on the front end*

When the Create an Account link is clicked, a User Registration form appears (see Figure 10-30) in which visitors can enter their information. All the fields marked with an asterisk (*) must be filled in; otherwise, an error will occur, and the visitor will be asked to provide the missing information.

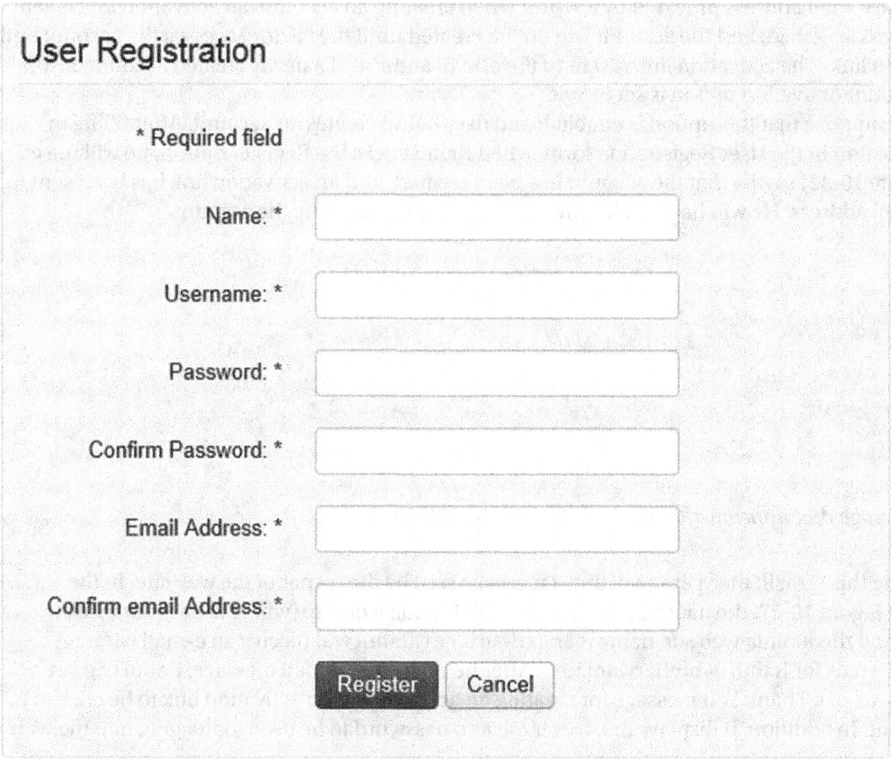

User Registration

* Required field

Name: *

Username: *

Password: *

Confirm Password: *

Email Address: *

Confirm email Address: *

Register   Cancel

Figure 10-30. User Registration form to create an account

Via the New User Registration Group drop-down list, you can select any of the predefined user groups shown in Figure 10-31 to define the default group for newly created accounts. (Refer to Chapter 5 for the rights and limitations of each user group).

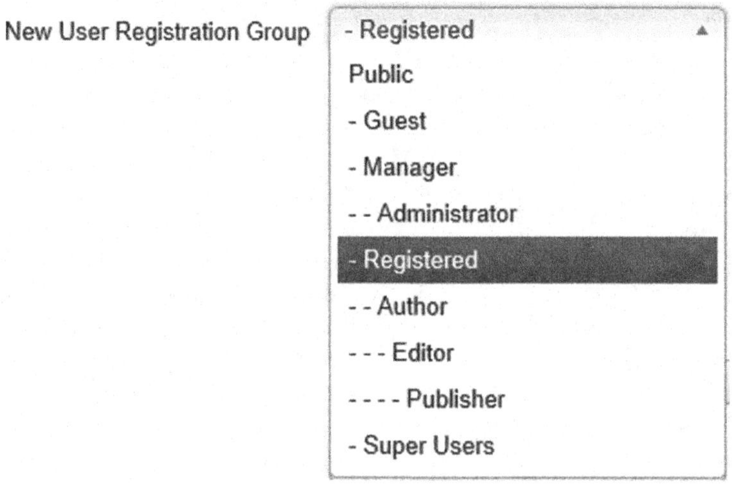

New User Registration Group

- Registered
Public
- Guest
- Manager
- - Administrator
- Registered
- - Author
- - - Editor
- - - - Publisher
- Super Users

Figure 10-31. Types of user groups for new users

To validate the e-mail address provided by a visitor when creating an account, an activation link is sent to the e-mail address specified, and the account will not be created until the visitor accesses the account and clicks the activation link. The activation link is sent to the e-mail address of a newly created account only if the New User Account Activation option is set to Self.

For example, suppose that this option is enabled, and user Rahul creates an account. After filling in the desired information in the User Registration form, when Rahul clicks the Register button, he will see a message (see Figure 10-32) saying that the account has been created, and an activation link has been sent to the specified e-mail address. He will have to click the activation link to activate the account.

> **Message** ✖
> Your account has been created and an activation link has been sent to the email address you entered. Note that you must activate the account by clicking on the activation link when you get the email before you can login.

Figure 10-32. *Message that appears after the sign-up form is submitted*

After accessing this e-mail, the visitor will find a message sent by the owner of the web site. In the example shown in Figure 10-27, the name of the owner of the Joomla web site (where the account was created) is bintu, and the Joomla web site name is bmharwani.net.Rahul will receive an e-mail with the subject "Account Details for Rahul at bmharwani.net." After he opens the e-mail message, Rahul will see a message that consists of a Thank You message for creating an account and an activation link to be clicked to activate the account. In addition, it displays the username and password to be used for logging into the web site in the future.

When the activation link is clicked, the user's account is activated, and an Activation Complete! message appears. The message also says that the user can now log in using the username and password supplied at the time of registration.

In the Users Configuration page, if the value of the New User Account Activation field is set to None, no activation link will be sent to the visitor's e-mail address; instead, the account will be directly activated.

To understand this better, let's set this field to No and click the Create an Account link from the Login module to create a new account. Assuming that the name of the user is Peter David, fill in the registration information as shown in Figure 10-33.

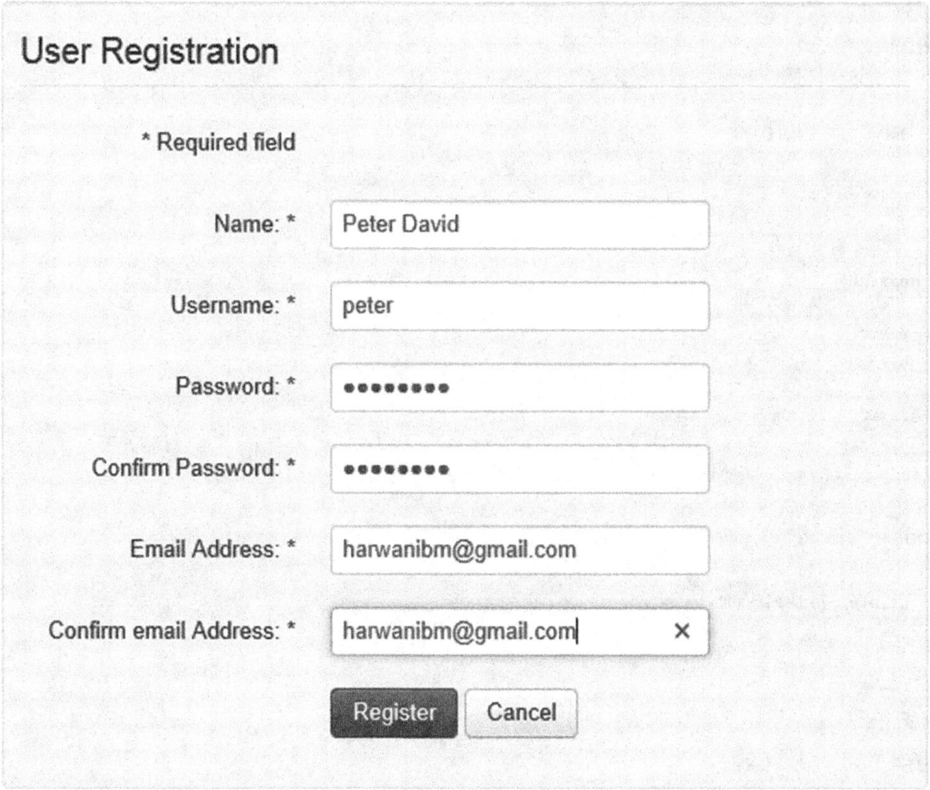

Figure 10-33. *Sign-up form for the user without the activation facility*

After the registration information is complete and the Register button is clicked, the message You May Now Log in Using the Username and Password You Registered With appears, as shown in Figure 10-34.

Figure 10-34. *Message to directly log in without the activation link formality*

The Front-end User Parameters option provides the user with the flexibility to edit the information specified during account creation from the front end. A user who successfully logs into the system sees an Edit Your Profile page (see Figure 10-35) that enables the user to see and edit the user information. Only if the value of this field is Yes will the user be able to edit the information. In addition to being able to edit personal information, the user can choose the type of editor (if the user is a member of the Author group or higher), the local time zone, the front-end language, and so on.

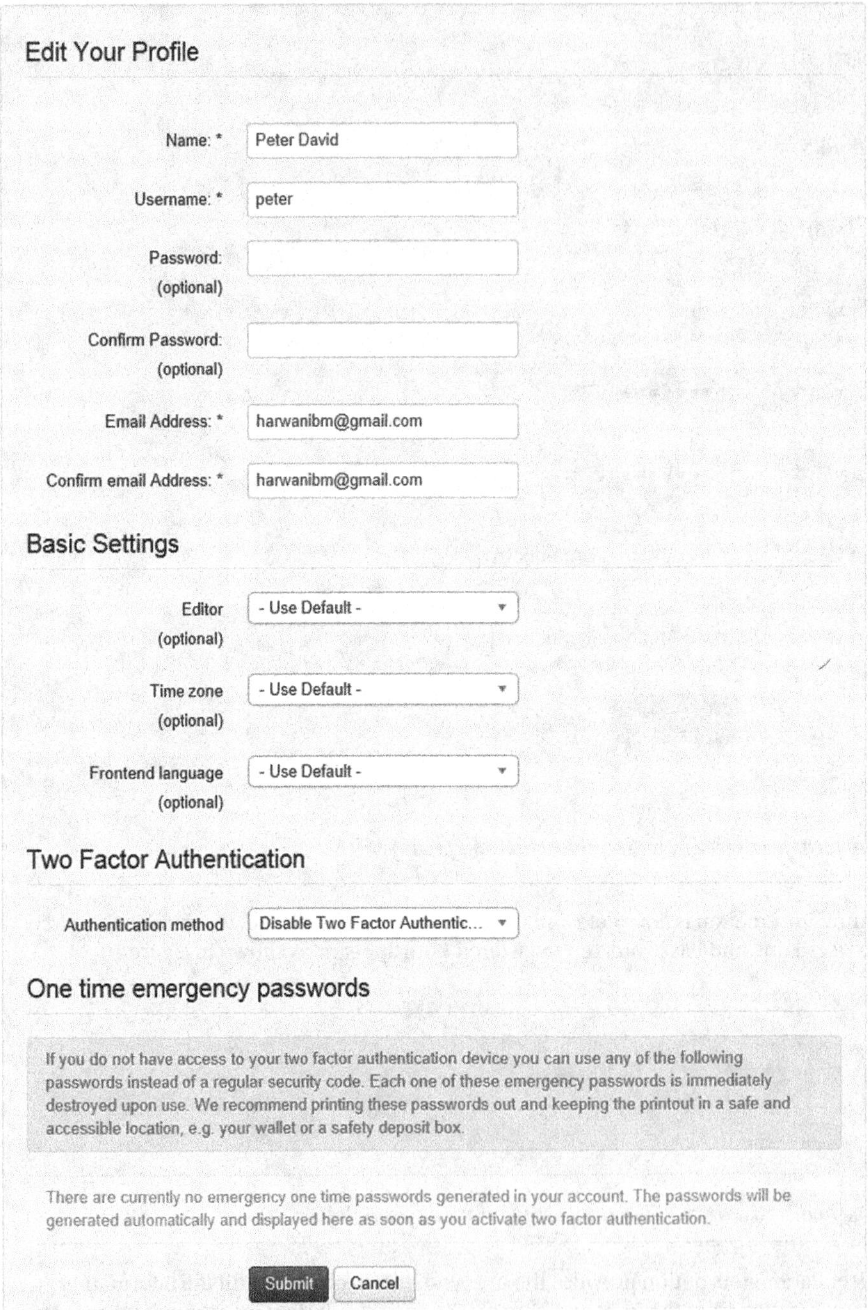

Edit Your Profile

Name: * Peter David

Username: * peter

Password:
(optional)

Confirm Password:
(optional)

Email Address: * harwanibm@gmail.com

Confirm email Address: * harwanibm@gmail.com

Basic Settings

Editor
(optional) - Use Default -

Time zone
(optional) - Use Default -

Frontend language
(optional) - Use Default -

Two Factor Authentication

Authentication method Disable Two Factor Authentic...

One time emergency passwords

If you do not have access to your two factor authentication device you can use any of the following passwords instead of a regular security code. Each one of these emergency passwords is immediately destroyed upon use. We recommend printing these passwords out and keeping the printout in a safe and accessible location, e.g. your wallet or a safety deposit box.

There are currently no emergency one time passwords generated in your account. The passwords will be generated automatically and displayed here as soon as you activate two factor authentication.

Submit   Cancel

Figure 10-35. *Editing a user's profile*

Configuring Media Manager

Media in a web site include images, banners, videos, songs, and so on. In Joomla, the media is managed via the Media Manager. You can configure Media Manager through Global Configuration. Open the Global Configuration page and from the list of components displayed on the left side, select the Media Manager component to open the Media Manager Options page.

The Media Manager Options page is used for setting certain checks on the files being uploaded to your web site. The idea is to upload only legal and verified files. The allowable file types and file sizes for uploads are set in Global Configuration, which you can access by clicking the Options button found in the toolbar. The options in the Media Manager Options page are shown in Figure 10-36 and explained following.

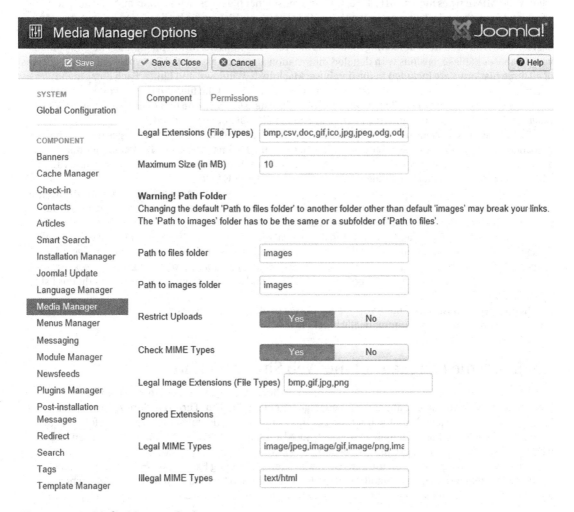

Figure 10-36. *Media Manager Options page*

The Legal Extensions (File Types) field contains the list of file types that users are allowed to upload. By default, Joomla allows the following basic image and document files: BMP, CSV, DOC, EPG, GIF, ICO, JPG, ODG, ODP, ODS, ODT, PDF, PNG, PPT, SWF, TXT, XCF, and XLS. You can edit this list to suit your needs.

The Maximum Size (in MB) field contains the maximum file size that users are allowed to upload. The default setting is 10MB. You can edit it according to your requirements.

In the Path to Images Folder field, you specify the path to the directory in which images are to be stored. The default is <Joomla! home>/images, but you can create a new folder to store your images and specify its path in this field to use it with the Media Manager. The images folder is used by Joomla, so you should not delete or rename this folder.

The Restrict Uploads option is used for restricting uploads to the server. If you set this to Yes, only authorized users will be able to upload documents or images to the web site. The default value of this option is Yes.

The Check MIME Types option is used for ensuring that the MIME files uploaded to your web site are valid. Valid MIME types include GIF, JPEG, PNG, and most other file types that support audio, video, and graphics. Recall that MIME files make it possible to include graphics, audio, and video to be sent over the Internet. To verify files, MIME Magic or File info is used. If the value of this field is set to Yes (the default), users will be restricted from uploading malicious files onto the web site. MIME Magic and File info contain vast databases of file extensions with detailed information about the associated file types. The file extensions of all three platforms are included in the database: Macintosh, Windows, and Linux. Each entry in the database contains information about the file format, a description of the file, and the program that opens the file. If the user tries to upload a file with an unknown file extension (i.e., one that doesn't exist in the MIME Magic or File info databases), an error will occur, and the file will not be uploaded.

The Legal Image Extensions (File Types) field allows you to specify the types of images that can be uploaded to your Joomla web site. It operates by checking the file image headers. By default, Joomla allows only images of type BMP, GIF, JPG, and PNG. For example, if you want to upload an image file with the extension .tiff, it will not be uploaded unless **tiff** is entered in this field.

The Ignored Extensions field is used for specifying the extensions that are to be ignored for MIME type checking. By default, this field is blank to indicate that no extensions are ignored, but you can always add an extension that you want to be uploaded without any checking.

The Legal MIME Types field contains the list of legal MIME types, making them valid for uploading. By default, Joomla automatically includes certain standard file types, including image/jpeg, image/gif, image/png, image/bmp, application/x-shockwave-flash, application/msword, application/excel, application/pdf, application/powerpoint, text/plain, and application/x-zip. You can edit this list to suit your requirements.

In the Illegal MIME Types field, you specify the list of illegal MIME types so that these types won't be uploaded. By default, Joomla automatically blocks text/HTML types.

Changing the Language of the Web Site Front End

It is always an advantage to display your site content in different languages. Let's install a language to see how the web site front end can appear in a language other than English. The extensions for almost all languages are freely available on the Internet. For this example, let's download the extension for French. The archive file for the French language is fr-FR_joomla_lang_full_3.4.1v2.zip, which you can find at http://joomlacode.org/gf/project/french/frs/. Download it to a local disk drive.

To install this language, open the Extension Manager by selecting Extensions ➤ Extension Manager. In the Install tab that is opened by default, click the Browse button to locate the French language archive file and click the Upload File & Install button to install this language in your web site, as shown in Figure 10-37.

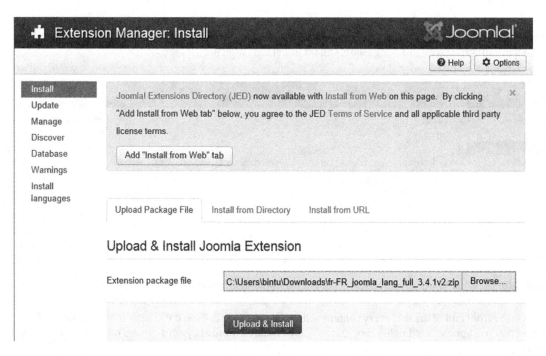

Figure 10-37. *Installing the French language pack*

You'll see the message Installing Package Was Successful, confirming that the French language pack was installed (see Figure 10-38).

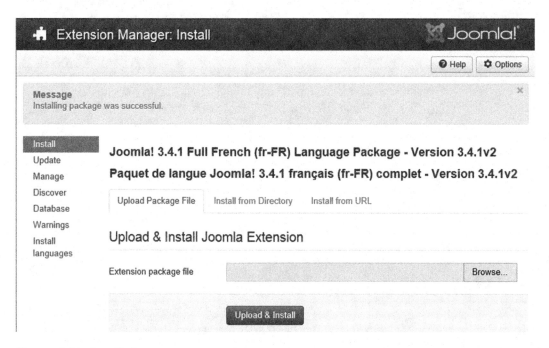

Figure 10-38. *Installation success message*

The Language Manager that you open by selecting Extensions ➤ Language Manager confirms the successful installation of the French language by displaying two language options: English and French (see Figure 10-39). The English language is still set as default language.

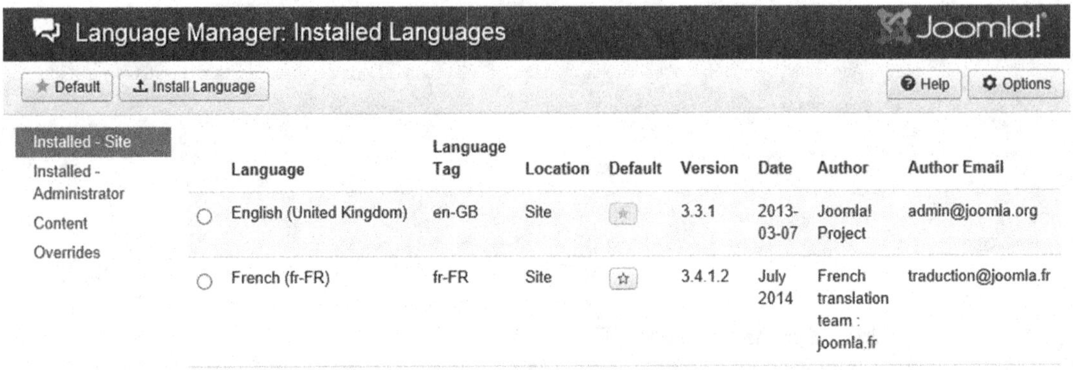

	Language	Language Tag	Location	Default	Version	Date	Author	Author Email
○	English (United Kingdom)	en-GB	Site	☆	3.3.1	2013-03-07	Joomla! Project	admin@joomla.org
○	French (fr-FR)	fr-FR	Site	☆	3.4.1.2	July 2014	French translation team : joomla.fr	traduction@joomla.fr

Figure 10-39. French now appears as an option in the frontend language list

On the front end of the site, every content will appear in English. Even if you search for a keyword, the output that will appear is in English. For example, if you search for the keyword *camera* on the site, you'll see the output shown in Figure 10-40.

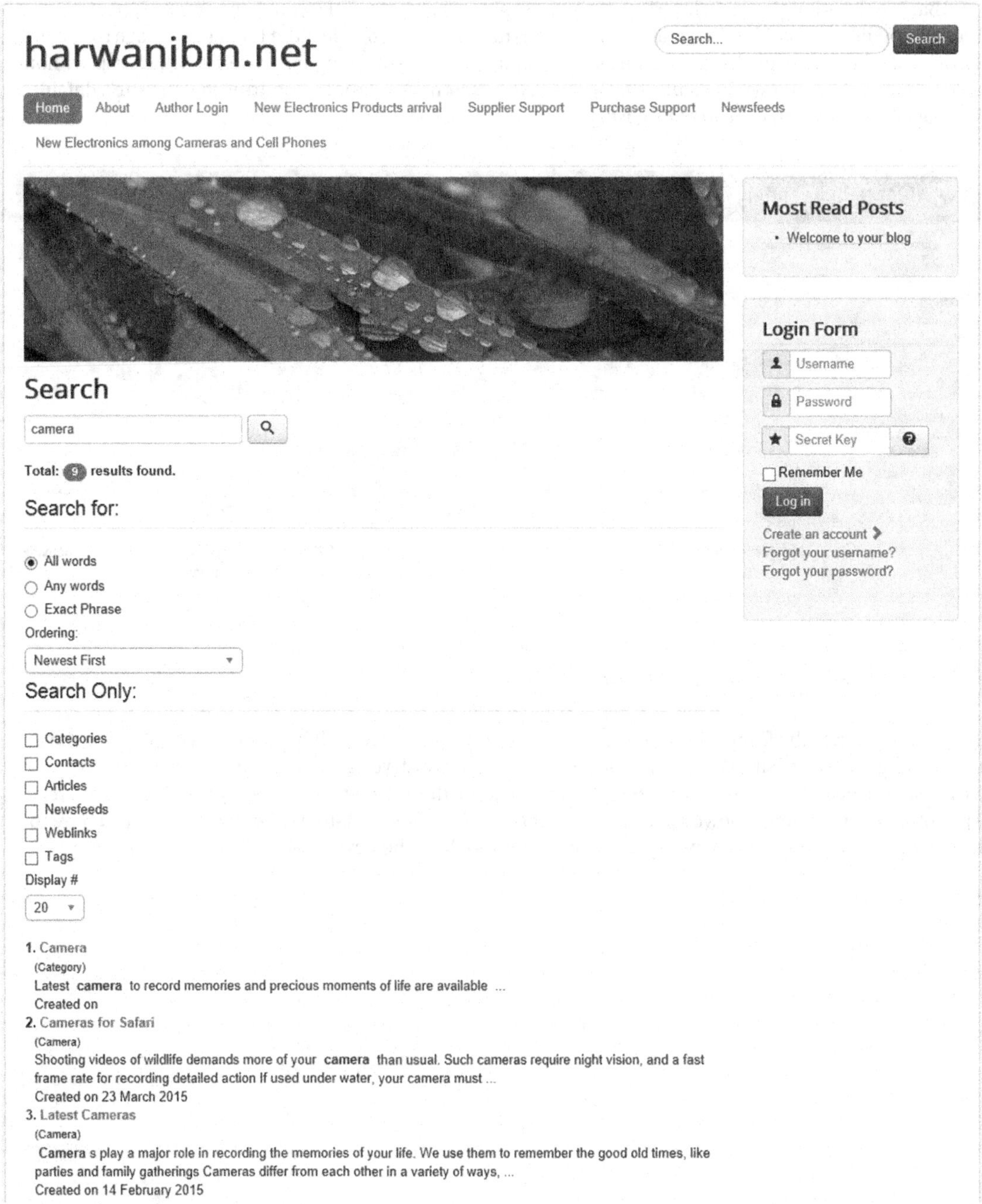

harwanibm.net

Search...   Search

Home   About   Author Login   New Electronics Products arrival   Supplier Support   Purchase Support   Newsfeeds

New Electronics among Cameras and Cell Phones

Most Read Posts

- Welcome to your blog

Search

camera   🔍

Total: **9** results found.

Login Form

👤 Username

🔒 Password

⭐ Secret Key   ❓

☐ Remember Me

Log in

Create an account ❯
Forgot your username?
Forgot your password?

Search for:

- ● All words
- ○ Any words
- ○ Exact Phrase

Ordering:

Newest First ▾

Search Only:

- ☐ Categories
- ☐ Contacts
- ☐ Articles
- ☐ Newsfeeds
- ☐ Weblinks
- ☐ Tags

Display #

20 ▾

1. Camera
(Category)
Latest **camera** to record memories and precious moments of life are available ...
Created on
2. Cameras for Safari
(Camera)
Shooting videos of wildlife demands more of your **camera** than usual. Such cameras require night vision, and a fast
frame rate for recording detailed action If used under water, your camera must ...
Created on 23 March 2015
3. Latest Cameras
(Camera)
Camera s play a major role in recording the memories of your life. We use them to remember the good old times, like
parties and family gatherings Cameras differ from each other in a variety of ways, ...
Created on 14 February 2015

Figure 10-40. *Search results in English*

Back to the administration interface (in Language Manager). To make your site content appear in French, you need to set it as the default language of the site. To do so, select the French language option from the list and click the asterisk (star) in the Default column. The French language asterisk, which was without color is now gold, as shown in Figure 10-41. The golden star next to French confirms that the site's default language is now French instead of English.

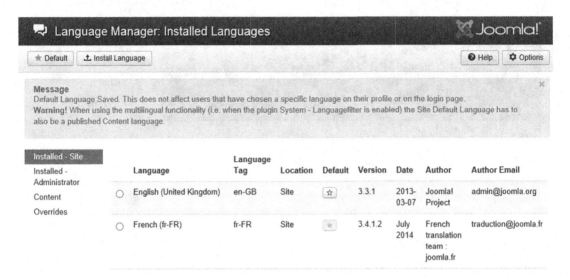

Figure 10-41. *Front end of web site changed to French*

Consequently, the front side content of the site is translated to French. With French declared as the default language of the site, if you search for the *camera* keyword, you get the results translated into French, as shown in Figure 10-42. Notice that everything, including the text on the search button, changes to French. The content of the articles, however, does not change. To translate the language of the articles, you have to install translation extensions, which you will learn how to do in the next section.

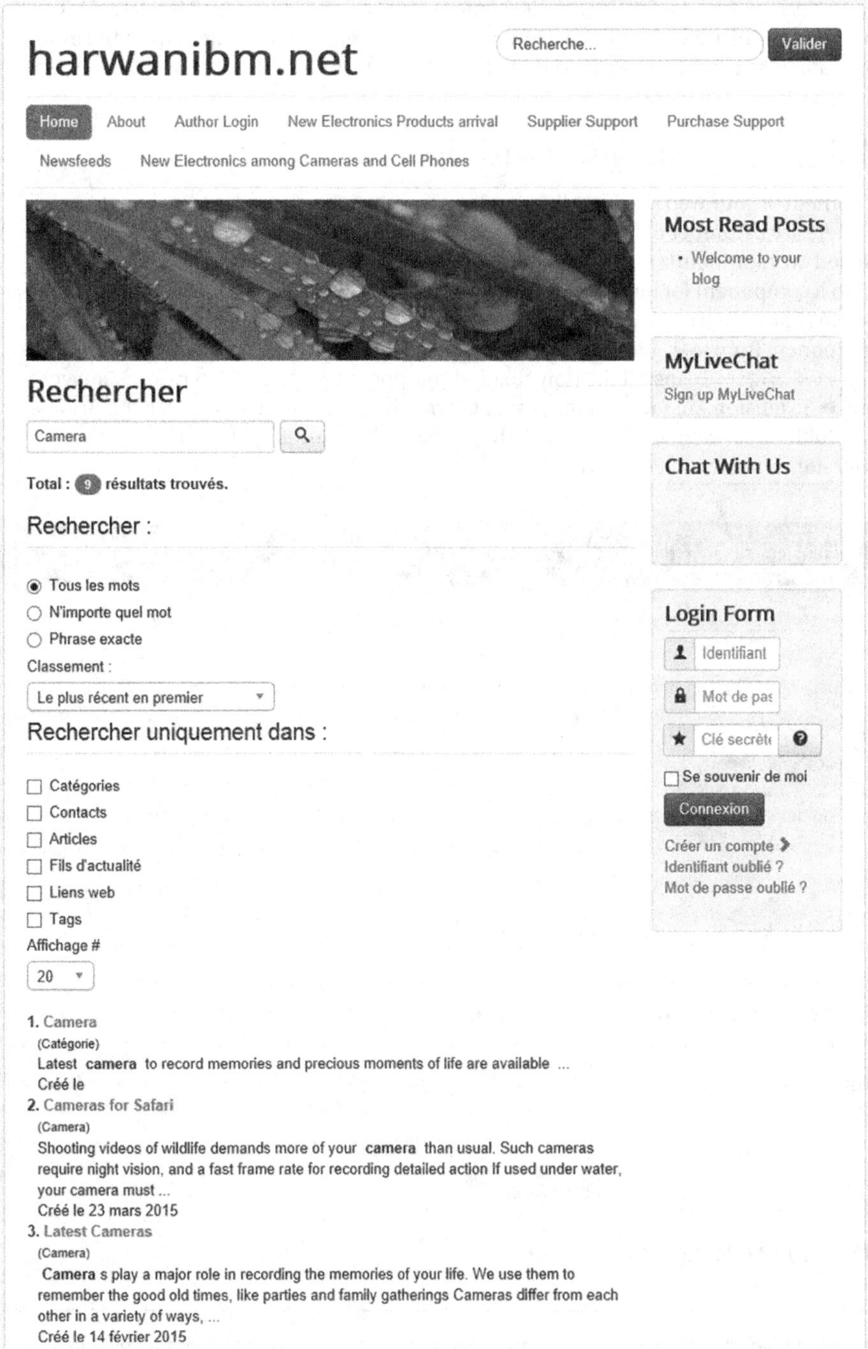

harwanibm.net

Recherche...   Valider

Home   About   Author Login   New Electronics Products arrival   Supplier Support   Purchase Support

Newsfeeds   New Electronics among Cameras and Cell Phones

Rechercher

Camera   🔍

Total : 9 résultats trouvés.

Rechercher :

- ⦿ Tous les mots
- ○ N'importe quel mot
- ○ Phrase exacte

Classement :

Le plus récent en premier

Rechercher uniquement dans :

- ☐ Catégories
- ☐ Contacts
- ☐ Articles
- ☐ Fils d'actualité
- ☐ Liens web
- ☐ Tags

Affichage #

20

1. Camera
(Catégorie)
Latest camera to record memories and precious moments of life are available ...
Créé le
2. Cameras for Safari
(Camera)
Shooting videos of wildlife demands more of your camera than usual. Such cameras
require night vision, and a fast frame rate for recording detailed action If used under water,
your camera must ...
Créé le 23 mars 2015
3. Latest Cameras
(Camera)
 Camera s play a major role in recording the memories of your life. We use them to
remember the good old times, like parties and family gatherings Cameras differ from each
other in a variety of ways, ...
Créé le 14 février 2015

Most Read Posts

- Welcome to your blog

MyLiveChat

Sign up MyLiveChat

Chat With Us

Login Form

- 👤 Identifiant
- 🔒 Mot de pas
- ★ Clé secrèt ❓
- ☐ Se souvenir de moi

Connexion

Créer un compte ❯
Identifiant oublié ?
Mot de passe oublié ?

Figure 10-42. *Search results in French*

With this procedure, you can translate your web site content into any one language. Also, translation can be performed from the administrative interface. How about translating the site content from the front side of the site, which enables visitors to choose the language to translate to?

Providing a Multilingual Facility to Visitors

You can translate the content of your web site into different languages to make it readable by people all around the globe. There are a number of freely available components on the Internet that can be downloaded and installed on your Joomla web site to translate web contents to different languages. This section will discuss such a component for language translations for your web site: JA Multilingual, which supports translations into41 languages.

Download the component from `www.joomlart.com/forums/downloads.php`. The downloaded archive file will be `com_jalang.v1.0.6.zip`. To install the downloaded component, open the Extension Manager by selecting Extensions ➤ Extension Manager. In the Install tab that is opened by default, click the Browse button to locate the JA Multilingual archive file and click the Upload File & Install button to install the component in your web site, as shown in Figure 10-43.

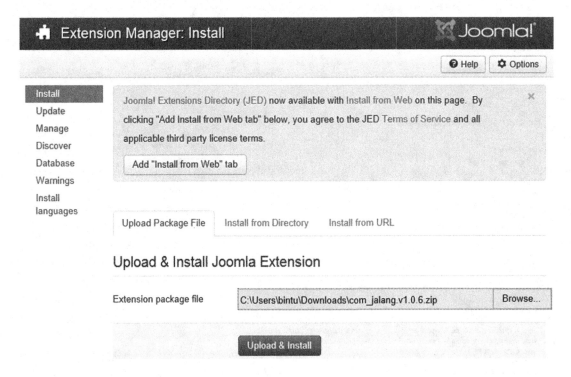

Figure 10-43. *Installing the JA Multilingual component*

▪ **Note**   Remember that third-party extensions are compressed files that you download from a developer's site directly to your computer. In most cases, you don't need to unzip the compressed files and can directly upload to Joomla.

If the component is successfully installed, you see the Installing Component Was Successful message shown in Figure 10-44.

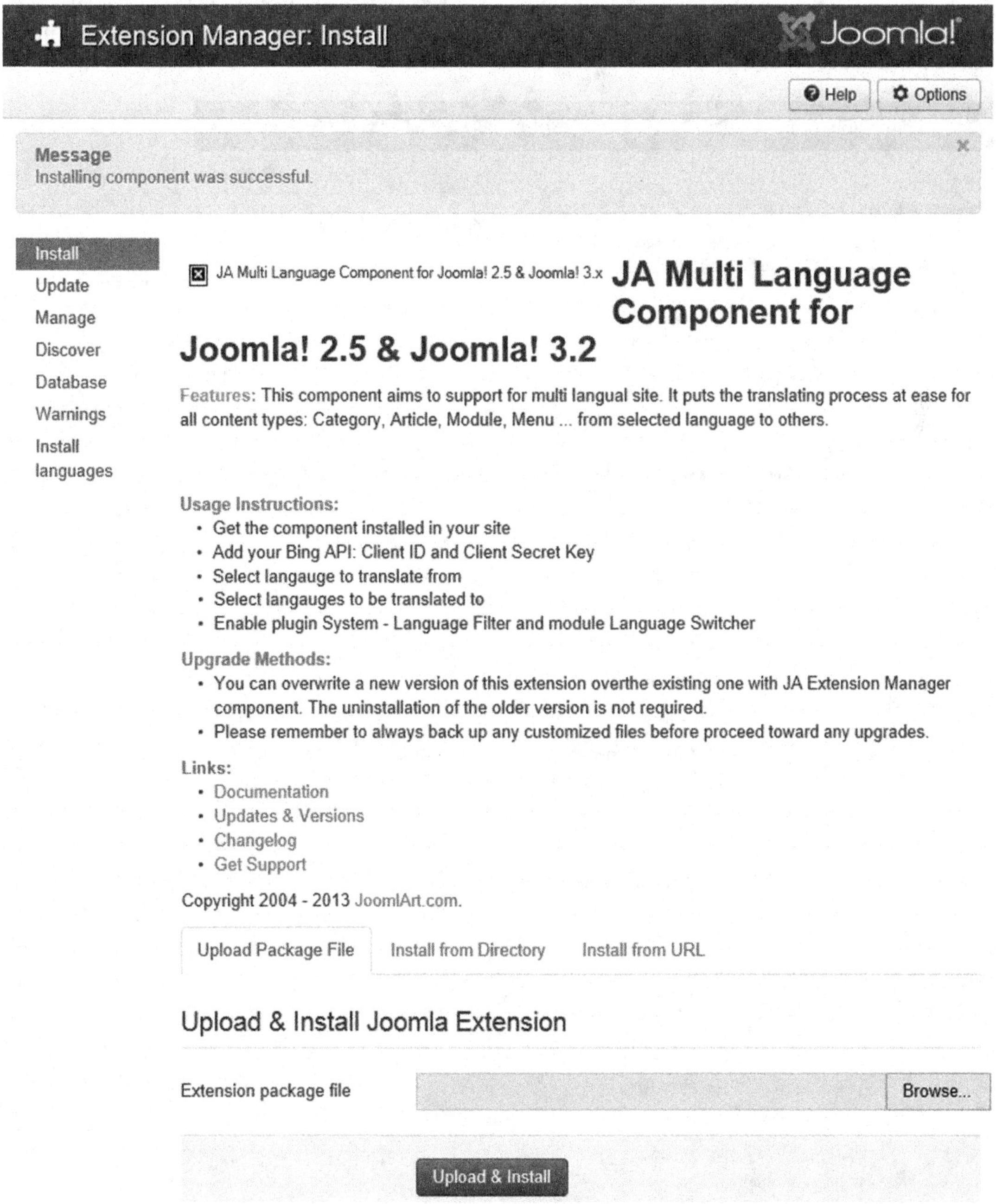

Extension Manager: Install   **Joomla!**

❓ Help   ⚙ Options

Message
Installing component was successful.   ✕

Install
Update
Manage
Discover
Database
Warnings
Install languages

☒ JA Multi Language Component for Joomla! 2.5 & Joomla! 3.x **JA Multi Language Component for Joomla! 2.5 & Joomla! 3.2**

Features: This component aims to support for multi langual site. It puts the translating process at ease for all content types: Category, Article, Module, Menu ... from selected language to others.

Usage Instructions:
- Get the component installed in your site
- Add your Bing API: Client ID and Client Secret Key
- Select langauge to translate from
- Select langauges to be translated to
- Enable plugin System - Language Filter and module Language Switcher

Upgrade Methods:
- You can overwrite a new version of this extension overthe existing one with JA Extension Manager component. The uninstallation of the older version is not required.
- Please remember to always back up any customized files before proceed toward any upgrades.

Links:
- Documentation
- Updates & Versions
- Changelog
- Get Support

Copyright 2004 - 2013 JoomlArt.com.

Upload Package File   Install from Directory   Install from URL

Upload & Install Joomla Extension

Extension package file   Browse...

Upload & Install

Figure 10-44. *Message confirming successful installation of the JA Multilingual component*

Open the component by selecting Components ➤ JA Multilingual. The Translation Manager will open with its Translate tab selected by default, as shown in Figure 10-45. The Translate tab indicates the default language. Translate to Field shows all the installed languages on the site and enables you to select the one in which you want to translate your site content. Because only French is installed, the field indicates that the site content can be translated only into French. The Component field shows the list of site components that can be translated to French.

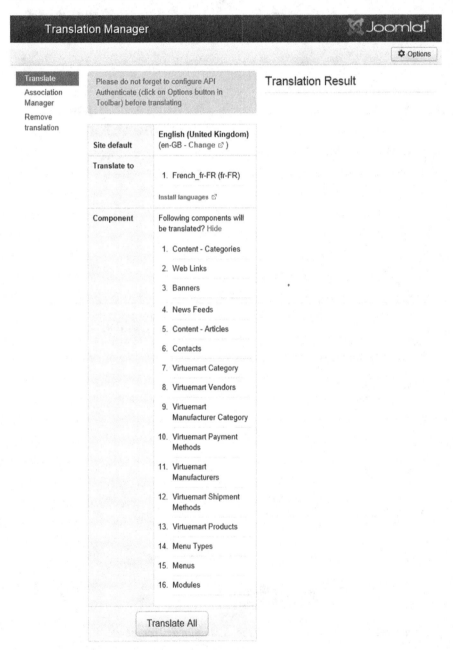

Figure 10-45. Translation Manager page

The JA Multilingual component supports two popular translation services: BING and Google. So before you click the Translate All button, you have to specify either of the following:

- Bing API Client ID and secret key
- Google API key

Here are the steps to get the Bing API and secret key:

1. Create a Microsoft account by visiting https://signup.live.com/ and signing up.

2. Login to Azure Marketplace by visiting https://datamarket.azure.com/ with the registered Microsoft account.

3. Visit https://datamarket.azure.com/account/keys to get your account key.

4. Register a new application with your key by accessing the link https://datamarket.azure.com/developer/applications.

5. Click the Edit button to get your Client ID and Client Secret.

6. Register the Bing translation service by visiting https://datamarket.azure.com/dataset/bing/microsofttranslator and registering a Bing translation service package. It provides a free package that allows you to translate two million characters per month. If your site database is too large, you can select a premium package.

Here are the steps to get the Google API key:

1. Visit https://cloud.google.com/console#/project, login with your Google account, and create a new project in Google Cloud Console.

2. Verify by phone to create a new project.

3. Open the project, select the APIs & auth ➤ APIs ➤ Translate API option, and then enable Translate API.

4. In the project, select APIs & auth ➤ Credentials, click the New Client ID option to create a new Client ID, and select Web Application platform.

5. Create a new API key by clicking the Create New Key button. Add the URL and then click Create. Copy the created API key.

6. Before you can start using the service, Google Translate API v2 requires billing information for all accounts. Go through the instructions and enable the billing that suits your needs.

7. To enable billing for your project, open your project, select Settings ➤ Enable Billing ➤. Fill in the info option and complete your transaction.

Now that you have created a Bing API Client ID and its secret key, click the Option icon from the toolbar at the top, select the Bing option from the Translation Service combo box, and enter the Bing API Client ID and its secret key in the fields that are displayed in Figure 10-46. Click the Save & Close button to save the information and go back to the Translation Manager page.

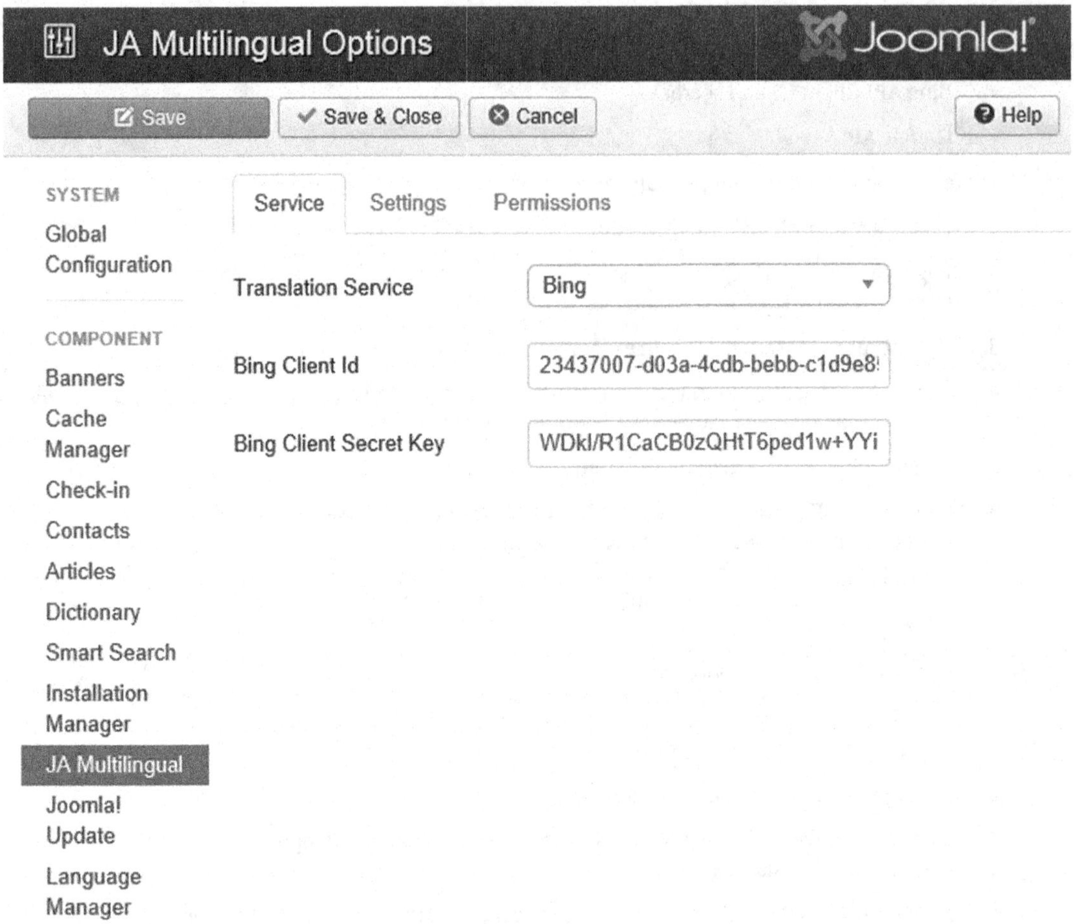

Figure 10-46. *JA Multilingual Options page*

You are now all set to translate your web site content, so select the Components ➤ JA Multilingual option to open the Translation Manager page. From the Translation Manager page, click the Translate All button to translate the site content into French. You can see the progress of the translation in the Translation Result column, as shown in Figure 10-47. You can also see which elements of the site were successfully translated and which could not be translated. You will get a success message for the elements that were successfully translated and a failed message for the elements that could not be translated.

Translation Manager

✿ Options

Translate
Association Manager
Remove translation

		Translation Result
Site default	English (United Kingdom) (en-GB - Change ⬩)	

Translate to

   1. French_fr-FR (fr-FR)

Install languages ⬩

Component   Following components will be translated? Hide

   1. Content - Categories

   2. Web Links

   3. Banners

   4. News Feeds

   5. Content - Articles

   6. Contacts

   7. Virtuemart Category

   8. Virtuemart Vendors

   9. Virtuemart Manufacturer Category

   10. Virtuemart Payment Methods

   11. Virtuemart Manufacturers

   12. Virtuemart Shipment Methods

   13. Virtuemart Products

   14. Menu Types

   15. Menus

   16. Modules

Translate All

Translation Result:

```
Start to translate for the
French_fr-FR language

[Started Translate The Table
categories]
[Started Translate The Table weblinks]
[Started Translate The Table banners]
[Started Translate The Table
newsfeeds]
[Started Translate The Table content]
----- Start Translating content:
Working on Your Site
Success
----- Start Translating content:
Welcome to your blog
Success
----- Start Translating content: About
your home page
Success
----- Start Translating content: Your
Modules
Success
----- Start Translating content: Your
Template
Success
----- Start Translating content:
Latest Cameras
Success
----- Start Translating content:
Cameras for Safari
Success
----- Start Translating content: Web
Cams - Video chatting
```

Figure 10-47. *Successful translation of web site content*

471

Now the entire web site exists in two languages: English and French. The Module Manager shown in Figure 10-48 shows the modules in English and their translated versions in French.

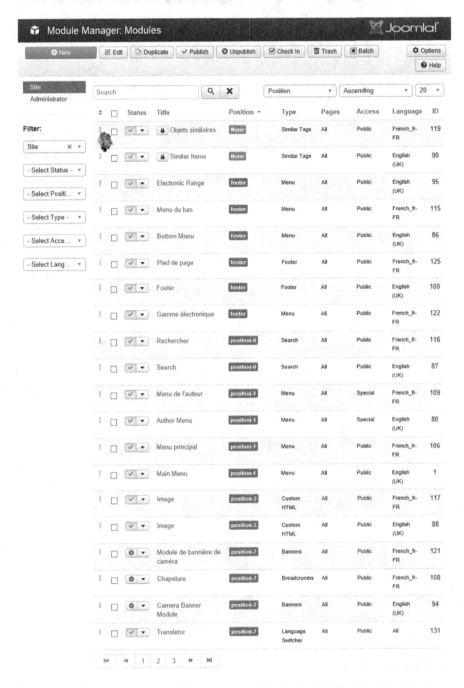

Figure 10-48. *Module Manager showing the modules in English and French versions*

The next step is to enable a plug-in called System - Language Filter. Open the Plugin Manager by clicking Extensions ➤ Plugin Manager. Search for the plug-in named System - Language Filter and ensure that it is enabled.

To enable visitors of your site to switch between different languages, you have to create a module that does this language-switching task. Open the Module Manager page and click the New button to create a new module. In the pop-up that prompts for the module type, select Language Switcher. In the Title field of the new module, enter any text; use **Translator** (see Figure 10-49).

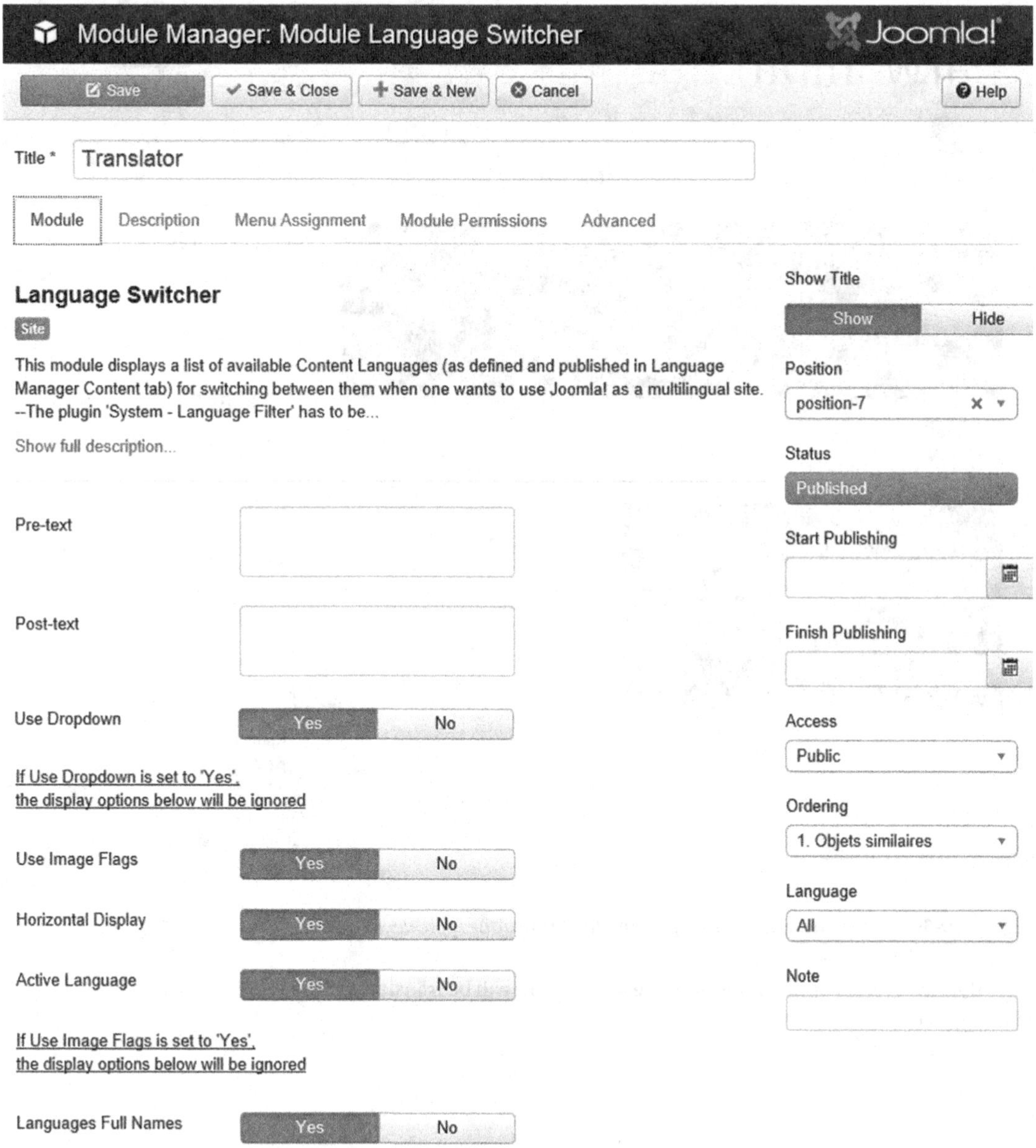

Figure 10-49. *Creating a new module based on the Language Switcher type*

In the Position combo box, you select the position for the new module. Chooseposition-7 (the right top side of the site). In the Language combo box, select All so that when you switch to any language, the module is enabled. Keeping the values of the rest of the fields to their defaults, click the Save & Close button to save the new module.

The front side of your site will now show a module called Translator with a combo box in it. Because only two languages, English and French, are installed on your site, the combo box will show only these two options. By default, the site content will appear in the default language (English), as shown in Figure 10-50.

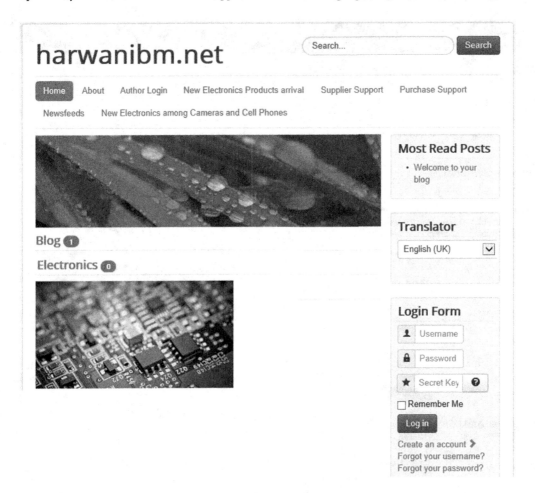

Figure 10-50. *Front side of the site displaying the Translator module*

After the French option is clicked, the site content will be translated into French, as shown in Figure 10-51.

Figure 10-51. *Web site content in French*

On the administrative interface and below the Translate tab that is opened by default are two more tabs: Association Manager and Remove Translation. The Association Manager tab is used to update translation manually. That is, you select the content type, and all content in your site that matches the selected content type will be listed (see Figure 10-52). Click the title of the desired content or click the Edit link (shown in the French column or any language column) in the row of the desired content to edit it.

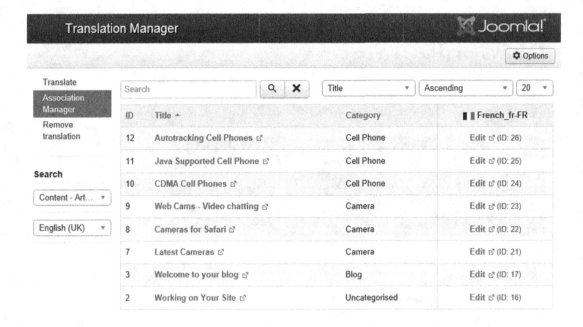

Figure 10-52. *Association Manager tab in Translation Manager*

After you select the Edit link of the "Autotracking Cell Phones" article, the article will open in French, as shown in Figure 10-53. You can edit the content if you want. After you make the desired changes in the content, click the Save & Close button at the top to save the changes.

Figure 10-53. *"Autotracking Cell Phones" article in French*

As its name suggests, the Remove Translations tab removes the implemented translations to start all over again. When you remove translations, you lose all the translated content, so you should make a backup before removing content. After doing so, click the Delete button in front of French in the Language box. The French translation will be removed. The Result column shows the impact of removing the translation; it shows the list of affected items (see Figure 10-54). After deleting the translated content, you can even uninstall the French language or you can stop after deleting the translated content.

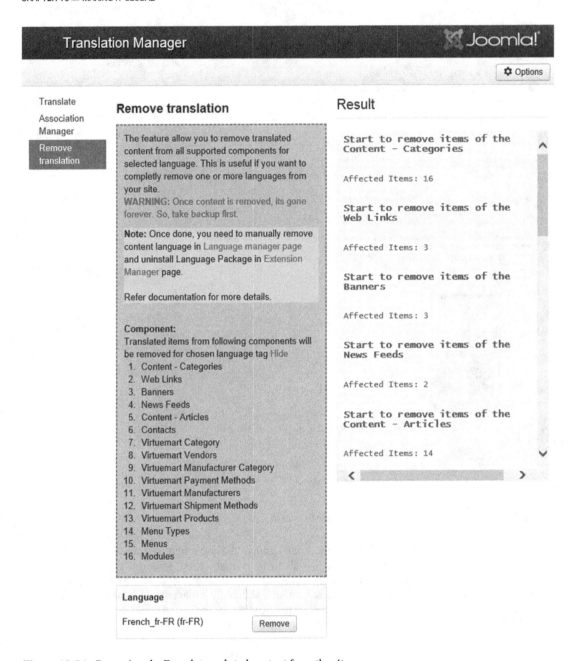

Figure 10-54. Removing the French translated content from the site

To uninstall the language, open the Extension Manager by selecting Extensions ➤ Extension Manager. In the Extension Manager page, select the Manage tab to display all the installed extensions. Search for the language package to uninstall. Select the check box of French_fr-FR and click the Uninstall button from the toolbar at the top. The French language pack will be uninstalled from your site.

Summary

This chapter dealt with Joomla's Global Configuration settings. You saw how to install an editor and how to make SEF URLs. You learned how to enable visitors to register on your web site, how an activation link is sent, and about its role in activating a new account. You saw how the language of the front end of your web site can be changed. To make your web site readable by everyone, you learned how to translate your web site contents into different languages.

I have tried my level best to make this concept easy and yet very detailed. I hope you have loved reading the book. Thanks.

Index

Web request life cycle, 10
Web site front end (Global configuration)
   French language pack, 461
   frontend language list, 462
   language option, 464
   message installation, 461
   search result, 462
Wrapper, 316
Wrapper module, 361

■ X, Y, Z

XAMPP
   administration
      language selection, 18
      status of services, 20
      welcome page, 19
   control panel, 15
      directory, 17
      status of services, 16
   database creation, 25

installation
   checkbox, 14
   completion screen, 14
   components, 12
   folder, 13
   setup wizard, 13
   welcome screen, 11
phpMyAdmin
   database management
      interface screen, 21
   default users, 22
   edit mode, 23
   message confirmation, 25
   mysql database, 22
   user table, 23
user authentication, 27
   authentication modes, 30
   login screen, 32
   MySQL root password, 30
   security status, 28
   welcome screen, 31

Get the eBook for only $5!

Why limit yourself?

Now you can take the weightless companion with you wherever you go and access your content on your PC, phone, tablet, or reader.

Since you've purchased this print book, we're happy to offer you the eBook in all 3 formats for just $5.

Convenient and fully searchable, the PDF version enables you to easily find and copy code—or perform examples by quickly toggling between instructions and applications. The MOBI format is ideal for your Kindle, while the ePUB can be utilized on a variety of mobile devices.

To learn more, go to www.apress.com/companion or contact support@apress.com.

Apress®
THE EXPERT'S VOICE™

Printed in the United States
By Bookmasters